HISTORY OF THE ROMAN REPUBLIC

THE HISTORY OF THE ROMAN REPUBLIC

A One-Volume Abridgment of *The History of Rome*

by

THEODOR MOMMSEN

Translated by W.P. Dickson

Edited by C. Bryans, F.J.R. Hendy & Arthur C. Howland

Foreword by Mart

First published 1906

This edition © 2022
Rogue Scholar Press
All Rights Reserved

ISBN: 978-1-954357-18-1

FOREWORD

The three volumes of Christian Matthias Theodor Mommsen's *Römische Geschichte* were published in 1856, forming a landmark account from the settlement of the Latin stock in Latium to the instauration of a military monarchy by Julius Caesar which would stretch across the entire Romano-Hellenic civilization. Mommsen's monumental historical labor strives to present a comprehensive picture of the political, military, social, cultural and ethnographic history of Rome, by surveying the fundamental character of the peoples of ancient Italy, class struggles and power dynamics, their institutions and culture, the hegemony of Rome in Latium and of Latium over the entire Italian peninsula, government and political life, economy and social troubles, law and justice, religion and customs, art, literature, science, spiritual life in a unified Italy, internal reform movements, party clashes, revolutionary periods, and the great wars that asserted their sovereignty over foreign contending powers. Such a comprehensive view could only be provided by the vast and sure erudition of a true archaeologist, the deep knowledge of old languages and customs of Italy by a historian whose reflexive mind could simultaneously combine that of a jurisconsult, philosopher and politician.

The origins of the work can be dated from an 1877 letter Mommsen addressed to Gustav Freytag, a Prussian writer and novelist. In it, Mommsen's dismissal from his professorship in Leipzig for his revolutionary views is shown to have prompted him to begin work on his magnum opus at the suggestion of the publishers Karl Reimer and Salomon Hirzel, after having been deeply impressed by his lecture on the Gracchian revolution.

For Mommsen, the revolution wrought by Tiberius and Gaius Gracchus forms the dramatic climax of the Roman story, and constitutes the conceptual base of his oeuvre. Mommsen's reflections on the roman revolutionary period are linked to his contemporaneous life, one which was brimming with narratives and interpretations of revolutions and revolutionary ages, seemingly tied to the German liberal. The crisis that Rome underwent during the final century of the Republic was depicted as a revolutionary period by the German historian, preceding Ronald Syme's work *The Roman Revolution* by more than 8 decades.

A parallel is drawn by Mommsen: the revolution carried out by the Gracchi would end in failure, just like the French Revolution. The uprising was, in the eyes of the historian, a legitimate one, one which represented the people over a closed oligarchy that had transgressed the earlier Roman conception of sovereignty, which rested upon the people.

> *"... the Roman community, just like the German, and probably like the oldest Indo-European community, was the true and ultimate holder of the concept of the sovereign state".*

The liberal interpretation of revolution and history is projected onto the final days of the Roman Republic, Rome came to resemble France at the turn of the eighteenth and nineteenth centuries: a dysfunctional nobility, failed reforms movements, revolutionary movements, *la Terreur.* Its historical culmination would come with the arrival of a Caesarist figure, terminating the Revolution. Mommsen's *History of Rome* was dominated by the conviction that the path from the Gracchi to Caesar was necessary and unavoidable, while positing that Roman popular sovereignty inevitably led to revolution. Here, the impact of Mommsen's own generational experiences is palpable: the typical liberal German outlook which saw the Revolutions of 1848 with disillusionment was now applied to the failed Gracchian revolution. Thus, Mommsen could be considered a Caesarist, no critique is levied against the institutions of the Principate and Caesar is portrayed as a Statesman embarked on a struggle for the military, intellectual and moral regeneration of his deeply decayed nation, in addition to the Hellenic nation which he regarded as inseparable to his own. In effect, during the last Century of the Republic and during the revolutionary period the Latin stock underwent an alarming depopulation forcing Caesar to take drastic action, like offering extraordinary rewards for the fathers of numerous families, as well as Latinisation.

Beyond the 19th Century German liberal constructs contained in the work and overt parallels to the epoch in which he lived (the German landed oligarchy is sometimes likened to the late-Republican oligarchy, the Gracchi to Babeuf), Mommsen's characteristic historical realist style can be found in all pages. German historian Heinrich von Seybel remarked thus on the work's apparent lack of artistic value and lyricism: "A book like Mommsen's *Römische Geschichte* is no consummate work of art but it contains a direction that, with a lively force, the enthusiasm of a new development, and the clarity of an irrevocable decision, aims for the ideal of a great classicism." Ranke's motto *labor ipse voluptas* embodies the abdication of the pursuit of genius and of literary masterpieces. Instead, the emphasis is shifted to industrious scholarly work of more rigorous material historicity. In a letter to Henzen, Mommsen justified and explained his style: "force the ancients to step down from the imaginary stage, on which the mass of the audience sees them, into the real world". Thus, Rome's domination was brought about by an amoral military assertion, shrewd and devious diplomacy, development of commerce, and the material aspects of national subordination and the exploitation of slaves and the lower classes. Eventually, during the last decades of the 19th Century, the style that made his work popular in Germany and abroad, i.e. realism and materialism, began to fade off and so did his fame, ousted by new historical trends: decadence, symbolism, naturalism.

Although Mommsen, the historian and minor political actor, was shaped by an era different from ours, belonging to a milieu that overcame the Romantic era and adhered to realism and liberal nationalism, his distinctive outlook towards the world can be of great use to the men of today. An immersion in the real can grant a new outlook towards our era: all utopias, ideological or religious consolations or romantic delusions are spared, an unromantic view of the world can subsequently emerge.

MART
AUGUST 2022

CONTENTS

PART I

LATIN SETTLEMENT AND CONQUEST OF ITALY
753-268 B. C.

PART II

CONQUEST OF THE MEDITERRANEAN STATES
264-133 B. C.

CONTENTS

PART III

THE REVOLUTION PERIOD. 133-78 B. C.

PART IV

FALL OF THE REPUBLIC AND ESTABLISHING OF THE MONARCHY. 78-44 B. C.

PART I

LATIN SETTLEMENT AND CONQUEST OF ITALY. 753-268 B.C.

HISTORY OF ROME

Chapter I

ITALY

THE division between ancient and modern history is not one of mere convenience; it has a reality, in that it marks the distinction in point of time, place, and character between the civilization of the old and new worlds.

Ancient history is in the main an account of the rise and fall of those peoples whose civilization had a common origin, and presented similar features. In each case, however, the individuality of each nation impressed its own peculiar stamp on the character of that civilization.

The Mediterranean Sea was the theater of the growth and decay of the great nations who may be included in the same cycle of civilization, and whose culture found its highest point in Thebes in Egypt, Carthage in Africa, Athens in Greece, Rome in Italy. When their work was finished, new peoples arose, a new cycle of civilization was begun, a new center was found in the Atlantic Ocean in place of the Mediterranean. The province of the Roman historian is to record the closing scene of the great drama of ancient history as enacted in Italy.

Geographically, this peninsula is formed by the mountain chain of the Apennines breaking off from the Western Alps and crossing the northern portion of the country in an easterly direction, thence turning southeast and south, and terminating finally at the strait that divides Italy from Sicily. It must be especially remembered that the ancient boundary of Italy on the north was *not* the Alps, but the Apennines; therefore, the flat country on the north, extending between the Alps and the Apennines as far down as the Abruzzi, does not belong geographically nor historically to the Italy of our history. As the Apennines nowhere rise precipitously, but inclose many valleys and tablelands connected by easy passes, the country is well adapted for human habitation. This is especially the case with the adjacent slopes and coast districts. On the east coast

stretches the plain of Apulia, on the south well-watered and fertile
lowlands adjoin the hill country of the interior, and on the west
we find, not merely the extraordinarily rich and irrigated lands of
Etruria, Latium, and Campania, but, owing to the action of the
sea and of volcanoes, the country is varied with hill and valley,
harbor and island.   Although Italy lacks the island-studded sea
which gave the Greeks their seafaring character, and is deficient
in bays and harbors, except on the southwest coast, yet it resembles
Greece in its temperate climate and wholesome mountain air, while
it excels it in rich alluvial plains and grassy mountain slopes.   All
Italian interests center in the west; the reverse is the case with
Greece.   Thus, the Apulian and Messapian coasts play a subordinate
part in Italian, as Epirus and Acarnania did in Greek history.   The
two peninsulas lie side by side, but turn their backs on each other,
and the Italians and Greeks rarely came into contact in the
Adriatic Sea.
     The history of Italy falls into two main sections, its internal
history down to its union under the leadership of the Latin stock,
and the history of its sovereignty over the world.   It must be borne
in mind that what has been called the conquest of Italy by the
Romans is really the consolidation and union of the whole Italian
stock—a stock of which the Romans were the most powerful branch,
but still only a branch.   Our attention must now be fixed on the first
of the two sections—on the settlement of the Italian stock: on its
external struggles for existence against Greek and Etruscan intruders; on its conquest of these enemies; finally, on its internal
strife, and the contest between the Latins and Samnites for the
leadership of Italy, resulting in the victory of the Latins, at the
end of the fourth century before Christ.
     With regard to the earliest migrations into Italy we have no
evidence to guide us, not even the uncertain voice of tradition.   No
monuments of a savage primitive race have ever been unearthed,
such as exist in France, Germany, and England.   But the remains
of the Italian languages show that the three primitive stocks were
Iapygian, Etruscan, and Italian.   The last is divided into two main
branches: Latin and Umbro-Samnite, or more fully that branch
to which the dialects of the Umbri, Marsi, Volsci, and Samnites
belong.   The center of Italy was inhabited, from a remote period,
by the two divisions of the Italian people.   Philological analysis
of the Italian tongue shows that they belong to the Indo-Germanic

family, and that the Italians are brothers of the Greeks and cousins of the Celts, Germans, and Slavonians.

In regard to the graver problems of life, in moral, social, political, and religious development, we find a marked difference between the Greeks and the Italians. In the Greek world we see the full and free play of individual life, and individual thought, whether in the political arena or that of literature, whether in the games at Olympia or in religious festivals. The whole was sacrificed to its parts, the nation to the township, the township to the citizen. Thus, solemn awe of the gods was lessened and at last extinguished by that freedom of thought which invested them with human attributes and then denied their existence. The Romans, on the contrary, merged the individual in the state, and regarded the progress and prosperity of the latter as the ideal for which all were bound to labor unceasingly. With them the son was bound to reverence the father, the citizen to reverence the ruler, all to reverence the gods. This distinction becomes more evident when we consider the length to which paternal and marital authority was carried by the Romans, and the merciless rigor with which a slave was treated by them. The meager and meaningless character of individual names among the Romans, when contrasted with the luxuriant and poetic fullness of those among the Greeks, points to the wish of the Romans to reduce all to one uniform level, instead of promoting the development of distinctive personality. But we must not forget that the basis was the same with both nations. In both, the clan arose from the family and the state from the clan; but, as the relations in a Roman household differed widely from those in a Greek, so the position of a clan, as a separate power, in a Greek, was far higher than in a Roman state. Again, although the fundamental ideas of the Roman constitution—a king, a senate, and an assembly authorized merely to accept or reject proposals submitted to it—are also found in Greek states, as in the earlier constitution of Crete, yet widely different was the development which these ideas received in each nation. So, too, in religion, both nations founded their faith on the same common store of symbolic and allegorical views of nature. But the Greek lost sight of the spiritual abstractions, and gave all the phenomena of nature a concrete and corporeal shape, clothing all with the riches of his poetic fancy. The Roman, casting aside all mythical legends of the gods, sanctified every action of life by assigning a spirit to everything existing—a spirit which came into being with it, and perished with it; and thus the very word Religio, "that which binds," shows what a hold this faith in the unseen and this power of spiritual abstraction had upon the Roman mind. Thus the two nations in which the civilization of antiquity culminated stand side by side, as different in development as they were in origin identical. The points in which the Hellenes excel the Italians are more universally intelligible, and reflect a more brilliant luster; but the deep feeling in each individual, that he was only a part of the community, a rare devotedness and power of self-sacrifice for the common weal, an earnest faith in its own gods, form the rich treasure of the Italian nation. Wherever in Hellas a tendency towards national union appeared, it was based not on elements directly political, but on games and art; the contests at Olympia, the poems of Homer, the tragedies of Euripides, were the only bonds that held Hellas together. Resolutely, on the other hand, the Italian surrendered his own personal will for the sake of freedom, and learned to obey his father that he might know how to obey the state. Amid this subjection individual development might be marred, and the germs of fairest promise might be arrested in the bud; the Italian gained in their stead a feeling of fatherland and of patriotism such as the Greek never knew, and, alone among all civilized nations of antiquity, succeeded in working out national unity in connection with a constitution based on self-government— a national unity which at last placed in his hands the mastery, not only over the divided Hellenic stock, but over the whole known world.

Chapter II

LATIN SETTLEMENTS AND ORIGIN OF ROME
753 B.C.

W E have no data enabling us to accurately determine the migration of the Italians into Italy. The Italian names Novla or Nola (new town), Campani, Capua, Volturnus, Opsci (laborers), show that an Italian and probably Latin stock, the Ausones, were in possession of Campania before the Samnite and Greek immigrations; but all traces of the Itali, who were the primitive inhabitants of the country subsequently occupied by the Lucani and Bruttii, were entirely obliterated by these two races. It is also not improbable that the Latins in primitive times spread over Latium, Campania, Lucania, and the eastern half of Sicily. But those settled in Sicily, Magna Graecia, and Campania came into contact with the Greeks at a time when they were unable to resist so superior a civilization, and were consequently, as in Sicily, completely Hellenized, or so weakened that they fell an easy prey to Sabine hordes. The Latins, however, who settled just north of Campania, in Latium, where no Greek colony was founded, succeeded in maintaining their ground against the Sabines and more northern foes. Latium itself is a plain traversed by the Tiber and Anio, bounded on the east by the mountains of the Sabines and Aequi, which form part of the Apennines; on the south, by the Volscian range, which is separated from the main chain of the Apennines by the ancient territory of the Hernici; on the west, by the sea, whose harbors on this part of the coast are few and poor; on the north, by the broad highlands of Etruria, into which it imperceptibly merges. This plain is dotted with isolated hills, and the Alban range, free on every side, stands between the Volscian chain and the Tiber. Here were settled the old Latins (Prisci Latini), as they were later on called, to distinguish them from the Latins settled outside Latium. But in early times the Tiber formed the northern boundary, and only the center of the region between the Tiber, the spurs of the Apennines, the Alban mount, and the sea, consisting of some seven hundred square miles,

7

formed Latium proper—the real plain land as it seems from the
height of the Alban mount.   This plain is broken by hills of tufa
of moderate height, and by deep fissures in the ground.   Owing to
this uneven character lakes are formed in winter, and as there is
no natural outlet for the water, malaria arises from the noxious
exhalations in summer heat.   This malaria the ancient inhabitants
avoided by wearing heavy woolen clothing, and by keeping a con-

ANCIENT LATIUM

stant blazing fire, and thus a dense population existed where now
no one can support a healthy life.

The conditions of early society among the settlers in Latium
must be a matter of conjecture.   There were a number of independent political communities called cantons, composed of little
villages.   The latter were in turn probably made up of family
groups whose association was based upon relationship and the need
of coöperation in getting a living, so that each village was a sort
of clan.   No doubt each canton had its local center, which served
alike as a place of meeting and of refuge; these were called, from
their position, mountain-tops (capitolia) or strongholds (arces).   In
time houses began to cluster round the stronghold, and were surrounded with the " ring " (urbs) ; thus the nucleus of a town was
formed, which tended gradually to absorb the different villages.

There can be little doubt that the Alban range, from its natural strength and advantages of air and water, was occupied by the first comers.   Here, among other ancient canton-centers, stood preëminent Alba, the mother-city of all the old Latin settlements. Therefore, when the various cantons, though each independent and governed by its own constitution of prince, elders, and general assembly of warriors, expressed their sense of the ties of blood and language by forming what is known as the Latin League, it was but natural that Alba should be the center of that league, and therefore president of the thirty cantons which composed it.   We have no certain knowledge as to the powers or legal rights this confederacy exercised over the various members.   Probably disputes between cantons were settled by the league, wars against foreign foes decided, and a federal commander-in-chief appointed. What we do know is that on the annual day of assembly the Latin festival was kept, and an ox sacrificed to the Latin god, Jupiter Latiaris.   Each community had to contribute to the sacrificial feast its fixed proportion of cattle, milk, and cheese, and to receive in return a part of the roasted victim.   During this festival a "truce of God" was observed throughout all Latium, and safe-conducts were probably granted, even by tribes at feud with one another. It is impossible to define the privileges of Alba, as presiding canton.   Probably it was a purely honorary position, and had no political signification, certainly none as denoting any sort of leadership or command of the rest of the Latin cantons.   But, vague as the outlines of this early canton life must necessarily be, they show us the one great fact of a common center, which, while it did not destroy the individual independence of the cantons, kept alive the feeling of national kinship, and thus paved the way for that national union which is the goal of every free people's progress.

In tracing the beginnings of Rome, her original constitution, and the first changes it underwent, we are on ground which the uncertain light of ancient tradition and modern theory has made most difficult, if not impossible to traverse with any certainty.   The very name of Romans, with which the settlement on the low hills on the left bank of the Tiber has so long been associated, was originally not Romans, but Ramnes (possibly "bushmen").   Side by side with this Latin settlement of Ramnians two other cantons settled, the Luceres and the Tities, the latter considered to be of Sabellian, not Latin, stock.   From the combination of these three arose Rome.

The unfavorable character of the site renders it hard to understand how the city could so early attain its prominent position in Latium. The soil is unfavorable to the growth of fig or vine, and in addition to the want of good water-springs, swamps are caused by the frequent inundations of the Tiber. Moreover, it was confined in all land directions by powerful cities. But all these disadvantages were more than compensated by the unfettered command it had of both banks of the Tiber down to the mouth of the river. The fact that the clan of the Romilii was settled on the right bank from time immemorial, and that there lay the grove of the creative goddess, Dea Dia, and the primitive seat of the Arval festival and Arval brotherhood, proves that the original territory of Rome comprehended Janiculum and Ostia, which afterwards fell into the hands of the Etruscans. Not only did this position on both banks of the Tiber place in Rome's hands all the traffic of Latium, but, as the Tiber was the natural barrier against northern invaders, Rome became the maritime frontier fortress of Latium. Again, the situation acted in two ways: Firstly, it brought Rome into commercial relations with the outer world, cemented her alliance with Caere, and taught her the importance of building bridges. Secondly, it caused the Roman canton to become united in the city itself far earlier than was the case with other Latin communities. And thus, though Latium was a strictly agricultural country, Rome was a center of commerce; and this commercial position stamped its peculiar mark on the Roman character, distinguishing them from the rest of the Latins and Italians, as the citizen is distinguished from the rustic. Not, indeed, that the Roman neglected his farm, or ceased to regard it as his home; but the unwholesome air of the Campagna tended to make him withdraw to the more healthful city hills; and from early times by the side of the Roman farmer arose a non-agricultural population, composed partly of foreigners and partly of natives, which tended to develop urban life.[1]

[1] One of the most potent influences in the growth of Rome was undoubtedly this habit of association engendered by her peculiar location. The settlements on neighboring hills, originally of separate cantons, were too near together to permit independence except at the cost of perpetual and mutually destructive warfare, so that the only alternative, that of union on a basis of equality of rights, was adopted. This at an early day broke down the political and religious exclusiveness characteristic of the Italian cantons and of all primitive communities and gave to the Romans a liberality of mind and an adaptability which was one of the chief elements of their success in dealing with other peoples. Rome thus absorbed other communities instead of destroying them.

Chapter III

THE ROMAN CONSTITUTION AND THE REFORMS OF SERVIUS TULLIUS

THE basis of the Roman constitution was the family, and the constitution of the state was but an expansion of that of the family. The head of the household was of necessity a man, and his authority alike as father or husband was supreme, and in the eye of the law as absolute over wife and child as over slave. Though a woman could acquire property, she was under the absolute dominion of her father, or, if married, under that of her husband, or, if he died, under the guardianship of her nearest male relations. This authority of the *pater familias* was alike irresponsible and unchangeable; nor could it be dissolved except by death. Although a grown-up son might establish a separate household of his own, all his property, however acquired, belonged legally to his father; and it was easier for a slave to obtain release from his master than for a son to free himself from the control of his father. A daughter, if married, passed out of her father's hand into that of her husband, to whose clan or gens she henceforth belonged. On the father's death the sons still preserved the unity of the family, nor did it become broken till the male stock died out, but, as the connecting links became gradually weaker in succeeding generations, there arose the distinction between members of a family, *agnati,* and members of a clan, *gentiles.* The former denoted those male members of a family who could show the successive steps of their descent from a common progenitor, the latter, those who could no longer prove their degree of relationship by pointing out the intermediate links of connection with a common ancestor. Slaves belonging to a household were regarded by the law, not as living beings, but as chattels, whose position was not affected by the death of the head of the house. Attached to the Roman household was an intermediate class of persons called clients ("listeners"), or dependents. These consisted partly of refugees from foreign states; partly of slaves living in a state of practical freedom; partly of persons who, though not free citizens of any community, lived in a condition of protected freedom. Although these formed with the slaves the familia, or "body of servants," and were dependent on the will of the head of the house or patron, their position was practically one of considerable freedom; and in the course of several generations the clients of a household acquired more and more liberty. Everyone who was a member of a Roman family, and therefore of one of the gentes, or clanships, whose union formed the state, was a true citizen or burgess of Rome. Everyone born of parents united by the ceremony of the sacred salted cake was also a full citizen; and therefore the Roman burgesses called themselves " fathers' children," *patricii,* as in the eye of the law they alone had a father. Thus the state consisted of gentes, or clans, and the clans of families, and although the relations of the various members of the household were not altered by their incorporation with the state, yet a son outside the household was on a footing of equality with the father in respect of political rights and duties. So, too, the various clients, though not admitted to the rights and duties proper to true burgesses, were not wholly excluded from participation in state festivals and state worship; and this would be especially true of those who were not clients of special families, but of the community at large.

Since the family served as the model for the constitution of the state, it was necessary to choose someone who should stand in the same relation to the body-politic as the head of the family did to the household. He who was so chosen rex, or leader, possessed the same absolute power over the state as the house-father had over his household, and, like him, ruled for life: there was no other holder of power besides him. His " command " (imperium) was all-powerful in peace and war, and he was preceded by lictors, or " summoners," armed with axes and rods on all public occasions. He nominated priests and priestesses, and acted as the nation's intercessor with the gods. He held the keys of the public treasury, and alone had the right of publicly addressing the burgesses. He was supreme judge in all private and criminal trials, and had the power of life and death; he called out the people for military service, and commanded the army. Any magistrates, any religious colleges, any military officers, that he might appoint, derived all their power from him, and only existed during his pleasure. His power only ended with death, and he appointed his successor, thus imparting a sense of permanence to the kingship, despite the personal change of the holders of the sovereign power. But, although the king's authority was so absolute, he never came to be regarded by the Romans as other than mortal, nor, as by divine right, higher and better than his fellow-citizens. This view of the kingship was at once the moral and practical limitation of its power. The king was the people's representative, and derived his power from them, and was accountable to them for its use and abuse. Moreover, the legal limitation to his power lay in the principle that he was entitled only to execute the law, not to alter it. Any deviation from the law had to receive the previous sanction of the assembly of the people and the council of elders. There is no parallel in modern life to the Roman family, or Roman state, or Roman sovereign.

The principle on which the division of the burgesses rested was that ten houses formed a clan, ten clans a wardship (curia), ten wardships the community. Each householder furnished a foot-soldier and each clan a horseman and senator. If communities combined, each was a part or tribe of the whole community. Originally each household had its own portion of land, but when households combined into a gens, each clan had its lands, and this system naturally extended to curies and communities, whether single or combined. Thus clan-lands formed in primitive times the smallest unit in the division of land. Although this division into ten curies early disappeared in Rome, we find it in later Latin communities, which always had one hundred acting councilors, each of whom was " head of ten households." This constitutional scheme did not originate in Rome, but was a primitive institution, common to all Latins. What the precise object and value of this division was we cannot now determine, and it is clear that any attempt to rigidly fix the number of households and clans must, through ordinary human accidents, have failed. The really important unit in the division was the curia, the members of which were bound by religious ties, and had a priest of their own. Military levies and money valuations were made according to curial divisions, and the burgesses met and voted by curies. Although all full citizens or burgesses were on a footing of absolute equality as regarded one another, the distinction between those who were burgesses and those who were not was most sharply and rigidly defined. If a stranger were adopted into the burgess-body he could not retain his rights as citizen elsewhere. If he did, he merely possessed honorary citizenship at Rome, and was entitled to the privileges and protection of a guest, not to the exercise of full citizen rights. There were no class privileges at Rome. All wore the simple woolen toga in public, although certain officers by virtue of their office were distinguished by dress. As the Latin immigrants had no conquered race to deal with, the nobility of Greece and the caste of India were unknown to them. The most important duty of the burgesses was military service, as they alone had the right of bearing arms. Hence the name *populus* ("body of warriors," connected with *populari*, "to lay waste"); hence, too, the name of *quirites* ("lancemen"), given them by the king. Other duties incumbent on the burgesses were such as the king laid upon them; among these was the all-important task of building walls, to which the name of *moenia* ("tasks") was given. As there was no state pay for services so rendered, there was no direct state expenditure of state taxation. The very victims for sacrifice were provided by the deposit, or cattle-fine, which the defeated party in a lawsuit was bound to pay. In cases of urgent need a direct contribution was levied, but this was regarded as a loan and repaid when times improved. Although the king managed the state exchequer, the state property, *e. g.*, the land won in war, was not identified with the private property of the king. His exchequer was filled partly by the land-taxes, *i. e.*, the scriptura, or pasture tribute, paid by those who fed cattle on the common pasture, and the vectigalia, or payment in kind in place of rent, by those who were lessees of the state lands; partly by gains in war; partly by harbor dues levied on the exports and imports of Ostia; partly, perhaps, by the tax which the non-burgesses settled at Rome paid him for protection. In addition to these duties the burgesses had also rights. They were convoked by the king in formal assemblies (comitia curiata) twice a year, or in such other meetings as the king thought fit to hold. They had no right of speech on such occasions, unless the king saw fit to grant it; their duty was merely to listen and return simple answers without discussion to the king's questions. As long as the king was executor of existing laws, no intervention was necessary on the part of the citizens; but where abnormal events arose which necessitated any change of or deviation from existing laws, the coöperation and assent of the burgess body was essential. The king put the question and the people returned answer; and the lex, or law, which was the outcome of this process, was not in its origin a command of a king, but a contract proposed by the king and

accepted or refused by his hearers. The citizens alone could allow
a man to make such a will as transferred his property on his death
to another; they alone could sanction the adoption of a man into
the burgess-body, or allow a burgess to surrender his rights as
citizen; they alone could pardon a condemned criminal, whence
arose the right of appeal, which was allowed only to those who
pleaded guilty. Thus far the assembly of the community, restricted
and hampered as it first appears, was yet from antiquity a constituent element of the Roman commonwealth, and was in law superior
to, rather than coördinate with, the king.

The origin of the senate can with probability be ascribed to
that remote period when each clan in Latium was under the rule
of its own elder. As the clans became amalgamated, the position
of such an elder was necessarily subordinated to that of the head
or king of the community; but that the senate was not a mere con-
clave of trusty councilors called into being by the king, but an institution as old as that of king and burgess-assembly, admits of
little doubt. It resembled the assembly of princes and rulers, gathered in a circle round the king as described by Homer. The number
was fixed at three hundred, corresponding to the three hundred clans
of which the three primitive communities, forming the whole state,
were composed. All senators sat for life; they were chosen by
the king, and it is only natural to suppose that, if originally the
senate consisted of the ancient body of clan elders, the king always
chose, when a senator died, a man of the same clan to fill his place.
The senators were, therefore, so many kings of the whole community, although the chief power, as in the household, was vested
in one of their body, namely the king; their insignia, though inferior to those of the king, were of the same character; the purple
border being substituted for the purple robe of the king, and the
red shoes of the senator being lower and less striking than those
which the king wore. Should the king die without appointing a
successor, one of the senators, chosen by lot as interrex, exercised
his authority for five days, and this interrex appointed the next,
thus passing on the five days' sovereign power to one of his own
body. Finally, one of these interreges, but never the one first
chosen, nominated the king, and his choice was ratified by the whole
assembly of the citizens. Thus the senate was the ultimate holder
of the ruling power, and was a guarantee of the permanence of the
monarchy. Further, it was the guardian of the constitution, ex-

amining every new resolution which the king suggested and the burgesses adopted, and having the right of vetoing these resolutions, should they appear to violate existing rights. The senate's consent had also to be obtained before war could be declared. And thus the senate's duty was to guard against any innovation or violation of the constitution, whether coming from king or burgess-assembly. In consequence of this power of the senate, or at least in close connection with it, arose the very ancient custom of the king's convoking the senate, and submitting to it the proposals he intended to bring before the citizens. By thus ascertaining the opinions of the individual members, the king avoided the possibility of any subsequent opposition from that body. On most questions, involving no breach of the constitution, the senate's part was doubtless merely that of compliance with the king's wishes. The senate could not meet unless convoked by the king, and no one might declare his opinion unasked; nor was the consultation of the senate on ordinary matters of state business legally incumbent on the king; but this consultation soon became usual, and from this usage the subsequent extensive powers of the senate were in great measure developed. To sum up, the oldest constitution of Rome was in some measure constitutional monarchy inverted. In the Roman constitution the community of the people exercised very much the same functions as belong to the king in England. The right of pardon, which in England is the prerogative of the crown, was in Rome the prerogative of the community; while all government was vested in the president of the state, whose royal power was at once absolute and limited by the laws. Further, in the relations of the state to the individual, we find that the family was not sacrificed to the community, but that, though power of imprisonment or death was vested in the state, no burgess could have his son or his field taken from him, or even taxation imposed on him. In no other community could a citizen live so absolutely secure from encroachment, either on the part of his fellows or of the state itself. This constitution was neither manufactured nor borrowed; it grew and developed with the growth and development of the Roman people, and as long as there existed a Roman community, in spite of changes of form, it was always held that the magistrate had absolute command, that the council of elders was the highest authority in the state, and that every exceptional resolution required the sanction of the sovereign, or, in other words, of the community of the people.

We have already stated that the earliest amalgamation in the history of Rome was that which blended together the Ramnes, Tities, and Luceres.   This was followed by the union of cantons located on the other hills in the same neighborhood, but no new tribe was added to the original three, the new burgesses being distributed among the existing tribes and curies.   Henceforth each of the three tribes contained two divisions or ranks, and these ranks were denoted by the names " first " (priores) and " second " (posteriores). But no increase was made in the number of the senate, the primitive number of three hundred remaining unchanged down to the seventh century of the city's history.   So also the magistrates or king's deputies remained the same.   This amalgamation increased the bulk, but did not change the character of the Roman state.   But another process of incorporation, the first steps of which may be traced to this period, and which proceeded very gradually, did profoundly affect the community.   We refer to the development of the *plebs*—a problem most intricate and elusive.   On a previous page the position of " clients " was described as twofold—that of those dependent on and protected by the master of the household, and that of those dependent on and protected by the state, *i. e.*, by the king. Every fresh amalgamation doubtless brought in an accession of clients, but the principal increase must have been due to the attraction that Rome, as a commercial center, possessed for foreigners, who became metics, or resident aliens, and to the influence of war, which while it transferred the citizens of conquered towns to Rome, at the same time thinned the ranks of the Roman citizens, who alone had the doubtful privilege of bearing the brunt of such wars.   In truth this latter fact was the chief cause in promoting the amalgamation of the clients and the citizens.   With the increase of the whole body of clients, and especially of that portion consisting of foreigners, attached as clients to the Roman state, but often retaining the citizenship of other communities, the old restrictions, which were more easily observed in the case of household clients, must have broken down.   Many, in fact, must have enjoyed practical freedom, though, of course, not the full rights of Roman citizens.   The immemorial principle of Roman law that, when once a master or owner had renounced his ownership, he could never resume it over the freedman or the freedman's descendants; the liberal concessions, made by Roman law especially to foreigners, as regarded marriage and the acquisition of property; the increasing number of manumitted

slaves; the influx alike of traders, and still more of Latins vanquished in war; the corresponding decrease of true Roman patricians, the constant vexation of the relations between client and
patron—these and other causes must have all sufficed to threaten a
revolution of the direst consequences to the Roman state. The new
name of plebes, or multitude (from *pleo, plenus*), by which the
clients were now called, was ominous, signifying, as it did, that the
majority no longer felt so much their special dependence as their
want of political rights.[1] The danger was averted by the reform
associated with the name of Servius Tullius, although the new
constitution assigned the plebeians primarily only duties, not rights.
Military service was now changed from a burden upon birth to a
burden on property. All freeholders, from seventeen to sixty years
of age, whether burgesses, metics, or manumitted slaves, provided
only they held land, were bound to serve; and they were distributed,
according to the size of their property, into five classes. The first
class, who were obliged to appear in complete armor, consisted of the
possessors of an entire hide of land, and were called classici. The
remaining four classes consisted of the respective possessors of
three-quarters, half, a quarter, or an eighth of a nominal farm, *i. e.*,
of a farm whose size served as the standard by which such divisions
were regulated (probably such a farm contained at least twenty
jugera [2]). The cavalry was dealt with in the same way: its existing six divisions, which retained their old names, were tripled; only
the richest landholders, whether burgesses or non-burgesses, served
as horsemen. All those who held land and were incapable of service, either from sex or age, were bound to provide horses and
fodder for special troopers. To facilitate the levying of the infantry, the city was divided into four parts. Each of these four divisions contributed a fourth part, not merely of the force as a whole,
but of each of its military subdivisions, and this arrangement tended
to merge all distinctions of clan and place, and also to blend, by its
leveling spirit, burgesses and metics into one people. The army
was divided into two levies: the first comprised the juniors, who
served in the field from their seventeenth to their forty-sixth year;
the second, the seniors, who guarded the walls at home. The whole
force of infantry consisted of four legions, each of 4200 men, or 42

[1] There are various other theories as to the origin of the plebeian class. For
a discussion of the question see Soltau, " Entstehung der alts römischen Volks-
versammlungen," Berlin, 1881.

[2] A jugera was approximately three-fifths of an acre.

centuries, 3000 of whom were heavy armed, and 1200 light armed; two of these legions were juniors and two seniors. Added to these were 1800 cavalry, thus bringing the whole force to about 20,000 men. The century, or body of one hundred, formed the unit of this military scheme, and by the arrangement above indicated there would be 18 centuries of cavalry and 168 of infantry. To these, other centuries of supernumeraries must be added, who marched with the army unarmed and took the place of those who fell ill or died in battle. The whole number of centuries amounted to 193 or 194; nor was it increased as the population rose. Out of this military organization arose the census or register of landed property, including the slaves, cattle, etc., that each man possessed, and this was strictly revised every fourth year. This reform, though instituted on purely military lines and for military purposes, had important political results. In the first place, every soldier, whether a full citizen or not, would be certain to have it in his power to become a centurion and, further, a military tribune. In the second, those rights which the burgesses had formerly possessed, not as an assembly of citizens in curies, but as a levy of armed burgesses, would now be shared by the whole army of centuries. These rights conferred the power on the military centuries of authorizing soldiers to make wills before battle, and of granting permission to the king to make an aggressive war. In the third place, although the rights of the old burgess-assembly were in no way restricted, there thus arose three classes: the full burgesses or citizens, the clients possessing freeholds, called later "burgesses without the right of voting," who shared in the public burdens, *i. e.*, military service, tribute, and task-work, and were, therefore, called municipals, and those metics who were not included in the tribes, and who paid protection-money, and were non-freeholders. Analogy from Greek states inclines to the view that this reform was modeled on Greek lines, and produced by Greek influence. The adoption of the armor and arrangements of the Greek hoplite system in the legion, the supply of cavalry horses by widows and orphans, point in this direction; moreover, about this time the Greek states in lower Italy adopted a modification of the pure clan constitution, and gave the preponderance of power to the landholders.

Chapter IV

ROME AND THE OTHER ITALIAN POWERS DURING THE REGAL PERIOD. 753-509 B.C.

THE steps by which Rome rose to the proud position of head state in Latium, the union of the Latin communities under her headship, the extension alike of Latin territory and of the city of Rome, and her early relations with the Etruscans and Greeks, cannot now be described, save in faint outline. We may, however, briefly summarize the results, the details of which have either been buried in oblivion or falsified by mythical legend. Firstly, those Latin communities situated on the Upper Tiber, and between the Tiber and the Anio—Antemnae, Crustumerium, Ficulnea, Medullia, Caenina, Corniculum, Cameria, Collatia, which on the east side sorely hampered Rome—were very early subjugated; the only one which retained its independence was Nomentum, probably by alliance with Rome. Constant war was waged between the Romans and the Etruscan people of Veii for the possession of Fidenae, on the left (Latin) bank of the Tiber, about five miles from Rome, but apparently without the Romans becoming permanent masters of this important outpost.

Secondly, Alba was conquered and destroyed; to her position as the recognized political head and sacred metropolis of Latium, Rome succeeded. Rome thus became president of the Latin league of thirty cantons, and the seat of the religious ceremonial observed at the Latin festival. An alliance was concluded on equal terms between Rome on the one hand and the Latin confederacy on the other, establishing lasting peace throughout Latium, and a perpetual league for offense and defense. Equality of rights was established between the members of this federation, alike as to commerce and intermarriage. No member of the league could exist as a slave within the league's territory, and, though every member only exercised political rights as member of the community to which he belonged, he had the private right of living anywhere he liked within the Latin territory; and, further, although

THE REGAL PERIOD

Latin law was not of necessity identical with Roman, the league naturally brought the two into more complete harmony with one another. The difference between the position occupied by Rome and that formerly held by Alba, was that the honorary presidency of the latter was replaced by the real supremacy of the former. Rome was not, as Alba, a mere member of the league, and included within it, but rather existed alongside it; this is shown by the composition of the federal army, the Roman and Latin force being of equal strength, and the supreme command being held by Rome and Latium alternately. In accordance with this principle, all land and other property acquired in war by the league was divided equally between Rome and Latium. Each Latin community retained its own independent constitution and administration, so far as its obligations to the league were not concerned; and the league of the thirty Latin communities retained its independence, and had its own federal council, in contradistinction to the self-government and council of Rome. As to the treatment of those Latin communities which, like Alba, were actually subjugated by Rome, the circumstances of each particular case doubtless decided the question, as to whether the inhabitants of a conquered town were forced to migrate to Rome, or allowed to remain in the open villages of their old district. Strongholds in all cases were razed, and the conquered country was included in the Roman territory, and the vanquished farmers were taught to regard Rome as their market-center and seat of justice. Legally they occupied the position of clients, though in some cases of individuals and clans full burgess-rights were granted; this was especially the case with Alban clans. The jealousy with which the Latin cantons, and especially the Roman, guarded against the rise of colonies as rival political centers is well shown in Rome's treatment of Ostia; the latter city had no political independence, and its citizens were only allowed to retain, if they already possessed, the general burgess-rights of Rome. Thus this centralizing process, which caused the absorption of a number of smaller states in a larger one, though not essentially a Roman nor even Italian idea, was carried out more consistently and perseveringly by the Roman than by any other Italian canton; and the success of Rome, as of Athens, is doubtless due to the thorough application of this system of centralization.

Thirdly, although Rome failed to master Fidenae, it kept its hold upon Janiculum, and upon both banks at the mouth of the

Tiber. In the direction of the Sabines and Aequi, Rome advanced her position, and, by the help of an alliance with the Hernici, held in check her eastern neighbors. On the south, constant wars, not without success, were waged against the Volscians and Rutulians; and in this quarter we first meet with Latin colonies, *i. e.,* communities founded by Rome and Latium on the enemy's soil, which shows that the earliest extension of Latin territory took place in this direction.

Fourthly, in addition to this enlargement of the Latin borders towards the east and south, the city of Rome, owing to its increase of inhabitants, and commercial and political prominence, needed new defenses. In consequence the Servian wall was constructed. enlarging the old Palatine city so as to include the Aventine, Coelian, Esquiline, Viminal, Quirinal and Capitoline hills, and the intervening spaces.[1] The citadel or acropolis of the city was removed from the Palatine to the Capitoline hill, which was easier to defend, and Janiculum, the hill on the opposite bank of the Tiber, was also fortified and united by a bridge with the southern bank.

Finally the relations of Rome during the regal period with the two foreign races with which her early history is interwoven must be considered. These races are the Etruscans and the Italian Greeks. A mystery shrouds the first people as to their origin, language, race-classification, and original home. Their heavy bodily structure, gloomy and fantastic religion, strange manners and customs, and harsh language, point to their original distinctness from all Italian and Greek races. No one has been able either to decipher the numerous remains of their language or to classify with precision the language itself. Whatever was their original home, the fact of the Etruscan dialect being still spoken in Livy's time by the inhabitants of the Raetian Alps, and of Mantua remaining Tuscan to a late period, proves that Etruscans dwelt in the district north of the Po, bounded on the east by the Veneti, and on the west by the Ligurians. To the south of the Po, and at its mouths, the Umbrians, who were the older settlers, were mingled with and under the supremacy of the Etruscan immigrants; and the towns of Hatria and Spina, founded by the Umbrians, and Felsina (Bologna) and Ra-

[1] It is necessary to remark that this enlarged Rome was never looked upon as the "city of seven hills," which title was exclusively reserved for the narrower old Rome of the Palatine. The modern list of the seven hills, as comprising those embraced by the Servian wall, viz., Palatine, Aventine, Coelian, Esquiline, Viminal, Quirinal, Capitoline, is unknown to any ancient author.

venna, founded by the Etruscans, point to this joint settlement; but the irruptions of the Celts forced the Etruscans early to abandon their position on the left bank of the Po, and later that on the right bank of that river.

The great settlement of the Tuscans in the land that still bears their name completely effaced all traces of Ligurian or Umbrian predecessors in that country, and maintained its position with great tenacity down to the time of the empire. Etruria proper was bounded on the east by the Apennines, on the north by the Arnus, on the south at first by the Ciminian forest, and later by the Tiber. The land north of the Arnus, as far as the mouth of the Macra and the Apennines, was debatable border territory, held now by Ligurians, now by Etruscans. The land between the Ciminian range and the Tiber, with the towns of Sutrium, Nepete, Falerii, Veii, and Caere, was occupied at a later date, possibly in the second century of Rome, and the Italian population there held its ground, though in a state of dependence. When the Tiber became the boundary, the relations between Rome and the Etruscan invader were on the whole peaceful and friendly, especially with the town of Caere. But where an Etruscan town threatened Rome's commercial position on the Tiber, as was the case with Veii, constant war naturally resulted. Any trace of Etruscans to the south of the Tiber must be ascribed to plundering expeditions by sea, never to regular land invasions; nor is there any reliable evidence of any Etruscan settlement south of the Tiber being planted by settlers who came by land.[2] Traditions indicate that Tuscan settlements took place in Rome; but the undoubted fact that a house of Etruscan origin—the Tarquins—held the royal scepter does not warrant the conclusion that the Etruscans ever were dominant in Rome. There is no evidence that Etruria exercised any essential influence on the language or customs or political development of Rome. The passive attitude of Etruria towards Rome was probably due to two causes, their struggles with the Celtic hordes from the North and their seafaring tendency, which is especially shown in their Campanian settlements.

The commercial instincts of the Etruscans caused them to form cities earlier than any other Italian race. Hence Caere is the first Italian town mentioned in Greek records. This same instinct disposed them less to war, and led them to employ mercenaries at a

---

[2] Others—*e.g.*, O. Müller and Pelham ("Encyclopædia Britannica")—hold the contrary view.

very early period. They were governed by kings with powers probably similar to those of Roman kings. They seem to have had a system of clans not dissimilar from that of the Romans, the nobles being marked off strictly from the common people. They were formed into loose confederacies, each consisting of twelve communities, with a metropolis and federal head, or high priest of the league. The whole nation was not embraced in one confederation, as the Etruscans in the north and those in Campania had leagues of their own, though these were so lax that they allowed, or rather preferred, that separate communities should carry on ordinary wars; nor did all the towns join, when, in exceptional cases, a war was resolved on by the confederacy. The Etruscan confederations appear to have been from the first deficient in a firm and paramount central authority.

When the tide of Greek invasion swept over Italy, it met a firm but not bitter resistance from the Latins and the inhabitants of the southern part of Etruria. Caere, in fact, attained its early prosperity by its tolerance of, and benefit from, commercial intercourse with the Greeks. But the " wild Tyrrhenians," alike on the banks of the Po and on the west coast, proved a deadly foe to the Greek intruders; they dislodged them from Aethalia (Elba) and Populonia. The depredations of Etruscan privateers were the dread of all Greek merchants, and caused the Greeks to call the western sea of Italy by their name (Tyrrhenum mare). Although the Etruscans failed to effect a settlement in Latium, or to dislodge the Greeks at Vesuvius, they held sway in Antium and Surrentum. The Volscians became their clients, and they founded a league of twelve cities in Campania. Their very piracy helped them to develop their commercial instincts; and, though at war with Italian Greeks, they were often on peaceful and intimate relations with Greece proper and Asia Minor. Their position as inhabitants of northern Italy from sea to sea, and thus commanding the mouths of the Po on the Adriatic and the great free ports on the western sea, as holding the land route from Pisae on the western coast to Spina on the eastern, and as masters in the south of the rich plains of Capua and Nola, gave them exceptional advantages, and the luxury thus speedily introduced was doubtless no small factor in their rapid decline. The part they played, as allies of the Phoenicians, and especially of the Carthaginians, in opposing Hellenic influence, belongs to another chapter; but the main result at first was to increase their trade and

THE REGAL PERIOD

establish their naval power. Corsica, with the towns of Alalia and Nicaea, became subject to them, while Carthage seized the sister island of Sardinia.

In regard to art and religion, Livy's statement that Etruscan culture was in early times the basis of Roman education, as Greek was in later days, cannot be accepted. The chief characteristic of the Etruscan religion was a gloomy mysticism, and Etruscan art exercised very little influence on that of the Italians. Their close commercial connection with Greece in early times accounts for certain resemblances in the art of the two countries, and Tuscan skill reached its height only in those districts towards the south where Greek influence was strongest. Far from being the most cultured people in the peninsula, the Etruscans must be assigned the lowest place in the history of Italian art.

The second foreign race which deeply affected the development of Rome was the Greek, which early established itself in southern Italy. All civilizing influences reached Italy by sea, and not by land; but it is remarkable that the Phoenicians, who established trading stations on almost every coast of the Mediterranean, have left only one trace in Italy. Their factory at Caere, however, was probably no older than the stations established by the Greeks on the same coast; and the name Poeni, which the Latins gave to the Phoenicians, was borrowed from the Greeks, and points to the probability that the Greeks introduced the Phoenicians to Italian knowledge. The name of the Ionian sea applied to the waters between Epirus and Sicily, and that of Ionian gulf, applied by early Greeks to the Adriatic, prove that seafarers from Ionia first discovered the southern and eastern coasts of Italy. Kyme (Cumae), the oldest Greek settlement in Italy, was founded by the town of the same name on the Anatolian coast. The Phocaeans are said to have been the first to explore the western sea, and doubtless they were soon followed by other Greeks, not only from Asia Minor, but from Greece itself and the larger islands of the Aegean. These, in their new homes in southern Italy or Magna Graecia, as it was called, and in Sicily, recognizing their community of character and interests, became blended together, as in our own time different settlers from the old world have combined in their new homes in North America. These Greek colonies may be grouped in three divisions. The original Ionian group included in Italy Cumae with the other Greek settlements at Vesuvius and Rhegium, and in Sicily Zankle (later

Messana), Naxos, Cantana, Leontini, and Himera. The Achaean
group embraced Sybaris and most of the cities of Magna Graecia.
The Dorian group comprehended Syracuse, Gela, Agrigentum, and
most of the Sicilian colonies; but in Italy it possessed only
Tarentum and Heraclea. As to the period at which these several
settlements took place, we rely on the fact that, while in Homer's
time Sicily and Italy were practically unknown, in Hesiod's poems
the outlines of these two lands are more clearly defined; and in the
literature subsequent to Hesiod a general and fairly accurate
knowledge appears to have been possessed by the Greeks. That
Cumae was the oldest Greek settlement in Italy is generally allowed; that between that settlement and the main Greek immigra-
tion into Sicily and lower Italy a considerable period elapsed is
also probable; but the first two dates in Italian history which can
be regarded as fairly accurate are the founding of Sybaris by the
Achaeans in 721 B.C., and that of the Dorian Tarentum in 708 B.C.

It is important to remember that the Italian and Sicilian
Greeks always retained the closest connection with their old homes,
and that therefore their history is always a history of Greeks, never
of true Italians or Sicilians. This is most clearly shown by the
league of the Achaean cities, comprising Siris, Pandosia, Metapontum, Sybaris with its offshoots Posidonia and Laus, Croton, Cau-
lonia, Temesa, Terina, and Pyxus; which, like the Achaean league
in the Peloponnese, preserved its own nationality, distinct alike from
the barbarians of Italy and the other Greek colonies. These
Achaean Greeks attained a very rapid prosperity, especially in the
case of Sybaris, Croton, and Metapontum; but they did so more
from the fertility of their soil, which they compelled the natives to
cultivate for them, than from their own efforts in commerce or
agriculture. This rapid bloom bore no fruit. Demoralized by a
life of luxury and indolence, these Italian Greeks produced no famous names in Greek art or literature, and their political constitution, sapped in the first place by the attempt of a few families under
the guise of Pythagorean philosophy to seize absolute power, and
later torn by party feuds, slave insurrections, and the grossest social
abuses, completely broke down. Thus the Achaeans exercised but
little influence on the civilization of Italy; and the bilingual mongrel
people, that arose out of the remains of the native Italians and
Achaeans and the more recent immigrants of Sabellian descent,
never attained any real prosperity.

The other Greeks settled in Italy had a very different effect on that country.   Although, unlike the Achaeans, they founded their cities by the best harbors, and mainly for trading purposes, they did not despise agriculture and the acquisition of territory.   The two cities of greatest influence on Italy were the Doric Tarentum and the Ionic Cumae.   The first named, from its possession of the only good harbor on the southern coast, from the rich fisheries on its gulf, from the excellence of its wool, and the dyeing of it with the purple juice of the Tarentine murex, rapidly acquired an unrivaled commercial position in the south of Italy.   The fact, moreover, that the Greeks planted no colony on the Italian shore of the Adriatic, and only two of importance on the Illyrian coast, viz., Epidamnus and Apollonia, caused Tarentum to have no small share in the Adriatic commerce, carried on by Corinth and Corcyra; and, as Ancona and Brundisium rose at a far later period, the ports at the mouths of the Po were the only rivals of Tarentum along the whole east coast. Her intercourse by land with Apulia sowed the seeds of civilization in the southeast of Italy; but it is noteworthy that, as a rule, the eastern provinces of Italy acquired the elements of civilization, not from the scanty Greek settlements on the Illyrian and Italian coasts of the Adriatic, but from the more numerous colonies on the west coast of Italy.   The people of Cumae, and of the other Greek stations near Vesuvius, attained a more moderate prosperity than either the Achaeans or Tarentines.   The district they occupied was small, and they contented themselves with spreading Greek civilization by peaceful commercial intercourse rather than by a policy of conquest and oppression.   There is no doubt that in very early times the western coast north of Vesuvius was visited by Greek voyagers, but the Latins and Etruscans successfully resisted the intruders, and north of Vesuvius no independent Greek community existed in historical times.   Nay, we may conclude that the danger from Greek depredations first turned the attention of the Italians in central Italy to navigation and the founding of towns; Spina and Hatria at the mouth of the Po, and Ariminum further south, were Italian, not Greek foundations.   Although this firm resistance was offered to the Greeks, yet, as far as Latium and southern Etruria were concerned, commercial intercourse was welcomed and fostered.   Caere, Rome, and the cities at the mouth of the Po, not only prospered commercially by this friendly connection, but, as their earliest traditions show, enjoyed religious intercourse with the Greek oracles of

Delphi and Cumae. The Greek voyagers met with a different treatment from the Etruscans proper, who wrested from their grasp the iron trade of Elba, and the silver mines of Populonia, and did not even allow individual traders to enter their waters. The union of the Etruscans with the Phoenicians, and the sudden rise of Carthage itself, arrested that Greek colonization which had, up to the middle of the second century of Rome, threatened to sweep the Phoenicians out of the Mediterranean. The establishment of Massilia, in 600 B.C., on the Celtic coast marks the limit of Greek enterprise; an attempt in 579 B.C. to settle at Libybaeum was frustrated by the natives and the Phoenicians, and a similar fate befell the Phocaeans at Alalia in Corsica, which they evacuated after a naval battle with the combined Etruscans and Carthaginians in 537 B.C., preferring to settle at Hÿele (Velia) in Lucania. In this struggle between the Greeks and the combined Etruscans and Phoenicians, Latium observed a strict neutrality, being on friendly and commercial relations with Caere, and Carthage on the one hand, and Velia and Massilia on the other. Although the Greeks did not give up the struggle, and even founded fresh stations, they no longer gained ground; and, after the foundation of Agrigentum in 580 B.C., they gained no important additions of territory on the Adriatic or on the western sea, and remained excluded from the Spanish waters as well as from the Atlantic ocean.

Chapter V

ESTABLISHMENT OF THE REPUBLIC
509-508 B.C.

THE close of the regal period, and the causes which led to the subsequent changes in the Roman constitution, render it necessary for us to revert to the internal state of Rome itself. Three distinct movements agitated the community. The first proceeded from the body of full citizens, and was confined to it: its object was to limit and lessen the life-power of the single president or king; in all such movements at Rome, from the time of the Tarquins to that of the Gracchi, there was no attempt to assert the rights of the individual at the expense of the state, nor to limit the power of the state, but only that of its magistrates. The second was the demand for equality of political privileges, and was the cause of bitter struggles between the full burgesses and those, whether plebeians, freedmen, Latins, or Italians, who keenly resented their political inequality. The third movement was an equally prolific source of trouble in Roman history; it arose from the embittered relations between landholders and those who had either lost possession of their farms, or, as was the case with many small farmers, held possession at the mercy of the capitalist or landlord. These three movements must be clearly grasped, as upon them hinges the internal history of Rome. Although often intertwined and confused with one another, they were, nevertheless, essentially and fundamentally distinct. The natural outcome of the first was the abolition of the monarchy—a result which we find everywhere, alike in Greek and Italian states, and which seems to have been a certain evolution of the form of constitution peculiar to both peoples. What is remarkable in the change at Rome, is that violent measures had to be adopted, and that the Tarquins, both the king and all the members of his clan, had to be forcibly expelled. The romantic details coloring this event do not affect the fact itself, nor are the reasons assigned by tradition undeserving of belief. Tarquin " the proud " is said to have neglected to consult the senate, and fill up the vacancies in it; to have pronounced sentences of death and confiscation without consulting his counselors; to have stored his own granaries, and exacted undue military service and other duties from the citizens.   The formal vow registered by each citizen that no king should even again be tolerated, the blind hatred felt at Rome ever afterwards for the name of king, the enactment that the " king of sacrifice " (*rex sacrorum*) should never hold any other office,—all these sufficiently testify to the exasperation of the people.   There is no proof that foreign nations took part in the struggle which ensued between the royal house and its expellers, nor can we regard the great war with Etruria in that light, since, although successful, the Etruscans neither restored the monarchy nor even brought back the family of the Tarquins.   The change, violently accomplished as it was, did not abolish the royal power ; the one life-king was simply replaced by two year-kings, called either generals (*praetores*) or judges (*judices*) or, more commonly, colleagues (*consules*).   Although, probably from the first, the consuls divided their functions—the one, for instance, taking charge of the army, the other of the administration of justice—such a partition was not binding, and each possessed and exercised the supreme power as completely as the king had done.   In consequence of this each consul could forbid what the other enjoined, and thus the consular commands, being both absolute, would, if they clashed, neutralize one another.   It is hard to parallel this system of co-ordinate supreme authorities, which, if not peculiarly Roman, was a peculiarly Latin institution.   The object clearly was to preserve the regal power undiminished, but, by doubling the holder of this power, to neutralize its effects.   The limit of a year, fixed for the duration of the consular office, was reckoned from the day of entry upon office to the day of the solemn laying down of power by the consuls ; and, as the consuls to a certain extent laid down their power of their own free will, and as, even if they overstepped the year's limit, their consular acts were still valid, they were not so much restricted directly by the law, as induced by it to restrict themselves.   Still, the effect of this tenure of office for a set term was to abolish the irresponsibility of the king, who, as supreme judge, had been accountable to no tribunal and liable to no punishment.   The consul, on the other hand, when his term had expired, and the protection given by his office had been removed, was liable to be called to account just like any other burgess.   Together with the

THE REPUBLIC

abolition of the monarchy, the ancient privilege of the king to have his fields tilled by the burgesses, and the position which the metics held as special clients of the king, naturally came to an end. The contrast between the old royal power and the new consular office was brought out more clearly by the following restrictions: The old right of appeal, which the king had granted or not at his pleasure in all criminal procedure, was now established by the Valerian law in 509 B.C.; the consul was now bound to grant this right to every criminal who was condemned to suffer capital or corporal punishment; unless, indeed, the sentence was pronounced under martial law. In token of this right, which before 451 B.C. was extended to cases of heavy fines, the consular lictors laid aside the axes, which had been the sign of the king's penal jurisdiction. The need of deputies, which had caused, but not compelled, the king to appoint a city-warden (*urbi praefectus*) to act in his absence, ceased with the substitution of two consuls for one king. If the consul in time of war did intrust the supreme command to a deputy, such a deputy was only adjutant or lieutenant of the consul. It is true that, in times of special emergency, the consuls could nominate a third colleague, who, under the name of dictator, revived the old single supremacy of the king, and who for the time was obeyed by the consuls and the whole state; but such an office was a special creation to meet an exceptional state of things. Although in the field a consul could delegate his functions to a deputy, at home he had no free will in the matter. The two questors ("trackers of murder"), whose appointment by the king to deal with criminal cases had not been obligatory although usual, became now regular state officers. The consul was obliged to nominate them, and their province was enlarged, so as to include the charge of the state treasure and state archives; their tenure of office, like that of the consuls, lasted for one year. On the other hand, the chief magistrate in the city had to act in person, or not at all, in those cases in which a delegation of his authority was not expressly incumbent on him. Thus in the home government no deputy acting for a city magistrate (*pro magistratu*) was possible, while military deputies (*pro consule, pro praetore, pro quaestore*) were only possible in the field, and had no power to act within the community itself. The consul retained the right, which the king had exercised absolutely, of nominating his successor, but he was bound to follow the expressed wishes of the community in his nomination. He might reject particular candidates, and at first even limit the choice to a list of candidates proposed by himself; and, what was more important, the candidate, once appointed, could never be deposed by the community. The consuls had not the right, which had belonged to the kings, of appointing the priests; the colleges of priests now filled up the vacancies in their own body, and the appointment of the vestals and single priests passed into the hands of the president, or pontifex maximus, now nominated for the first time by the pontifical college. Thus the supreme authority in religion was separated from the civil power, and the semi-magisterial position of the pontifex maximus is a further proof of the wish to impose limits on the consular power. The insignia of the consul were markedly inferior to those which had distinguished the king. The lictor's ax was taken away, the purple robe of the king was replaced by the purple border of the consul's toga, the royal chariot was abolished, and the consul was obliged, like every other citizen, to go on foot within the city.

We have above alluded to the revival of the royal power in the person of the dictator. His other title, "master of the army" (*magister populi*), as also that of his chief assistant (*magister equitum*, "master of the horse"), coupled with what we know about the circumstances and causes of his appointment, prove that the dictatorship was an essentially military institution. No doubt it was designed to obviate the disadvantage of divided power in the field, and its restriction to a maximum limit of six months indicates that the office was not to last longer than the duration of a summer campaign. The dictator was nominated by one of the consuls; and, as their colleague, he was obliged to lay down his office when they did. All magistrates were subject to him, and no appeal was allowed from his sentence; the community had no part in his election. The consuls, then, were, with certain restrictions, what the kings had been, the supreme administrators, judges, and generals; in matters of religion, too, they offered prayers and sacrifices for the community, and with the aid of skilled interpreters ascertained the will of the gods. The very restrictions which hampered the consuls could, in time of need, be broken through by the dictatorship, and Rome could see again, under a new name, the absolute authority of the king. In this way the problem of legally retaining and practically restricting the regal authority was solved in genuine Roman fashion, with equal acuteness and simplicity, by the nameless statesmen who worked out this revolution.

A further change of great importance followed the new powers given to the community as a whole. The right of annually electing the consuls, and of deciding, upon appeal from a criminal, the life or death of a citizen, gave the public assembly something more than the passive formal part in state-administration which it had played under the kings. The growth, wealth, and importance of the plebs, and the necessity of their help in making the reform, rendered it impossible for all power to remain in the hands of the smaller body of the patriciate, which by this time had practically become an order of nobility. Therefore the new community was extended so as to embrace the whole body of plebeians; all the non-burgesses, who were neither slaves nor citizens of foreign states, living at Rome under the *jus hospitii,* were admitted into the curies, and the old burgesses, who had hitherto formed the curies, lost the right of meeting and passing resolutions. Further, the curiate assembly (*comitia curiata*) had thus lost its fundamental character of burgesses belonging to different clans, and included many plebeians, who belonged to no clan, but were legally on an equal footing with the most aristocratic citizens. To obviate the results of such a democratic leveling, all political power was taken away from the comitia curiata, and was transferred to the assembly of the centuries (*comitia centuriata*); that is, to the assembled levy of those bound to military service, who now received the rights, as they had previously borne the burdens, of citizens. This body, originally constituted for purely military purposes, now decided cases of appeal, nominated magistrates, adopted or rejected laws. There was no debate in this assembly, any more than in that of the curies; but the constitution of the assembly gave the preponderance of power to the possessors of property, and the peculiar system, by which the decision of an election was often determined by the voting of the first centuries, gave a manifest advantage to the possessors of property, whose centuries had the privilege of giving their votes first.

The prerogatives of the senate were increased by the reform of the constitution. In addition to its old rights of appointing the interrex, and of confirming or rejecting the resolutions passed by the community, the senate could now either reject or confirm the appointment of the magistrates elected by the public assembly. The senate was still composed exclusively of patricians, but on occasions when its advice was asked, side by side with the patres, or true patrician senators, a number of non-patricians were admitted and "added to the senate-roll" (*conscripti*). These plebeians were not by this admission placed on a footing of equality; they did not become true senators, and were not invested with the senatorial insignia; they had no share in the magisterial prerogatives of the senate, nor were they allowed to express their opinion on those occasions when the senate met in the character of a state-council, and discussed what advice should be tendered the community: they were simply silent voters in the divisions of the house, and called " foot-members " by the proud nobility, or " men who voted with their feet." Still, this admission of plebeians into the senate-house was a most important step, and one fraught with no slight consequences. The consuls in office did not vote, but they selected the new members of the senate, alike the patres and the plebeian conscripti, although they were no doubt more restricted by the opinions of the nobility in their selection than the king had been. Two rules early obtained; that the consulship entailed upon the holder of it admission to the senate for life; that vacancies in the senate were not filled up at once, but on the occasion of the census, taken every fourth year, when the roll of senators was revised and completed. The number of senators remained unchanged, and, from the fact that the conscripti were included in the number, we may infer the diminution of the number of patriciate clans. It is easy to see what an immense preponderance of power the revolution gave the senate. Its right of rejecting the proposals of the comitia centuriata, its position as adviser of the chief magistrate, its tenure of office for life, as contrasted with the annual duration of magistracies,—all tended to place the government in its hands. But what chiefly did so, was the fact that the consul ruled for but a brief space, and was, on the expiration of his term of office, merely one of the nobility; and thus, even if a consul were inclined to question the senate's influence, he lacked the first element of political power, viz., time; while his authority was paralyzed alike by the priestly colleges and his own colleague, and, if need be, could be suspended by the dictatorship. The result was that the senate became the real governing power, and the consul subsided into a president, acting as its chairman and executing its decrees. The senate also drew into its own hands the management of the state finances, by causing the consul to commit the administration of the public chest to two quaestors, who naturally became dependent on the senate.

THE REPUBLIC

The revolution thus accomplished at Rome was, as we have seen, conservative in its character, in that the fundamental elements of the old constitution were retained. It was, in fact, a compromise between the two state parties—the old burgesses and the plebeians—who, for the time being, sank their party quarrels, and united under the pressure of the common danger of a despotism. The necessity of their coöperation caused those mutual concessions we have described above, and the importance of the revolution lay far more in the indirect effects of those concessions than in the limit of time imposed on the supreme magistracy. Among these indirect effects was the rise of the Roman citizens in the later sense of the term. The plebeians had hitherto been little better than aliens or metics in the eye of the law. Now they were enrolled in the curies as citizens, they voted in the common assembly and in the senate, and they were protected by the right of appeal. The elevation of the old burgess-body, or patriciate, into an exclusive aristocracy was another result of the revolution. The very incorporation of the plebeians into the burgess-body caused the patres to close up their ranks, and hold stubbornly to the privileges that remained to them; the admission of new clans into their body, which had not been very rare under the kings, now ceased. Although the plebeians might become military officers and senators, they could hold no public magistracy or priesthood: and the patres still maintained the legal impossibility of marriage between their order and the plebeians. It further became necessary to define the distinction between the enlarged burgess-body and those who were now the non-burgesses. To this epoch, therefore, we may trace back—in the views and feelings of the people—both the invidiousness of the distinction between the patricians and plebeians, and the strict and haughty line of demarcation between cives Romani and aliens.

The provinces of civil and military authority were now finally separated. The power of the consul within the city limits was restricted by law, as shown above; his power as general was absolute. Therefore the general and the army could not in their military capacity enter the city proper, unless allowed to do so. Thus the distinction between quirites and soldiers became deeply rooted in the minds of the people.

Viewing the revolution as a whole, its immediate effect was to establish an aristocratic government, by making the senate practically supreme. But the germs of a more representative constitution were visible. The enrollment of the plebeians among the burgesses, the admission of certain of them to the senate, were victories of happy augury for the future. Those plebeian families admitted on account of their wealth or position into the senate naturally held aloof from the mass of the plebs. In addition to this distinction in the plebeian body, there arose another out of the system of voting in the comitia centuriata, which placed the chief power in that class of farmers whose property was in excess of that of the small freeholders, but inferior to that of the great proprietors; and this arrangement further enabled the seniors, although less numerous, to have as many voting divisions as the juniors. While in this way the ax was laid to the root of the old burgess-body and their clan-nobility, and the basis of a new burgess-body was laid, the preponderance in the latter rested on the possession of land and on age, and the first beginnings were already visible of a new aristocracy, based primarily on the consideration in which the families were held—the future nobility.

Chapter VI

THE TRIBUNATE OF THE PLEBS AND THE DECEMVIRATE. 495-449 B.C.

AT the beginning of the last chapter we noted the importance of the struggle which was intimately connected with land-occupation. Before proceding to describe the constitutional changes which arose from this struggle, we must revert for a time to the original land-tenure among the Romans, and, as far as possible, strive to clearly present the main features of this most difficult and important question. From the first, agriculture was felt to be the main support and fundamental basis of every Italian commonwealth. The Roman state in particular secured by the plow what it won by the sword; it felt that the strength of man and of the state lay in their hold over the soil; and this feeling caused the state to avoid, if possible, the cession of Roman soil, and caused the farmers to cling tenaciously to their fields and homesteads. The main object of war was to increase the number of freeholders; this object was also evident in the Servian constitution, which showed the original preponderance of the agricultural class in the state; and which, by its division of the community into " freeholders " and " producers of children " (*proletarii*), without reference to their political position, proved that a large portion of the landed property had passed into the hands of non-burgesses. This division, by imposing upon the freeholders the duties of citizens, paved the way, as we have seen, to conceding them political rights. In the earliest times no burgess had any special property in land : all arable land was the common possession of the several clans; each clan tilled its own portion and divided the produce among its constituent households. When and how the distribution of land among the individual burgesses was made we cannot tell—at any rate it was previous to the Servian constitution; and that same constitution leads us to conclude that the mass of the land was divided into medium-sized farms of not less than 20 jugera, or 12½ acres. Landed estates were successfully guarded against excessive subdivision by custom and

the sound sense of the population.   Evidence is also furnished by
the Servian constitution that even in the regal period of Rome there
were small cottagers and garden proprietors, with whom the mat-
tock took the place of the plow.   In addition to the ordinary farmers, it is clear from the same constitution that large landed proprietors had also come into existence—partly perhaps from the nu-
merical inequality of the members of the various clans, when the
clan-lands were divided among the members; partly, too, from the
great influx of mercantile capital into Rome.   But, as we cannot
suppose that there were many slaves at this time, by whose labor
such large estates were afterwards worked, we must conclude that
a landowner assigned lots to tenants of such portion of his estate as
he could not farm in person.   Such tenants were composed of
decayed farmers, clients, and freedmen, and formed the bulk of the
agricultural proletariate.   They were often free men, and were then
called "tenants on sufferance" as their possession was only held at
the pleasure of the owner.   For this usufruct of the soil the tenant
did not necessarily pay rent in kind, and, when he did, his position
was not quite the same as that of the lessee of later times.   The
relation between the landlord and his tenants was all the closer,
because the landlords did not employ middlemen, but lived themselves on their estates, and took the greatest interest in the welfare
of those dependent on them; their lodging in the city was only for
business purposes, and for avoiding, at certain seasons, the un-
healthful atmosphere of the country. Such slaves as were employed
were, as a rule, of Italian race, and must have occupied very different relations towards their masters from those held by Syrians and
Celts in later days.   It was from these large landowners, and the
system above described, that there sprang up in Rome a landed,
and not an urban, nobility; and further, these tenants-on-sufferance
were of the greatest service to the state, in furnishing trained and
intelligent farmers to carry out the Roman policy of colonization. A
sharp line divided arable from pasture land.   The latter belonged to
the state and not to the clan, and was consequently not subjected to
the distribution, which has been described above.   The state used
such land for its own flocks and herds which were intended for sacrifices and other purposes, and which were kept up by cattle-fines;
and such land was also used by individuals who paid a certain tax
(*scriptura*) for the right to graze their cattle on the common pasture.   This right was a special privilege of the burgess, and was

never granted to a plebeian, except under extraordinary circumstances. In the regal period such common pasture land was probably not extensive, and, as a rule, any conquered territory was parceled out as arable land, originally among the clans, and then among individuals. This description of land tenure in the earliest period now allows us to resume our history at the point of our digression.

Although the new government at Rome passed certain measures—such as the reduction of port-dues; the state-purchase of corn and salt, so as to supply the citizens at reasonable prices, the addition of a day to the national festival, the limitation of the magisterial power of fining,—which seemed intended for the good of the more numerous and less wealthy classes, unfortunately such regulations were exceptional. The object of the kings had probably been to check the power of capital and increase the number of farmers. The object of the new aristocratic government was to destroy the middle classes, and especially the smaller independent farmers; and thus to develop the power of the capitalists, and of large landowners, and to increase the number of the agricultural proletariate. Out of this action on the part of those in power arose the evil influence of the capitalists. The extension of the financial province of the state treasury to such matters as the purchase of grain and salt caused the state to employ agents, or middlemen, to collect its indirect revenues and more complicated payments. These men paid the state a set sum, and farmed the revenues for their own benefit. Thus there grew up a class of tax-farmers and contractors, who, in the rapid growth of their wealth, in their power over the state, to which they appeared to be servants, and in the absurd and sterile basis of their moneyed dominion, are completely on a parallel with the speculators on the stock-exchange of the present day.

The mismanagement of the public land brought out these evils most clearly. The patricians now claimed the sole right of the use of the public pasture and state lands: a right which, as shown above, belonged by law to every burgess. Although the senate made exceptions in favor of the wealthy plebeian houses, the small farmers and tenants-on-sufferance, who needed it most, were excluded from the common pasture. Moreover, to oblige men of their own order, the patrician quaestors gradually omitted to collect the pasture-tax, and thus diminished the state revenues. And further, instead of making fresh assignations of land, acquired by conquest, to the poorer citizens, the ruling class introduced a pernicious system of what was practically permanent occupation, on the condition of the state receiving from the occupier one-tenth of corn, or one-fifth of oil and wine. Thus the system of " precarium," or tenure-on-sufferance, above described, was now applied to the state lands; and not only did this tenure become permanent, but it was allowed only to the privileged patricians and their favorites; nor was the collection of the fifths or tenths enforced with more rigor than that of the pasture-tax. Thus the smaller landholders were deprived of the usufructs which were their right as burgesses, were more heavily taxed in consequence of the lax collection of the revenues from the use of the public land, and lost the old outlet for their energies, which had been provided by the assignations of land. Added to these evils was the system of working large estates by slaves, which at this time was introduced, and which dispossessed the small agrarian clients, or free laborers. Moreover, owing to the enforced absence from his farm in time of war, and the exorbitant taxation and other state-imposed works which war entailed, the farmer often lost possession of his farm, and was reduced to the position of bondsman, if not slave, of his creditor. This creditor was often a capitalist, to whom speculation in land offered a new and lucrative field; if left as nominal proprietor, and actual possessor of the farm, the debtor was perhaps saved from utter ruin, but was demoralized by the consciousness that his person and estate really belonged to another, and that he was entirely dependent on his creditor's mercy. The misery and distress caused by these evils threatened to annihilate the middle class of smaller farmers, and matters were not long in coming to a crisis. About 495 B.C. a levy was called for. Owing to the exasperation produced by the strict enforcement of the law of debt, the farmers refused to obey. One of the consuls, Publius Servilius, induced them to do so, by suspending the law and liberating the imprisoned debtors. On their return from the field of victory, the other consul, Appius Claudius, enforced the debtor-laws with merciless rigor. The war was renewed in the following year; and this time the authority attaching to the dictatorship and the personal popularity of the dictator, Manius Valerius, were found necessary to win over the reluctant farmers. Victory again was with the Roman army; but on its return the senate refused to agree to the reforms proposed by the dictator. On the news of this refusal reaching the army, arrayed outside the city gates, the whole force left its general and encampment, and marched to a hill between the Tiber and the Anio. This celebrated secession, to what was afterward called "the sacred mount" (Mons Sacer), was terminated by the mediation of the dictator and the submission of the senate. The consequences of the movement undertaken by the multitude without a settled leader, and accomplished without bloodshed, were felt for many centuries. It was the origin of the tribunate of the plebs.

The following were the chief characteristics of the tribunate. The two tribunes were of plebeian rank, and elected by the plebeians assembled in curies. Their power was confined to the city's limits, and thus could not oppose the military imperium of the consul, which was all-powerful outside those limits, nor the authority of the dictator, whether exercised inside or outside the city. Within these limits the tribunes stood on an equal and independent footing with the consuls, and had the right to cancel any command, issued by a magistrate, upon a formal protest from the burgess aggrieved by such a command. This power of intercession made it possible for the tribunes to bring the ordinary administration and execution of the law to a deadlock while an appeal against the sentence of a judge or decree of the senate was being investigated. Their judicial powers, owing to the vague and ill-defined laws touching offenses against order, and crime against the community, were alike extensive and arbitrary. They could by their messengers summon before them any burgess, even the consul, arrest him on refusal, imprison him, or allow him bail pending investigation, and finally sentence him to death or the payment of a fine. An appeal from their sentence was heard, not by the whole body of burgesses, but by the whole plebeian body, and the tribunes defended themselves before this assembly in case of such an appeal. Out of this right of defense sprang the right of holding assemblies of the people, and addressing them on other matters, a right expressly guaranteed to the tribunes by the Icilian law of 492 B.C., which rendered liable to severe punishment anyone who interrupted a tribune while speaking, or who bade the assembly disperse. They could take the vote of the people at such meetings, and the "plebiscites," or resolutions thus passed, soon came to have a force and validity which did not properly belong to them. Lastly, the persons of the tribunes were declared inviolable, and the man who laid hands on them was counted accursed in the sight of gods and men.

This outline of the tribunician power serves to show that it was really a copy of the consular power. In both cases the Roman check of intercession, or veto, plays a prominent part; as one consul could veto his colleague, so one tribune could thwart the other. The special power of vetoing the consul, or any other state magistrate, belonged to the tribune, in virtue of his position as protector and counsel of the plebs. Again, the duration of office was limited to a year in both cases, and in both cases the holder of the office could not be deposed. Further, in their criminal jurisdiction, two aediles were associated with the tribunes, just as two quaestors had been attached to the consuls; but the consul submitted to the prohibition of the tribune, while the tribune was unrestricted by any such prohibition from the consul. Still, although a copy, the tribunician power presented a contrast to the consular. It was essentially negative, while that of the consuls was essentially positive. The consuls alone were magistrates of the Roman people, as being elected by the whole burgess-body, and not merely by the plebeians. Therefore the consul alone had the outward insignia of office; the tribune lacked official attendants and the purple-bordered robe, and had no seat in the senate. Thus in this remarkable institution absolute prohibition was in the most stern and abrupt fashion opposed to absolute command; the quarrel was settled by legally recognizing and regulating the discord between rich and poor.

It remains for us to consider what was the political value of the tribunate. Springing as it did from the miseries caused by over-taxation, the baleful system of credit, and the pernicious occupation of the state lands, it yet put no stop to these evils. The reason of this is simply that the wealthy plebeians had as much interest in these abuses as the patricians. The good that the office might do in individual cases of hardship, and in helping plebeians to gain admission to state offices, was more than counterbalanced by the evil of rendering the administration of criminal law subject to the party passion of politics. For party purposes, too, the tribunes could employ their power to veto, and throw out of gear the machine of state, and thus pave the way for that very tyranny which they were created to render impossible. In the latter days of the republic we shall find that this was the very course they pursued; and the odium thus incurred found expression in the contemptuous definition of the tribunate as a " pestiferous power, the offspring of sedition, with sedition for its end and aim." The events which followed the institution of the tribunes indicate a state of organized civil war between the two parties of the state. Among minor conflicts stands out the story of Gaius Marcius, surnamed Coriolanus, from the storming of Corioli. Romance has doubtless colored his bitter opposition to the tribunes in 491 B.C., his expulsion by them from Rome, his return at the head of the Volscian army, his withdrawal on the appeal of his mother, his death at the hands of the exasperated Volscians; but the truth of these disgraceful conflicts between the Roman orders remains unshaken. The murder of the tribune, Gnaeus Genucius, who had dared to impeach two men of consular rank in 473 B.C., had a more lasting result, giving rise two years later to the Publilian law. The proposer of this law, Volero Publilius, who was tribune in 471 B.C., established in the first place the comitia tributa,[1] or plebeian assembly of tribes. Hitherto the plebeians had voted by curies, and numbers alone had determined their decision. The clients of patrician families voted in these assemblies, and thus enabled the nobility to exercise no small influence on the result. The new plebeian assembly was composed solely of those who were freeholders, and thus excluded the great majority of freedmen and clients, as well as all the patricians. Owing to this the comitia tributa was practically an assembly of the independent middle class, and was, owing to its exclusion alike of patricians and non-freeholder plebeians, less representative of the burgesses than the assembly of curies had been. In the second place we must ascribe, if not directly to the provisions of the Publilian law, at least indirectly to its effects, the fact that the resolutions of the plebs (plebiscita) were recognized as legally binding on the whole community, and had the same validity as the decrees of the comitia centuriata. Probably, also, the increase of the number of tribunes from two to five was due to this law, and their election was now transferred to the comitia tributa. Previous to this outcome of party triumph and party legislation, a far wiser and far more serious attempt to deal with the real source of evil was made by Spurius Cassius, a patrician of the patricians, and personally illustrious by two triumphs. He proposed to reform the public land system by distributing a portion of it among the needy citizens; but the cry of "king" was raised, and the commons, irritated by the proposed association of the Latins in the distribution,

---

[1] The origin of the comitia tributa is a much disputed question. For another view of the question see Ihne, "Early Rome," 144-147.

and ever ready to believe that royal power was being aimed at, refused to save their champion. Cassius fell, and his law was buried along with him; but its specter thenceforward incessantly haunted the eyes of the rich, and again and again it rose from the tomb against them, until, amid the conflicts to which it led, the commonwealth perished.

Later, in 462 B.C., a further attempt to abolish the tribunate came from one holding that office. Gaius Terentilius Arsa proposed to nominate a commission of five men for the purpose of preparing a legal code which should bind the consuls in the exercise of their judicial powers. Ten years of party strife elapsed before this proposal was carried into effect, and during that strife two concessions were made to induce the plebeians to give up this legal code. In 457 B.C. the tribunes were increased from five to ten; in 456 B.C., the Aventine, which had hitherto been sacred ground and uninhabited, was distributed among the poorer burgesses, for them to build on and occupy. But these concessions did not turn aside the plebs. The legal code was agreed to, and in 451 B.C. ten men were elected by the centuries, for the purpose of drawing it up. These decemvirs had full powers as supreme magistrates in the place of the consuls; no appeal was allowed in their case; the tribunate was suspended; and, what was more important, plebeians, as well as patricians, were eligible for the new office. The first plebeians were elected at the second election in 450 B.C., and these were the first non-patrician magistrates of the Roman community. The object of this new creation was to substitute a limitation of the consular powers by written law for the more turbulent veto of the tribunes. The pledge given by the decemvirs not to infringe the liberties of the plebs did not, perhaps, imply the abolition of the tribunate; but a wise compromise would doubtless have brought this about, had the decemvirs retired when their task was done. In 451 B.C. the law, engraven on ten tables of copper, was affixed in the Forum to the rostra in front of the senate-house. Two more tables were added in the following year, and thus originated the first and only legal code of Rome—the Twelve Tables. The changes introduced by this code were of a comparatively slight character; the maximum of interest was fixed at ten per cent., and the usurer was rendered liable to heavy penalties. The legal distinction between freeholders and non-freeholders was retained, as also the invalidity of marriage between patricians and plebeians. The chief feature was the denial of appeal to the comitia tributa in capital cases, and the confirmation of it in the case of the comitia centuriata. The political significance of this code lay not so much in the particulars of its legislation, as in the fact that the consuls were now bound to administer justice according to set forms and rules; while the exhibition of the code in public subjected the administrator to the control of the public eye. The downfall of the decemvirs, who under various pretexts refused to abdicate their office, has been ascribed by legend to the tyranny of their chief, Appius Claudius. The murder of Lucius Siccius Dentatus, the bravest soldier in Rome, and a former tribune, was laid at the door of the decemvirs; and the act of the centurion Lucius Verginius, who slew his own daughter to save her from the brutal lust of Appius, caused the storm of popular indignation to break forth. The two armies, which a double war against the Sabines and Volscians had called into the field, on hearing the story from Verginius and Lucius Icilius, the betrothed lover of the dead maiden, straightway left their camps, and once more seceded to the Sacred Mount. They there nominated their tribunes, and, as the decemvirs still remained obstinate, returned to the city, and encamped on the Aventine. The decemvirs now gave way, and Appius Claudius and Spurius Oppius put an end to their lives, while the remaining eight went into exile. It is hard to believe that the decemvirate, one of the triumphs of the plebs, was abolished by that body. Possibly the whole story is a myth of the aristocrats. The overthrow of the decemvirate would more naturally have come from the patricians. A subsequent contest may possibly have ensued to force the patricians to restore the tribunate, resulting in the victory of the plebs, and in the compromise which was confirmed by the Valerio-Horatian laws, the so-called Magna Charta of Rome.

At any rate the tribunate was restored, and, under the Valerio-Horatian laws, gained the following new powers in 449 B.C.: The consuls were forced to administer justice in accordance with the twelve tables of the decemvirs; to compensate for the loss of right of appeal in capital cases to the comitia tributa, every magistrate, the dictator among the rest, was obliged to allow the right of appeal; the tribunes could, as before, inflict fines without limitation, and submit their sentences to the comitia tributa; the management of the military chest was taken from the consuls, and intrusted to two quaestors, who were chosen by the whole body of freeholders, both patrician and plebeian; the votes of this assembly were taken by

districts, which gave the plebeian farmers far more weight than they
possessed in the comitia centuriata; the tribunes were allowed to
sit on a bench at the door of the senate-house, and thus have a share
in the proceedings of that body. And from this important concession gradually arose the principle, that the tribune could by his
veto stop any resolution of the senate or of the public assembly.
No attempt to abolish this magistracy was ever from this time forward made in Rome.

Chapter VII

STRIFE OF PATRICIANS AND PLEBEIANS
445-265 B.C.

THE contest between the patricians and plebeians was not yet ended. For two hundred years the bitter strife continued; each successive struggle wrested from the old aristocracy one or more of their dearly loved privileges, until at last not one remained, save that which birth alone gives and naught can take away, the exclusive pride of caste. To present a continuous history of the internal strife of parties, it will be necessary to confine this chapter to a narrative of the inner life of Rome, and to summarize as briefly as possible the events of each blow to the patrician power, and the results of the conflict as a whole. The history of Rome's foreign relations, although they exercised no slight influence on her internal discord, must be reserved for another place.

Social discontent, rather than political, had given rise to the tribunician movement, a movement viewed with suspicion by wealthy plebeians as well as by patricians. Doubtless some of the leading plebeians had supported their less powerful brethren in the struggle, whether from motives of justice or self-interest. But, now that the office of tribune was firmly established, the whole plebeian body, comprising both those wealthier families and the general mass of the citizens, became firmly united together, and used the tribunate as a lever to remove the political disabilities of their order. The first blow was dealt by the Canuleian law in 445 B.C. This law legalized the validity of marriage between a patrician and plebeian, giving the children of such a marriage the rank of their father. It further yielded to the demand of the plebeians to be admitted to the consulship by a compromise which sought to retain many of the privileges of the office for the patricians. Each year the people were to vote whether there should be the usual consuls or whether their place should be taken by six military tribunes. In the latter case the plebeians were eligible to the office, but the military tribunes

were not to enjoy all the honors of the consuls. They could not cele-
brate triumphs or have their ancestors' images set up in the family
hall and exhibited on public occasions, nor could they speak or
vote in the senate—rights which the regular consuls enjoyed. During the period of nearly eighty years, from 444 B.C. to the
throwing open of the consulship to the plebeians by the Licinian
law in 367 B.C., we find that the military tribunes were elected fifty
times, and the patrician consuls twenty-three times. The miserable
shifts by which the patricians thus sought to baffle their opponents
found further expression in the creation of the censorship in 435
B.C. The two officers, or "valuers" (*censores*), thus created, were
chosen from the patricians, and held office for a period of not more
than eighteen months. They had charge of the registration of the
whole body of citizens for the purposes of taxation, and the duty
of ascertaining the age and property of each man, and of assigning him his proper position on the burgess-roll. This task had
hitherto been managed by the consuls every fourth year. The
censorship, although at this period lacking its subsequent importance
and moral supremacy, from its influence in filling up the vacancies
in the senate and the equites, and from its power to remove persons
from the lists of senators, equites, and burgesses, came to be regarded as the palladium of the aristocracy. The second great victory over the patricians was gained in 421 B.C., when the questorship was thrown open to the plebeians. Hitherto the consuls had
nominated the two city questors, who had charge of the public
money; their election was now transferred to the same body which
elected their two colleagues who had charge of the military chest.
Thus the plebeians became eligible for the first time to one of the
ordinary magistracies, although we do not find that they were able
to avail themselves of this privilege until 409 B.C., when they
secured three places out of the four. In their bitter resistance to
the plebs the aristocracy had resort to every artifice which could
influence elections; the aristocratic colleges of priests, under the
guise of religion, seconded the bribery and intimidation freely
practiced on the electorate. Laws could be arrested, elections made
null and void, by the convenient discovery of portentous omens,
whether from the flight of birds or other phenomena. The blood
of Rome's best and bravest citizens was shed in the vain hope of
stemming the tide of plebeian victory.

At last a solution of the troubles arising from political discontent and social wretchedness sprang out of the combination of the chief plebeians with the farmers. This solution was found in the famous proposals brought forward in 377 B.C. by the tribunes Gaius Licinius and Lucius Sextius. Their proposals were that the military tribunes should be abolished, and that at least one of the consuls should be a plebeian; that plebeians should be admitted to one of the three great priest-colleges, viz., that of the custodians of the oracles; that no one should keep on the common pasture-land more than a hundred oxen and five hundred sheep, or hold more than five hundred jugera (about three hundred acres) of the state lands left free for occupation; that every landlord should be obliged to employ in land cultivation a certain number of free laborers, in proportion to that of his rural slaves; that debtors should be relieved by the deduction of the interest already paid from the capital, and by arranging set terms for the payment of arrears.

The three watch-words of this great movement were clearly social reform, civil equality, the abolition of privilege. The hereditary distinctions associated with the curule magistracy, the right to speak in the senate-house, the possession of spiritual dignities, were no longer to be the exclusive property of the nobles. Social distress was to be relieved, and the poorest burgess was to have his rightful share in those lands from which the selfishness of the rich had so long excluded him. That the patricians struggled hard to prevent these proposals becoming law is not surprising; but that they were passed, after a struggle of eleven years, in 367 B.C., proves the strength of the united forces of the farmers and rich plebeians. The passing of these laws was marked by founding the Temple of Concord at the foot of the Capitol—the last act of the aged warrior and statesman Marcus Furius Camillus, who perhaps trusted that the struggle, too long continued, was now at an end. But the patrician spirit still showed itself in the creation of a third consul, or, as he was usually called, a pretor. However, this office among others was thrown open to the plebeians in 337 B.C., having remained in the hands of the aristocracy only twenty-nine years. The last blows which destroyed aristocratic exclusiveness were that by which the dictatorship was thrown open to the plebeians in 356 B.C.; that which gave the plebeians access to the censorship in 351 B.C.: that dealt by the Publilian law in 339 B.C., which ordained that at least one of the censors must be a plebeian; and that which rendered it impossible for the senate to reject a decree of the community by compelling that body to give their consent before-hand to any measures which might be passed by the comitia tributa. The next blow, aimed at the religious privileges of the patricians, fell later. In 300 B.C. the Ogulnian law increased the number of pontifices from five to eight, and that of the augurs from six to nine, and distributed the stalls in the two colleges between the patricians and plebeians. Lastly, owing to another secession of the plebs, the final blow was given by the law of the dictator Quintus Hortensius, in 287 B.C. This law declared that the decrees of the plebs, passed in their tribal assembly, should have equal force with the decrees of the whole populus, or community. Thus it was brought about that those very burgesses who had once exclusively possessed the right of voting, no longer had even a vote in that assembly whose resolutions were binding on the whole state.

The end had at last come to a strife of two hundred years. The clan nobility, as such, was no longer a political factor in the Roman Republic; but, although its power and privileges were gone, its exclusive patrician spirit was ever a disturbing element of discontent in the public and private life of Rome. To understand rightly the history of Rome in the third and second centuries B.C., we must never overlook this sulking patricianism; it could, indeed, do little more than irritate itself and others, but this it did to the best of its ability.

It remains for us to estimate the result of these changes, as to whether they checked social distress and established political equality.

It cannot be said that any lasting benefit was enjoyed by the poorer classes from the new laws. No legislation could really check the system of large estates, or the employment of slave-labor, without at the same time shaking the foundations of the civil organization of that time, in a way that would entail far-reaching consequences. The true advantages of the reform legislation obtained by the alliance of the poor farmers and the rich plebeians accrued to the latter alone. Relief for the former came not from legislation, but from the successes of Rome, and the necessity of sending out large colonies to consolidate the Roman rule in Italy. Added to this, the general increase of prosperity from successful war and commerce, and the flourishing condition of the state finances, must have lightened the burdens of the farmers, and diffused material well-being among the whole community.

As to political equality, it was now practically attained. In the eye of the law, at least, all arbitrary distinctions were abolished. The different gradations, which age, wisdom, and wealth always produce in society, were lessened by the system that pervaded Roman life. That system aimed rather at a uniform level of ability than at bringing into prominence those more highly gifted. Rich and poor alike lived frugal lives, avoiding even the luxury of silver plate. From the last war with Veii down to that against Pyrrhus, the farmers played a more important part than the old patriciate; the exploits of a plebeian, like Decius, and of a poor farmer, like Manius Curius, now began to take equal rank with, and even eclipse, those of the noblest aristocrat. But, great as the strides to this republican equality were, the government still remained aristocratic. The mere opening of state magistracies to the humblest and poorest burgess does not remove the difficulties which always hinder the rise of a man from the ranks. Moreover, a new aristocracy, consisting of the wealthy plebeians, had existed from the first, and now developed fresh powers. Their policy had always followed lines distinct from, and often opposed to, that of the plebs. This new aristocracy coalesced with the old patriciate, and largely adopted its views, and soon practically took its place. A natural result of this development was the rise of a new opposition. This new democratic party was formed no longer of plebeians, as such, but of the lower classes and the small farmers. But, fortunately for Rome, her struggles with foreign foes caused the leaders of the two new state parties to forego their quarrels in the face of a common danger; and thus we find the patrician Appius Claudius uniting with his personal foe, the farmer Manius Curius, for the purpose of crushing Pyrrhus. The breach was already formed; but the adversaries still shook hands across it.

Finally, let us consider what effect the political abolition of the old nobility had upon the relations between the burgesses, the magistrates, and the senate. Although the powers of the burgess assemblies were increased in certain directions, chiefly with respect to the number of magistrates nominated by them, they did not as a rule interfere with the administration of government. They kept a firm hold on their right to declare war, and occasionally settled disputes between the governing powers, when appealed to by the disputants, and in 390 B.C. they even annulled a decree of the senate. The Hortensian law probably marks the extension of the powers of the comitia tributa, which came to be consulted as to the conclusion of peace and alliances. Still, the influence of these assemblies on public affairs towards the close of this period began to wane. This was mainly due to the extension of the bounds of Rome, whose burgess-body no longer composed a city, but a state. Thus the interest felt in their proceedings on ordinary occasions was comparatively slight, inasmuch as only those residing in the capital as a rule attended. Moreover, the magistrate who convoked the assembly could prevent all discussion; hence the assemblies became mere instruments in his hands, and played a passive part, neither helping nor hindering the administration of the government.

With regard to the Roman magistrates, a great loss of power was the outcome of party contests. The close of the struggle left the consular power subdivided and weakened. Jurisdiction, city police, election of senators and equites, the census and financial administration, were all transferred to magistrates elected by the community, and occupying a position coördinate with, rather than subordinate to, the consuls. In addition to this creation of collateral standing offices such as the pretorship, the senate now annually defined, though it did not directly assign, the different departments of the consuls; and the senate no longer allowed the consuls to conclude peace, without first receiving instructions from the assembled senators. Lastly, the senate could in emergencies sustain a consul by creating a dictator; and, although nominally designated by the consul, the consul-elect was, as a rule, really chosen by the senate. Even the dictator's power was no longer regarded as absolute and unlimited. The definition of the functions of the dictator, as of that of the consul and other magistrates, came to be regarded as a constitutional necessity. Thus we find in 363 B.C., and again in 351 B.C., a dictator appointed for a special and limited duty, such as the performance of a religious ceremony. Moreover, restrictions were imposed in 342 B.C. by plebiscites, enacting that no one should hold two magistracies in the same year, and that the same man should not hold the same office twice within a period of ten years. Later, again, in 265 B.C., the Marcian law forbade anyone holding the censorship twice. Although the rule forbidding pluralism, *i.e.*, the holding of two offices at the same time, was strictly observed, we frequently find instances of a relaxation of the other restriction. The change, which thus transformed the supreme power of the state into a limited magistracy with definite functions, also affected the tribunate. Now that this office had accomplished the purpose for which it had been used, by securing the abolition of the legal disabilities of the commons and of the privileges of the old nobility, the original object of the tribunate as counsel and protector of the humblest and weakest was as odious to the new plebeian aristocracy as it had been to the patrician. Therefore, under the new organization the office lost its old character of a weapon of opposition, and became an instrument of government. The tribunes no longer sat on a bench at the door of the senate-house, but took their seats by the side of the other magistrates, and took part in the discussions. Like the other acting magistrates, they did not during their year of office vote in the senate, but they had the right of convoking it, of consulting it, and of procuring decrees from it. Thus, by becoming magistrates of the state, the tribunes for the time lost their old revolutionary and obstructive character, and paved the way for the steady growth of the power of the new aristocracy; indeed, the tribunes were, as a rule, members of that body. Yet the preservation and the associations of the name of tribunate might well forbode danger in the future. For the moment, however, and for a long time to come, the aristocracy was so absolutely powerful, and so completely possessed control over the tribunate, that no trace is to be met with of a collegiate opposition on the part of the tribunes to the senate. What opposition did arise came from single independent tribunes, and was easily crushed, often by the aid of the tribune-college itself.

The real governing power became vested in the senate. The Ovinian law, probably passed soon after the Sexto-Licinian laws, regulated the composition of that body. All who had been curule ediles, pretors, or consuls became members. The action of the censors was in this way greatly restricted, although it was still their duty to fill up all the vacancies which remained after the abovementioned officers had been placed on the senatorial roll. Even in making this selection the censors were bound by oath to choose all the best citizens. Moreover, usage, if not law, seemed to have ordained that burgesses, who had filled a non-curule office, or who were eminent for personal valor, or who had saved the life of a fellow-citizen, should be selected for the honor. Those thus chosen by the censor voted, but took no part in debate. The main part of the senate, whose election was determined by the Ovinian law, and not by the selection of the censors, and who held the reins of government, were in this way indirectly elected by the people. The

Roman government in this way made some approach to, although
it did not reach, the great institution of modern times, representative popular government, while the aggregate of the non-debating
senators·furnished—what it is so necessary, and yet so difficult to
get in governing corporations—a compact mass of members, capable of forming and entitled to pronounce an opinion, but voting
in silence. No magistrate submitted a proposal to the people without, or in opposition to, the senate's opinion; if he did so, the
senate, by means of the vetoing power of the magistrates and the
annulling powers of the priests, easily thwarted him; and in extreme cases the senate could refuse to execute the decrees of the
people. Through the presiding magistrate the senate practically
exerted a paramount influence on the elections, and, as was shown
above in the case of the consuls, bore no small part in settling what
was to be the special sphere of the elected magistrates. Further,
the senate acquired the right, which by law belonged only to the
community, of extending the term of office to the consul or pretor,
acting outside the city's limits; and the consul or pretor, whose
term was thus prolonged, was said to be acting " in a consul's
or pretor's stead " (*pro consule, pro praetore*). From the year
307 B.C. the term of the commander-in-chief was regularly prolonged by a mere decree of the senate. Finally, as regards administration, war, peace, and alliances, the founding of colonies, the
assignation of lands, and the whole system of finance, the senate
became practically supreme. Great as the powers intrusted to the
senate were, the senate proved fully worthy of the trust. Although
it is clear that the steps above described arrested the free action of
the burgesses, and reduced the magistrates to mere executors of the
senate's will, the assembly, by its ability to govern, justified its
usurpation of power. Its members owed their position to merit
and the people's choice, not to birth; those unworthy of their high
position were liable to removal by the censors every fifth year.
Their life-tenure of office freed them from the necessity of trimming
their sails to the shifting breeze of public opinion, and gave them
a complete control over the executive magistrates, whose office annually changed hands. This continuity of existence rendered possible a firm, unwavering, and patriotic foreign policy; and never
was a state more firmly and worthily represented in its external
relations than Rome in its best times by its senate. We cannot
deny that, in matters of internal administration, the senate too

often favored the selfish interests of the moneyed and landed aristocracy, which was largely represented in that body. But, when
we consider its conduct as a whole, we must allow that the Roman
senate was the noblest organ of the nation, and in consistency and
political sagacity, in unanimity and patriotism, in grasp of power,
and unwavering courage, the foremost political corporation of all
times—still even now " an assembly of kings," which knew well how
to combine despotic energy with republican self-devotion.

Chapter VIII

FALL OF ETRUSCAN POWER AND THE COMING OF THE CELTS. 500-343 B.C.

THE last three chapters have been devoted to the internal struggles of Rome, and their political results; we can now turn to the external history both of Rome and of Italy. Two notable events meet our eyes—firstly, the collapse of the Etruscan power: secondly, the incursions of the Celts. About 500 B.C. the Etruscans had reached their zenith of prosperity. Allied with the Carthaginians, who were absolute masters of Sardinia, and had a firm foothold in Sicily, they ruled the Etruscan and Adriatic seas. Although Massilia retained her independence, the seaports of Campania and of the Volscian land, and the island of Corsica, were in their hands. The possession of Latium, which interposed a firm barrier between Etruria proper and the Tuscan settlements in Campania, was naturally of the utmost importance; and, for a short time, the conquest of Rome by Lars Porsena in 507 B.C. seemed to open out a prospect of the realization of Tuscan supremacy in Italy. But the advance of the victorious Etruscans into Latium received a check beneath the walls of Aricia, from the timely succor of the people of Cumae in 506 B.C. The end of this war is unknown; possibly the disgraceful terms of the peace, which Rome had concluded with Lars Porsena the previous year, were somewhat modified; but, for a time at least, Latium was in imminent danger of being reduced to subjection by Etruscan arms. Fortunately, however, for Rome, the main strength of the Etruscan nation was diverted from Latium, and called to do battle elsewhere; while Veii and the neighboring towns grappled with Rome, the rest of the Etruscans were engaged in another cause.

The arrest of Greek colonization by the combined Etruscans and Carthaginians has been already described; a more deadly blow, on a far grander scale, if we may believe tradition, threatened the whole Greek world. The simultaneous defeat of the Persians at Salamis and the Carthaginians at Himera by the rulers of Syracuse and Agrigentum, Gelon, and Theron, in 480 B.C., utterly crushed the great combination of Persians, Carthaginians, and Etruscans against liberty and civilization. Six years later the Cumaeans and Hiero of Syracuse vanquished the Etruscan fleet off Cumae; and the rise of Syracuse to the chief power in Sicily, and of Tarentum to the leading position in the south of Italy, put an end to the maritime supremacy of both Etruscans and Carthaginians. Syracuse in 453 B.C. ravaged the island of Corsica and the Etrurian coast, and occupied Elba; and later, in 415 to 413 B.C., the Athenian expedition against Syracuse, which received support from Etruscan galleys, ended in ignominious failure, and left Syracuse free to turn on her old enemy with redoubled vigor. Dionysius, who reigned from 406 to 367 B.C., founded Syracusan colonies on the Illyrian coast at Lissus and the island of Issa, and on the eastern coast of Italy at the ports of Ancona, Numana, and Hatria; thus ousting the Etruscans from the Adriatic. In addition to this, he captured, in 358 B.C., Pyrgi, the rich seaport of Caere, a blow from which the Etruscans never recovered. Later, too, when the death of Dionysius and the ensuing political troubles of Syracuse opened the way to Carthaginian arms, we find that the revival of maritime supremacy by Carthage brought no similar revival to their old allies the Etruscans. On the contrary, the relations between the two powers had become so strained, that in 310 B.C. Tuscan men-of-war assisted Agathocles of Syracuse in his war against Carthage, and the old alliance was thus severed. This rapid collapse of the naval power of the Etruscans was due in great measure to the fact that, at the same time that they were struggling with the Sicilian Greeks by sea, they were assailed on all sides by foes on land. During the period of the combination of Persians, Carthaginians, and Etruscans, above alluded to, a bitter war raged between Rome and Veii from 483 to 474 B.C. Its result was so far favorable to Rome that the Etruscans gave up Fidenae, and the district they had won on the right bank of the Tiber. Moreover, the Samnites attacked the Etruscan settlements in Campania; Capua fell in 424 B.C., and the Etruscan population was extirpated or expelled. But in northern Italy a new nation was knocking at the gates of the Alps. It was the Celts; and the brunt of their inroad fell first upon the Etruscans.

The character of the Celtic nation, their origin, and the part they played in Italian history at this period now claim our attention.

Nature, though she lavished upon the Celts her most brilliant gifts, had denied them those more solid and enduring qualities which lead to the highest human development, alike in morality and politics. They preferred a pastoral life to an agricultural, and had none of that attachment to their native soil which characterized the Italians and the Germans. Their fondness for congregating in towns and villages did not lead them to develop political constitutions. As a nation they had little sense of unity; their individual communities were equally deficient in sincere patriotism, consistent purpose, and united effort. Ever ready to rove, they were the true soldiers-of-fortune in antiquity, and possessed all the qualities of good soldiers, but of bad citizens,—qualities which explain the historical fact that the Celts have shaken all states and founded none. These people at a very early period settled in modern France; from there they crossed over to Britain in the north, and in the south passed the Pyrenees, and contested the possession of Spain with the Iberian tribes. Our history is immediately concerned with their movements in the opposite direction, when, leaving their homes in the West, they retraced their steps and poured over the Alps in ceaseless streams. Their hordes, on passing the Graian Alps by the little St. Bernard, first formed the Celtic canton of the Insubres, with Milan as its capital. The canton of the Cenonmani, with the towns of Brescia and Verona, soon followed. The Ligurians were dislodged, and the possessions of the Etruscans on the left bank of the Po were soon wrested from their grasp; Melpum fell, and soon the invaders crossed the Po, and assailed the Etruscans and Umbrians in their original home. Isolated roving bands no doubt reached the borders of Etruria proper, and about the middle of the fourth century the Tuscan nation were practically restricted to that land which still bears their name. About the year 426 B.C. the Etruscans were thus engaged in war with three enemies: in the north with the encroaching Celts; in the south with the Samnites, who had invaded Campania; and with the Romans. A fresh outbreak of hostilities between Rome and Veii was due to the revolt of the people of Fidenae, who had murdered the Roman envoys and called in the help of Lars Tolumnius, king of Veii. This king was slain by the consul Aulus Cornelius Cossus, and the war ended favorably to the Romans. After a truce, during which the position of Etruria grew more and more critical, war broke out again in 406 B.C. between Rome and Veii: the latter received support from

Capena and Falerii, but, owing to their struggles with the Celts, and their dislike for the regal form of government in Veii, the Etruscan nation as a whole gave no aid to the hard-pressed Veientines. The city fell in 396 B.C., and was destroyed by the triumphant Romans, to whom the heroism of Marcus Furius Camillus had first opened up the brilliant and perilous career of foreign conquest. Tradition tells us that Melpum and Veii fell on the same day; whether this be so or not, the double assault from the north and the south, and the fall of the two frontier strongholds, were the beginning of the end of the great Etruscan nation. For a moment, however, it seemed as if the folly of Rome was destined to turn aside from the head of the Etruscans the sword of the foreign barbarian. In 391 B.C. Clusium, situated in the heart of Etruria, was hard pressed by the Celtic Senones; so low was Tuscan pride, that Clusium begged aid from the destroyers of Veii. Rome, however, in place of substantial help, dispatched envoys, who attempted to impose on the Celts by haughty language; when this failed, the envoys violated the law of nations by fighting in the ranks of the men of Clusium. To the demand of the barbarians for the surrender of these envoys the Romans refused to listen. Then the Brennus, or king of the Gallic host, abandoned the siege of Clusium, and turned against Rome. The battle of the Allia in 390 B.C., and the capture and destruction of Rome, taught the Romans a bitter lesson. The horrors of this catastrophe, the burning of the city, the saving of the Capitol by the sacred geese, and the brave Marcus Manlius, the scornful throwing down into the scale of the Gallic sword, have left a lasting impression on the imagination of posterity; but the victory of the Gauls had no permanent consequences —nay, it only served to knit more closely the ties of union between Latium and rebuilt Rome. The Gauls often returned to Rome during this century. Camillus, indeed, crowned his great career by defeating them at Alba in 367 B.C.; the dictator Gaius Sulpicius Peticus routed a Gallic host in 358 B.C., and eight years later Lucius Furius Camillus, the son of the celebrated general, dislodged the Gauls from the Alban mount, where they had encamped during the winter. But these plundering incursions only served to make all Italy regard Rome as the bulwark against the barbarians, and thus to further her claim, not only to supremacy in Italy, but also to universal empire. The Etruscans had attempted to recover what they had lost in the Veientine war, while the Celts

were assailing Rome. When the barbarians had departed, Rome
turned once more on her old enemy. The whole of southern Etruria,
as far as the Ciminian range, passed into Roman hands, and the
advanced frontier line was secured by the fortresses of Sutrium and
Nepete, established respectively in 383 and 373 B.C. Moreover,
four new tribes were formed in the territories of Veii, Capena,

THE PEOPLES OF EARLY ITALY
343 — 290 B.C.

and Falerii, in 387 B.C., and the whole country became rapidly
Romanized. A revolt of Tarquinii, Falerii, and Caere, about 358
B.C., against Roman aggression was soon crushed; and Caere had
to cede half its territory, and withdraw from the Etruscan league.
The relation of political subjection in which Caere stood to Rome
was called " citizenship without the power of voting " (civitas sine
suffragio) ; thus the state lost its freedom, but could still administer
its own affairs. This occurred in 351 B.C.; and eight years later

Falerii withdrew from the Etruscan league, and became a perpetual ally of Rome. Thus the whole of southern Etruria became subject to Roman supremacy.

Gradually the conflicts in northern Italy ceased, and the various nations settled side by side within more defined limits. The stream of Celtic immigrations over the Alps flowed back; whether from the desperate efforts of the Etruscans, and the strong barrier of the Romans, or from some causes operating on the other side of the Alps, we cannot determine. In a general way the Celts now ruled between the Alps and the Apennines, and as far south as the Abruzzi: but their dominion did not sink deep into the land, nor had it the character of exclusive possession. In the flat country occupied by the Celts Etruscan settlements still existed. Mantua was a Tuscan city even in the days of the empire, as also was Hatria on the Po; and Etruscan corsairs still rendered the Adriatic unsafe far on into the third century B.C. Further, although mere fragments of the former supremacy of the Etruscans were now left in these districts, such civilization as we find among the Celts and Alpine peoples was due to Tuscan influence. To this we must ascribe the fact that the Celts in the plains of Lombardy abandoned their roving warrior-life, and permanently settled in that district. But the Etruscan nation was now hemmed in on all sides. Its possessions in Campania, and in the district north of the Apennines and south of the Ciminian forest, were lost forever—its day of power had passed away. Socially and politically the whole nation had completely degenerated. Unbounded luxury and gross immorality had eaten out the heart of the people. Gladiatorial combats first came into vogue among the Etruscans; sensual indulgence of every sort sapped the nation's vigor. The abolition of royalty, which had been carried out in every city about the time of the siege of Veii, introduced the worst form of aristocratic government. The federal bond had always exercised but little restraint; now the abuse of power by the nobles caused social revolution and bitter distress. The energies of the nation were broken from the day of Veii and of Melpum. Earnest attempts were still once or twice made to escape from the Roman supremacy, but in these instances the stimulus was communicated to the Etruscans from without—from another Italian stock, the Samnites.

Chapter IX

ADVANCE OF ROME TO THE CONQUEST OF ITALY.
500-290 B.C.

WE have now reached a turning-point in the fortunes of Rome. In the last chapter it was shown that she had abandoned her old defensive attitude towards Etruria, and had succeeded in annexing the southern portion of that country, and in repelling the restless Celtic hordes. Her next foes are no longer foreign intruders, but men of her own stock, or of Italian race.

We may briefly summarize the steps by which Rome became mistress of Italy as follows: The subjugation of the Latins and Campanians; the gallant struggles of the Samnites, both on their own behalf and on behalf of the rest of the still independent Italians; and the invasion and defeat of Pyrrhus. With regard to the first point, we must for a moment revert to the old position of Rome in Latium, as exercising a hegemony, based upon complete equality between the Roman state on the one hand and the Latin confederacy on the other. That these relations were violently shaken by the abolition of the monarchy at Rome we know from tradition, which has painted in glowing colors the victory at Lake Regillus, gained by the Romans about 499 B.C. More certain proof is afforded by the renewal of the perpetual league between Rome and Latium by Spurius Cassius six years later. At what time the rest of Latium followed Rome's lead and abolished the regal power we do not know, but probably this took place at an early period. Although we are without definite information on each point, it is easy to understand how the basis of equal rights soon became impracticable; how Rome not only bore the brunt of most of the wars, but also naturally appropriated the substantial fruits of the victories; how she not only decided the question of war or peace, but practically appointed from her own body the federal generals and chief officers, and assumed the direction of every campaign, and how in founding colonies she supplied most of the colonists.

Although the public rights of the federal Latins were thus encroached upon, their private rights remained the same. To whatever federal town a Latin migrated, he was a passive burgess, could hold property, marry, make wills; and, though not eligible for office, he shared in all other political rights and duties, and could vote in the comitia tributa, if not in the other assemblies.

Long ere the allied Latins dared penetrate Etruria, they successfully extended their power towards the east and south. The Sabines between the Tiber and Anio offered but a feeble resistance to the confederate arms, possibly owing to the fact that the Sabine hordes were pouring into lower Italy. It was not even found necessary to plant colonies in this Sabine land to keep it in subjection. Their neighbors, the Aequi, on the upper Anio, and the Volscians on the coast, proved far tougher foes. In their constant struggles with these two peoples, the Romans and Latins made it their chief aim to sever the Aequi from the Volsci. This object they partly obtained by planting Latin colonies at Cora, Norba, and Signia, about 495 B.C., and still more by forming a league with the Hernici in 486 B.C.; the accession of this state isolated the Volscians, and formed a bulwark against the Sabellian tribes on the south and east. The power of the Aequi was thus broken, but it was not till the system of fortresses or colonies had been extended throughout the Volscian land that the Volsci ceased to resist. Chief among these colonies were Velitrae, founded in 494 B.C., Suessa Pometia and Ardea in 442 B.C., Circeii in 393 B.C.; and finally, after two great victories, won by the dictator Camillus in 389 B.C., and the dictator Aulus Cornelius Cossus in 385 B.C., the Pomptine territory was secured by the founding of the fortresses Satricum in 385 B.C., and Setia in 382 B.C., and the territory itself was distributed into farm allotments and tribes about 383 B.C. These successes of the league, which now embraced Rome, Latium, and the Hernici, only rendered it more liable to disunion. The allies felt all the more acutely the overshadowing burden of Rome's increased power, and were naturally indignant at her overbearing acts of injustice. A glaring instance of wrong was the appropriation by Rome of a border territory between the lands of the people of Aricia and Ardea, to which both cities laid claim, and had called in Rome to act as arbiter in 446 B.C. Dissensions, owing to this, arose in Ardea between the aristocratic party, which held to Rome, and the popular party, which sided with the Volscians. The chief cause of the disruption of the league was the absence of a common foe. The capture of Rome by the Celts, and the appropriation by Rome of the Pomptine territory caused the most famous Latin towns to break off from their alliance. Separate wars, in consequence, occurred with the revolted towns—with Lanuvium, 383 B.C.; Praeneste, 382-380 B.C.; and Tusculum, 381 B.C. The latter was reduced to the position of a municipality, and was incorporated in the Roman state with the full rights of Roman citizenship, retaining certain powers of self-government. This was the first instance of a municipium in its later sense. In addition to these towns, Tibur, in 360 B.C., and some of the colonies planted in Volscian land, revolted from Rome; and Tibur even made common cause with the again advancing Celtic hordes, whom the dictator Ahala defeated in 360 B.C. But, owing to the want of concert between the various Latin cities, Rome subdued each separately, and also proved victorious in the later and severer struggle with her allies, the Hernicans, from 362-358 B.C. In the latter year the treaty between Rome and the Latins and Hernicans was renewed, but the terms were doubtless greatly to Rome's advantage.

To this period must be referred the closing of the Latin confederation, which took place about 384 B.C. Probably this was in no small degree the cause of the revolt of Latium above described. The league, as now constituted, included thirty towns with full Latin rights. In addition, there were the colonies founded by Rome and the Latin league. A second class of seventeen towns had no right of voting, but shared in the Latin festival. Such communities as were subsequently founded, e. g., Sutrium, Nepete, Cales, and Tarracina, were not incorporated in the league; nor were those communities whose independence was afterwards taken away, such as Tusculum and Satricum, erased from the list. The geographical limits of Latium were fixed by the closing of the league. Moreover, in the case of all Latin communities subsequently founded, right of commerce and marriage was granted to them only in relation to Rome; they could not enjoy the interchange of these privileges with any other Latin community. Further, all special leagues between Latin communities, irrespective of Rome, were for the future prevented, as being dangerous to Rome's preëminence. Owing also to Rome's influence, ediles were created in the Latin communities, and their constitutions were remodeled on the Roman pattern. After the fall of Veii and the conquest of Pomptine land, Rome tightened the reins of government over the practically subject Latins; and the exasperation arising therefrom caused Latin volunteers to join foreign foes in their conflicts with Rome; and, in 349 B.C., the Latin league refused the Romans its regular contingent. The defeat of the Aurunci and the capture of Sora in 345 B.C. had advanced Roman arms to the Liris. Thus Rome was brought into contact with the Samnites and the struggle with this brave people now claims our attention.

The Samnites were a people belonging to the Umbrian branch of the Italian stock who had settled in the mountainous regions of the interior to the east of Latium and Campania. They were for the most part a simple race of sturdy husbandmen united in a loose confederacy wherein no one community preponderated, as did Rome in Latium. The policy they pursued was the exact opposite of that of Rome. They were content with the defense of their territory, and rarely sought to enlarge it; and new lands gained were the result of adventurous bands who left their homes in search of plunder, and were left to their own resources by their native state. Thus their gains were not direct gains to the Samnite nation, while Rome secured every success by a system of colonization. The movements of the Samnites had hitherto been partly checked by the Greeks and Etruscans. The rapid collapse of the Etruscans, and the decline of the Greek colonies from 450-350 B.C., left them free to march west and south. Capua was captured by them in 424 B.C.; four years later they dealt a fatal blow to the Campanian Greeks by taking Cumae. It is about this time that another Samnite stock, called Lucanians, made its appearance in southern Italy. The Lucanians proved too powerful for the demoralized Greeks; and, despite the united efforts of the chief Achaean cities, who reconstructed their league in 393 B.C., in a very short time but few Greek towns remained. Their speedy downfall was due in great measure to the fact that Dionysius the elder, of Syracuse, sided with the Lucanians against his countrymen. Even Tarentum, powerful and warlike as she was, was forced to turn for aid to her mother country.

Thus, at the period when Roman power began to advance southward, the Samnites and their kinsfolk the Lucanians and Bruttians had practically swept over the whole of southern Italy. Isolated Greek towns continued to exist, such as Tarentum, Thurii, Croton, Metapontum, Heraclea, Rhegium, and Neapolis; some

of these retained their independence. Other Greek cities, such as
Cumae, Posïdonia, Laus, and Hipponium, were under Samnite rule.
In this way mixed populations arose; this was especially the case
with the bilingual Bruttii, and in a lesser degree with the Samnites
in Lucania and Campania. The very extent of the Samnite conquests, owing to the want of a settled policy, and of some bond by
which the Lucanians, Bruttians, and Samnites proper might be
closely united, proved a source of weakness rather than strength.
The space they occupied was out of proportion to their numbers,
and the hold they exercised over their possessions was loose and
insecure. Moreover, Greek culture exercised a fatal influence on
the Samnite nation. Thus in Campania the Samnite population of
Capua, Nola, Nuceria, and Teanum adopted Greek manners, and a
Greek form of constitution. Capua became notorious for its wealth
and luxury, for its gladiatorial combats, and its warlike, if dissolute,
youth whose plundering excursions to Sicily and other places had
no small effect on the history of Italy. The Campanian Samnites
—especially in Capua, where Etruscan influences still lingered—
thus completely changed their old habits of life; and, though they
did not lose their love of enterprise and bravery, they were unable
to resist the demoralizing influences with which they were there
surrounded. The same result in a lesser degree is observable in the
Lucanians and Bruttians. Treasures of Greek art have been discovered in their tombs, and they abandoned their old national mode
of writing for that of the Greeks. The stock inhabiting Samnium
proper alone retained its old character, and was free from all the
debasing effects of a superior but immoral civilization. The Hellenized Samnites of Campania soon learned to fear their hardier
and purer kinsmen in Samnium, who, pouring down from their
mountain strongholds, ravaged the rich plains of their weaker
brethren.

Roman interference sprang from this very cause. The
Sidicini in Teanum, and the Campanians in Capua, called in Rome
to protect them against the Samnites in 343 B.C. When Rome
at first refused, the Campanians offered to submit to Roman supremacy; this offer was too tempting to be rejected. Rome and
Samnium, whether after a campaign or not is doubtful, came to
terms; Capua was left under Roman, and Teanum under Samnite sway, and the upper Liris was left in Volscian hands. Both
sides were glad to lay down arms—the Samnites, because Tarentum

CONQUEST OF ITALY

was threatening her Sebellian neighbors; the Romans, because a fresh storm was brewing in Latium. The old grievances of the Latin towns were aggravated by the prospect of Roman rule extending to the south of them, and once more they broke into open revolt. All the original Latin communities, except the Laurentes, took up arms against Rome; but all the Roman colonies in Latium, except Velitrae, remained firm to the Roman side. Capua seized the opportunity to get rid of Roman rule, and other Campanian cities joined the revolted Latins. The Volscians also felt that still another chance was given them of recovering their liberty; but the Hernici and the Campanian aristocracy did not unite with the insurgents. The battle of Trifanum in 340 B.C., gained by Titus Manlius Torquatus over the joint forces of the Latins and Campanians, broke the neck of the rebellion. The old Latin league was dissolved in 338 B.C., and was changed from a political federation into a mere association for religious purposes. The Latin communities were isolated from one another by the application to the whole of Latium of the principle which was introduced in the case of those colonies founded after the closing of the Latin league in 384 B.C. Moreover, each community had to form a separate alliance with Rome, as the old confederacy no longer existed. In certain cases harsh measures were adopted. Tibur and Praeneste had to give up part of their territory to Rome. Colonists were sent to Antium, the most important and strongest town of the Volscians; and the town was treated as Tusculum had been in 381 B.C. Lanuvium, Pedum, Aricia, and Nomentum also lost their independence and became Roman municipia. Velitrae lost its walls, and its senate was deported to the interior of south Etruria, while the town was probably treated as Caere had been in 351 B.C. The land thus acquired by Rome was partly distributed among Roman citizens, and two new tribes were instituted in 332 B.C., thus bringing the total up to twenty-nine. The decoration of the orators' platform in the Forum with the beaks of the galleys of Antium by the dictator Gaius Maenius, in 338 B.C., and the erection of a column in the Forum to his honor, attested the Roman sense of the great results achieved by this war. Roman rule was secured in similar fashion in the Volscian and Campanian provinces. A number of towns, among which were Capua, Fundi, Formiae, and Cumae, became dependent on Rome in the same way that Caere was. Privernum, under Vitruvius Vaccus, struck the last blow for Latin freedom;

but in 329 B.C. the town was stormed, and its leader executed. About ten years later two new tribes were formed out of the numerous settlers planted in the Falernian and Privernate territories. The two strong colonies of Cales, in the middle of the Campanian plain, and Fregellae, commanding the passage of the Liris, finally secured the newly won land. These were founded in 334 and 328 B.C. respectively. The Romans even established a garrison in Sora, which properly belonged to Samnite territory. This steady pursuit of a far-reaching policy of colonization secured to Rome what she won on the field of battle, and contrasts strongly with the unsteady violence and loose grasp of the Samnite nation. It is clear that the Samnites must have been alarmed at the advance of the Romans, but with the exception of garrisoning Teanum they did little to prevent it. The Samnite confederacy allowed the Roman conquest of Campania to be completed before they in earnest opposed it; and the reason for their doing so is to be sought partly in the contemporary hostilities between the Samnite nation and the Italian Hellenes, but principally in the remiss and distracted policy which the confederacy pursued.

While Rome had been securing her hold in the center of Italy, the Samnite tribes of the Lucanians and Bruttians had been engaged in constant struggles with the Italian Greeks in the south, and especially with Tarentum. So hard pressed was the latter city that she called in the aid of the Spartan king, Archidamus, who was defeated by the Lucanians on the same day as Philip conquered at Chaeronea, in 338 B.C. Alexander, the Molossian, uncle of Alexander the Great, proved far more successful in his championship of the Greek cause in southern Italy. Not only did he capture Consentia, the center of the Lucanians and their confederates, but he defeated the Samnites who brought aid to the Lucanians, and subdued the Daunians and Messapians, who had made common cause with the Sabellian tribes against the Greeks. His successes, however, alarmed the Tarentines, who turned against their commander; and his scheme of founding a new Hellenic empire in the West was cut short by the hand of an assassin in 332 B.C. His death left the Lucanians and other Sabellian tribes again paramount . in the south of Italy, and destroyed all hopes of a combined resistance from the Greek cities.

We have already shown that war was sooner or later unavoidable between Rome and the Samnites, as the latter were the only

CONQUEST OF ITALY

power capable of disputing with Rome the supremacy of Italy. Had the Samnites been able to count on the active coöperation of all Sabellian tribes, of the Lucanians and Bruttians, as well as of the smaller cantons, such as the Vestini, Frentani and Marrucini— had they, further, been able to persuade the Greeks of Campania and of southern Italy to sink minor differences in the face of a common danger—had they been able to rouse at once the Etruscans in the north, and the still chafing and indignant Latins, Volscians, and Hernicans, Rome might no doubt have succumbed. But such combinations belong rather to the imagination of the historian than to the facts of history. The immediate cause of the outbreak of war lay in the two independent Greek cities of Campania, Palaeopolis and Neapolis. Rome was scheming to obtain possession of these towns, and the Samnites combined with the Tarentines to prevent them. A strong garrison was placed in Palaeopolis by the Samnites. The Romans laid siege to the town; and thus war began, nominally against the people of Palaeopolis, really against the Samnites, in 327 B.C. Palaeopolis, weary alike of the foes without and the Samnite garrison within, got rid of the latter by stratagem, and concluded peace with Rome on the most favorable conditions in the following year. The Campanian Greeks generally followed the example of Palaeopolis, and held to the Roman side; and Rome still further attained her object of isolating Samnium, by detaching the Sabellian towns to the south of the Volturnus— Nola, Nuceria, Herculaneum, and Pompeii—through the influence of the aristocratic party in those cities. By the same means Rome secured an alliance with the Lucanians, who were the natural allies of the Samnites. This alliance was of great importance, as it left Rome free to turn all her attention to Samnium, while the Samnite ally, Tarentum, was occupied with guarding herself against Lucanian inroads.

It is not necessary to recount in detail all the events of this war, which lasted seven and thirty years. The isolated position of the Samnites, the disasters that befell them in quick succession, the humble request they made for peace in 322 B.C., the rejection of the same by the Romans; the desperate resistance and brief success of Samnite arms at the Caudine Pass, under the brave Gavius Pontius, in 321 B.C.; the refusal of the senate to recognize the agreement made by the defeated generals, mark the first period of the war. When it was renewed, the Samnites occupied Luceria in

Apulia, the attempt to relieve which town had caused the Romans
the disaster in the pass of Caudium; and they captured Fregellae,
and gained over the Satricans. Lucius Papirius Cursor now was
placed in command of the Roman forces, and took Luceria in 319
B.C., having received no small assistance from the people of Arpi
and other Apulians. Roman successes followed this important capture, and Satricum was recovered and severely punished. For a
moment, indeed, fortune deluded the Samnites with hopes of victory. The frontier towns of Nuceria and Nola sided with them.
Sora, on the upper Liris, expelled the Roman garrison. The Auso-
nians on the coast and at the mouth of the Liris threatened to rise,
and the Samnite party in Capua began to bestir itself. But the
recapture of Sora in 314 B.C., the cruel suppression of the Ausonian
revolt, the execution or voluntary death of the leaders of the Samnite party in Capua, the defeat of the Samnite army before the walls
of that city, the treaty with Nola which detached that city forever
from the Samnites in 313 B.C., and the fall of Fregellae in the same
year, turned the tide of war once more in Rome's favor, and placed
Apulia and Campania in her hands. Her position was secured by
the usual process of founding new fortresses; *e.g.,* Luceria in
Apulia, Saticula on the frontier of Campania and Samnium, In-
teramna, and Suessa Aurunca on the road from Rome to Capua.
Appius Claudius, the censor, completed in 313 B.C. the great military
road from Rome to Capua, across the Pomptine marshes. Thus
by roads and fortresses Samnium was now cut off, and the ultimate
object of the subjugation of Italy was within Rome's grasp.

The close of the second period of the war exhibits an attempt
at coalition—which at the outset might have rescued Italy.
Tarentum, indeed, practically continued an inactive spectator of
the contest; with childish arrogance its rulers had, in 320 B.C.,
ordered the Roman and Samnite armies in Apulia to lay down their
arms; but, when Rome refused, Tarentum lacked the courage and
sense of honor to declare war. Towards the close of the war she
once more invoked Greek aid against the Lucanians, and the Spartan prince Cleonymus succeeded in compelling the latter to make
peace with Tarentum; but he did not dare to enter on the more
perilous course of actively siding with the Samnites against Rome.
But in the north and center of Italy the ignoble example of Tarentum found no imitators. The Etruscans in 311 B.C. made one more
fiery effort for freedom, and for two years the Roman frontier-

fortress of Sutrium was hotly besieged. But all was in vain; in
310 B.C. Quintus Fabius Rullianus penetrated for the first time
Etruria proper, marching through the Ciminian forest, and at the
Vadimonian Lake crushed the roused Etruscans. The three most
powerful towns, Perusia, Cortona, and Arretium, made peace with
Rome; and two years later, after another defeat, Tarquinii followed their example, and the Etruscans laid down their arms.
Meanwhile the Samnites abated not their exertions; but their
hopes, based on Etruscan aid, were rudely dashed to the ground by
the terrible battle in 309 B.C., in which the very flower of their army
—the wearers of striped tunics and golden shields, and the wearers
of white tunics and silver shields—was extirpated by Lucius
Papirius Cursor. Too late to save them came the allied forces of
the Umbrians, the Marsi, and Paeligni, and, later, the Hernicans,
who all rose against Rome—too late, for the Etruscans had already
cowered back into inaction. The first three peoples were soon mastered by Roman arms; but for a moment the rising of the Hernicans in the rear of the Roman army threatened destruction. But
Anagnia, the chief Hernican city, fell; and two consular armies
penetrated the fastnesses of Samnium, and took the Samnian capital,
Bovianum, by storm in 305 B.C. A brief peace, on moderate terms,
ensued, not only with Samnium, but with all the Sabellian tribes;
and about the same time, owing to the withdrawal of the Spartan
Cleonymus to Corcyra, Tarentum, whose part in the contest we have
already described, came to formal terms with Rome.

Rome lost no time in turning her victory to good account. In
the first place, she dissolved the Hernican league, and punished those
communities which had revolted, by taking away their autonomy
and giving them citizenship without voting power. Those Hernican
communities which had not joined in the revolt remained with their
old rights. In carrying out her wise policy of subjugating central
Italy, Rome severed the north of Italy from the south, and prevented the inhabitants from being in direct touch with one another.
The old Volscian land was completely subdued and soon Romanized, by planting a legion of four thousand men in Sora on the
upper Liris, by making Arpinum subject, and taking away a third
of its territory from Frusino. Two military roads ran through the
country separating Samnium from Etruria: the northern one which
was afterwards the Flaminian, covered the line of the Tiber, passing
through Ocriculum to Nequinum, which was later called Narnia,

when the Romans colonized it in 299 B.C. The southern road, afterward called the Valerian, commanded the Marsian and Aequian land, running along the Fucine Lake by way of Carsioli and Alba, in both of which towns colonies were planted. Thus, when we remember the roads and fortresses which already commanded Apulia and Campania, it is easy to see that Samnium was enclosed by a net of Roman strongholds. Such a peace was more ruinous than war, and the proud and heroic Samnites viewed it in that light.

We have now reached the third and final period of their brave but ill-fated struggle. This time the Samnites, taught by experience, brought pressure to bear on the Lucanians, and secured their alliance; strong hopes were entertained, not only of a rising in central Italy, but of active aid from the Etruscans and from mercenary Gauls. War broke out afresh in 298 B.C., and the first move was the suppression of the Lucanians by Roman arms, and two Samnite defeats in the following year. The superhuman efforts of the Samnite nation put three fresh armies into the field, and their general, Gellius Egnatius, who led an army into Etruria, caused the Etruscans to rise once more and take into their pay numerous Celtic bands. The Romans strained every nerve to meet the threatened danger; and, by sending part of their forces into Etruria, drew off a portion of the Etruscan forces which were encamped with the Samnites and Gauls near Sentinum, in Umbria, on the eastern slope of the Apennines, in 295 B.C. It was here that the two consuls Publius Decius Mus and the aged Quintus Fabius Rullianus encountered the confederate army; and it was here that the heroic death of Publius Decius rallied the Roman legions when wavering before the Gallic hordes, and at the cost of nine thousand Roman lives gained a victory, which broke the coalition and made Etruria sue for peace. The Samnites, however, met their fate with a spirit unbroken by disaster, and in the following year gained some successes over the Roman consul, Marcus Atilius; but in 293 B.C. the battle of Aquilonia dealt a blow to the Samnites from which they never recovered; and, though in their mountain strongholds they continued the struggle till 290 B.C., deserted by all to whom they looked for aid, decimated and exhausted by a war which had lasted thirty-seven years, they at last concluded an honorable peace.

For Rome, their great antagonist, was too wise to impose 'disgraceful or ruinous conditions. Her object was to secure forever what she had already subjugated. With this end in view, two fortresses, Minturnae and Sinuessa, were established on the Campanian coast in 295 B.C. All the Sabines were forced to become subjects in 290, and the strong fortress of Hatria was established in the Abruzzi, not far from the coast, in 289 B.C. Still more important was the colony of Venusia, founded with twenty thousand colonists in 291 B.C., which, standing on the great road between Tarentum and Samnium, at the borders of Samnium, Apulia, and Lucania, kept in check the neighboring tribes, and interrupted the communications between Rome's two most powerful enemies in southern Italy. Thus the compact Roman domain at the close of the Samnite wars extended on the north to the Ciminian forest, on the east to the Abruzzi, on the south to Capua, while the two advanced posts, Luceria and Venusia, established towards the east and south on the lines of communication of their opponents, isolated them on every side. Rome was no longer merely the first, but was already the ruling power in the peninsula when, towards the end of the fifth century of the city, those nations which had been raised to supremacy, by the favor of the gods and by their own capacity, began to come into contact in council and on the battlefield; and as at Olympia the preliminary victors girt themselves for a second and more serious struggle, so on the larger arena of the nations, Carthage, Macedonia, and Rome now prepared for the final and decisive contest.

Chapter X

WAR WITH PYRRHUS—UNION WITH ITALY
280-268 B.C.

THE preceding chapter presented the chief features of that career of conquest which left Rome without a rival in Italy. But before her position was firmly and permanently established, and before the various Italian races were united under her rule, one more step remained, and one more struggle had to be decided. The interest of this final phase in the subjugation of Italy is chiefly due to the romantic charm of the name of Pyrrhus. The personal qualities and adventurous enterprises of Pyrrhus himself cannot but excite our imagination and kindle our sympathies. Of still greater moment is the fact that this was the first occasion on which Roman and Greek influences met in conflict; that from Pyrrhus date Rome's direct relations with Greece; that the struggle between phalanxes and cohorts, between a mercenary army and a militia, between military monarchy and senatorial government, between individual talent and national vigor, was first fought out in the battles between Pyrrhus and the Roman generals. The victory on this occasion, as on all others, rested with Roman arms, but the victory was of a different character from that over Gauls and Phoenicians; for in the end the subtle charm of Hellenic ideas and Hellenic life amply avenged the physical and political inferiority of the Greek to the Roman.

For the sake of chronological sequence it will be well to reach the causes which brought Pyrrhus to Italy before we narrate his previous career or estimate his position in history.

The peace with Samnium had scarce been concluded when the storm broke out afresh, and this time from a new quarter. The Romans had granted the Lucanians, in consideration of their services in the Samnite war, the Greek cities in their territory. In consequence of this, Thurii, among other cities, was attacked by the Lucanians and Bruttians, and reduced to great extremities. Thurii appealed for protection to Rome; and Rome, feeling that the fortress of Venusia enabled her to dispense with the Lucanian alliance, granted the appeal. The Lucanians and Bruttians, thus foiled by the Romans, proceeded to form a new coalition against their old allies, and at the same time opened the campaign by a fresh attack on Thurii about 285 B.C. This coalition was at once joined by the Etruscans, Gauls, Umbrians, and Samnites. The last-named, exhausted and hemmed in on all sides as they were, could render but little assistance. But in the north, under the walls of Arretium, the Roman army, led by the praetor Lucius Caecilius, was annihilated by the Celtic Senones, who were in the pay of the Etruscans.

As reprisals a terrible revenge was executed on the Senones in 283 B.C., by the consul Publius Cornelius Dolabella, who carried fire and sword through their territory, and completely expelled the whole Celtic tribe from Italy. Their Celtic kinsmen and neighbors, the Boii, at once joined the Etruscans, and a mighty combined army marched to wreak vengeance on Rome; but two battles, one near Lake Vadimo in 283 B.C., and another near Populonia in the following year, crushed this combination, and caused the Boii to conclude a separate peace with Rome. The Romans were now free to prosecute with vigor the war in southern Italy. Thurii was relieved and the Lucanians utterly defeated in 282 B.C.; the most important places—Locri, Croton, Thurii, and Rhegium—were garrisoned. That part of the Adriatic coast which had been occupied by the Senones was secured by a colony planted in the seaport of Sena, the former Senonian capital. A Roman fleet sailed from the Tyrrhene Sea to take up its station in the Adriatic, and, on its way, anchored in the harbor of Tarentum. The time had at last arrived for the supine people of Tarentum to shake off their lethargy; but their awakening came too late. Old treaties had forbidden Roman men-of-war from sailing beyond the promontory of Lacinium. Fiery appeals by mob-orators excited the Tarentine multitude to such a degree of senseless passion that it rushed down to the harbor, fell upon the unsuspecting Romans, and seized their ships and crews after a sharp struggle. The wanton outrage was followed up by the surprise of Thurii and the severe punishment of its inhabitants. Notwithstanding this violent breach of all civilized law, the Romans displayed great moderation and forbearance in the terms they offered Tarentum. But all negotiations failed, and the Roman consul, Lucius Aemilius, entered Tarentine territory in 281 B.C. It was clear that Tarentum could not resist Rome single-handed, and the fear of the demagogues as to the vengeance which Rome would exact drove them to urge the completion of the alliance with Pyrrhus on the terms proposed by the Epirot king.

At this point we must revert to the previous history of the man whose name has cast a halo of romance upon this war. Born in 320 B.C., Pyrrhus, when but six years old, was by his father's downfall deprived of his hereditary throne among the Molossians of Epirus, and subjected to the many vicissitudes that befell all those engaged in Macedonian politics. Trained in the campaigns of the veteran Antigonus, one of Alexander's chief generals, universally admired by the Alexandrian court of Ptolemy, whither the battle of Ipsus brought him as a hostage, he was restored to his native land and kingdom of Epirus in 296 B.C., through the influence of Ptolemy, who wished to counteract the growing power of the Macedonian ruler, Demetrius Poliorcetes. Aided by the brave Epirots, whose loyalty and enthusiasm were fired by their young ruler, " the eagle of Epirus," as they styled him, extended his dominions. When Demetrius was driven from his throne in 287 B.C., Pyrrhus was summoned to wear the royal diadem of Philip and of Alexander.

No worthier successor could have been found. But Macedonian jealousy, and that national feeling which could not brook a foreign leader, caused him to resign the kingdom after a short reign of seven months. The colorless life of an Epirot king could not satisfy the ambition of such a man as Pyrrhus. Conscious of his great powers as a general, fired with a desire to imitate the great Alexander, Pyrrhus eagerly embraced the opportunity that now offered itself of founding an Hellenic empire in the West. In estimating the possibilities of success, and the historical position of Pyrrhus himself, we cannot but feel that the attempt to draw a comparison between him and Alexander completely fails. Alexander was at the head of a powerful and well-officered Macedonian army; he was the foremost general and most gifted statesman of his time; his own dominions were secured by the powerful army he left behind him; the foes he went to encounter were such as, long inured to despotism, knew nothing of national independence and national vigor, and regarded with indifference a change of despots. In the case of Pyrrhus none of these advantages existed.

Despite his noble descent, his strategic ability, his pure and chivalrous nature, he was but a soldier of fortune, a king of mountain-tribes, a man whose chances of success depended on mercenaries and foreign alliances, and on his ability to keep together a coalition of secondary states. Wide-reaching as was his scheme of founding a great Hellenic empire in the West, it was the unreal dream of a romantic adventurer, not the possible and practicable aim of a powerful conqueror and statesman.

When once Tarentum had signed the treaty with Pyrrhus, the arrival of Cineas, the confidential adviser of Pyrrhus, and of his general, Milo, in 281 B.C., with three thousand Epirots, put an end to all further vacillation. Pyrrhus himself landed early in the following year, with a mixed force of various Greek tribes, amounting in all to about twenty thousand infantry, two thousand archers, five hundred slingers,' three thousand cavalry, and twenty elephants. The boasts which the Tarentine envoys had made, of the huge confederate army ready to take the field in Italy, were soon proved to be utterly fallacious. In the north, the Etruscans alone were still in arms, but misfortune attended every effort they made. The Tarentines, who had hoped that Pyrrhus would take all the blows while they shared the spoil, found their master in the eagle of Epirus. They were called upon to serve; and the foreign soldiers were quartered in their houses, and foreign guards set over their gates. The strictest military government everywhere prevailed; and all the clubs, theaters, and amusements of the pleasure-loving Tarentines were ruthlessly suspended.

Special exertions were made by Rome to meet the new danger. In 280 B.C., on the banks of the Siris, near Heraclea, the Roman consul, Publius Laevinus, first measured swords with a Greek army under the greatest general of the day. After a stubborn contest, varied by many vicissitudes of fortune, the elephants of Pyrrhus decided the issue. The losses of the Romans, estimated from fifteen to twenty thousand, were almost equaled by those of Pyrrhus. But the value of winning the first battle was at once shown by the fact that the Lucanians, Bruttians, Samnites, and all the Greek cities joined Pyrrhus. The Latins, however, remained firm, and the frontier fortress, Venusia, although completely hemmed in by enemies, refused to desert Rome. Pyrrhus saw that his hopes lay in securing favorable terms from the Romans, while the impressions of the battle of Heraclea were still vivid. He commissioned Cineas, whose rhetorical powers were famous, to go to Rome and demand the freedom of all Greek towns, and the restitution of the territory taken from the Samnites, Daunians, Lucanians, and Bruttians. The leniency and respect shown by Pyrrhus towards his Roman prisoners, and the persuasive arts of Cineas, made the senate waver, but the undaunted energy of the blind and aged Appius Claudius, who had been censor in 312, and consul in 307 and 296 B.C., and who had caused himself to be carried into the senate-house at this critical moment, revived the true Roman spirit in the hearts of his audience. The proud answer was given that Rome could not negotiate with foreign troops as long as they were on Italian soil. This answer, then heard for the first time, passed thenceforth into a maxim of state.

Pyrrhus now marched upon Rome, hoping by this step to shake the allegiance of her allies and to terrify the capital. Roman courage, however, was proof alike against the flatteries of Cineas and the armed threats of Pyrrhus. No Latin ally, no Campanian Greek state joined him; moreover, the Etruscans at this time concluded peace with Rome, and thus set free the army of the consul Tiberius Coruncanius. Three armies, one in his rear under Laevinus, and two in the vicinity of the capital, barred his progress. After surprising Fregellae and reaching Anagnia, the king was forced to retrace his steps without striking a decisive blow. At the approach of winter he returned to his old quarters in Tarentum. In the spring of 279 B.C. Pyrrhus resumed the offensive, and met the Roman army in Apulia near Ausculum. The allied forces of Pyrrhus amounted to about seventy thousand infantry, eight thousand cavalry, and nineteen elephants. The Romans with their confederates were not inferior in number; and as a protection against the elephants they had invented a sort of war-chariot, armed with projecting iron poles and movable masts, capable of being lowered, and fitted with an iron spike. Pyrrhus also had copied the Roman system of maniples, and placed companies on the wings of the phalanx, with spaces between them, in imitation of the cohorts. For two days the battle raged; at last the elephants, as at Heraclea, forced back the Roman line, and Pyrrhus remained in possession of the field.

This defeat cost the Roman forces some six thousand lives; but Pyrrhus himself was wounded. Nor was the victory decisive enough to break up the Roman confederacy, and thus further the political designs of the Epirot king. Forced by his wound to renounce the campaign and remain inactive in Tarentum, Pyrrhus soon perceived that the losses he had sustained and the petty quarrels and hatred of discipline which characterized his allies, rendered all chances of ultimate success with his present resources out of the question. The condition of the Sicilian Greeks gave him an opportunity of leaving Italy, and of this he gladly availed himself.

After the death of Agathocles of Syracuse, in 289 B.C., Carthage had made great strides in the subjugation of Sicily. No resistance could be offered by the smaller Greek cities, whose government, whether under demagogues or despots, was always equally incapable. Agrigentum had fallen, and Syracuse was now hard pressed by the victorious Carthaginians. In the hour of her peril Syracuse acted as Tarentum had done; she offered the supreme power to Pyrrhus. Thus fortune, by placing in his hands at the same moment Tarentum and Syracuse, seemed to give to Pyrrhus a great opportunity of realizing his mighty schemes. One effect of this union of Italian and Sicilian Greeks under one head was to bring into closer relations Carthage and Rome. An offensive and defensive treaty was concluded between them, in 279 B.C., against Pyrrhus, binding each party to assist the other in case of attack, and binding both states not to conclude a separate peace with Pyrrhus. Messana, which had previously been seized by the Mamertines, who were the Campanian mercenaries of Agathacles, in fear of the vengeance of Pyrrhus joined the Romans and Carthaginians, and thus secured for them the Sicilian side of the straits. A strong Carthaginian fleet proceeded to blockade Syracuse, while at the same time a land army laid siege to it, in 278 B.C. Pyrrhus was therefore forced to desert the Lucanians and Samnites, and content himself with occupying Tarentum by a garrison under Milo, and Locri with a force under his son Alexander. He himself set sail with the rest of his troops for Syracuse in the spring of 278 B.C. During his absence from Italy the Romans, exhausted by their previous struggles, allowed the war to drag on, without being able to completely expel the troops left behind by Pyrrhus. Heraclea, indeed, made peace with Rome in 278, and Locri slaughtered its Epirot garrison in 277 B.C.; but Milo retained his hold of Tarentum, and made successful sorties against the Romans. Ignorance of the art of besieging towns, and the want of a fleet, made the capture of Tarentum almost impossible; and the Carthaginians, owing to their disasters in Sicily, were unable to render any real assistance. Pyrrhus, on landing at Syracuse, met with complete success. At the head of the Greek cities he wrested from the Carthaginians almost all that they had won. To cope with their powerful fleet and capture the all-important position of Lilybaeum, Pyrrhus built himself a fleet, and in 276 B.C. seemed to have within his grasp the realization of his aims. But his methods of governing Sicily were those which he had seen Ptolemy practice in Egypt: personal favorites, not native Greeks, exercised absolute authority as magistrates and judges in the various cities; his own troops acted as garrisons, and his own acts were arbitrary and despotic to the last degree.

His reign thus became more detested than even the threatened Carthaginian yoke had been, and negotiations were entered into by the principal Greek cities with the Carthaginians. To this error Pyrrhus added a second. Instead of securing his rule in Sicily, expelling the Carthaginians and capturing Lilybaeum, he turned his thoughts once more to Italy. Possibly a sense of honor and the cry of his old allies, the Lucanians and Samnites, moved him to do so; but the folly of the step was at once apparent. When once it was known that he had set sail for Italy, towards the close of 276 B.C., all the Sicilian cities revolted, and refused to grant him money or troops; and thus the enterprise of Pyrrhus was wrecked, and the plan of his life irretrievably ruined; he was thenceforth an adventurer who felt that he had been great, and was so no longer. Foiled in an attack on Rhegium, he surprised Locri, and avenged himself on the treacherous inhabitants. In the spring of 275 B.C. he marched to the aid of the hard-pressed Samnites, and near Beneventum, on the Campus Arusinus, he fought his final battle on Italian soil. The very elephants which had won his previous victories proved the cause of his defeat by attacking their own side. Unable any longer to keep the field, or to get reinforcements from abroad, Pyrrhus left Italy, and once more took part in Greek politics. He even succeeded in recovering the whole of his former kingdom, and in paving the way for a return to the throne of Macedonia. But his successes bore no lasting fruit, and he perished ingloriously in a street fight at Argos, in 272 B.C.

With the battle of Beneventum and the departure of Pyrrhus the war in Italy came to an end. Milo, who had been left behind in Tarentum, made over that city to the Roman consul Lucius

UNION WITH ITALY

Papirius in 272 B.C., on hearing of his master's death. He thus prevented the citizens from surrendering the town to the Carthaginians, who had entered the harbor with a fleet, and secured for himself and his troops a free departure. The Carthaginians, thus frustrated in their attempt to gain a foothold in Italy, pretended that their presence was merely due to their wish to help the Romans. The gain to Rome from the act of Milo can scarcely be overestimated. In the same year the Samnites, Lucanians, and Bruttians laid down their arms. Rome was now mistress of all Italy. New colonies and new roads held in a firm grip the conquered territories. Paestum and Cosa in Lucania, Beneventum and Aesernia to command Samnium, Ariminum, Firmum in Picenum, and Castrum Novum to hold in check the Gauls, were all established in the ten years from 273-264 B.C. Preparations were made to continue the southern highway to the seaports of Tarentum and Brundisium, to colonize the latter seaport and make it the rival of Tarentum. Wars with small tribes whose territory was encroached upon were caused by the construction of these fortresses and roads, and Rome's dominion was thus extended from the Apennines to the Ionian Sea. Nor did she solely confine her attention to the development of her power by land.

At this time Carthage was practically paramount in the western water of the Mediterranean. Even Syracuse gradually ceased to compete with her; Tarentum, owing to the Roman occupation, was no longer formidable; the naval power of Etruria had long been broken, and the Etruscan island of Corsica lay open to the ships of Carthage. The constant struggles by land had caused the Roman fleet to dwindle in neglect, until about 350 B.C. it reached its lowest point of inefficiency. A treaty with Carthage in 348 B.C. bound Roman ships not to sail beyond the Fair Promontory (Cape Bon) on the Libyan coast; a like stipulation with Tarentum excluded Roman ships from the eastern basin of the Mediterranean.

As soon as able, Rome made efforts to free herself from this humiliating position. The chief towns along the Tyrrhene and Adriatic Seas were colonized, and thus protected the coasts from invasion and pillage. The Roman navy was in part revived, and the war-ships taken from Antium in 338 B.C. served as a nucleus for this purpose. Such Greek cities as were admitted into a state of dependence on Rome furnished a certain number of vessels as a war contribution. In 311 B.C. two masters of the fleet were created by a special resolution of the burgesses, and the Roman fleet lent assistance in the Samnite war at the siege of Nuceria. But the renewal of the treaty with Carthage in 306 B.C. shows how little Rome really accomplished. Although continuing to improve the state of her navy, she was allowed to trade only with Sicily and Carthage, and was thus restricted to the narrow space of the western Mediterranean.

It remains for us to consider the political effect of the mighty changes consequent upon the establishment of Roman supremacy in Italy. We do not know with exactness what privileges Rome reserved for herself as sovereign state. It is certain that she alone could make war, conclude treaties, and coin money; and that, further, any war or treaty resolved upon by the Roman people was legally binding on all Italian communities, and that the silver money of Rome was current everywhere in Italy.

The relations of the Italians to Rome cannot in all cases be precisely defined, but the main features are as follows. In the first place, the full Roman franchise was extended as far as was compatible with the preservation of the urban character of the Roman community. Those who received this franchise may be divided into three classes. First, all the occupants of the various allotments of state lands, now embracing a considerable portion of Etruria and Campania, were included. Second, all the communities which, after the method first adopted in the case of Tusculum, were incorporated and completely merged in the Roman state. As we have seen this course had been followed in the case of many of the original members of the Latin league; it was now, in 268 B.C., pursued with regard to all the Sabine communities and many of the Volscian. Finally, full Roman citizenship was possessed by the maritime or burgess colonies which had been instituted for the protection of the coast. In these towns the young men were exempted from service in the legions, and devoted all their attention to guarding the coasts.

Thus the title of Roman citizen in its fullest sense was possessed by men dwelling as far north as Lake Sabatinus, as far east as the Apennines, and as far south as Formiae. But within those limits isolated communities, such as Tibur, Praeneste, Signia, and Norba, were without the Roman franchise; while beyond them other communities, such as Sena, possessed it.

In the next place, we must distinguish the various grades of subjection which marked all the communities not honored with the full Roman franchise. As in the case of the recipients of full citizenship, so here we may make a threefold division. To the first division belong the Latin towns: these retained their Latin rights; that is, they were self-governing and stood on an equal footing with Roman citizens as regards the right of trading and inheritance. But it is important to observe that the Latins of the later times of the Republic were no longer for the most part members of the old Latin towns, which had participated in the Alban festival, but were colonists planted in Latium by Rome, who honored Rome as their capital and parent city, and formed the main supports of Roman rule in Latium. Indeed, the old Latin communities, with the exception of Tibur and Praeneste, had sunk into insignificance. It was but natural that the Latin colonies, issuing as they did from the burgess-body of Rome, should not rest content with mere Latin rights, but should aim at the full rights of Roman citizens. Rome, on the other hand, now that Italy was subjugated, no longer felt her former need of these colonies; nor did she deem it prudent to extend the full franchise with the same freedom as she hitherto had done. A line was now strictly drawn, and all members of autonomous communities founded after 268 B.C. could no longer by settling in Rome become municipes or passive burgesses with the power of voting in the comitia tributa. Men of eminence, *e.g.*, public magistrates, in such communities were alone in future eligible to the Roman franchise. By these means the old power of migration to Rome was somewhat restricted, and a jealous guard was set upon the privilege of becoming a full Roman citizen.

To the second division belong those towns whose inhabitants were passive citizens of Rome (*cives sine suffragio*). They were liable to service in the Roman legions, and to taxation, and were included in the Roman census. A deputy or prefect appointed annually by the Roman pretor administered justice according to laws which were subjected to Roman revision. In other respects they retained their old form of government and appointed their own magistrates. Caere was the first town to be placed on this footing; afterwards Capua and other more remote towns were treated in the same way.

In the third and last division we may include all allied communities which were not Latin states; the relation of these towns to

Rome was defined by separate treaties, and therefore varied in accordance with the terms imposed by such agreements.

No doubt all national leagues, such as the Samnite and Lucanian, shared the fate which had earlier befallen the Latin and Hernican confederations; and any movements which might tend to bind one community with another, whether by rights of intermarriage or of acquisition of property or by common council-chambers, were doubtless suppressed by the vigilance of Rome. Further, all the Italian communities were obliged to equip and furnish at their own expense contingents in time of war. Those Latin towns classified above in the first division furnished a definitely fixed number of infantry and cavalry which acted on the wings of the Roman legion and were therefore named " wings " and " winged cohorts." The same duty was imposed on most of the allied communities classified in the third division, such as Apulians, Sabellians, and Etruscans.

Further, the passive citizens defined in the second division were, as above stated, bound to serve in the ranks of the Roman legions, while the duty of supplying ships of war fell almost entirely on the Greek cities. Such were the leading features of the Roman government of Italy, the details of which can no longer be ascertained. In addition to breaking up all existing confederacies, and thus splitting up the subject states into a number of smaller communities, Rome fostered schisms and factions among them. In pursuance of the same object the government of all dependent communities was now placed in the hands of the wealthy and leading families, whose interests were naturally opposed to those of the multitude, and who were inclined to favor Roman views. Capua, whose nobles had sided with Rome throughout the war against the revolted Latins and Campanians, furnished a notorious instance of this policy. Special privileges and pensions were granted by Rome to the Campanian aristocracy. But the great wisdom and moderation of Rome is shown by the fact that she either extended to these dependent states the Roman franchise, or allowed them to retain a certain amount of self-government, and gave them a share in the successes of Rome. Thus in Italy, at least, no community of Helots existed, nor, which was equally important, was there any tributary state; for Rome with a wise magnanimity never assumed that most dangerous of rights, the right of taxing any of her Italian subjects. Rome exercised control and supervision over the

UNION WITH ITALY

various Italian communities by means of the four quaestors of the fleet, who had a district and residence outside Rome assigned them by law. In addition, the chief magistrate of every community had to take a census of his state every fourth or fifth year; by this means the Roman senate was kept informed of the resources in men and money of the whole of Italy.

Politically united under the leadership of Rome, the various tribes inhabiting Italy now began to realize more completely and feel more intensely their unity as a nation. This feeling must have first sprung into existence from the contrast presented by the Greeks, and must have been heightened by the danger with which the Celts threatened all Italians equally. It found expression in two names, which now began to be applied to all the peoples inhabiting Italy. The name of Italians, which was originally a Greek term, became current everywhere, and Italia, originally limited to the modern Calabria, was now used of the whole land. The name of Togati, or " men of the toga," was now for the first time used to designate all the Italians, and thus sharply contrasted them with the Celtic "men of the hose " (Braccati). This common use by all of the Latin toga—the right to wear which was an exclusive privilege of the Roman citizen—seemed to point to the day when the Latin language would be regarded as the mother-tongue of every Italian: the germs of the Latinization of the whole peninsula were already planted; time alone was needed for their development.

It had taken Rome 120 years to complete the union of the Italian peninsula, broken up as it was by mountain ranges and naturally favoring the formation and preservation of various isolated states. But a union it was, rather than a subjugation, and each nation was left to the practical management of its own affairs. Content with self-government, the various communities, for the most part, easily bore the yoke of Roman supremacy. Eventually all the municipal towns received the full Roman franchise (90 B.C.), and thus established the municipal principle of government which endures to the present day.

The recognition of Rome's new position as one of the great powers in the political world was first marked by an embassy sent from Alexandria to Rome in 273 B.C., primarily with a view to settling commercial relations. Egypt was at that time at variance with Carthage touching Cyrene, and with Macedonia touching her predominating influence in Greece; the complications that were

eventually to arise between Rome and Carthage for the possession
of Sicily, and between Rome and Macedonia for the sovereignty of
the Adriatic coasts, were doubtless foreshadowed even then, and

may well have suggested an alliance with Egypt. The new struggles which were preparing on all sides could not but influence
each other; and Rome, as mistress of Italy, could not fail to be
drawn into the wide arena, which the victories and projects of
Alexander the Great had marked out as the field of conflict to his
successors.

PART II

CONQUEST OF THE MEDITERRANEAN STATES. 264-133 B.C.

Chapter XI

CARTHAGE. 500-264 B.C.

WE now turn our eyes to a race of people widely differing from any in Italy in nature and origin, *viz.*, the Carthaginians. Belonging to the great Semitic race, which has ever, as though from some instinctive sense of its wide diversity, kept itself severed from the European nations, Carthage was one of the numerous settlements of the enterprising Phoenicians. This particular branch of the Semitic stock issued forth from its native land of Canaan or "the plain," and spread further west than any other people of the same race. Utilizing to the full the excellent harbors, and the bountiful supply of timber and metals of their own country, the Phoenicians early attained an unrivaled position in the ancient world as the pioneers of commerce, navigation, manufacture, and colonization. In the most remote times we find them in Cyprus and Egypt, Greece and Sicily, Africa and Spain, and even on the Atlantic Ocean and the North Sea. The field of their commerce reached from Sierra Leone and Cornwall in the west, eastward to the coast of Malabar.

But the one-sided character that marks the development of the great nations of antiquity is especially visible in the case of the Phoenicians. We cannot ascribe to them the credit of having originated any of the intellectual or scientific discoveries which have been the glory of other members of the Semitic family. Their religious conceptions were gross and barbarous; their art was not comparable to that of Italy, still less to that of Greece; their knowledge of astronomy and chronology, of the alphabet, of weights and measures, was derived from Babylon. No doubt, in their commercial dealings, the Phoenicians spread valuable germs of civilization, but rather as a bird dropping grain than a husbandman sowing seed. They never civilized and assimilated to themselves the nations with which they came into contact.

Moreover, politically, the Phoenicians were, like the rest of their race, without the ennobling idea of self-governed freedom. A policy of conquest was never in their eyes to be compared with a policy of commerce. Their colonies were factories. The power to trade with natives was bought too dear if it entailed constant war and the interruption of peaceful barter. Thus they allowed themselves to be supplanted in Egypt, Greece, Italy, and the east of Sicily, almost without resistance; and in the great naval battles at Alalia in 537 B.C., and at Cumae in 474 B.C., for the supremacy of the western Mediterranean, the brunt of the struggle with the Greeks fell upon the Etruscans, and not on the Phoenicians. In the great Sicilian expedition, which ended in their defeat at Himera by Gelo of Syracuse in 480 B.C., the African Phoenicians only took the field as subjects of the Great King, and to avoid being obliged to aid him in the East instead of the West. This was not from want of courage or national spirit; indeed, the tenacity and obstinacy with which the race has ever held to its feelings and prejudices as a nation far exceeds the pertinacity of any European people: it was rather due to their want of political instinct and of the love of liberty. No Phoenician settlements attained a more rapid and secure prosperity than those established by the cities of Tyre and Sidon on the south coast of Spain and the north coast of Africa. Here they were out of the reach of the Great King and of Greek rivals, and held the same relation to the natives as the Europeans held to the American Indians. Although not the earliest settlement, by far the most prominent was Karthada, " the new town," or Carthage. Situated near the mouth of the river Bagradas, which flows through the richest corn district in North Africa, on rising ground which slopes gently towards the plain and ends in a seagirt promontory, commanding the great roadstead of North Africa, the Gulf of Tunis, Carthage owed its sudden rise to preëminence even more to the natural advantages of its situation than to the character of its inhabitants. Even when restored, Carthage at once became the third city in the Roman empire; and in our day, on a far worse site, and under far less favorable conditions, a city exists in that district, whose inhabitants number one hundred thousand. We need no explanation, then, of the commercial prosperity of ancient Carthage; but we must answer the question raised by its development of political power, a development never attained by any other Phoenician city.

At the outset Carthage pursued the usual passive policy of

CARTHAGE

Phoenician cities. She paid a ground-rent for the space occupied by the city to the native Berbers, the tribe of Maxitani or Maxyes; and she recognized the nominal supremacy of the Great King by paying tribute to him on different occasions. It gradually, however, became clear to the Carthaginians that, unless they undertook the task of repelling Greek influences and Greek migrations, the Phoenicians would be supplanted in Africa, as they had already been in Greece, Italy, and Sicily. The colony of Cyrene threatened their very stronghold and imperiled their existence. The Carthaginians, therefore, undertook the task; and by about 500 B.C., after a long and obstinate struggle, they had to a great extent effected their purpose, and set bounds to Greek invasion. These successes changed the character of the city itself; it no longer aimed at being merely preëminent in commerce, but at establishing an empire as mistress of Libya and of part of the Mediterranean.

About the year 450 B.C. the Carthaginians refused any longer to pay rent for the soil they occupied to the natives, and were thus enabled to prosecute agriculture on a greatly extended scale. Capital thus found a new outlet, and the rich soil of Libya was cultivated on a system similar to that employed by modern planters. Single landowners appear to have employed on their estates no fewer than twenty thousand slaves. Moreover, the native Libyan farmers were subdued, and reduced to the position of fellahs, who paid a fourth of the produce of their soil as tribute to their new masters, and served as a recruiting ground for the Carthaginian armies. The Nomads, or roving pastoral tribes, were driven back into the deserts and mountains, or were compelled to pay tribute and supply soldiers. Finally, the Carthaginian rule embraced the other Phoenician settlements in Africa, or the so-called Liby-Phoenicians. These states, with the exception of Utica, the ancient protectress of Carthage, lost their independence, and had to pull down their walls and to contribute a fixed sum of money and a definite number of soldiers. But they did not pay a land-tax, nor were they subject to the recruiting system like the subject Libyans; and they enjoyed equal legal privileges and right of intermarriage with the Carthaginians.

Thus Carthage became the capital of a great North African empire, extending from the desert of Tripoli to the Atlantic Ocean; on the west in Morocco and Algiers, indeed, she merely held a belt along the coast, but on the east in the region of Tunis she extended her sway far into the interior. In the words of an ancient writer, the Carthaginians were changed from Tyrians into Libyans. The Phoenician tongue and civilization were, at any rate among the more advanced natives, adopted in Libya. The rise of Carthage was synchronous with a decline of the great cities in the mother-country, Tyre and Sidon; and from the first-named most of the powerful families emigrated to their prosperous daughter city.

In addition to the empire in Libya we must bear in mind the parallel growth of the maritime and colonial dominion of Carthage. The early Tyrian settlement at Gades (Cadiz) was the chief

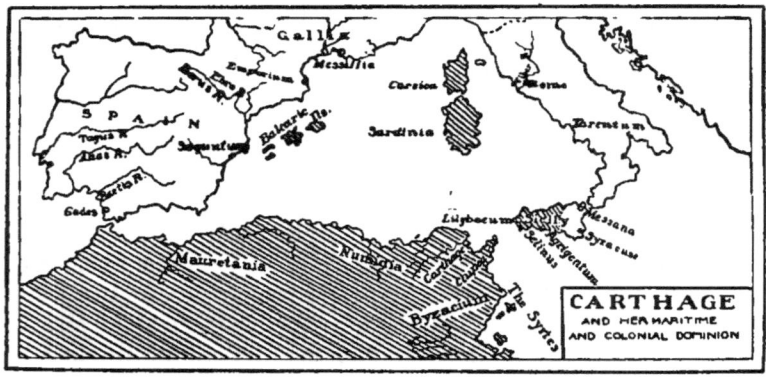

CARTHAGE AND HER MARITIME AND COLONIAL DOMINION

Phoenician colony in Spain. By a chain of factories on the west and east of Gades, and by the possession of the silver mines in the interior, the Phoenicians occupied nearly all the modern Andalusia and Granada. Although not strictly under the rule of Carthage, no doubt Gades and the other stations in Spain fell under her hegemony. The island of Ivizo and the Baleares were early occupied by the Carthaginians, partly as fishing-stations, partly as outposts against the Greek colony of Massilia, with which Carthage was ever at war. Moreover, about 500 B.C., the Carthaginians established themselves in Sardinia, the natives of which island retired before them into the mountainous interior, just as the Numidians withdrew to the borders of the African desert. The fertile districts of the Sardinian coast were cultivated by imported Libyans, and colonies were planted at Caralis (Cagliari) and other points. They also held the west and northwest coast of Sicily, to-

CARTHAGE

gether with the smaller adjacent islands of the Aegates, Melita, Gaulos, Cossyra; the station at Motya, and later at Lilybaeum, preserved their communication with Africa, as those at Panormus and Soluntum did with Sardinia. For a long period, down to the Athenian expedition to Sicily (415-413 B.C.), the Greeks and Carthaginians seem to have agreed to tolerate one another in Sicily.

All these possessions served not only as commercial centers, but as pillars of the Carthaginian supremacy by sea. The western straits of the Mediterranean were practically closed to other nations, and in the Tyrrhene and Gallic seas alone the Phoenicians had to endure the rivalry of foreign fleets. As long, indeed, as the Etruscan power counterbalanced the Greek in those waters, Carthage could afford to remain passive; but on the fall of the Etruscans and the rise of the naval power of Syracuse, a great contest ensued between Dionysius of Syracuse (406-367 B.C.) and Carthage, in the course of which all the smaller Greek cities in Sicily were either totally destroyed, e. g., Selinus, Himera, Agrigentum, Gela, and Messana, or reduced to a state of utter prostration. The island was partitioned between the Syracusans and Carthaginians, and on several occasions each side in turn was on the point of completely expelling its rival from the island. But gradually the balance inclined in favor of the Carthaginians, and, after the failure of the attempt of Pyrrhus to restore the Syracusan fleet, the Carthaginians commanded without a rival the whole western Mediterranean; and their efforts to occupy Syracuse, Rhegium, and Tarentum show the extent of their power, and the objects they had in view. They shrank from no violence in their attempt to monopolize the whole trade of the West; any foreigner sailing towards Sardinia and Gades, if apprehended, was thrown into the sea, and the treaty of 306 B.C. closed every Phoenician port except that of Carthage against Roman vessels, which forty-two years before had been allowed to trade with the ports in Spain, Sardinia, and Libya.

The constitution of Carthage was described by Aristotle as having changed from a monarchy to an aristocracy, or as a democracy inclining toward oligarchy. The conduct of affairs was directly vested in the hands of a council of elders, which consisted, like the Spartan gerusia, of two kings, annually nominated by the citizens, and of twenty-eight elders, also annually chosen by the same body. All the chief business of state was transacted by this council, and the general and his chief officers, who were always "elders," were appointed by it. The kings seem to have had comparatively little power, and acted as supreme judges. The general was much more of an autocrat, and is described by Roman writers as a dictator; the term of his office was not fixed, but the gerusiasts attached to him as sub-commanders must have restricted his power, and on laying down his office he had to give an official account of his actions.

But over the gerusia and the magistrates was the body of the Hundred and Four, or the judges, the bulwark of the Carthaginian oligarchy. Although there is considerable obscurity as to the mode of their election and the length of their tenure of office, we may infer from the name of senators, given them by the Greeks and Romans, that they practically held office for life, and that they were elected by some method of coöptation. At first intended to act as political jurymen and hear the accounts of, and, if necessary, punish the general, or any of the gerusiasts, the judges gradually came to interfere in all legislation and thus usurp the functions of those gerusiasts whom they controlled. We can thus easily understand how the generals and statesmen of Carthage were perpetually hampered in council and action by the fear of this control.

The body of citizens seems to have exercised very little influence in Carthage. Although the people were consulted in the election of a general, their opinion was only taken after the general had been nominated by the gerusia. On other questions the people were only consulted if the gerusia thought fit, so that, viewing the Carthaginian constitution as a whole, we may conclude that the government was one of capitalists, such as would arise in a city where there was no rich middle class, but merely a city rabble on the one hand and a class of great merchants, planters, and noble governors on the other.

Regarded from a financial point of view, Carthage stands pre-eminent among the states of antiquity. Polybius calls it the wealthiest city in the world, and indeed it rivaled the London of our own times. The high pitch reached by the Carthaginians in the art of husbandry is attested by the agricultural treatise of Mago, the textbook not only of Carthage, but of Rome, which was translated into Greek and edited in Latin by the express order of the Roman senate, for the benefit of Italian landholders. The close connection between agriculture and the management of capital was a special feature of their enlightened system; no one held more land than he could thoroughly manage. Thus enriched at home by the well-nigh inexhaustible resources of fertile Libya, whose horses, oxen, sheep, and goats excelled those of all other lands, and drawing a huge rental from her subjects, while abroad she held in her hands the trade and manufactures of the interior as well as of the coasts of the western Mediterranean, Carthage occupied a commercial position up to that time unrivaled in the ancient world; and the whole carrying trade between East and West became more and more concentrated in her single harbor. For science and art Carthage was chiefly indebted to Hellenic influences, and rich treasures were carried off to Carthage from Sicilian temples. Native intellect was subservient to the interests of capital: and therefore her literature bore chiefly upon agriculture and geography, and such subjects as advanced commerce. The same utilitarian view of education caused the Carthaginians to pay special attention to the knowledge of foreign languages. In consequence of the huge accumulation of wealth in the city no direct taxation was found necessary; and after the second Punic war, when the power of Carthage was broken, it was found possible, by a stricter administration of the finances, to meet the current expenses and pay the yearly installment of $240,000 to Rome without levying any tax. Carthage anticipated the economic principles of a later epoch in her financial management of loans and currency. In fact, if government had resolved itself into a mere mercantile speculation, never would any state have solved the problem more brilliantly than Carthage.

Some comparison between the resources of Rome and Carthage will be a fitting close to this chapter. Both cities were purely agricultural and mercantile, art and science in both playing a subordinate and wholly practical part. In Rome the landed interest still preponderated over the moneyed; in Carthage the reverse was the case. In the former the great mass of citizens tilled their own fields; in the latter the agricultural interest was centered in the hands of large landholders and slave-owners. Thus at Rome, owing to the fact that most of the citizens held property, the tone was conservative; in Carthage the majority held no property, and were therefore moved alike by the bribes of the rich and the reform-

cries of the democrats.   Rome still prescribed pristine frugal simplicity in her mode of life; Carthage was the victim of opulence and
luxury.

Politically, the constitution of both was aristocratic.   The
judges of Carthage and the senate of Rome governed on the same
system of police-control.   In both cities the individual magistrate
was subject to the control of the governing board, but the cruel
severity and absurd restrictions visible in the Carthaginian system
contrast very unfavorably with the milder and more reasonable
powers of the Roman council.   Moreover, the Roman senate was
open to and filled by men of eminent ability, representatives of the
nation in the truest and best sense, while the Carthaginian senate
exercised a jealous control on the executive, and represented only a
few leading families, and was inspired by a sense of mistrust of all
above and below it.   Hence the steady unwavering policy of Rome,
and the confidence and good understanding generally existing between the senate and its magistrates; while at Carthage a wavering
half-hearted policy was pursued, and the best officers were generally
at feud with the governing body at home, and were thus forced to
join the reform or opposition party.   Again, as to their treatment
of subject states, Rome threw open her citizenship to one district
after another, and made it even legally attainable by the Latin communities; Carthage never allowed such a hope to be entertained,
still less to be realized.   Rome granted a share in the fruits of
victory, and sought to create a party in each state favorable to her
own interests; Carthage reserved to herself all the spoils of victory,
and took away from all cities the freedom of trade.   Rome allowed
a shadow of independence even to the lowest grade of her subject
states, and imposed a fixed tribute on none; Carthage enforced a
heavy tribute on even the old Phoenician cities, with the exception
of Utica, and treated subject tribes as state slaves.   Thus every
African community, with the above exception, would have profited
by the fall of Carthage, whereas every state in Italy would have
lost rather than gained by a rebellion against Rome.   The strength
of the Roman alliance was shown in the war against Pyrrhus; the
landing of Agathocles and Regulus in Africa, and the mercenary
war, proved the hollow and rotten nature of the Carthaginian confederacy.   In Sicily alone Carthage pursued a wiser and milder
policy, owing to her inability to take Syracuse, and thus there was
always a party there favorable to her interests.

The state revenues of Carthage were far superior to those of Rome, but the sources of that revenue—tribute and customs—were exhausted far sooner than those of Rome, and the Carthaginian mode of conducting war was far costlier than the Roman.

Though very different, the military resources of the two rivals were not unequally balanced. Carthage, at the time of her conquest, still numbered 700,000 citizens, and at the close of the fifth century she could put into the field an army of 40,000 hoplites. Rome's advantage lay not so much in the superiority of numbers, as in the superior physique and character of the Roman husbandman. Neither the Carthaginians nor the Liby-Phoenicians were naturally soldiers; the flower of the Carthaginian armies consisted of the Libyans, who made good infantry, and were unsurpassed as light cavalry. Aided by the forces of the dependent tribes of Libya and Spain, and by the famous slingers of the Baleares, as well as by mercenary foreigners, the Carthaginians could raise their armies to almost any strength; but a long and dangerous interval must elapse before such hosts could be collected, and, when assembled, they lacked that unity of interests and those ties of fatherland which made the Roman army so formidable. Moreover, the relations between the Carthaginian officers and the mercenary and Libyan troops were marked by a callous indifference on the one hand and a dangerous and mutinous dissatisfaction on the other. Officers broke their word to the troops, and even betrayed them,—wrongs which were bitterly avenged by Libyan insurrections. Great efforts were always made by the Carthaginian government to remedy the defects of their military system. Not only were the army chests and magazines kept fully stored, but special attention was paid to all machines of war, and to the use of elephants. As the Carthaginians did not dare to fortify their dependent cities, owing to their fear of their subject states, they spared no pains in making Carthage impregnable. Rome, on the other hand, allowed most of the subject towns to retain their walls, and secured her power by a chain of frontier fortresses throughout Italy. The great strength of Carthage lay in her war-marine, composed of ships and sailors unrivaled in the world. Ships with more than three banks of oars were first built at Carthage, and her quinqueremes were better sailors than the Greek ships of war. In this point Rome was no match, and could not at this period venture into the open sea against her rivals.

To sum up, the resources of the two great powers were at the outset very equally matched; but the danger of Carthage lay in the want of a land army of her own, and of a confederacy of states resting on a secure and self-supporting basis. It was plain that neither Rome nor Carthage could be seriously attacked except in the home of her power; but, in the one case, almost insuperable obstacles met the invader; while, in the other, half his task was accomplished as soon as he had set foot on African soil.

Chapter XII

THE FIRST PUNIC WAR. 264-241 B.C.

AS was but natural, the first conflict between Rome and Carthage had its origin in the island which lay between Italy and Africa. After Pyrrhus had been driven from Sicily and Italy in 275 B.C., the Carthaginians were left masters of more than half the island, and were in possession of the important town of Agrigentum. Syracuse retained nothing but Tauromenium and the southeast of the island. We have above alluded to the roving and mercenary character of the Campanian youth, who, feeling no strong attachment to their native land, had ever been willing to join the forces of Greek adventurers. On the death of Agathocles a band of these mercenaries had, by an act of odious treachery, seized Messana, and in a short time these Mamertines, or men of Mars, as they styled themselves, became the third power in Sicily. Their increasing strength was not unwelcome to the Carthaginians, who gladly saw a new and hostile power established close to Syracuse. Hiero, the new ruler and able general of Syracuse, made great efforts to restore the city to its former eminence, and to unite the Sicilian Greeks. Being at peace for the time with the Carthaginians, he turned his arms against Messana, at the very time that Rome was taking vigorous measures against the Campanian kinsmen of the Mamertines, who had established themselves in Rhegium.

Hiero succeeded in shutting up the Mamertines in their city, and was on the point of successfully terminating a siege which had lasted some years, when the Mamertines in their dire strait turned for help to Rome, and offered to deliver their city into her hands. It was a moment of the deepest significance in the history of the world when the envoys of the Mamertines appeared in the Roman senate. If the Romans acceded to their request, they would not only do violence to their own feelings of right and wrong, by receiving into alliance a band of adventurers stained with the worst crimes, whose very kinsmen in Rhegium they had just

punished for the same offense, but they would throw aside their
views of establishing a mere sovereignty in Italy for the wider and
more dangerous policy of interference with the outside world—a
policy which could not fail to bring them into complicated relations
with powers strictly outside their own land.   A war with Carthage,
serious as it might prove, was not the only result that might follow
such a step; no one could calculate the consequences of so bold a
leap in the dark.   After long deliberation the senate referred the
matter to the citizens; and they, fired by a consciousness of what
they had already achieved, and by a belief in their future destiny,
authorized the senate in 265 B.C. to receive the Mamertines into the
Italian confederacy, and to send them aid at once.

When the Roman force dispatched to carry out this policy
reached Rhegium it was learned that Carthage had been called in to
mediate between Syracuse and Messana, and that the town was now
in possession of a Carthaginian garrison.   It was the fear of just
such a result that had first induced the Romans to interfere in the
affair of the Mamertines.   Without delay, therefore, the expedition crossed the strait and took forcible possession of Messana.

Carthage declared war 264 B.C., and a strong fleet under
Hanno, the son of Hannibal, blockaded Messana.   At the same
time a Carthaginian land army laid siege to the town on the north
side, and Hiero undertook the attack on the south side of the city.
But the Roman consul, Appius Claudius Caudex, crossed over from
Rhegium, and, uniting his forces with those of Claudius, surprised
the enemy, and succeeded in raising the siege.   In the following
year Marcus Valerius Maximus defeated the allied armies of
Carthage and Syracuse.   Upon this Hiero went over to the Roman
side, and continued to be the most important and the firmest ally
the Romans had in the island.   The desertion of Hiero and the
success of Roman arms forced the Carthaginians to take refuge in
their fortresses; and the succeeding year, 262 B.C., practically saw
the close, for the time being, of the war in Sicily.

The whole island passed into the hands of the Romans, with
the exception of the maritime fortresses, held by the firm grip of
Hamilcar, and the coast towns, which were awed into obedience
by the all-powerful Carthaginian fleet.   The real difficulties of the
war were at last beginning to be realized by the Romans, and the
necessity of a fleet was clearly recognized.   Not only was it impossible for them completely to subdue Sicily while Carthage ruled

the sea, but their own coast was continually ravaged by Carthaginian privateers, and their commerce was well-nigh ruined. Therefore they resolved to build a fleet of one hundred quinqueremes and twenty triremes. A stranded Carthaginian man-of-war served as a model to the Roman shipbuilders, and in the spring of 260 B. C. the great task was accomplished, and the fleet launched. It has been seen in what poor estimation the Romans held naval matters, and even now, not only the sailors, but also the naval officers, were almost exclusively drawn from their Italian allies. To compensate for their ignorance of nautical tactics and maneuvers, the Romans made great use of soldiers; and by lowering flying-bridges on to the Carthaginian ships, and fastening them with grappling-irons, they reduced the fight to a land conflict, making it possible to board and capture the enemy's ships by assault. The first great trial of strength took place at Mylae, a promontory to the northwest of Messana, where the Roman fleet under Gaius Duilius encountered the Carthaginian fleet under the command of Hannibal. The Carthaginians, despising their awkward-looking opponents, fell upon them in irregular order; but the boarding-bridges gave the Romans a complete victory, the moral effect of which was far greater than the victory itself. In spite of this success, however, the war dragged on without any decisive action, Hamilcar maintaining himself in Sicily with great skill. At last, weary of this unsatisfactory state of things, the Romans determined to strike at Carthage in her native land. In the spring of 256 B.C. a powerful fleet of 330 ships set sail for Africa; on the way it received on board at Himera, on the south coast of Sicily, four legions under the command of the two consuls, Marcus Atilius Regulus and Lucius Manlius Volso. The Carthaginian fleet, consisting of some 350 ships, had taken up its station at Ecnomus to protect its native shores; thus, when the two fleets met, each side must have numbered little less than one hundred and fifty thousand men. After an obstinate struggle, in which both sides suffered heavily, the Romans gained the day; and the consuls, having deceived the Carthaginians as to their place of landing, disembarked, without any hindrance from the enemy, on the eastern side of the gulf of Carthage, at the bay of Clupea. An entrenched camp was formed on a hill above the harbor, and so confident were the Romans rendered by the success of their plan that half the army and most of the fleet were recalled home by the senate. Regulus remained in Africa with 40 ships, 15,000 infantry, and 500 cavalry. The terror-stricken Carthaginians did not dare to face the Romans in the field; the towns everywhere surrendered, and the Numidians rose in revolt against Carthage. Cowed by this accumulation of disasters, the proud Phoenician city sued for peace, but the exorbitant terms proposed by Regulus were little calculated to render such a solution possible. Under the spur of dire necessity, Carthage evinced that energy and enthusiasm which on such occasions often marks Oriental nations. Hamilcar, the hero of the guerrilla war in Sicily, appeared on the scene with the flower of his Sicilian troops; gold purchased the support both of Numidian cavalry and of Greek mercenaries, among whom was the Spartan Xanthippus, famous for his knowledge and skill in the art of war. During the energetic preparations of Carthage, Regulus remained idle at Tunis; he still pretended to besiege Carthage, and did not even take measures to secure his retreat to the naval camp at Clupea.

His folly cost him dear. In the spring of 255 B.C. the Carthaginians were in a position to take the field; and Regulus accepted battle without waiting for reinforcements. Roman courage availed not against the superior tactics of Xanthippus. Outflanked and surrounded by the Numidian horse, crushed and completely broken up by the elephants, the Romans were almost annihilated. The consul was one of the few prisoners; about two thousand fugitives reached Clupea in safety. On the news of this disaster reaching Rome, a large fleet at once started to save the remnant shut up in Clupea. After defeating the Carthaginians off the Hermaean promontory, the Roman ships arrived at Clupea, and carried off what remained of the army of Regulus. Content with accomplishing this, they sailed homeward, and thus evacuated a most important position, and left their African allies to Carthaginian vengeance. To crown the misfortunes of Rome, a terrible storm destroyed three-fourths of their fleet, and only eighty ships reached home in safety.

Carthage took a stern vengeance on the revolted Numidians, and filled her exhausted treasury with the heavy fines in money and cattle which she exacted from her rebellious subjects. Able now to assume the offensive, she dispatched Hasdrubal, son of Hanno, to Sicily, with a force especially strong in elephants. He landed at Lilybaeum, and Sicily once more became the theater of the war. A new Roman fleet of three hundred ships was dispatched thither in the incredibly short space of three months; and the Carthaginian stronghold of Panormus, with many other places of minor importance, fell into the hands of the Romans. But by land no progress was made, and the Romans did not dare to risk a battle in the face of the overwhelming numbers of Carthaginian elephants. The year 254 B.C. passed by; and the next year, while returning from a plundering expedition to the coast of Africa, the Romans lost 150 vessels in another storm, owing to their obstinate refusal to allow the pilots to take their own course. The senate, utterly downcast by this disaster, reduced their fleet to sixty sail, and limited themselves to the defense of the coast and the convoy of transports. The land war in Sicily was more successful. In 252 B.C., Thermae, the last Carthaginian position on the north coast, and the island of Lipara, yielded to Roman arms; and in the following year the consul Gaius Caecilius Metellus gained a great victory over the Carthaginian army under the walls of Panormus, owing to the disorder of the elephants, which charged their own side. The Carthaginians could no longer take the field, and in a short time they only retained their hold on Drepana and Lilybaeum. The Romans refused the Carthaginian proposals for peace in 249 B.C., and concentrated all their efforts on the capture of Lilybaeum. This was the first great siege undertaken by Rome; but the greater adroitness of the Carthaginian sailors and the ability of Himilco, the commander of Lilybaeum, parried all the efforts of the Romans both by sea and land. Foiled in their efforts to take the city by assault, they were forced to attempt to reduce it by blockade; but they were unable to completely prevent Carthaginian ships from running into the harbor with supplies from Drepana, while the light Numidian cavalry made all foraging both difficult and dangerous on land. In addition, disease, arising from the malaria of the district, thinned the ranks of the Roman land army. Weary of the tedious blockade, the new consul, Publius Claudius, attempted to surprise the Carthaginian fleet as it lay at anchor before Drepana. Completely outmaneuvered by the Phoenician admiral, Atarbas, the Roman consul fell into the trap set for him, and only escaped by prompt flight himself. Ninety-three Roman vessels, with the legions on board, were captured, and the Carthaginians won their first and only great naval victory over the Romans. Lilybaeum was thus set free from the blockade by sea; in fact, the remains of the Roman fleet were in their turn blockaded by the Carthaginian vice-admiral, Carthalo. The latter also took advantage of the folly of the second consul, Lucius Junius Pullus, who was in charge of a second Roman fleet, intended to convey supplies to the army at Lilybaeum. Carthalo met this fleet off the south coast, sailing in two squadrons at some distance from each other; interposing his own ships between the squadrons, he forced both to run on shore. A violent storm completed the work begun by Carthaginian assaults, and both squadrons were completely wrecked, while the Carthaginians easily weathered the storm out on the open sea.

Now, if ever, was the time for Carthage to humble her great antagonist. During a war of fifteen years the Romans had lost four fleets, three with armies on board; and one land army had been destroyed in Libya. This, added to the many minor losses by disease, guerrilla warfare, battles by sea and land, had reduced the burgess-roll, from the years 252-247 B.C. alone, by about forty thousand men, without reckoning the losses of the allies, who bore the whole brunt of the war by sea. The loss of ships and war-material, and the utter paralysis of trade, had inflicted incalculable damage. Moreover, every method and every plan had been tried, and Rome was no nearer the end than she was at the outset of the war. In utter despondency the senate no longer felt equal to the task of subduing Sicily; the fleet was discarded, and the state ships were placed at the disposal of privateer captains, whose unaided valor might perhaps compensate in some degree for the feebleness of the senate. The miserable indolence and weakness of the Carthaginian government alone saved Rome: relieved of the necessity of self-defense, the Carthaginians imitated the example of their enemy, and confined their operations by land and sea to the petty warfare in and around Sicily.

The next six years of uneventful warfare, from 248-243 B. C., reflect little credit on Carthage, and still less on Rome. Hamilcar, named Barak or Barca (*i. e.*, lightning), the Carthaginian commander in Sicily, alone showed proper energy and spirit. Aware that the infantry of Carthage were no match for the Roman legions, and aware that his mercenaries cared as little for Carthage as for Rome, he proved that personal attachment to a general could compensate in the minds of his soldiers for the want of ties of nation and country. He established himself on Mount Ercte, and later captured the town of Eryx, and from these strong positions he carried on a plundering warfare, and levied contributions from the plains, while Phoenician privateers ravaged the Italian coast. The Romans were unable to dislodge him from either of his positions, and every day threatened to bring fresh defeat and disgrace to the Roman arms. This gloomy aspect of affairs was completely changed, not by the energy of the Roman government, but by the noble patriotism of individuals. By private subscription a fleet of two hundred ships, manned by sixty thousand sailors, and fitted out with the greatest care, was raised and presented to the state. This fleet, under the consul Gaius Lutatius Catulus, had no difficulty in occupying the harbors of Drepana and Lilybaeum, and prosecuted the siege of both places with great vigor. Carthage, taken by surprise, dispatched a weak fleet with supplies to the beleaguered towns, and hoped to effect a landing without interference from the Romans. They were, however, intercepted and forced to accept battle off the small island of Aegusa, in the spring of 241 B.C. The result was never doubtful, and the Romans gained a complete and decisive victory. The last effort of the Roman patriots had borne' fruit; it brought victory, and with victory peace.

Peace was concluded at last on terms not wholly unfavorable to Carthage. Sicily, however, had to be abandoned, and Hamilcar was forced by the incapacity of others to descend from the positions he had occupied for seven years with such conspicuous success. In addition to Sicily, Carthage ceded all the islands between Sicily and Italy. She was also condemned to pay a war indemnity of about four million dollars, a third of which was to be paid down at once, and the remainder in ten annual instalments. But Hamilcar refused to accede to certain demands of the Roman consul, and the independence and integrity of the Carthaginian state and territory was expressly guaranteed. Both Rome and Carthage bound themselves not to enter into a separate alliance with any dependency of the other, nor in any way to encroach on the rights which each exercised in her own dominions. The dissatisfaction of the patriotic party at Rome was so great that at first the public assembly refused to sanction the proposed terms of peace. But a commission was appointed to settle the question on the spot in Sicily, and practically the proposals of Catulus were adopted, and Hamilcar, the unconquered general of a vanquished nation, delivered up to the new masters of Sicily the fortresses which had been in the possession of the Phoenicians for at least four hundred years; and in 241 B.C. the West had peace.

The severe struggle, which thus ended in the extension of Roman dominion beyond Italy, throws a strong and by no means favorable light on the Roman military and political system. Notwithstanding the noble patriotism and heroic energy often exhibited by the citizens, we cannot fail to mark the miserable vacillation shown by Rome in the conduct of this war. The fact is that the organization of the Roman senate and of the military system were only adapted for a purely Italian policy, and a purely continental war. The wide area of the battlefield, the necessity of a fleet, the siege of maritime fortresses, were all hitherto unknown to the Romans. For the solution of such problems the senate, from its composition and ignorance, was quite unfitted: moreover, the system of choosing a new commander every year, often to reverse the plans of his predecessor, was manifestly absurd. The noble creation of this war—a Roman fleet—was never truly Roman; Italian Greeks commanded, and subjects, nay even slaves and outcasts, composed the crews; naval service was always held in slight esteem when compared with the honor of the legionary. The general, again, as we see in the case of Regulus, could not change his tactics to suit the exigencies of the moment. The old idea that any citizen was fit to be a general was true only in rustic warfare, while the notion that the chief command of the fleet should be regarded as a mere adjunct of the chief command of the land army excites our wonder and ridicule. To the energy of her citizens, and still more to the terrible blunders of her adversaries, Rome owed her victorious issue from the first Punic war.

In the years that followed this peace Rome gradually extended her dominion to what we may term the natural boundaries of Italy, to the Alps in the north and to Sicily in the south. On the expulsion of the Phoenicians, Rome contented herself with allowing her steadfast ally, Hiero, to retain his independence as ruler of Syracuse, and of the neighboring districts of Elorus, Neetum, Acrae, Leontini, Megara, and Tauromenium; the rest of Sicily she permanently appropriated. Meanwhile Carthage, in consequence of her cowardly and miserly attempt to dock the pay of the mercenaries of Hamilcar, was engaged in a deadly conflict with her revolted soldiers and her Libyan dependencies, among whom the revolution spread far and wide. The city of Carthage itself was

FIRST PUNIC WAR

besieged, and not only in Libya, but even in Sardinia, the insurgents looked to Rome for aid. Rome, although she refused to succor the revolted Libyans, availed herself of the treachery of the Sardinian garrisons, and seized possession of that island in 238 B.C.; shortly afterwards she added Corsica to her new possessions. Carthage, restored by the genius of Hamilcar to her full sovereignty in Africa, demanded in 237 B.C. the restitution of Sardinia; but she did not dare to take up the gage of battle which was promptly thrown down by Rome; and therefore she had to submit to the cession of Sardinia, and in addition, to pay 1200 talents ($1,460,000).

The acquisition of Sicily and Sardinia caused an important change in the Roman method of administration, and one which marked the difference between Italy and the provinces, between the conquests of Rome in her own proper land of Italy and those she made across the sea. The necessity of some special magistrate for these transmarine regions caused the appointment of two provincial pretors, one for Sicily, and one for Sardinia and Corsica; the coasts of these latter islands alone were occupied, and with the natives of the wild interior perpetual war was waged. The two pretors exercised powers very similar to those of the consuls in early times; the pretor was commander-in-chief, chief magistrate, and supreme judge. One or more questors were assigned to each pretor, to look after the finance-administration. With the exception of this difference in the chief power, the same principles were adhered to as those which Rome had observed in organizing her dependencies in Italy. All independence in external relations was taken away from the provincial communities; every provincial was restricted, as regards the acquisition of property, and perhaps the right of marriage, to his own community. But in Sicily, at least, the cities retained their old federal organization, and their harmless federal diets: the power of coining money was probably withdrawn. The land, however, was left untouched, and each Sardinian and Sicilian community retained self-administration and some sort of autonomy. A general valuation corresponding to the Roman census was instituted every fifth year, and all democratic constitutions were set aside in favor of aristocratic councils.

Another *de facto* distinction, of great importance, between the Italian and transmarine communities, was that the latter furnished no fixed contingent to the army or fleet of Rome; they lost the right of bearing arms, and could only use them in self-defense when called upon by the pretor. In lieu of a contingent they paid a tithe of their produce and a tax of five per cent. on all articles of commerce exported or imported; these taxes were not new to the Sicilian Greeks, who had paid them to the ruling power, whether the Persian king, Carthage, or Syracuse. Certain communities were no doubt exempted from these imposts; Messana, for instance, was enrolled in the Roman alliance, and furnished its contingent of ships; other towns, such as Segesta and Halicyae, Centuripa and Alaesa, and Panormus, the future capital of Roman Sicily, though not admitted as confederates of Rome, were exempted from taxation. But on the whole the position of Sicilian and Sardinian communities was one of tributary subjection, not of dependent alliance.

By the possession of Sicily, Sardinia, and Corsica, Rome might now call the Tyrrhene Sea her own. On the east coast the founding of Brundisium in 244 B.C. had from the first established Roman supremacy; the quarrels of the Greek states prevented any rival power arising in Greece itself. But the Adriatic Sea was a prey to Illyrian pirates, and hordes of these tribes, in their dreaded Liburnian galleys, defied all authority and ravaged every coast. They established themselves in Phoenice, the most flourishing town in Epirus, and at length took possession of the rich island of Corcyra. Urgent appeals from hard-pressed Greek settlements on the Adriatic coast, and constant complaints from Italian mariners, at last caused Rome to interfere, and to send an embassy to Agron, king of Scodra and Illyria, with demands that he should put the evil down. His refusal was met with an insulting threat from one of the Roman envoys, for which all the ambassadors paid with their lives. A Roman fleet, with an army on board, appeared to succor the hard-pressed town of Apollonia in 229 B.C., and the corsairs were completely vanquished and their strongholds razed to the ground. The territory of the sovereigns of Scodra was greatly restricted by the terms imposed by Rome, and much of the Illyrian and Dalmatian coasts, together with several Greek cities in that quarter, was practically reduced under Roman sway, or attached to Rome under forms of alliance. The Greeks submitted with a good grace to the humility of seeing their countrymen delivered from the scourge of piracy by barbarians from across the sea, and admitted the Romans to the Isthmian games and the

FIRST PUNIC WAR

Eleusinian mysteries. Macedonia was too weak to protest by aught but words, and that part she disdained to play.

With the exception of a six-days' war with Falerii in 241 B.C., nothing broke the peace of Italy proper. But matters were not so settled in the northern district between the Alps and the Apennines, where strong Celtic races still held their ground. It was but natural that Rome should now wrest the gates of the Alps from the grasp of these barbarians, and make herself mistress, not only of the mighty river, navigable for 230 miles, but of the largest and most fertile plain in the then civilized Europe. The Celts, indeed, had begun to stir in 238 B.C., and two years later the army of the Boii, united with the Transalpine Gauls, encamped before the walls of Ariminum. Fortunately for Rome, exhausted as she then was by her struggle with Carthage, the two Celtic hosts turned on one another, and thus freed Rome from the threatened danger. In 232 B.C. the Celts, weary of waiting for the outbreak of that con- test for Lombardy, which they perceived was inevitable, resolved to strike the first blow. All the Italian Celts, except the Cenomani and Veneti, took part in the war against Rome; advancing to the Apennines in 225 B.C., from which quarter the Romans did not expect an attack, they ravaged Etruria up to the walls of Clusium, and by a clever strategy almost succeeded in cutting off one Roman army before the other could relieve it. Failing in this attempt, the Celts retreated, but were intercepted at Telamon by some legions which had crossed from Sardinia and landed at Pisae. The consul Gaius Atilius Regulus commanded this force, and at once made a flank attack with his cavalry; he fell in the engagement, but his colleague, Papus, at the head of the Italian army, now came into action. Despite their desperate resistance against the double at- tack, the Celts were utterly defeated, and all the tribes south of the Po submitted in 224 B.C. The next year saw the struggle re- newed on the northern side of the river. The valor of the Roman soldiers redeemed the blunder of their general, Gaius Flaminius, and turned what nearly proved a defeat into a glorious victory over the Insubres. Many conflicts took place in 222 B.C., but the cap- ture of the Insubrian capital, Milan, by Gnaeus Scipio, put an end to their resistance. Thus the Celts of Italy were completely vanquished, and though in the most northern and remote districts Celtic cantons were allowed to remain, in all the country south of the Po the Celtic race gradually disappeared. By extensive as-

signations of land in the country between Picenum and Ariminum;
by carrying the great northern highway, or " Flaminian Road," on
from Narnia across the Apennines to Ariminum on the Adriatic

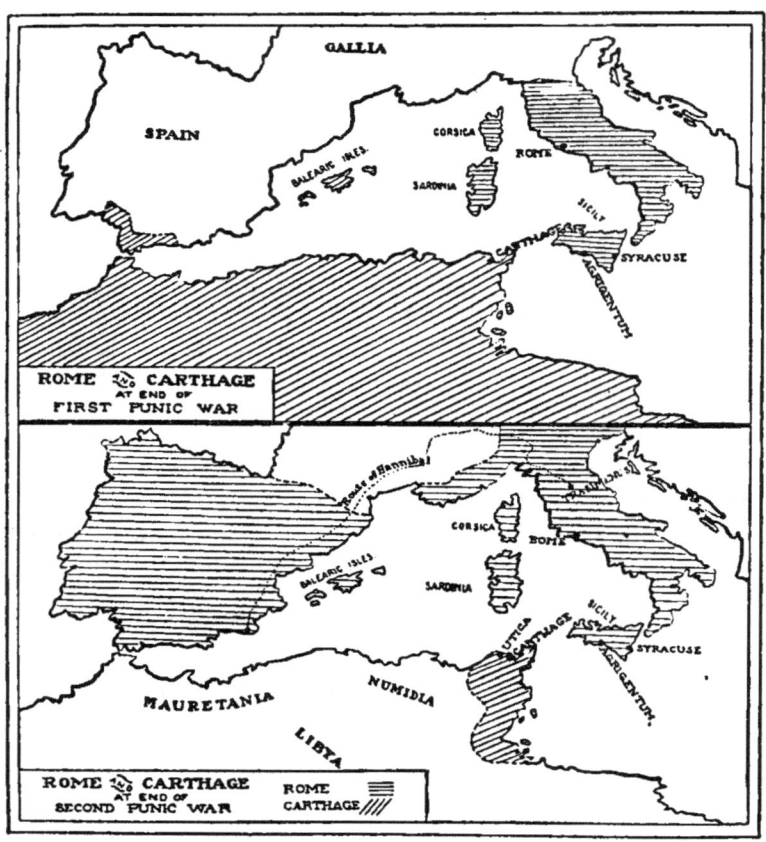

coast; by planting fortresses and Roman townships, *e. g.,* Placentia
and Cremona on the Po itself, in the newly acquired territory, the
Romans showed their determination to reap the fruits of their late
conquests; but a sudden event checked them while in the full tide
of their prosperity.

Chapter XIII

THE SECOND PUNIC WAR. 218-202 B.C.

THE most shallow-minded Carthaginian can scarcely have regarded the peace with Rome in 241 B.C. as likely to prove lasting. Carthage had, no doubt, long been divided into two parties, the one eager for political reform, the other striving to retain the close oligarchical constitution. These two parties were now further rent asunder by the cry for war and the demand for peace. To the latter, or peace-party, belonged the gerusia and Council of a Hundred, under the leadership of Hanno; to this party the timorous and indolent, the worshipers of money and place, naturally attached themselves. The war-party found its chief support in the democratic leaders and military officers, among whom Hasdrubal and Hamilcar were preëminent; the wisest, most far-seeing, and most patriotic Carthaginians lent their aid to this section of the state. The successful conclusion of the war against the revolted Numidians, while it made clear to all the genius of Hamilcar Barca, brought out in odious contrast the miserable incapacity of Hanno, and the utterly corrupt and pernicious character of the ruling oligarchy. Great prominence was thus given to the patriotic party, and, although political reform was impracticable, while Rome was all-powerful and gave her countenance to the treacherous oligarchs, important changes were effected in the military system of Carthage. Hanno was deposed from his command, and Hamilcar was nominated commander-in-chief of all Africa for an indefinite period. He could only be recalled by the vote of the popular assembly, and the choice of a successor was made to depend, not on the magisterial board at home, but on the decision of the officers serving in the army. Apparently Hamilcar was invested with these dictatorial powers for the purpose of superintending the border-warfare with the Numidians; but we shall see what a different view he took of the charge committed to him.

The task set Hamilcar of saving the state by means of the army was calculated to try to the uttermost the abilities of that great man. Not only had he to construct an army out of poor material, and to pay his mercenaries out of an ill-supplied chest, but he had also, as leader of a party, to please and delude in turn the venal multitude at home, whose fickle devotion he knew but too well how to appraise. Although still a young man, Hamilcar possibly foreboded his premature fate, and, ere he left Carthage, he bound his son Hannibal, then nine years of age, by the most solemn oath to swear eternal enmity to Rome, and thus transmitted to his children his schemes, his genius, and his hatred. At the head of a strong army, and accompanied by a fleet under his son-in-law, Hasdrubal, Hamilcar marched westwards, apparently against the Libyans in that quarter; suddenly, without any authority from the government, he crossed over into Spain, and there laid the foundations of the Spanish kingdom of the Barcides. Of his personal achievements we have no details, save that Cato the Elder, on seeing the still fresh traces of his work, exclaimed that no king was worthy to be named by the side of Hamilcar Barca. After nine years of constant war with the Spanish native tribes, when he was beginning to see the result of all his labors, he fell fighting, in 228 B.C.

For the next eight years his son-in-law, Hasdrubal, carried on his plans in the same spirit. The adroit statesmanship of Hasdrubal consolidated the Carthaginian kingdom in Spain which the generalship of Hamilcar had founded. The fairest regions of Spain, the southern and eastern coasts, became Carthaginian provinces; towns were founded, chief of which was Cartagena, on the only good harbor on the south coast, whose silver mines, then first discovered, a century later produced a yearly yield of more than $1,800,000. The revenues of the province not only paid for the maintenance of the army, but enabled Hasdrubal to remit a large sum to Carthage every year. The revival of commerce, which thus recouped in Spain what it had lost in Sicily and Sardinia, was in itself a sufficient reason for the non-interference of the home government with the plans of Hamilcar and Hasdrubal.

We must ascribe the inaction of Rome during such a long period of brilliant Carthaginian successes to the ignorance of the Romans, who knew very little of so remote a country as Spain, and who, no doubt, at first regarded with contempt the reports furnished them by their spies in Carthage. In 226 B.C., however, the senate warned Hasdrubal not to pass the Ebro, and received into alliance the two Greek towns on the east coast of Spain,

SECOND PUNIC WAR

Saguntum and Emporiae; by fixing this limit to the Carthaginian advance the Romans intended to secure a basis of operations in the country between the Ebro and the Pyrenees, should occasion arise for their active interference in Spain. The delay of the Romans in beginning the second Punic war was due to many causes, but chiefly to their inability to form a true conception of the great scheme which the family of Barca was pursuing with such success. The policy of the Romans was always more remarkable for tenacity, cunning, and consistency than for grandeur of conception or power of rapid organization.

So far fortune had smiled on the Carthaginians. It was not fated that Hasdrubal should attempt to realize the dream of his great predecessor. In 220 B.C. he fell by an assassin's hand, and his place was filled by Hannibal, the eldest son of Hamilcar, then in his twenty-ninth year. Despite his youth, the man thus chosen by his comrades-in-arms was fully worthy of their confidence. Nature had bestowed upon him gifts both mental and physical, which were no mean qualifications for his mighty task; education and association had completed nature's work. Brought up from his infancy to cherish thoughts of vengeance on Rome, trained as a soldier in early youth under his father's eye, already highly distinguished, as the commander of the Spanish cavalry, alike for personal bravery and for the higher qualities of a leader, Hannibal was specially fitted to carry out the great projects of his father. Anger, envy, and meanness have written his history, but have not been able to mar the pure and noble image which it presents. Combining in rare perfection discretion and enthusiasm, caution and energy, Hannibal was marked in a peculiar degree by the Phoenician characteristic of inventive craftiness. Every page of the history of the period attests his genius as a general, and his gifts as a statesman were, after the peace with Rome, no less conspicuously displayed in the reform of the Carthaginian constitution, and in the unparalleled influence which, as a foreign exile, he exercised in the cabinets of the Eastern potentates. The power which he wielded over men is shown by his incomparable control over an army of various nations and many tongues—an army which never, in the worst times, mutinied against him. He was a great man; wherever he went he riveted the eyes of all.

Hannibal resolved at once to begin the war, while the Celts in Italy were still unsubdued, and while a war between Rome and

Antigonus Doson, the far-seeing ruler of Macedonia, seemed imminent. Unfortunately the death of the latter reduced Macedonia
to silence; while the death of Hasdrubal had again brought the
peace-party in Carthage to the helm of the state. But Hannibal
was not to be deterred by the opposition of the miserable politicians
at home. Having in vain tried to provoke the people of Saguntum
to break the peace, he attacked the town in 219 b.c. on the pretext
that the Saguntines were oppressing a native tribe subject to
Carthage. The authorities at home, whose sanction Hannibal had
purposely refused to wait for, did not dare to oppose the war thus
begun. Owing to the supineness of the Romans, who were engaged in war with the Illyrian brigands, Saguntum fell after a
siege of eight months, and the rich spoils sent home to Carthage
roused the people to such a pitch of enthusiasm that they accepted
the challenge of war from the Roman envoys, who had been sent
to demand the surrender of Hannibal, in the spring of 218 b.c.

Hannibal intrusted the safety of Spain to his younger brother,
Hasdrubal, and sent home about 20,000 men to defend Africa. The
fleet remained in Spain to secure the communications between that
country and Africa. Two smaller fleets were dispatched, the one
to ravage the coast of Italy, the other to attempt to surprise Lilybaeum, and to renew the war in Sicily. Hannibal himself, relying
on the enmity of the Celts and Ligurians to Rome, determined to
make northern Italy the meeting-place, where all foes of Rome
might unite and aid him in the achievement of his great enterprise.
It is not clear why he chose the land-route, the old pathway of
Celtic hordes, in preference to that by sea; for neither the maritime
supremacy of the Romans nor their league with Massilia, could
have prevented a landing at Genoa.

In the spring of 218 b.c., with a force of 90,000 infantry,
12,000 cavalry, and 37 elephants, he set out from Cartagena to
cross the Ebro, and he inspired all his soldiers with enthusiasm by
pointing out the main plan and object of his undertaking. Distracted by the unexpected nature of the danger which threatened
them, the Romans seem to have been but little prepared with a
settled plan of war, and to have fatally delayed both in aiding
Saguntum and in meeting Hannibal on the Ebro; the losses inflicted on Hannibal by the native tribes, when he forced the passage
of that river, show clearly where the Romans ought to have first
opposed him. Part of his troops he left behind to secure the newly

won country between the Ebro and the Pyrenees, part he sent home on reaching that chain of mountains; with the rest, amounting to 50,000 infantry and 9000 cavalry, all veterans, he crossed the Pyrenees, nor did he meet with any serious resistance until he reached the Rhone, opposite Avignon; there he was met by a levy of the Celts, but, outwitting them, he crossed the river before the arrival of the consul, Publius Cornelius Scipio, who had delayed at Massilia, and reached the Alps in safety. He had the choice of three routes in crossing this mighty barrier. The coast-route was, however, out of the question, as it was not only barred by the Romans, but would also have taken him away from his destination. The remaining two routes at that time consisted of the pass of the Cottian Alps (Mont Genèvre), which, though shorter, passes through a difficult and poor mountain country, and of the pass of the Graian Alps (the little St. Bernard). This, though longer, is far the easiest to traverse; and the route by this pass leads through the broadest and most fertile of the Alpine valleys; moreover, the Celts favorable to Hannibal inhabited the country on the Italian side of the little St. Bernard, while the Cottian pass led directly into the territory of the Taurini, a Celtic tribe at feud with the Insubres, who were Hannibal's allies. Thus every circumstance tended to make Hannibal choose the pass of the Graian Alps. [1]

The march along the Rhone toward the valley of the upper Isère, through the rich country of the Allobroges, brought the Carthaginian army, after sixteen uneventful days, to the foot of the Alps, and there the first dangers were encountered from some cantons of the Allobroges, who made constant assaults on the army during its ascent of the first Alpine chain, and during the descent of the precipitous path that trends sheer down to the lake of Bourget. A welcome rest in the fertile valley of Chambéry gave Hannibal time to repair his losses in beasts of burden and horses. Marching up the Isère, the army now entered the territory of the Ceutrones, whose courteous hospitality did but mask their coming treachery. On reaching the narrow track that led to the summit of the St. Bernard, Hannibal found the pass occupied on both sides, and in the rear, by the perfidious Ceutrones. His forethought in

[1] Various geographical questions connected with Hannibal's campaigns, such as the route followed through the Alps and later on through the Apennines, the details of the battles of Trebia, Trasimene, Cannae, etc., are still unsettled and matters of much dispute.

sending forward the baggage and cavalry saved him from the intended robbery of his supplies; but all along the line of his ascent constant conflicts caused not only loss of men and beasts, but confusion and utter despondency in his soldiers' hearts. At last, however, the summit was reached, and after a brief rest the perilous descent began; here the late season, with its fresh mantle of September snows, proved more terrible than the treacherous attacks of barbarians. But all difficulties gave way before the iron will and unshaken confidence of the great general, and at last the shattered army enjoyed a nobly earned repose in the plain of Ivrea, quartered in the villages of the friendly Salassi, clients of the Insubres. Fortunately for Hannibal, no Roman troops were stationed so far north to await his arrival. The Alps were crossed, and Hannibal had attained his object; but to this end he had sacrificed more than half his infantry and three thousand cavalry. The military value of this wonderful achievement may well be called in question, but the courage, skill, and masterly execution of the plan by Hannibal himself admit of no doubt. The grand idea of Hamilcar, that of taking up the conflict with Rome in Italy, was now realized. It was his genius that projected this expedition, and the unerring tact of historical tradition has always dwelt on the last link in the great chain of preparatory steps, the passage of the Alps, with a greater admiration than on the battles of the Trasimene lake and of the plain of Cannae.

Hannibal's arrival in Italy disconcerted the Roman plans. The army of Publius Scipio had already landed in Spain, under the command of Gnaeus, the brother of Publius. The latter, on being foiled by Hannibal at the passage of the Rhone, had himself returned to Pisae with a few troops, and was now in command of the Roman force in the valley of the Po. The army of the other consul, Tiberius Sempronius, had been fortunately delayed in its intended attack on the African coast by the descent of the Carthaginian fleet on Sicily, and was now recalled to northern Italy, but the surprise of the Romans enabled Hannibal to rest his troops after the passage of the Alps and to cement his alliance with the Celts and Ligurians before encountering the famous legions of the Republic.

The two armies met in the plain between the Ticinus and the Sesia, not far from Vercellae, and Scipio was decisively beaten, owing to the overpowering force of the light Numidian cavalry.

SECOND PUNIC WAR 117
218-217 B.C.

Scipio himself was severely wounded, and only saved by the spirited devotion of his son, then a youth of seventeen. He at once wisely recrossed the Po, and, followed by Hannibal, took up a strong position on the hills behind the Trebia. Here he was joined by the second army under Sempronius, and thus strengthened and occupying a highly advantageous position, the Romans might await with confidence the next move of Hannibal. Fortunately for the latter, Scipio's wound caused the sole command to devolve on Tiberius Sempronius, who was fired with impatience to avenge the previous defeat on the Ticinus and the desolation of the villages of such Celts as still remained loyal to Rome. Drawn on by the simulated flight of the enemy's cavalry, the Romans crossed the Trebia in hot pursuit, and suddenly found themselves face to face with the whole army of Hannibal drawn up for battle. The Roman cavalry proved no match for their opponents; but the stubborn courage of the infantry resisted every attack both of foot and horse, until a picked force of two thousand Carthaginians under Mago by an attack in the rear decided the day. Even then the first division of the Roman infantry, ten thousand strong, cut their way through the midst of the enemy and succeeded in reaching the fortress of Placentia. The losses of Hannibal in battle fell chiefly on the Celts, but many of his veterans and all his elephants, except one, perished afterwards of fatal diseases caused by the cold and wet of that bitter December day. The victory made Hannibal master of northern Italy, and the Celtic insurrection spread far and wide without let or hindrance from Roman arms. Hannibal bivouacked for the winter where he was, and organized the Celtic accessions to his army, which are said to have numbered more than sixty thousand infantry and four thousand cavalry.

Despite this brilliant success Hannibal was probably well aware of his true position in Italy. He knew that his chance of ultimate victory depended rather on political than military achievements, upon the gradual loosening and breaking up of the Italian confederation: as long as that confederation remained united, and confronted him with its vastly superior resources, he no doubt felt that with his inferior infantry, with his precarious and irregular support from home, with the capricious aid of the fickle Celts, he had no hope of humbling to the dust his proud antagonist. Owing to this conviction, Hannibal's conduct of the war in Italy is marked by a constant change both of the theater of war and of the plan of operations, and also by an earnest endeavor to turn every success to good account by posing as the liberator of Italian cities from the tyranny of Rome. With this object in view he released all the Italian prisoners without a ransom, and charged them to report that he waged war against Rome, not Italy, whose saviour and restorer of ancient powers and independence he professed himself. The Roman prisoners, on the other hand, he loaded with chains as slaves.

In the early spring of 217 B.C. Hannibal set out from the Po; and at a point as far west as possible he crossed the Apennines, while the new consul, Gaius Flaminius, lay idle at Arretium. His army suffered terrible hardships on the other side of the mountains when struggling through the low-lying and flooded country extending between the Serchio and Arno, and Hannibal himself lost the sight of one eye from ophthalmia. However, at last he reached the rich land at Faesulae, where he encamped, having thus completely baffled the consul Flaminius.

The latter, raised by the popular party at Rome to a second consulship, did not wait for his colleague, Graeus Servilius, to leave his useless post at Ariminum, and join him. Fired by his ambition to justify the good opinion of the democrats, and stung by the sight of the devastation which marked far and wide the line of Hannibal's march through Etruria, Flaminius hastily followed, and overtook Hannibal in the district of Cortona. Here Hannibal had chosen his field of battle—a narrow defile between two steep mountains, closed at its outlet by a high hill, and at its entrance by the lake Trasimene. Here he prepared an ambush for the enemy, into which the Roman army in the heavy mist of an early morning marched unsuspectingly and was almost entirely annihilated. Fifteen thousand Romans fell, and among them the consul; and as many more were captured: while Hannibal's loss was but fifteen hundred. The vanguard of the Romans, six thousand strong, proved once more the irresistible might of the legion, and cut its way through the opposing infantry; but they were next day surrounded and made prisoners of war by Maharbal, at the head of a squadron of cavalry. About the same time the cavalry of the army of Servilius, which had been sent forward to support Flaminius, fell in with the enemy and was cut to pieces. All Etruria was lost; and the Romans broke down the bridges over the Tiber, and nominated Quintus Fabius Maximus dictator, to make all preparations for the defense of the city, upon which it was supposed Hannibal would at once march.

Hannibal, however, knew better; suddenly marching through Umbria, he carried fire and sword through the territory of Picenum, and then gave a much-needed rest to his army on the shores of the Adriatic. More than this, he here adopted the marvelously bold experiment of reorganizing his Libyan infantry, after the Roman fashion, and of equipping them with the arms taken from the Roman spoils. From here, too, he sent messages of his victory by sea to Carthage. After a sufficient rest and practice of the new method of warfare, he marched slowly along the coast into southern Italy. His hope that the Italian confederacy would now break up was not fulfilled: not a single community entered into alliance with the Carthaginians.

A new general of very different tactics now confronted Hannibal, in the person of the dictator Quintus Fabius. Elected to counteract the demagogic spirit which had given the consulship to Flaminius, he was as opposed in strategy as in policy to his predecessor. Determined to avoid a pitched battle and to wear out Hannibal by small conflicts and deprivation of provisions, Fabius followed Hannibal as he marched over the Apennines into the heart of Italy and made a futile attempt on the loyalty of Capua. Bitter indeed must have been the feelings of the Roman soldier as from the heights along which Fabius marched was visible the flaming track of ruin and desolation throughout Samnium and Campania, beneath the devastating blight of the Numidian horsemen. At last, however, the patient policy of Fabius seemed to grasp its reward. When Hannibal, foiled in his attempt on Capua, began to retreat, Fabius intercepted his route near Casilinum by strongly garrisoning that town on the left bank of the Volturnus, and occupying the heights commanding the right bank with his main army, while a division blockaded the road along that river. All his efforts were, however, baffled by the famous ruse of Hannibal, who caused his light-armed troops to climb the heights immediately above the road, and drive before them a number of oxen with lighted faggots on their horns. The Romans, thinking that they saw the whole Carthaginian army marching off during the night by torchlight, abandoned their blockade of the road, and made for the heights. Hannibal thus gained a free passage for his main army, and on the morrow easily disengaged his light troops;

then marching northeast, and laying all the country under contribution as he marched, he proceeded to entrench himself for the winter in the plains of Apulia at Gerunium. Huge stores of grain and supplies were daily amassed by detachments sent out for that purpose.

Marcus Minucius, the master of the horse, in the absence of the dictator, formed a camp not far off, in the territory of the Larinates; and by some successful engagements with Carthaginian detachments he caused the storm, which had long been brewing at Rome, to break out against Fabius and his policy. The Roman legions felt that they had borne long enough the passive attitude of vigilant observation, and had too long acquiesced in the sight of all Italy spoiled by the invader without striking a blow in her defense. Indeed, the policy of Fabius not only did not save Rome, but never really hindered Hannibal from carrying into execution any single operation he had planned. The outcry at Rome gave rise to the absurd resolution of the people, by which Minucius was appointed co-dictator with the same powers as Fabius, but with a diametrically opposite policy. Minucius, in his eagerness to give effect to his spirited policy, was soon lured into a foolish attack, and only escaped annihilation by the timely rescue of Fabius. Rome, now thoroughly aroused, haughtily declined the offers of money from Hiero of Syracuse, and from the Greek cities in Italy, and determined to send out such a force as had never before been seen: consisting of eight legions, each raised a fifth above the normal strength, with a corresponding number of allies. Weary of the dictatorship, and bitterly distrusting the senate, the people in 216 B.C. elected Marcus Terentius Varro as consul, whose sole recommendation was his low origin and hot-headed zeal for the popular cause. His colleague was the able Lucius Aemilius Paulus, whose candidature was supported, and with great difficulty carried, by the senatorial party.

Hannibal had already resumed the offensive in Apulia, and, marching south from Gerunium, took the citadel of Cannae, which commanded the plain of Canusium. Hither came the two new consuls with a united army of eighty thousand infantry and six thousand cavalry, as compared with the forty thousand infantry and ten thousand cavalry of Hannibal. Paulus saw that the wide, open plain was very favorable to the superior horse of his enemy, and therefore constructed two camps higher up the river, the larger on the right bank, the smaller on the left of the Aufidus, hoping thus to compel Hannibal to retire from his position. But the soldiers and his hot-headed colleague were impatient of camp-work, and longed to measure swords with the hated foe. At early dawn, on one of the days on which Varro held the supreme command, the Romans crossed over the river, then almost dry, and took up position near their smaller camp in the wide plain that stretches westward from Cannae. The Carthaginians followed them, and Hannibal formed his infantry in crescent shape, with the Celtic and Iberian troops in the center to meet the first shock of the serried ranks of the enemy; the light Numidian horse occupied the open space in the plain facing the Italian cavalry under Varro; the heavy cavalry under Hasdrubal occupied the ground near the river on the right, and faced the less numerous Roman horse under Paulus. The Roman legions easily overthrew the Celts and Iberians, and pressed on into the center to complete their success. On the left wing the cavalry action was undecided, but on the right Hasdrubal completely scattered and cut down the Roman horse. Meanwhile the Roman infantry had become wedged in by their eager efforts to follow up their first success, and were unable to deploy their ranks so as to meet the attacks of the Libyan infantry, who closed in upon all sides. At this crisis, Hasdrubal, who had previously completely routed the horse under Varro and left their pursuit to the light Numidian horse, made a third and final charge on the confused ranks of the Roman infantry. All was lost, and the Romans merely stood to be butchered. The army was an-nihilated: seventy thousand Romans lay on the field, while Hannibal lost but six thousand, two-thirds of whom were Celts. Paulus was among the slain, as also the pro-consul Gnaeus Servilius, who had led the infantry, and eighty men of senatorial rank. Varro was not ashamed to survive the disaster, and, saved by his swift steed, reached Venusia; and the senators, with a noble, if to us ironical, generosity, met him at the gates of Rome, and thanked him for not having despaired of the safety of the state. In addition to those slain on the field of battle, most of the division guarding the Roman camp were made prisoners; and, as if to crown the disasters of Rome, a little later a legion sent to Gaul fell into an ambush, and was completely destroyed, together with its general, Lucius Postumius, the consul-designate for the coming year.

Now at last there seemed good hope of realizing that great political combination for the sake of which Hannibal had invaded Italy; his army had nobly performed its task, and opened the way for the union of the eastern and western foes of the proud city. In one essential quarter, indeed, all chance of succor had been for the time destroyed. Gnaeus Scipio had met with great success in Spain, and was not only master of the country north of the Ebro, but with the aid of his brother Publius, had in 217 B.c. crossed that river, after inflicting a severe defeat on the Carthaginian fleet at its mouth, and advanced as far as Saguntum. Further, in the following year, almost at the same time as the great victory of Cannae, the two Scipios totally defeated Hasdrubal, when attempting to cross the Ebro and bring a fresh army across the Pyrenees to his brother's aid. As far as Africa was concerned, Hannibal had received all the assistance he could hope for from home, though he was continually pinched for want of money wherewith to pay his soldiers. The news of the victory of Cannae made Carthage resolve to send him reinforcements of money and men, and to prosecute the war with energy both in Italy and Spain. Now, too, Philip of Macedon formed his long-deferred alliance with Carthage, and undertook to land an army on the east coast of Italy, in return for the restoration of the lands in Epirus, which had been wrested from Macedonia by the Romans. Moreover, Hieronymus, the young and incapable successor of the shrewd Hiero, joined the side of the Carthaginians; and the united fleet of Syracuse and Carthage at once rendered the position of the Romans at Lilybaeum most critical. But, above all, signs were at last visible that the Italian confederacy was losing its cohesion, and throwing off its allegiance to Rome. Most of the Italian towns of southern Italy passed over to the side of Hannibal. The aristocratic party in all these places vehemently opposed the change of sides, and their bitter opposition, especially in Capua, produced internal conflicts, which greatly lessened the advantage derived by Hannibal from these secessions. On the other hand, the south Italian and Campanian Greeks remained firmly loyal to Rome, despite their perilous position and the attacks of Hannibal; naturally, too, all the Latin colonies in southern and central Italy presented an unyielding front to the enemy.

Such were the direct consequences of the day of Cannae, a cruel but just punishment for the grave political errors of the

Roman people. The war with Hannibal had revealed, with fatal clearness, the absurdity of the method of electing generals, and the still greater danger of such a method when, as in the case of the two consuls Flaminius and Varro, it became the tool of party and the two-edged instrument of demagogism. It was clear that political struggles must cease to dictate the policy of the war, and that all elements must unite to preserve the state. The noble and patriotic manner in which the senate performed its task, and healed the party quarrels by abstaining from all recriminations, constitutes its glorious and imperishable honor. Quintus Fabius took the lead in all the defensive measures, and the praetor, Marcus Claudius Marcellus, whose destination previous to the battle of Cannae had been Sicily, was appointed to the chief command of the hastily collected army. Every nerve was strained to gather troops and supply arms. All those above boyhood were called out, debtor-serfs and criminals were armed, and even eight thousand slaves were incorporated in the army. All proposals from Hannibal touching a ransom of captives were contemptuously rejected; no word, no action, was suffered to have even the semblance of a thought of peace, while Hannibal was still in Italy and Cannae unavenged.

From this point on the war in Italy flagged, and, in spite of various military successes, Hannibal's power began to decline. He had gained all that he could hope for by mere force of arms, but the Roman confederation in central Italy still presented an unbroken front to his invincible army. The great difficulty of taking fortified towns prevented a single battle from being so decisive as it is in our own days. Further, Rome had grown wiser, and the selection of Marcus Claudius Marcellus as commander of the forces in Italy contributed in no small degree to Rome's preservation. Hannibal could no longer count either on the inaction of the Roman armies or on the fatal mistakes of ignorant generals. In 215 B.C. the Romans took the field with three armies in Campania. A fourth, meanwhile, under the pretor Marcus Valerius, had taken up its position at Luceria, and in conjunction with the force under Marcellus caused great annoyance to Hannibal's allies in Apulia and Lucania. To relieve these, Hannibal attacked Marcellus and suffered defeat beneath the walls of Nola. These misfortunes obliged Hannibal to evacuate Campania and march to Arpi, where he might in person put a stop to the further progress of the Romans in Apulia. One of the Roman armies followed him, leaving the

other two to arrange for the attack on Capua in the coming
spring.

It was clear to Hannibal that the offensive was no longer possible, and that each day the defensive became more difficult. The
accomplishment of his purpose depended on the strenuous co-
operation of the government at Carthage, on the success of the
Carthaginian generals in Spain, and on the long-promised aid of
Philip of Macedon. But the peace party in Carthage, after the
first impressions of the victory of Cannae had died away, regained
the ascendency, and, with the exception of a small force of four
thousand Africans, no adequate reinforcements reached Hannibal
from Carthage. Had he been able to bring into play the united
forces of Carthage, Spain, Sicily, and Macedonia, the overthrow of
Rome would have been well-nigh certain; but in no quarter did
matters go well for him. The activity and success of the two
Scipios in Spain held Hasdrubal in check. The assassination of
Hieronymus at the close of the same year left the state of Syracuse
in great confusion, though the city still held true to the Carthaginian
alliance. Marcellus himself was sent over to finish the war in
Sicily in 214 B.C. Owing to the dread of Roman vengeance and
the passionate enthusiasm for liberty which Hannibal's emissaries
had excited in the Syracusan multitude, Marcellus was obliged
to lay siege to the city, and after eight months to convert the
siege into a blockade. The defense of Syracuse was notable
alike for the famous ingenuity of the great engineer, Archimedes, and for the efforts made by Carthage in its behalf, but
neither availed against Roman pertinacity. In 212 B.C. Syracuse
surrendered and was completely sacked by the soldiers of Marcellus,
Archimedes being among the slain. The city was deprived of its
freedom and was classed among the communities that paid tribute
to Rome.

All Sicily seemed lost to the Carthaginians, whose force at
Agrigentum, under Hanno and Epicydes, dared not make a move
against the triumphant Romans. But Hannibal's influence, and the
ability of one of his Libyan cavalry officers, Mutines, whom Hannibal sent from Italy, carried on a guerrilla warfare throughout the
island with great success. Mutines, at the head of the Numidian
cavalry, even succeeded in worsting Marcellus himself. Jealousy,
however, arose between him and Hanno, and the latter deposed
him from the command of the cavalry, placing his own son in the

position.   Mutines in disgust delivered up Agrigentum to the Romans and thus put an end to the war in Sicily, which henceforth remained entirely under Roman rule.

Hannibal might with good reason have looked for more substantial aid from Macedonia.   In Greece generally there was a strong outburst of national patriotism; internal discord had been healed and peace established in 217 B.C. between Philip and the Aetolian league.   But in Greece, as in Carthage, a national leader was wanting to give effect to the national ardor of the moment. After a futile attempt to take Apollonia in 216 B.C., and after constantly threatening but never daring to carry out his promised descent on the east coast of Italy, Philip made a useless attack on the Roman possessions in Epirus in 214 B.C.   The energetic action of the Romans, who crossed over from Brundisium and stormed his camp, cowed him back into inaction.   Nor was he roused out of this inertness until a coalition, headed by the Aetolians, and joined by the old Greek enemies of Macedonia, and supported by Rome, forced him to bestir himself.   In the long and dreary war that followed he repelled the attacks of his foes with vigor and success, but Hannibal soon ceased to look eastward for aid.   Worn out by useless conflicts, at last Philip made peace with the Aetolians in 205 B.C., and then with Rome: a peace favorable, indeed, to Philip, in so far as it left matters in much the same position as they were at the beginning of the war; but disastrous to him and to the Greek nation as a whole, since by it the grand and just combination which Hannibal had projected, and all Greece had for a moment joined, was shattered irretrievably.

In Spain the struggle was sharpest, and was marked by the vicissitudes incidental to the character of the country and habits of the people.   Neither Rome nor Carthage had brought into Spain a force sufficiently powerful to terminate the contest; therefore both sides had to have recourse to native help; but the natives regarded neither side with ardent partisanship, and they were never to be depended upon for persistent and united action.   For a time, indeed, the two Roman generals, Publius and Gnaeus Scipio, were brilliantly successful; but in 211 B.C. Hasdrubal, brother of Hannibal, after suppressing the revolt of Syphax in Africa, which had been stimulated by the Romans, crossed back into Spain and annihilated the army of the two Scipios, who lost their lives in the fatal battle.

In the following year Rome was enabled, by the fall of Capua, to dispatch a force of 12,000 men, under the pro-pretor Gaius Claudius Nero, to check the Carthaginian advance in Spain. Nero was not unsuccessful on the field, but his strategic ability was more than counterbalanced by his harshness and inability to deal with the natives. The senate, aware of the great exertions which were being made in Carthage to send Hasdrubal and his brilliant African ally, Massinissa, with a powerful army across the Pyrenees to Italy, resolved to send an extraordinary general with a numerous force to Spain. His nomination, if we may credit the story, was left to the people. At first no one in Rome offered himself as a candidate; but at last Publius Scipio, son of the Publius Scipio who had fallen in Spain, although not properly qualified for the office, came forward. The youth, personal beauty, enthusiasm, military distinction gained on the fields of Trebia and Cannae, and political eminence of Publius Scipio were of themselves calculated to deeply impress the people of Rome; the thought that a youth of twenty-seven, who had merely held the offices of edile and military tribune, was thus suddenly raised to the highest and proudest office in the state at a time of great peril, and was going forth to avenge a father's death, rendered that impression indelible, and has colored the story with romantic details. Although lacking the energy, iron will, and statesmanlike grasp of such men as Caesar and Alexander, Publius Scipio was eminently calculated to inspire others with his own enthusiasm. His personal qualities, both of appearance and manner; his graceful oratory; his happy union of Hellenic culture and Roman patriotism; above all, his intense belief in himself as one specially favored by the gods, served to cast a romantic glamour round his name, and to kindle in men's hearts a fervent belief that a true prophet and divinely inspired saviour had arisen to give victory and peace to his country.

On being elected general, Scipio proceeded to Spain in 210 B.C., accompanied the pro-pretor Marcus Silanus, and by his friend Gaius Laelius as admiral, with a strong force and well-filled chest. He at once successfully executed one of the boldest *coups-de-main* known in history. All the three Carthaginian generals were at least ten days' march from Nova Carthago. Suddenly, early in the spring of 209 B.C., Scipio appeared before the weakly garrisoned town with his whole army and fleet. By engaging the attention of the garrison with an attack from the land side, Scipio had no difficulty in scaling the undefended walls from the harbor side, where at ebb-tide a land passage was left open to his troops. The capture of the Carthaginian capital, apart from the immense stores thus thrown into the conqueror's hands, completely restored Roman prestige in Spain. Scipio's command was indefinitely prolonged, and not only were the passes of the Pyrenees, and all the country north of the Ebro, secured, but incursions were successfully made into Andalusia. Rendered over-confident by success, Scipio extended his operations over too large an area, and, when in Andalusia, he encountered Hasdrubal Barca at Baecula, in 208 B.C., on his march northward to his brother's aid. Scipio claimed the victory, but Hasdrubal attained his object, and succeeded in crossing the Pyrenees, and taking up his quarters in Gaul for the winter. The two following years fresh armies were sent from Carthage, but Scipio defeated them, and in 206 B.C. Spain became a Roman province. Scipio resigned his command in that year and returned to Rome, while Mago the Carthaginian commander, collecting what ships and troops he could, set sail for northern Italy.

Meanwhile the great conflict in Italy had been continued without interruption, but it would be tedious to follow in detail the course of military events from the battle of Cannae to that of the Metaurus. At no time did the genius of Hannibal display itself to greater advantage than in this period when, deprived of all outside help, he supported himself in Italy against the whole power of Rome. Little by little, however, he was driven into the southern portion of the peninsula; Capua was taken by the Romans and cruelly punished for its defection, and, though some of the Greek cities opened their gates, Hannibal could only play a waiting game and expect the promised succor from his brother in Spain.

The material distress of Rome was terrible: the exchequer was utterly impoverished, the lands lay fallow, and starvation was only averted by corn-supplies from Egypt; the pay of the soldiers was greatly in arrear, and the country villages, no longer smiling homes of farmers, were nests of beggars and brigands. Still more ominous was the fact that the allies of Rome began to weary of the struggle, and even Latium to waver in her allegiance. In 209 B.C. many of the Latin communities announced that henceforth they would neither send contingents, or contributions, and that Rome must carry on the struggle single-handed. Fortunately the colonies in Gaul, Picenum, and southern Italy, with Fregellae at their head, refused to adopt so short-sighted a policy, but Arretium gave dangerous signs that the Etruscans were preparing to rise once more in aid of Hannibal.

In the midst of all these difficulties and signs of coming trouble, the news arrived that Hasdrubal had crossed the Pyrenees in the autumn of 208 B.C., and that Rome would have to face, next year, both sons of Hamilcar in Italy. Thus, at last, it seemed as if Hannibal was destined to reap the reward of his long and patient waiting. Rome once more called out twenty-three legions. Hasdrubal, however, was too quick for them, and ere the Romans could occupy the outlets of the Alpine passes, news came that he had reached the Po, that the Gauls were flocking to his standard, and that Placentia was invested. Marcus Livius hastened to the northern army: while his colleague Gaius Nero, with the aid of the force at Venusia under Gaius Hostilius Tubulus, obstructed the advance of Hannibal. The latter marched from the Bruttian territory and fought an indecisive engagement with Nero at Grumentum; he succeeded, however, in his object, and by a flank march reached Apulia, and encamped at Canusium. Nero followed, and took up his position opposite to him.

While the two armies remained idly facing one another, Nero had the good fortune to intercept the all-important dispatch from Hasdrubal, acquainting Hannibal with his intention to meet him at Narnia. Nero thereupon made his bold and famous march with a picked force of seven thousand men, and joined Marcus Livius in the north at Sena Gallica: he left behind him the bulk of his army strongly entrenched against attack, and, what was more important, he left Hannibal unconscious of his departure and ignorant of Hasdrubal's intention. The two consuls at once marched against Hasdrubal, and found him crossing the Metaurus. Hasdrubal tried to avoid a battle, but, being deserted by his guides, made the best provision for the inevitable. A flank attack by Nero decided the hotly contested day. Hasdrubal scorned to survive the disaster, and his army was destroyed.

The defeat and death of Hasdrubal, in 207 B.C., solved the mighty question of the triumph or humiliation of Rome. After fourteen days' absence Nero again reached his old station at Canusium, and confronted the unconscious Hannibal in Apulia. With him, in ghastly fashion, he brought the news of Hasdrubal's defeat, and the overthrow of all Hannibal's plans and hopes. Hannibal retired to the Bruttian territory; while Rome, overjoyed at the relief from the terrible strain of past years, and conscious that the peril was over, resumed business and even pleasure as in time of peace, and made no great effort to finish the war. Thenceforth the struggle languished in Italy, nor could all the superior force of his opponents compel Hannibal to shut himself up in fortresses or to leave Italian soil.

We have now reached the final scene of this great contest. Publius Scipio, who had returned from Spain in the previous year, was chosen consul in 205 B.C. His popularity with the multitude made him no favorite with the senate, whose members viewed with suspicion his Greek refinement and modern culture, and not unjustly criticised his leniency and indulgence towards his officers and his conduct of the war in Spain. Moreover, the senate was averse to an expedition into Africa as long as Hannibal was in Italy, and was specially disinclined to intrust it to Scipio, who had shown too clearly a tendency to slight the constitutional authority of the senate and to rely on his fame and popularity with the masses. At last, however, Scipio was intrusted with the task of building a fleet in Sicily, and raising an army, of which the two legions in Sicily formed the nucleus. The fleet was ready in forty days, and seven thousand volunteers responded to the call of their beloved commander.

In the spring of 204 B.C. Scipio set sail with 30,000 men, 40 ships of war, and 400 transports, and landed unopposed at the Fair Promontory near Utica. He was at once joined by his old foe Massinissa, who had been driven from his kingdom by the combined armies of Carthage and Syphax. The latter had embraced the side of Carthage, and, as a reward, had caused Carthage to renounce her old ally Massinissa. The arrival of Syphax with a powerful army, and his junction with the Carthaginian force stationed to oppose Scipio, caused the Roman general to abandon the siege of Utica, and to entrench himself for the winter on a promontory between Utica and Carthage. Fortune, however, never failed to smile on Scipio, and, under cover of proposals for peace, Scipio succeeded in surprising both camps on the same night, and in utterly routing the two armies. Reinforcements at this moment arrived, consisting of a Macedonian corps under Sopater, and of Celtiberian mercenaries. The Carthaginians, thus strengthened, resolved to venture on a pitched battle in the "Great Plains," five days' march from Utica. Scipio was completely successful, and Syphax fell into his hands.

The peace party at Carthage now tried to reverse the Barcid policy, and sued for peace. The terms proposed by Scipio were so moderate that the peace faction were for accepting them at once. But the patriotic party had not lost hope, and during the negotiations recalled Hannibal and Mago from Italy. The latter, however, after striving for three years to form a coalition in northern Italy against Rome, had just been defeated near Milan, and during his voyage home died of a wound received in that battle. Hannibal at once embarked at Croton, and, after an absence of thirty-six years, returned once more to his native land in 203 B.C. The Roman citizens breathed freely when the mighty Libyan lion, whose departure no one even now ventured to compel, thus voluntarily turned his back on Italian ground. To mark the occasion, a grass wreath, the highest distinction possible in the Roman state, was presented to the veteran Quintus Fabius, then nearly ninety,— his last honor, for in the same year he passed away.

Hannibal's arrival in Africa ignited the torch of war once more. The people of Carthage refused to ratify the peace practically concluded, and the seizure of a ship of war with Roman envoys on board broke the armistice. Scipio, in just wrath, ravaged the valley of the Bagradas, and penetrated the interior, when his course was arrested by Hannibal. After fruitless negotiations both armies prepared for a decisive battle at Zama, in 202 B.C. By a skillful disposition Scipio managed that the elephants of the enemy should pass through his lines without breaking them: forcing their way to the side, these unwieldly creatures threw the cavalry of Hannibal into disorder, and the far more numerous horse of Massinissa easily scattered the Carthaginian squadrons. The infantry battle was most bloody and severe: nor did the veterans of Hannibal ever flinch until the cavalry of Massinissa, returning from pursuit, surrounded them on all sides. The Phoenician army was annihilated and Cannae avenged. Hannibal with a few men escaped to Hadrumetum.

Peace was now inevitable if Carthage was to be saved from destruction. The terms proposed by Scipio, and subsequently ratified by the senate, were: the cession of the Spanish possessions and the islands of the Mediterranean; the transference of the kingdom of Syphax to Massinissa; the surrender of all ships of war except twenty, and an annual contribution of two hundred talents ($240,000) for the next fifty years; an engagement not to make war against Rome or her allies, and not to wage war in Africa beyond the Carthaginian boundaries without the permission of Rome.   The practical effect of these terms was to render Carthage tributary and to deprive her of her political independence.   The terms of this peace have often been considered too light, and they served as a handle to the charge that Scipio, in his eagerness to secure for himself the glory of finishing the war, forgot what was due to Rome.   A true estimate of the peace and of its effect on the future position of Carthage inclines rather to the view that these terms were the outcome of the nobleness of the two greatest men of the age, and a recognition on the part of Scipio of the crime of blotting out one of the main props of civilization merely to gratify the petty ferocity of his fellow-countrymen.   The noble-mindedness and statesmanlike gifts of the great antagonists are no less apparent in the magnanimous submission of Hannibal to what was inevitable than in the wise abstinence of Scipio from an extravagant and insulting use of victory.

It remains for us to sum up the results of this terrible war, which for seventeen years had devastated the lands and islands from the Hellespont to the Pillars of Hercules.   Rome was henceforth compelled by the force of circumstances to assume a position at which she had not directly aimed, and to exercise sovereignty over all the lands of the Mediterranean.   Outside Italy there arose the two new provinces in Spain, where the natives lived in a state of perpetual insurrection; the kingdom of Syracuse was now included in the Roman province of Sicily: a Roman instead of a Carthaginian protectorate was now established over the most important Numidian chiefs: Carthage was changed from a powerful commercial state into a defenseless mercantile town.   Thus all the western Mediterranean passed under the supremacy of Rome.   In Italy itself, the destruction of the Celts became a mere question of time: the ruling Latin people had been exalted by the struggle to a position of still greater eminence over the heads of the non-Latin or Latinized Italians, such as the Etruscans and Sabellians in lower Italy.   A terrible punishment was inflicted on the allies of Hannibal.   Capua was reduced from the position of second city to that of first village in Italy: the whole soil, with a few exceptions, was declared to be public domain-land, and was leased out to small occupiers. The same fate befell the Picentes on the Silarus. The Bruttians became in a manner bondsmen to the Romans, and were forbidden to carry arms. All the Greek cities which had supported Hannibal were treated with great severity: and in the case of a number of Apulian, Lucanian, and Samnite communities a loss of territory was inflicted, and new colonies were planted. Throughout Italy the non-Latin allies were made to feel their utter subjection to Rome, and the comedies of the period testify to the scorn of the victorious Romans.

It seems probable that not less than three hundred thousand Italians perished in this war, the brunt of which loss fell chiefly on Rome. After the battle of Cannae it was found necessary to fill up the hideous gap in the senate by an extraordinary nomination of 177 senators: the ordinary burgesses suffered hardly less severely. Further, the terrible strain on the resources of the state had shaken the national economy to its very foundations. Four hundred flourishing townships had been utterly ruined. The blows inflicted on the simple morality of the citizens and farmers by a camp-life worked no less mischief. Gangs of robbers and desperadoes plundered Italy in dangerous numbers. Home agriculture saw its existence endangered by the proof, first given in this war, that the Roman people could be supported by foreign grain from Sicily and Egypt. Still, at the close and happy issue of so terrible a struggle, Rome might justly point with pride to the past and with confidence to the future. In spite of many errors she had survived all danger, and the only question now was whether she would have the wisdom to make a right use of her victory, to bind still more closely to herself the Latin people, to gradually Latinize all her Italian subjects, and to rule her foreign dependents as subjects, not as slaves,—whether she would reform her constitution and infuse new vigor into the unsound and fast-decaying portion of her state.

Chapter XIV

A REVIEW OF THE WEST AND EAST. 201-194 B.C.

THE war with Hannibal had interrupted Rome in the extension of her dominion to the Alpine boundary of Italy; that task was now resumed. The Celts, aware of the coming vengeance, had again taken up arms in 201 B.C. The insurrection spread far and wide, and Celtic and Ligurian bands sacked Placentia and invested Cremona in the following year. A great battle before the latter city ended in their overthrow, but the struggle continued until 193 B.C. before these people were finally subdued. The Romans intended that the Transpadane Celts should serve as a bulwark against the incursions of northern tribes. It seems that the Celtic nationality in these districts rapidly became submerged in the all-absorbing spread of Latin influence. The terror of the Roman name penetrated even beyond the Alps, and by the founding of Aquileia, about 183 B.C., the Romans showed their determination to close the gates of the Alps forever against the northern nation. New means of communication were opened up by the extension of the Flaminian road, under the name of the Aemilian, from Ariminum to Placentia, and by the reconstruction of the Cassian Way from Rome to Arretium. The result was that the Po, and not the Apennines, now divided Celtic from Italian land, and that south of the Po the old name of Ager Celticus, applied to the district between the Po and the Apennines, ceased to have any meaning.

The same policy was pursued with the Ligurian tribes occupying the hills and valleys in the northwestern highlands of Italy. Some were extirpated, others transplanted, and the mountainous country between the valley of the Po and the Arno was practically cleared. The fortress of Luna was established in 177 B.C., to act as a bulwark against the Ligurians, and as a port for ships sailing to Massilia or Spain. With the more western Ligurian tribes in the Genoese Apennines and the Maritime Alps conflicts were incessant, but no permanent results were effected. Wars, too, of a similar character were waged in Corsica and Sardinia, where the natives in the interior were continually hunted down by Roman troops.

With regard to Carthage, Rome's great aim was to keep suspended over her head the fear of a declaration of war. Massinissa was established close at her doors as a most powerful Numidian chief, and Carthaginian territory was constantly exposed to the spoliations of the Libyan and Numidian tribes, who exulted in thus retaliating on their old tormentors for their former sufferings. Carthage bore every insult with true Phoenician patience. Her embassies and complaints to Rome had no effect, save that of making her victor more resolved in this short-sighted policy of humiliation. One man, however, still remained at Carthage, a just object of dread to his enemies. Hannibal had already overthrown the rotten oligarchy and instituted the most beneficial political and financial reforms. By checking the embezzlement of the public moneys it was soon found that the tribute to Rome could be paid without extraordinary taxation. Hannibal was doubtless reorganizing Carthage to be ready for the complications which he saw must arise for Rome in the East. We cannot wonder that the Romans at last insisted on the surrender of Hannibal, in 195 B.C., which demand he anticipated by a speedy flight to the East, and thus left to his ancestral city merely the lesser disgrace of banishing its greatest citizen forever from his native land, of confiscating his property, and of razing his house. The profound saying, that those are the favorites of the gods on whom they lavish infinite joys and infinite sorrows, thus verified itself in full measure in the case of Hannibal. Even after his withdrawal, Rome, still not content, adopted a course of perpetual irritation against Carthage. Jealous of her financial prosperity, which remained unshaken by the loss of political power, Rome was ever the credulous receptacle of every rumor of Carthaginian perfidy and intrigue.

Unwilling to have any possessions of her own in Africa, Rome established the great Berber chief Massinissa in his new Numidian kingdom. This remarkable man was in every way fitted for the post. Thoroughly conversant with Carthage, in which city he had been educated, and with whose armies he had fought both as friend and foe, fired with bitter hatred of the Carthaginian oppressor, both as a native African and as a prince personally wronged, gifted with a physique which knew no fatigue, and with a nature that recked not of scruple or honor, Massinissa became the soul of his nation's revival; and, during ninety years of unimpaired life and sixty years of vigorous reign, was completely successful in consolidating the vast kingdom of which he was the founder.   By the addition of the kingdom of Syphax, who died in captivity in Rome, and by occupying the old Sidonian city of Great Leptis and other districts, Massinissa held rule from the Mauretanian to the Cyrenaean frontier, and enclosed the Carthaginian territory on all sides; indeed, he fixed his eyes on Carthage as his future capital.   Under his example the Berber became converted from a nomad shepherd into a farmer and settled citizen; the Numidian hordes of plunderers became trained soldiers, worthy to fight by the side of Roman legions; Cirta, his capital, became the seat of Phoenician civilization, which the king carefully fostered, with a view, perhaps, to the future extension of his power over Carthage.   Thus the Libyan language, nationality, and manners, after so many years of degradation, reasserted their position, and made themselves felt even in the old Phoenician cities.

In Spain the Greek and Phoenician towns along the coast at once submitted to the Romans, and were absorbed in their civilization.   On the other hand, the natives, especially in the west and north and in the interior, were a perpetual thorn in the side of the Romans, nor was it even safe for a Roman governor to travel without a strong escort.   Bound together by all-powerful laws of chivalry, proud of their military honor, fired with a love of war and change, the barbaric Spaniards were utterly devoid of political instinct, and could neither submit to military discipline nor political combination.   Thus in Spain there was no serious war nor real peace.

The Romans divided the peninsula into two provinces, and while the governor of Hither Spain, the modern Arragon and Catalonia, was ever occupied with quelling Celtiberian revolts, his colleague in Further Spain, which comprised the modern Andalusia, Granada, Murcia, and Valencia, was similarly busy in attempts to hold in check the Lusitanians. Necessity thus compelled the Romans to adopt a new policy—to maintain a standing army of four legions in the country; hence it was in Spain that the military occupation of the land on a large scale first became continuous, and that the military service first acquired a permanent character.   The obvious danger of withdrawing or even changing every year a large portion of the forces in so remote and turbulent a country forced the

Romans to adopt this course. Thus service in Spain became very
odious to the Roman people, who now learned that dominion over a
foreign nation is a burden not only to the slave, but also to the
master. Reality was first given to the Roman rule in the peninsula by the valor of Quintus Fulvius Flaccus in 181 B.C.; and
two years later, his successor, Tiberius Gracchus, achieved results
of a permanent character, not merely by force of arms, but by his
adroit comprehension of the Spanish character. By inducing
Celtiberians to serve in the Roman army, by settling free-booting
tribes in towns, by wise and equitable treaties, Gracchus made the
Roman name not only feared but liked, and his own memory was
ever held dear by the natives.

The Spanish provinces were governed on principles similar to
those which were observed in Sicily and Sardinia; but the Romans
proceeded with great caution, and often conceded considerable
privileges to Spanish towns, such as the right of coining their own
money. The old Carthaginian imposts of fixed money payments
and other contributions were retained, instead of the tithes and
customs paid by Sicilian and Sardinian communities. The grave
fault of changing the pretors every year was still committed,
and that in spite of the Baebian law, which in 192 B.C. prolonged the command of Spanish governors for two years. On the
whole, Spain, notwithstanding its mines both of iron and silver,
was a burden rather than a gain to the Roman state; but probably
the chief reason for its retention as a province was the fear that,
if left unoccupied, it might serve another foe as it had served
Hannibal, and act as a basis of operations against the sovereignty
of Rome.

We must now turn our eyes eastward, and see how those complications arose which involved Rome in the Macedonian and
Asiatic wars. Macedonia, alone of all the Greek states, had preserved that national vigor which made the Greek race so famous in
earlier days. Philip V. ruled not only over Macedonia proper, but
over all Thessaly, Euboea, Locris, Phocis, and Doris, and held
many isolated and important positions in Attica and the Peloponnese, of which the chief were Demetrias in Magnesia, Chalcis in
Euboea, and Corinth, "the three fetters of the Hellenes." His
real strength, however, lay in his hereditary kingdom of Macedonia
proper. It is true that this land was very sparsely populated, but
the national character of its loyal and courageous people, never

shaken in their fidelity to their native land and hereditary form of government, places the Macedonians almost on a level with the Romans themselves; in particular, the regeneration of the state after the storm of Celtic invasion in 278 B.C. was as honorable as it was marvelous.

The huge unwieldy empire of Asia, pretending to stretch from the Hellespont to the Punjab, was in reality an aggregate of states in different stages of dependence, or rather a conglomeration of insubordinate satrapies and half-free Greek cities. Along the coast the Great King vainly endeavored to expel the Egyptians; on the eastern frontier he was perpetually harassed by Parthians and Bactrians; while in Asia Minor the Celtic hordes had settled on the north coast and the eastern interior, and on the west the Greek cities were constantly trying to assert and make good their independence. Indeed, in Asia Minor the king's authority was little more than nominal except in Cilicia, Phrygia, and Lydia, for the powerful kingdom of Pergamus embraced a large portion of the west, and a number of cities and native princes practically owned no lord. Egypt, on the other hand, presented a marked contrast to the loose organization of Asia. Under the prudent Lagidae, Egypt had been welded into a firmly united and compact state, incapable of revolt or disruption under the worst misrule. The objects of the Ptolemies' policy were not, like the Macedonian or Persian, vague dreams of universal empire, but definite and capable of realization. The whole traffic between India and the Mediterranean was in the hands of the rulers of Egypt, and owing to their excellent geographical position, whether for defense or attack, the Egyptians established themselves not only in Cyrene, but in Cyprus and the Cyclades, on the Phoenician and Syrian coast, on the whole of the south and west coast of Asia Minor, and even in the Thracian Chersonese. The finances of Egypt were most flourishing, and Alexandria, the seat of the Ptolemies, attracted all the learning, whether scientific or literary, of the time. The mutual relation of these three great Eastern powers was naturally one of antagonism and rivalry; but Egypt, as a maritime power, and the protectress of the Asiatic Greek towns and minor states, was the foe of both Macedonia and Asia, while the two latter powers, though rivals, were ready to combine against Egypt, their common enemy.

In addition to the various states of the second rank in Asia Minor, such as Atropatene, Armenia, Cappadocia, Pontus, and

Bithynia, there were three powerful Celtic tribes who had settled with their national customs and constitution in the interior.   From their barbarous strength and free-booting habits they were the constant terror of the more degenerate Asiatics.   It was due to his successful opposition to these hordes that Attalus was raised from the position of a wealthy citizen to that of king of Pergamus.   His court was a miniature Alexandria, and, as the patron of art and science, and from his retention, when king, of his simple citizen character, Attalus may not inaptly be styled the Lorenzo de' Medici of antiquity.

In Greece proper we find a great decay of national energy. The Aetolian League, whose policy was alike hostile to the Achaean confederacy and to Macedonia, would have proved of far more service to the Greek nation had not its members pursued a system of organized robbery, and by their unfortunate policy prevented any union of the whole Hellenic race.   In the Peloponnese the Achaean League had knit together the best elements of Greece, and breathed new life and true patriotism into the nobler portion of the Hellenes.   But, owing to the selfish diplomacy of Aratus and the foolish invocation of Macedonian interference to settle its disputes with Sparta, the league had become entirely subject to Macedonian influence, and had admitted Macedonian garrisons into its chief fortresses.   Sparta alone of the other Peloponnesian states showed any vigor, and under the unscrupulous Nabis daily increased its strength.   The commercial prosperity enjoyed by Byzantium, the mistress of the Bosporus, and by Cyzicus, on the Asiatic side of the Propontis, was at this time very considerable; but they were both eclipsed by Rhodes, which had secured the carrying trade of all the eastern Mediterranean.   Aided by her fleet and the courageous temper of her citizens, Rhodes was the champion of all the Greek maritime cities, and, though as a rule pursuing a policy of neutrality and of friendly relationship with the neighboring powers, she did not shrink, if need be, from adopting sterner measures.   The Rhodians became the leaders of a league of the chief Greek cities scattered along the coasts and islands of Asia Minor and elsewhere, such as Sinope, Lampsacus, Halicarnassus, Chios, and Smyrna. This league upheld with success the cause of freedom against the attacks of neighboring tyrants, and securely fostered the arts of peace and the old Greek spirit, uncontaminated by the tyranny of a dissolute soldiery or the corrupt atmosphere of an Eastern court.

Such, then, was the state of things in the East when Philip of Macedon was induced to break down the wall of political separation, and to interfere in the West. The miserable incompetence he had shown in the first Macedonian war, 215-205 B.C., and the contemptible indolence which caused him to utterly disappoint Hannibal at a critical period, have been already pointed out. Now, however, though Philip was not the man needed at this juncture, he exhibited none of those faults which had marred his first war with Rome. Philip was a true king in the worst and best sense of the term. Inflated with arrogance and pride, incapable of taking advice or brooking opposition, he was utterly callous to the lives and sufferings of those about him; bound by no sense of moral tie or obligation, the slave of passion, combining in singular fashion sagacity and resolution with supineness and procrastination, he was yet gifted with the valor of a soldier and the eye of a general; jealous of his honor as a Macedonian king, he could rise to a spirited and dignified public policy; full of intelligence and wit, he won the hearts of all whom he wished to gain.

At the present moment Philip directed his attentions to Egypt. About 205 B.C. he had formed an alliance with Antiochus of Asia to break up the Egyptian state, now ruled over by Ptolemy Epiphanes, a child five years old, and to divide the spoil. In 201 B.C. Philip had begun his task of plunder, and crossing to Asia had proceeded to make war upon the Greek cities on the coast. Chalcedon saved itself by submission, but Cius and Thasos were stormed and sacked. Rhodes, at the head of her league, declared war against Philip; she was joined by Byzantium and Attalus of Pergamus. Several indecisive battles were fought at sea; towards the close of the year Philip withdrew to Macedonia, where his presence was urgently needed.

At this point the Romans thought right to interfere. They could not view with indifference the possible extension of Philip's power, the conquest of Rhodes and Egypt, the fall of Cyrene, and the future peril of all the Greek cities, whose protectors they claimed to be, and they could not honorably refuse aid to Attalus of Pergamus, who had been their staunch ally since the first Macedonian war. The policy of interference in the East was not actuated by greed for further conquest, but was dictated by necessity; it redounds to the senate's honor that it resolved to prepare for war with Philip at a time when the Roman citizens were thoroughly weary of and exhausted by one transmarine war, and when such a war was sure to rouse a storm of popular disapprobation.

At first, indeed, the Romans lacked a pretext for war. Their ambassador, sent to Abydus, after the capture of that city by Philip in 200 B.C., was politely reproved by the Macedonian king for attempting to interfere with his designs. The Athenians, however, had at this time put to death two Acarnanians who strayed into their mysteries. The Acarnanians at once invoked Philip's aid, and he proceeded to lay waste Attica. Athens applied for help to Rome, and the popular assembly was at 'length induced by various concessions to ratify the declaration of war by the senate, in 200 B.C. These concessions were chiefly made at the expense of the allies, who had to supply the garrison service in Gaul, Lower Italy, Sicily, and Sardinia; volunteers alone, as was alleged, were enrolled for the Macedonian campaign. Two of the six legions, thus called out, embarked at Brundisium under the leadership of the consul Publius Sulpicius Galba.

The position of Philip was very critical. Antiochus stood aloof; Egypt, despite its anxiety to keep a Roman fleet out of Eastern waters, was utterly estranged from Philip by his recent scheme of partition; the Rhodian confederacy of Greek cities was also, owing to recent events, a pronounced enemy; while in Greece itself many of the most powerful states were ready to welcome the Romans as deliverers, and the Acarnanians and Boeotians alone remained the steadfast allies of Macedonia. The Achaean League, previously estranged by the murder of Aratus, had, under the able leadership of Philopoemen, revived its military power and freed itself from the oppressive influence of Macedonia. Aware of the danger to Greece of invoking Roman aid, this league attempted in vain to mediate between Philip and Rhodes, and in despair remained neutral, awaiting the coming of the Roman troops with undisguised but inactive dread. Thus Philip, by his cruelty and arrogance, had alienated all those Eastern powers which at this critical hour should have proved his staunchest allies in repelling the common danger to Greek freedom and independence.

The Roman army under Galba effected very little, and the result of the first year of the war was on the whole favorable to Philip. A second campaign conducted by a far abler officer, the Consul Titus Quintius Flamininus, was more successful, and the Achaean League went over to the Roman side. Finally, in 197 B.C.,

Flamininus succeeded in bringing Philip to a decisive engagement in the district of Scotussa. The battle takes its name from the steep height of Cynoscephalae, which, lying between the two camps, was the scene of the first encounter between the vanguards of both armies. Owing to the success of the Macedonians at the outset, Philip was encouraged to risk a battle with his whole force, and, after a fierce conflict, in which the phalanx exhibited its ancient prowess, Philip was utterly defeated, and escaped to Larissa.

At this defeat, even his most staunch allies, the Acarnanians, submitted to Rome; resistance was no longer possible. The terms imposed do honor to the Romans. They gave no ear to the malignity of the Aetolians, who demanded the annihilation of the Macedonian kingdom; for they clearly saw that it alone could serve as a bulwark against the encroaching Celts and Thracians. A commission of ten was appointed, at the head of which was Flamininus, to settle the complicated affairs of Greece. The result of their deliberations was the decision that Philip should give up all his possessions in Asia Minor, Thrace, Greece, and the islands of the Aegean; that he should pay a contribution of a thousand talents ($1,220,000); that he should conclude no foreign alliances without Rome's consent, and wage no foreign wars; that he should enter into the Roman alliance, and send a contingent when required; that the Macedonian army should not exceed five thousand men, nor its fleet five decked ships; that the territory of Macedonia should remain unimpaired, with the exception of some small strips and of the revolted province of Orestis.

With regard to the disposition of the possessions thus ceded by Philip, Rome, having learned by experience in Spain the doubtful value of transmarine provinces, kept none of the spoil for herself, and decreed freedom to the Greek states—a freedom rather in name than deed, when we consider the value of it to a nation devoid of all union and unity. Athens received the three islands of Paros, Scyros, and Imbros, as a reward for the hardships she had suffered and for the many courtesies she had shown to Rome. All Philip's possessions in the Peloponnese and on the Isthmus were ceded to the Achaean League, which was thus practically made ruler of the Peloponnese: but scant favor was accorded to the boastful and greedy Aetolians, who incorporated Phocis and Locris, but were not suffered to extend their power to Acarnania and Thessaly.

Nabis of Sparta obstinately refused to give up Argos to the

Achaean League, and only yielded to a powerful display of Roman arms; and, though his banditti were dispersed and Sparta captured, both the city and Nabis himself were left intact, the conquerors only requiring the cession of his foreign possessions and his adherence to the usual stipulations touching the right of waging war and of forming foreign alliances.

Peace was thus, outwardly at any rate, established among the petty Greek states. Flamininus acted with great fairness and patience throughout, and strove as far as possible to mete out justice to the claims of each Greek state. He showed an especially wise and tolerant moderation in his punishment of the rebellious Boeotians, who, in their eagerness to attach themselves again to Macedonia, did not refrain from putting to death isolated bands of Roman soldiers.

In 194 B.C. Flamininus, after holding a conference of all the Greek states at Corinth, withdrew his troops from every fortress and departed homeward, thus giving the lie to the Aetolian calumny that Rome had inherited from Philip " the fetters " of Greece.

We cannot doubt the nobleness and sincerity of the Roman endeavor to set Greece free; the reason of its failure was the complete demoralization of the Greek nation. In truth, the necessities of the case demanded the permanent presence of a superior power, not the pernicious boon of a fictitious freedom; the feeble policy of sentiment, with all its apparent humanity, was far more cruel than the sternest occupation. History has a Nemesis for every sin —for an impotent craving after freedom, as well as for an injudicious generosity. The Nemesis in this case was the war with Antiochus of Asia.

Chapter XV

WAR WITH ANTIOCHUS AND THE FINAL CONQUEST OF THE EAST. 192-168 B.C.

ANTIOCHUS had long fixed his eyes upon the Syrian coast, which had been wrested from Asia by the Egyptians, and had seized the occasion of Philopator's death, in 205 B.C., to concert measures with Philip for the partition of the kingdom of the Ptolemies. But he lacked the foresight to make common cause with Philip in repelling Roman interference, and had taken advantage of the second Macedonian war to secure Egypt for himself. At first he attacked the Egyptian possessions in Cilicia, Syria, and Palestine, and by a victory gained in 198 B.C., near the sources of the Jordan, he became absolute master of the two latter countries. He then proceeded with a strong fleet to occupy all the districts on the south and west coasts of Asia Minor, which had formerly belonged to Egypt, but had virtually fallen under the dominion of Philip. Rome had, however, bidden Philip to withdraw from these possessions, and to leave them free and untouched, and now Antiochus came forward to take Philip's place as the oppressor of the Greek cities and free kingdoms in those lands.

Already, in 198 B.C., Attalus of Pergamus had applied to Rome for aid against Antiochus; and in the following year the Rhodians openly protected the Carian cities of Halicarnassus, Caunus, Myndus, and the island of Samos against the attacks of the Great King. Other cities, such as Smyrna and Lampsacus, took heart to resist Antiochus, and they, one and all, called upon Rome to give effect to her promise that they should be free, and to prove that neither Macedonian tyrant nor Asian despot should be suffered to endanger Greek life and liberty. Rome, however, was slow to answer such a call; nor did she resort to other measures than those of diplomacy, when Antiochus, in 196 B.C., landed in Europe and invaded the Thracian Chersonese, and took active measures to convert Thrace into a dependent satrapy on the plea that he was merely reasserting his claim to the land conquered by his ancestor Seleucus.

The delay of the Romans in forcibly opposing Antiochus, who plainly showed his designs not only on Asia Minor, but also on Greece, may be ascribed partly to their weariness of war, but chiefly to the vain wish of Flamininus to pose as the liberator of Greece and the extinguisher of the war in the East.   Flamininus was thus induced to withdraw all the Roman garrisons from Greece in 194 B.C., and to blind the Romans to the fact that the embers of war still smoldered, soon to be rekindled into a flame by his own vanity and by the senate's culpable negligence.

In the year previous to the withdrawal of the Roman troops from Greece, Antiochus had accorded an honorable reception to the exiled Hannibal, which in itself was tantamount to a declaration of war; but Flamininus refused to regard it as such, and contented himself with addressing mere verbal remonstrances and demands to Antiochus.   The latter did not fail to profit by the respite unexpectedly granted him by the Roman evacuation of Greece.   He made alliances with all the states of Asia Minor and Greece that would listen to his proposals, and events soon reached such a pass that a rupture between the two nations became inevitable.   After some fruitless discussion at Ephesus between the envoys of Rome and the Great King, war was declared in 192 B.C.

The attitude of Philip of Macedon, of Eumenes, of the Achaean League, Rhodes, and Egypt, who all sided with Rome, showed at once how futile would be the attempts of Antiochus in Europe. Notwithstanding this he crossed the Aegean and anticipated his enemies by occupying Euboea and part of Thessaly.   On the approach of the Roman army he retired to Thermopylae, but, being defeated there, was forced to withdraw from Europe altogether. Some time was now occupied by the Romans in a naval warfare for the purpose of clearing the Aegean Sea of the enemy's ships and opening the way to an invasion of Asia.   The conduct of the war on land had been intrusted to Scipio Africanus, conqueror of Zama.   In 190 B.C. he crossed the Hellespont and met the army of the Great King near Magnesia, at the foot of Mount Sipylus, not far from Smyrna.   The cumbrous masses of the Asiatic troops proved their own destruction: the flower of their army, drawn up in Macedonian phalanx, was foiled in its efforts to reach the Roman legions by the confusion of their own light troops, and by the absence of the heavy cavalry under Antiochus, which had rushed off in pursuit of a small Roman squadron.   At last the phalanx was broken up by its own elephants, and the whole army scattered in utter rout.

The losses of Antiochus have been estimated at fifty thousand, those of the Romans at three hundred foot soldiers and twenty-four horsemen. Peace was concluded on the terms proposed by Scipio before the battle, by which Antiochus was condemned to pay all the costs of the war and to surrender the whole of Asia Minor. Antiochus himself was soon after, in 187 B.C., slain, while plundering a temple of Bel in Elymais, at the head of the Persian Gulf. With the day of Magnesia, Asia was erased from the list of great states; and never perhaps did a great power fall so rapidly, so thoroughly, and so ignominiously as the kingdom of the Seleucidae under this Antiochus the Great.

The final settlement of Asia was determined by a commission presided over by Volso. The sum to be paid by Antiochus was fixed at fifteen thousand Euboic talents ($18,000,000); all possession in Europe, and all the country in Asia Minor west of the river Halys and the mountain chain of the Taurus, were now ceded by the Great King; lastly, certain restrictions were imposed upon his rights of waging war and of navigating the sea. Even beyond the boundaries of the Roman protectorate, Ariarathes, king of Cappadocia, though mulcted in a light fine for his alliance with Antiochus, retained his kingdom and was practically independent of Antiochus; moreover, the two satrapies of Armenia now rose under Roman influence into independent kingdoms. Prusias, king of Bithynia, was allowed to keep his possessions intact; nor were the Celts ousted from their territory, though bound to refrain in the future from sending out armed bands and levying blackmail from the Asiatic Greeks. The Greek cities, which were free and had joined the Romans, were confirmed in their ancient freedom and exempted from tribute to the various dynasts of Asia Minor; this exemption was not, however, extended to those which paid tribute to Eumenes. Rhodes obtained Lycia and the greater part of Caria as a reward for her zealous assistance. But the largest share of the spoil fell to the king of Pergamus. Eumenes received the Thracian Chersonese and the greater part of Asia Minor west of the Halys, the protectorate over and right of receiving tribute from such Greek cities as were not made absolutely free, and a contribution of nearly five hundred talents from Antiochus. Thus he was nobly recompensed for his sufferings and devotion to the Roman cause, and thus the kingdom of the Attalids became in Asia what Numidia was in Africa—a powerful state dependent on Rome, capable of acting as a check upon Macedonia and Syria without needing Roman support. Rome thus adhered strictly to its policy of acquiring no transmarine possessions, and in 188 B.C. the fleet and land army evacuated Asia.

The war with Antiochus had naturally agitated the ever quarrelsome and excitable states in European Greece. The Aetolians, who had tried to rekindle the flame of war by attacks on Philip of Macedon, were soon compelled to utter submission by the combined arms of the Roman consul, Marcus Fulvius Nobilior, and the Macedonians and Achaeans. The possessions taken from the Aetolians were divided among the allies of Rome, who reserved for herself nothing but the two islands of Cephallenia and Zacynthus. Neither Philip nor the Achaeans were satisfied with their share of the spoil. The last-named were foolish enough to attempt to display their independence of Rome, and with a quasi-patriotic zeal to desire an extension of their power; though indignant at the advice of Flamininus to content themselves with the Peloponnese, and at the refusal of Rome to enlarge the territory of their league, they proved their incapacity to govern what they already possessed by constant quarrels with Sparta and Messene. The senate, after vain attempts to arbitrate, at last grew weary of these petty disputes, and left the Achaeans and the Greek states generally to settle such trifles among themselves.

After the defeat of Antiochus, Hannibal had taken refuge with Prusias, the king of Bithynia, and had successfully aided him in his wars with Eumenes. Now he, the only being on earth who was still a source of terror to Rome, was hunted down by his old enemies in a way unworthy of so great a nation, and compelled to take poison, dying in 183 B.C., at the age of sixty-seven.

About the same time died his great rival and lucky victor, Publius Scipio. The favorite of fortune, he had added to the empire of Rome, Spain, Africa, and Asia; and yet he, too, like Hannibal, spent his last years in bitter trouble and disappointment, a voluntary exile from the city of his fathers, for which he had spent his life, but in which he had forbidden his own remains to be buried. We do not exactly know what drove him from Rome. The charges of peculation brought against him and his brother Lucius were no doubt empty calumnies, but his arrogance and proud belief that he was not as other men had doubtless raised many enemies, while his own wish to sacrifice everything to the promotion of his own family caused general distrust of his political aims.   It is, moreover, the distinguishing characteristic of such natures as that of Scipio—strange mixtures of genuine gold and glittering tinsel— that they need the good fortune and the brilliance of youth in order to exercise their charm, and, when this charm begins to fade, it is the charmer himself that is most painfully conscious of the change.

Thus ended this Asiatic war.   A significant indication of the feeble and loose organization of the kingdom of the Seleucidae is the fact that it, alone of all the great states conquered by Rome, never after the first conquest made a second appeal to arms.   But Rome had not yet done with her troubles in the East; and her unjust treatment of Philip of Macedon in return for his staunch support during the war with Antiochus soon caused another outbreak in that quarter.   All the states in Greece now seized the opportunity of damaging their ancient oppressor, and of reviving the anti-Macedonian feeling by constant complaints to the Roman senate; but the irritation and annoyance thus caused to Philip was as nothing compared with the indignation he felt at the extension of the kingdom of Eumenes.   The Attalids had ever been the bitterest foes of Macedonia, and, now that their power was revived and increased under the protecting arm of Rome, Philip's thirst for revenge went beyond all limits of prudence.   On hearing of some fresh invectives which had been launched against him in the Thessalian assemblies he replied with the line of Theocritus: "What! thinkest thou that all my suns are set?" a reply which showed that he had determined once more to put all to the hazard. In these later days, however, Philip displayed a caution and an earnest perseverance in his preparations which at an earlier date might have changed the world's history.   He even curbed his proud temper so as to pretend complete submission to Rome, and delayed the breaking out of war by the agency of his son Demetrius, who during his residence as a hostage at Rome had won great popularity with the leading Romans.   Perseus, the eldest son, fearing that Philip would disinherit him in favor of Demetrius, persuaded his father to put the latter to death, on the false charge that he was intriguing with Rome against Macedonia.   Philip learned too late the plot of the fratricide, but died himself, in 179 B.C., before he could punish the crime.

Thus Perseus succeeded to the throne, a man remarkable for his personal prowess and steady perseverance, and incapable of being turned aside, as his father had been, by the vicious allurements of pleasure. He entered on all his father's schemes with resolute determination, and to the outward eye of.his countrymen he seemed the man needed for the great work of liberation from the yoke of Rome. But he lacked the genius and elasticity of Philip. He could devise plans and persevere in his preparations for their execution, but when the time came for action he was frightened at his own handiwork. As is the case with all narrow minds, the means became to him the end; when imminent peril demanded the use of the treasures which he had amassed for the war with Rome, Perseus could not find the heart to part with his golden pieces.

The wise measures of Philip, in founding towns, encouraging marriage, and in developing the finances of his country during twenty years of peace, had rendered the power of Macedonia at least twice as strong as it had been at the outbreak of the second Macedonian war. Perseus now possessed an army of thirty thousand troops, independent of auxiliaries, a treasury capable of paying both this army and ten thousand mercenaries for ten years, and, above all, a devoted and loyal people. The attempts, however, to raise a coalition against Rome, and thus carry out the schemes of Hannibal, failed. In Greece it is true that the sentiments of every state were gradually veering round to the side of Perseus, whose name was not stained, as that of his father had been, by atrocious and bloodthirsty deeds. Every Greek now saw the true meaning of the freedom granted by Rome, and that the restoration of Hellenic nationality by a foreign power involved a contradiction in terms. The efforts of Eumenes, who tried by gifts and favors to conciliate the Greeks in Asia Minor, and to reconcile them to the arrangements made by Rome, were received with every sign of scorn and contempt.

But the support from the Greek cities and states, whether of Greece proper or Asia Minor, was but a broken reed whereon to lean. More important was the success which attended the efforts of Perseus to stir up the barbarian tribes living near the Danube and in Illyria, and the close alliance he formed with the brave Cotys, ruler of the Odrysians and of all eastern Thrace. By public proclamation he gained over to his side all the Greeks who, owing to political and other offenses, and still more owing to debt, had been exiled. From these and other causes the whole of Greece was once more in a state of ferment. Rome saw that she could delay no longer; and the advent of Eumenes in person, with a long list of grievances and a true account of the state of affairs in Greece, caused the senate to resolve on war in the autumn of 172 B.C.

Perseus, instead of acting at once and occupying Greece by the aid of the Macedonian party in each state, frittered away his time in discussions with Quintus Marcius Philippus, whose aim was to cause Perseus to delay active operation until the Roman legions arrived. This foolish delay on the part of Perseus ruined his chance of support from the Greek states and confederacies. The Aetolian League chose Lyciscus as its new strategus, a thorough partisan of Rome; and the Boeotian confederacy suddenly collapsed completely on the complaint of a Roman envoy touching two of their cities, Haliartus and Coronea, which had entered into engagements with Perseus.

In June, 171 B.C., the Roman legions landed, and Perseus, owing to his utter remissness, found himself alone. Fortunately for him, the Roman consul, Publius Licinius Crassus, was grossly incompetent, and, had Perseus followed up his first success, gained near Larissa, by assuming the offensive, no doubt all Greece would have at once followed the example of the Epirots and revolted. Crassus signalized his shameful command by forcing the small Boeotian town of Coronea to capitulate, and by selling its inhabitants into slavery. His successor, Aulus Hostilius, was equally unsuccessful, and was twice easily repulsed in attempting to enter Macedonia; while his colleague, Appius Claudius, commanding the western army, met with nothing but reverses. Moreover, the Roman name, hitherto distinguished in the East by the honorable probity of its political transactions, was now stained by treacherous and underhand dealing with various Greek states. Two campaigns had served to show the completely demoralized and disorganized condition of the Roman army, which was only saved from destruction by the inability of Perseus to change his plan of defensive warfare to one of a vigorous offensive.

A third campaign was scarcely more successful, but in 168 B.C. a very different Roman general appeared on the scene, in the person of Lucius Aemilius Paulus, son of the consul who fell at Cannae—a man full of vigor despite his sixty years, and utterly incorruptible. He soon turned the position of the enemy and forced them to retreat to Pydna. Here the decisive battle was fought, and the Macedonian phalanx, after dispersing the Roman vanguard and endangering the whole army, lost its formation on the uneven ground, and was cut down to a man; twenty thousand Macedonians fell, and eleven thousand were made prisoners. Perseus fled with his cavalry and treasure to Samothrace, and soon after surrendered, weeping, to the Romans; he died a few years later, at Alba on the Fucine Lake.

Thus perished the empire of Alexander the Great, 144 years after his death. Macedonia was henceforth abolished, and the united kingdom was broken up into four republican leagues, which paid to Rome half the former land-tax; right of intermarriage between the members of different leagues was forbidden, and every measure was taken to prevent a revival of the ancient monarchy. The Romans gained their object, and from that day to this Macedonia has possessed no history.

Illyria, whose king Genthius was taken prisoner, and whose capital Scodra was captured by the pretor Lucius Anicius, was treated in the same way as Macedonia had been. It was split up into three free states; its piratical fleet was confiscated, and an end was thus put to the depredations of Illyrian corsairs.

In the treatment of the rest of the Greek world, Rome now discarded the sentimental policy of Flamininus, and determined to reduce all Greek states to the same humble level of dependence. It was clear that with the abolition of Macedonia the kingdom of Pergamus, as exercising a check on that power, ceased to be a necessity. The Romans therefore proceeded to circulate strange, though utterly unfounded, reports as to the loyalty of Eumenes; they attempted to set his brother Attalus against him by granting Attalus favors and inciting him to establish a rival throne; they declared Pamphylia independent, and, when the Galatians overran Pergamus, they, after a pretense of mediation, declared them independent also. Eumenes set sail for Italy to remonstrate; but the senate suddenly decreed that no kings in future were to come to Rome, and sent a questor to meet Eumenes at Brundisium. Eumenes, taking the hint, declared that he was satisfied, and returned home; he clearly saw that all equality of alliance was at an end, and that the time of impotent subjection to Rome had now come for himself as for all other free states.

The high-spirited Rhodians were the next to suffer. Deluded by the consul Quintus Marcius, who had pretended to wish for their

mediation in the war with Perseus, they just before the battle of
Pydna sent envoys to the Roman camp and the Roman senate,
saying that the Macedonian war was injurious to their commercial
interests, and that they would declare war against the side which
refused at once to make peace. This miserable republican vanity
soon changed to humble entreaty, when the Romans, after the battle
of Pydna, threatened the Rhodians with war. The senate, glad of
an excuse to humiliate the haughty merchant city, deprived Rhodes
of all her possessions on the mainland, and, by the erection of a free
port at Delos, so damaged Rhodian commerce that the yearly re-
ceipts from customs sank at once from $205,000 to $30,000.

In Greece itself severe measures were taken. Seventy towns
in Epirus were plundered, and the inhabitants, to the number of
150,000, were sold into slavery. Trials for high treason took place
in all parts of Greece, owing to the existence of a Macedonian party
in every city. A very large number of suspects from Achaia,
Aetolia, Acarnania, and Lesbos were deported to Italy, partly, perhaps, to escape the bloodthirsty zeal of such men as the Aetolian
strategus Lyciscus.

An opportunity had, moreover, been given Rome to interfere
once more in the East. During the third Macedonian war Antiochus Epiphanes, king of Asia, or, as it was now called, Syria,
seized the occasion to carry out the traditional policy of the Seleucidae and to conquer Egypt. When he was on the eve of success,
and was lying encamped before Alexandria, a Roman envoy arrived
shortly after the battle of Pydna, and drawing a circle round the
king, warned him at once to restore all that he had conquered and
to evacuate Egypt. With this warning Antiochus was forced to
comply; and Egypt at once submitted to the Roman protectorate.

Every state in the world now did homage to Rome, and the
most obsequious flattery met the ears of the Roman senate. Nor
was the moment ill-chosen; from the battle of Pydna Polybius
dates the full establishment of Rome's universal empire. All subsequent struggles were rebellions, or wars with nations beyond the
pale of Graeco-Roman civilization. The whole civilized world
recognized in the Roman senate the supreme tribunal for kings and
nations; to acquire its language and manners foreign princes and
noble youths resided in Rome. Only once was a real attempt made
to get rid of Roman dominion—by Mithradates, king of Pontus.

The battle of Pydna marks the last occasion on which the senate
still adhered to the state maxim that Rome should, if possible, hold

no possessions and maintain no garrisons beyond the Italian seas, but should keep in check the numerous dependent states by a mere political supremacy. The treatment of Macedonia and other states after the battle of Pydna shows that Rome had at last recognized the impracticable nature of this protectorate; the necessity of her constant intervention had proved to Rome that the effort to preserve vanquished states, even at the cost of faithful allies, was a failure. Signs were now forthcoming that by gradual steps these client-states would be reduced to the position of subjects. When we review the extension of Rome's power from the conquest of Sicily to the battle of Pydna, it becomes clear that the universal empire of Rome was a result forced upon the Roman government, without, and even in opposition to its wish—certainly it was not a gigantic plan contrived and carried out by a thirst for territorial aggrandizement. All that the Roman government wished for was the sovereignty of Italy; and they earnestly opposed the extension of this sovereignty to Africa, Greece, and Asia, from the sound view that they ought not to suffer the kernel of their empire to be crushed by the shell. Their blind hatred of Carthage led them into the error of retaining Spain, and of assuming in some measure the guardianship of Africa; their still blinder enthusiasm for Greek freedom made them commit the equal blunder of conferring liberty everywhere on the Greeks.

The policy of Rome was not projected by a single mighty intellect and bequeathed by tradition from generation to generation; it was the policy of a very able but somewhat narrow-minded deliberative assembly, which had far too little power of grand combination, and far too much of an instinctive desire for the preservation of its own commonwealth, to devise projects in the spirit of a Caesar or a Napoleon. The universal empire of Rome was, in fact, based on the political development of antiquity in general. In the ancient world balance of power was unknown, and every nation's aim was to subdue his neighbor or to render him harmless. Though we may sentimentally mourn the extinction of so many richly gifted and highly developed nations by the supremacy of Rome, we must bear in mind that that supremacy was not due to a mere superiority of arms, but was a necessary consequence of the international relations of antiquity generally; and therefore the issue was not one of mere chance, but the fulfillment of an unchangeable and therefore endurable destiny.

Chapter XVI

THE GOVERNMENT AND THE GOVERNED

AMID the din of arms and constant succession of victories, it is difficult to trace the secret and silent growth of those changes which were fraught with such momentous consequences to the Roman constitution. The new aristocracy, consisting of the old patrician families and of those plebeians who had become united with the old patricians, gradually gathered in its grasp the reins of government. The leaders of the plebeian element of the aristocracy were most zealous in maintaining the barrier of caste, and in assigning a political significance to those outward badges, such as the ius imaginum, the laticlave, the gold rings, and the bulla, which had originally merely distinguished the higher from the lower patrician families. The senate and the equestrian order[1] were no longer organs of the whole state, but organs of the aristocracy. In each case this change was due to the power of the censorship. Everyone who had held a curule magistracy[2] had a legal claim to a vote and seat in the senate; but the censor had the power of summoning men to become members of that body, and of striking off the names of such as were unworthy of so high a position. Inasmuch as the election to a curule office and the choice of censor really lay in the hands of the senate, it was but natural that curule magistrates and censors were chosen out of the ranks of the nobility, and thus practically gave a strong aristocratic character to the composition of the senate. So, too, the censors selected the members of the equestrian centuries, and no doubt, as a rule, had regard to the birth and position of the members they selected, rather than to their military capacity. Thus the equestrian order

---

[1] The equestrian order was originally made up of those citizens who served as the cavalry contingent of the legions. As this service presupposed considerable wealth, and as in the comitia centuriata they voted by themselves in the eighteen equestrian centuries into which they were divided, they came to be looked upon as a wealthy, privileged class of nobles, a little inferior to the senators, but far superior in rank to the ordinary plebeians.

[2] The curule officers were the dictator consuls, pretors, censors, and ediles.

became a stronghold of the aristocracy. The distinction between classes was further rendered more marked by the unwise change introduced by the great Scipio in 194 B.C. This change separated the special seats assigned to the senatorial order from those occupied by the mass of the people at the national festivals.

The office of censor, owing to these changes, became invested with a peculiar glory of its own, as the palladium of the aristocratic order, and great efforts were made to resist attacks on the censorship or judicial prosecution of unpopular censors, and to prevent opponents of the aristocracy from holding this office. An important check, moreover, was placed upon the censor himself by the usage which obliged him to specify the grounds on which he erased the name of senator or knight. The nobility, in order to keep the government in their own hands, were naturally averse to appointing more magistrates than the growth of Roman power rendered unavoidable. The appointment, in 243 B.C., of two pretors in the place of one, and the assignation of all lawsuits between Roman citizens to the city pretor (*praetor urbanus*) and of all lawsuits between men who were not Roman citizens to his colleague (*praetor peregrinus*) was manifestly inadequate to the growing needs of the state. Further, the attempt to govern the four transmarine provinces by the appointment of four pretors in 197 B.C. showed a desire to limit the number of magistrates who were outside the immediate control of the senate, rather than a real grasp of the requirements of the new empire. A more serious evil was the election of the twenty-four military tribunes. *i. e.*, of the whole military staff, by the comitia tributa; thus the choice of officers became subject to the evils of popular election, and every effort was made by the aristocracy to secure the position for members of their own order, and to make the military tribunate the stepping-stone in the political career of young nobles. In serious wars, *e. g.*, in 171 B.C., it was found necessary to suspend this system, and to restore to the general the power of electing his own staff.

Owing to the aristocratic spirit that pervaded every section of the government, the chief magisterial offices of consul and censor not only centered in the hands of a limited number of gentes, but, what was worse, in the hands of particular families. This was markedly the case in the policy of the Scipios and the Flaminini. Moreover, a serious laxity began to prevail in the management of the public money; and, although embezzlement was still rare among

Roman officials, the corruption prevalent in the provinces could not fail to react with pernicious effect on the pretors and their retinue. The relations of Rome to her allies and dependents, both within and outside Italy, gradually underwent a change. In the first place, such communities as had been passive burgesses of Rome, and had sided with Hannibal, *c. g.*, Capua, lost their Roman citizenship, while other communities which had remained true to Rome acquired the full franchise; thus, except in isolated cases, the position occupied by passive burgesses ceased to exist. Admission to the Roman franchise became more and more difficult; and the tendency arose on the part of the Roman citizens to separate themselves, not only from the mass of Italians, but even from their old Latin allies, whose staunch support had saved the state in the war with Hannibal. The chief burdens of war, of garrison duty, and of the Spanish service, now fell upon the allies, while the Roman citizens appropriated most of the spoil and of the honors and advantages that accrued from the successes won by the arms of their allies. Indeed, the Latins, though of course far removed from the servile position held by the Bruttians and other communities, felt that the distinction between themselves and the mass of the Italian confederacy was being abolished, and that they were fast becoming the subjects, instead of the privileged allies, of Rome.

A far graver error was the retention of the old constitution, which Carthage had established in Sicily, Sardinia, and Spain: by retaining the tribute imposed by their predecessors, the Romans renounced their old policy of having no tributary subjects; and by applying this method to Hither Spain, Macedonia, and Illyria, they clearly adopted the dangerous and demoralizing expedient of making money out of their new possessions. It is true that the governors were legally bound to administer their office with honesty and frugality, and it is equally true that many, like Cato in Sardinia, scrupulously observed the legal injunction. But the temptation was too great; the control exercised by the senate over the governors was of necessity very lax, and the complaints of the governed, unless the severity and rapacity of the pretor had exceeded all ordinary limits, met with but scant attention. Moreover, the governor could not be called to account during his term of office, and the charges laid against him were, as a rule, heard by a jury consisting of men of his own order, and therefore little inclined to visit the offender with severe punishment. We can, then, scarcely doubt that, owing to the feeble control exercised by the senate, and the absolute nature of the governor's provincial office, and, still more, owing to the corrupt servility of those whom he governed, it was a rare thing for governors to return home with clean hands.

A wholesome corrective to the abuse of the senatorial power, theoretically at least, still existed in the assemblies of the people. But this period exhibits to us the growing unimportance, nay impotence, of the popular comitia. The reason is plain. With the extension of the Roman suffrage, not only throughout Latium, Sabina, and a part of Campania, but to the new colonies founded in Picenum and across the Apennines, the burgess-body no longer consisted of farmers living within easy distance of the capital. Thus the decision of the great questions of foreign policy rested with men scattered over Italy, who met together in the capital by mere chance, and who were unable by previous consultation to arrive at some joint course of action and to show an intelligent grasp of the weighty questions submitted to their judgment. As a rule, then, the people played a passive part on such occasions, and ratified without discussion the proposals made to them by the senate.

Again, out of the old clients of powerful houses now arose a city rabble, whose votes in the comitia were becoming of even more importance than those of the scattered burgesses, and were employed by the aristocracy to counterbalance the independence of the farmers. Systematic corruption began to be practiced upon these clients by the sale of grain at low prices, by an increase of festivals and holidays, and by gladiatorial shows, in order that the aristocratic candidate might secure his election to the offices of state at the expense of his poorer rival. The spoils of war were even employed to corrupt the soldiers, and the stern refusal of Lucius Paulus to turn his victory at Pydna to such base uses almost cost him the honor of a triumph. It was but natural that such corruption should work the decay of the old warlike spirit, and that cowardice should stain the honor of the Roman officers and soldiers.

Another sign of the universal degeneration was the miserable love for petty distinctions: triumphs were granted to the victor of Ligurian or Corsican robbers; statues and monuments became so common that it was said to be a distinction to have none; men received permanent surnames from the victories they had won; and among the lower orders equal anxiety was manifested to mark their social grade by trifling badges.

The party of opposition in the state was composed of two elements of widely different character.   In the first place, there was the patriotic party, whose cry for reform arose from a genuine distrust and hatred of the prevailing corruption.   The moving spirit and typical representative of this party was Marcus Porcius Cato (234-149 B.C.).   This rough Sabine farmer had been induced to enter upon a political career by a noble of the old stamp, Lucius Valerius Flaccus.   He saw active service throughout the whole of the second Punic war, and in all countries and in every capacity had won equal distinction.   He was the same in the Forum as in the battlefield.   His prompt and intrepid address, his rough but pungent rustic wit, his knowledge of Roman law and Roman affairs, his incredible activity and his iron frame, first brought him into notice in the neighboring towns; and when at length he made his appearance on the greater arena of the Forum and the senate-house in the capital, constituted him the most influential pleader and public orator of his time.   Thoroughly narrow in his political and moral views, and having the ideal of the good old times always before his eyes and on his lips, he cherished an obstinate contempt for everything new.   Deeming himself entitled, by virtue of his own austere life, to manifest an unrelenting severity and harshness towards everything and everybody; upright and honorable, but without a glimpse of any duty beyond the sphere of police discipline and of mercantile integrity; an enemy to all villainy and vulgarity as well as to all genius and refinement ; and, above all things, a foe to those who were his foes, he never made an attempt to stop evils at their source, but waged war throughout life against mere symptoms, and especially against persons.   Not only did he attack the most powerful aristocrats, such as the Scipios and the Flaminini, but he never shrank from abusing his own supporters did he deem they deserved it.   Still, so staunch were the farmers in their support, that when Cato and his friend and colleague, Lucius Flaccus, stood as candidates for the censorship in 184 B.C., all the exertions of the aristocrats were powerless to prevent their return.

The reforms introduced by Cato and his party were aimed at arresting the spread of decay and at checking the preponderating influence of the aristocracy in politics.   In view of the first object, police regulations were enacted to restrict the luxurious style of living, and to introduce a frugal economy into Roman households. More successful and more practical were the efforts made to revive the farmer class by founding Latin colonies in the north, and by large and numerous assignations of the domain land.   Although Cato failed to carry his proposal to institute four hundred new equestrian stalls, and thus remedy the decline of the burgess cavalry, the necessities of war had long before compelled the government to reduce the rating which allowed a man to serve in the army from $210 to $30, and to abolish the other qualification of free birth.   The admission of the poor and of freedmen into the army gave them a new importance in the state, and was one of the chief causes of the changes introduced into the comitia centuriata.   These changes, accomplished about 241 B.C., at the close of the first Punic war, placed all five classes composing the comitia on an equal footing as regarded number of votes, and took away from the equites their old priority in voting, and gave the freedmen the same power as the freeborn.

This reform was the first victory won by the new democracy over the aristocracy, but its effects were greatly neutralized by the fact that, though priority of voting was taken away from the equites or aristocratic voters, it was still confined to a division chosen by lot from the first or richest class; and further, the equalization of the freedmen with the freeborn was set aside twenty years later, in 220 B.C., by the censor Gaius Flaminius, and the freedmen were excluded from the centuries.   A proof that the reform did not at any rate greatly affect the power of the aristocracy is furnished by the fact that the second consulship and second censorship, although in law open to both patricians and plebeians, were almost invariably filled by patricians; the second consulship was held by patricians down to 172 B.C., and the second censorship down to 131 B.C.

Viewed as a whole, the reforms of Cato and his party, distinguished as they were by great energy and a noble wish to counteract the evident evils of the time, were unfortunately marred by a want of clear insight into the source of those evils, and by the failure to devise, in a large and statesmanlike spirit, some comprehensive plan for their remedy.

In the second place, the party of opposition contained a far less reputable element, the outcome of the city rabble.   The spirit of demagogism was abroad; men, cursed with a love of empty speechmaking, pretended to be ardent reformers, but in their harangues dwelt only on the excessive powers of the aristocratic government and on the rights of the citizens, not on the urgent need for moral reform in every section of the state. The evils which arose out of this new spirit have already been indicated in the history of the war with Hannibal: the appointment of mere party leaders, such as Flaminius and Varro, to the supreme command; the absurd decree which made Minucius co-dictator with Fabius in 217 B.C., and which gave the deathblow to the dictatorship; the charge of embezzlement laid against Marcellus in 219 B.C.,—these and other acts all proceeded from the wanton interference of the demagogues. The citizens were even tempted to interfere with the administration of the finances, the oldest and most important prerogative of the government; and, in 232 B.C., Gaius Flaminius, owing to the fatal obstinacy of the senate, went to the burgesses with his proposal to distribute the domain-lands in Picenum. Nor was this new system of politics confined to its author, Gaius Flaminius; aristocrats, such as Scipio, in their efforts to place themselves and their families in a position superior to that of the rest of the senate, condescended to vie with demagogues in their flattery of the city rabble. We have already pointed out the impotence of the comitia; as a rule, indeed, the burgesses had the good sense and sufficient patriotism to give a hearty support to that senate which had weathered the storm of Hannibal's invasion. But appeals to selfishness and avarice could not fail to demoralize the best citizens; and sudden caprice or violent outbursts of jealousy or hatred from time to time showed that the old foundations of the Republic were being undermined. To the later generations, who survived the storms of revolution, the period after the Hannibalic war appeared the golden age of Rome, and Cato seemed the model of the Roman statesman. It was in reality the calm before the storm, and the epoch of political mediocrities. The seeming outward stability of the Roman constitution, during the years 266-146 B.C., was a sign, not of health, but of incipient sickness and revolution.

A review of this period would be incomplete unless it presented a brief notice of the economic troubles produced by the system of farming on a large scale, and by the power of capital. The importation of corn from the provinces, and the sale of it at a merely nominal price for the benefit of the idle proletariat of the capital, naturally ruined the market for the growers of Italian corn. The evil was all the worse and all the more inexcusable in a country like Italy, where there were hardly any manufactures, and, consequently, no large industrial population whose needs, as in England, could not be supplied by home-grown grain. On the contrary, agriculture was the mainstay of the Roman state, and the short-sighted policy of the government in this matter sacrificed the soundest to the most worthless part of the nation. The small farmers were gradually ruined, and their holdings became merged in the large estates of the landlords, who, by cultivating their lands by means of large gangs of slaves, were able to produce at a cheaper rate than the farmer. But even the large landlord was unable to compete with foreign grain, and devoted himself almost entirely to stock-raising and the production of oil and wine; and thus it was that arable land to a great extent was converted into pasture, while, owing to the increased use of slaves, free labor became almost unknown. The power of the capitalist was alike evinced in the speculative management of land, in the increase of money-lenders, and in the enormous extent of all mercantile transactions; and, as in the end the gains from commercial enterprise flowed into Rome, the result was that Rome, compared with the rest of the world, stood as superior in point of wealth as in political and military power. In fact, the whole Roman nation became possessed with the mercantile spirit, and, while money served to create a new social barrier between rich and poor, that deep-rooted immorality, which is inherent in an economy of pure capital, ate into the heart of society and of the commonwealth, and substituted an absolute selfishness for humanity and patriotism.

Moreover, the very population of Italy began to decline, and Cato and Polybius agree in stating that at the end of the sixth century of the city Italy was far weaker in population than at the end of the fifth; and although it was, in the first instance, the two long wars with Carthage that decimated and ruined both the burgesses and the allies, the Roman capitalists beyond doubt contributed quite as much as Hamilcar and Hannibal to the decline in the vigor and the numbers of the Italian people.

Chapter XVII

THE SUBJECT COUNTRIES DOWN TO THE GRACCHAN
EPOCH. 168-133 B.C.

BEFORE we enter upon the period of change which takes its name from the family of the Gracchi, it is necessary to present a picture of the state of things in the subject countries. Trivial and dreary as the separate conflicts in these remote lands between weakness and power may seem, yet collectively they are of great historical significance; and the reaction which the provinces exercised on the mother country alone renders intelligible the condition of Italy at this period.

At first the only two recognized provinces of Rome, if we except what may be regarded as the natural appendages of Italy, *i. e.,* Sicily, Corsica, and Sardinia, were the two Spains; and they were the scene of many wars and the cause of much trouble to Rome. In 154 B.C. the peaceful state of the Spanish provinces, which had lasted for nearly thirty years, was broken by the successful invasion of the Lusitanians. The complete defeat of the governor of Farther Spain, in 153 B.C., emboldened the Celtiberians to join against the common foe; and the successes achieved by the powerful tribe of the Arevacae over the Consul Quintus Fulvius Nobilior even eclipsed the previous victories of the Lusitanians. But the advent of Marcus Claudius Marcellus, who combined skillful generalship with humane treatment, terminated the Celtiberian war in 151 B.C. After a brief interval of peace another outbreak occurred, due to the weakness and perfidy of the Roman commanders. The withdrawal of the regular military forces during the last Macedonian and Punic wars in 149 B.C., and the appearance of a Spanish national leader in the person of the famous Viriathus, gave a dangerous character to the revolt. It seemed as if at last Spain had found a champion able to break the fetters of Rome; general after general, army after army, both in northern and southern Spain, recoiled in utter discomfiture before the ability and enthusiasm of the Spanish leader. For about ten years (148-139 B.C.) Viriathus was the acknowledged king of the Lusitanians, though never distinguished by any badge from the meanest soldier—a true hero, remarkable alike for his physical and mental qualities. In the end his brilliant and noble career was, as often happened in Spain, cut short by the hand of the assassin, three of his intimate friends having sold the life of their lord to the Roman consul, Quintus Servilius Caepio, in return for their own safety. With the death of Viriathus the war in Lusitania came to an end, and two years later the Celtiberians in the north were reduced by the consul Quintus Caecilius Metellus.

The struggle with the town of Numantia was more serious. The incapable consul, Quintus Pompeius, after several severe defeats, agreed to come to terms with its invincible inhabitants; but in fear of the reckoning that awaited him at home for thus concluding peace, he at the last moment took refuge in a base falsehood, and denied the agreement he had made. The matter was referred to the senate, who supported their guilty consul, and ordered his successor, Marcus Popilius Laenas, to continue the war. The total incompetence of the Roman generals and the demoralized condition of their armies caused the war to drag on, amid disgrace and disaster, from 137-134 B.C. In the latter year Scipio Aemilianus, the first general in Rome, was sent out, and after reorganizing the Roman army by treatment alike severe and contemptuous, he set about the task of subduing the brave Numantines. After a heroic defense, the city, utterly exhausted by famine and pestilence, fell in the autumn of 133 B.C., and its fall reëstablished the supremacy of Rome in Hither Spain. A senatorial commission was shortly after sent to Spain, and the provinces were reorganized. Thanks to the efforts of Scipio and other governors the country gradually became exceedingly prosperous, and despite the guerrilla warfare ever waged by the half-subdued native tribes, it was the most flourishing and best organized country in the Roman dominions.

Far more insupportable was the condition—intermediate between formal sovereignty and actual subjection—of the African, Greek, and Asiatic states. These had neither independence nor peace. In Africa there was constant war between Carthage and Numidia; in Egypt the rulers of that country and Cyrene were ever disputing for the possession of Cyprus; in Asia almost every petty kingdom was torn by intestine struggles, and several were at war with one another. The interference of Rome, constantly invoked, only made matters worse. Rome neither resigned her authority nor displayed sufficient force to bring the ruled into subjection. It was the epoch of commissions. Commissioners went to and fro, reporting and giving orders, to which the Asiatic states, feeling secure from their very remoteness, as a rule paid no attention. The Roman government conferred neither the blessings of freedom nor of order. It was clear that this state of things must be put an end to, and that the only way to do so was by the conversion of the client states into Roman provinces. The only question was whether the Roman senate would perceive the necessity of the task, and would put its hand to the work with the requisite energy.

In Africa we have to record the last act of the terrible Carthaginian drama. The Romans saw with ill-concealed envy the increasing prosperity of their old rival, though hampered in every way by the encroachments of Massinissa. At the head of the second commission, sent from Rome in 161 B.C., to settle points of dispute between the Numidian king and Carthage, was the aged Cato, whose inveterate hatred of Carthage was aroused afresh by the sight of her great commercial prosperity. Opposed though he was by the larger-minded Scipio Nasica, Cato had no difficulty in finding men at home ready to support his view that Rome could know no security until Carthage was destroyed, and among his most ardent supporters were the bankers and rich capitalists of Rome, who saw that the wealth of Carthage must revert to themselves.

An opportunity for putting the policy of Cato into effect soon arose. In 154 B.C. Massinissa appealed to Rome to act once more as arbiter between him and Carthage, and pointed out that the leaders of the patriotic party in Carthage, Hasdrubal and Carthalo, were amassing stores and collecting troops in violation of the treaty with Rome. The Carthaginians were ordered to destroy their naval stores and dismiss their troops; but the spirit of the people was roused, and the demand was rejected and preparations made to wage war against Massinissa. In 152 B.C. hostilities began, and owing to the miserable incapacity of Hasdrubal, Massinissa gained a complete victory.

The Romans now conceived that the hour had come to deal the death blow to their old antagonist. By making war upon an ally of Rome, Carthage had broken one of the stipulations of their treaty, and had thus given Rome a plausible pretext for war, and from the feeble display of arms she had made against Massinissa, Carthage seemed a certain and easy victim. In vain the Carthaginians made every submission to avert the threatened blow, and war was declared in 149 B.C. After dallying with the wretched envoys sent from Carthage, the Roman consul, Lucius Marcius Censorinus, who had landed at Utica, at last revealed the dire purpose of the senate, and bade the envoys tell the gerusia that Carthage must be evacuated and surrendered to destruction. At this the frenzied enthusiasm of the Phoenician race once more blazed forth. The most marvelous efforts were made to secure the defenses of the city, and to repair the blunder which had surrendered all the arms and dismantled the battlements in obedience to the Roman demands.

Meanwhile, the Roman consuls were deluded by pretended embassies, and though but a few miles distant, had no idea what was happening in the Phoenician capital. The precious respite was turned to good account: day and night the work of forging arms and catapults never flagged. Young and old, women and children, were all fired with the same zeal and the same hatred. With incredible speed the work was finished, and the city and its inhabitants ready for the struggle. Art had rendered the naturally strong site of Carthage well-nigh impregnable, and the two consuls, Manius Manilius and Lucius Censorinus, on realizing their blunder and attempting to prosecute the siege, soon found out how utterly incompetent they were for the task. After losses by assaults and disease the Romans were compelled, by the death of Massinissa in 149 B.C., to suspend all offensive operations. The youthful Scipio, who was serving as a military tribune, alone retrieved the honor of the Roman name, both by his personal bravery and his politic dealings with the native Numidians.

The following year saw two new commanders, Lucius Piso at the head of the land army, and Lucius Mancinus in charge of the fleet: they achieved even less than their predecessors and neglected the siege of Carthage for attacks on smaller towns, which as a rule were unsuccessful. A Numidian sheik passed over to the Carthaginian side with eight hundred horse, and negotiations were entered into with the kings of Numidia and Mauretania. At this juncture the Romans adopted the extraordinary measure of giving the command to Scipio Aemilianus, and thus made him consul without his having held the preliminary office of edile. His arrival in 147 B.C. completely changed the aspect of affairs. Mancinus was rescued from a position of great danger on an isolated cliff, and the siege of Carthage was once more begun in real earnest. Scipio first constructed a large camp across the isthmus which connected Carthage with the mainland, and then blocked up the entrance to the harbor by a mole of stone ninety-six feet in breadth. This latter operation the Carthaginians neutralized by cutting a new canal, thus gaining a new outlet into the harbor. But Scipio at last succeeded in his object, and completely blockaded the city by land and sea, leaving famine and pestilence to complete what he had begun.

In the spring of 146 B.C. the city wall was scaled, and for six days the famished inhabitants continued a· terrible but hopeless struggle from house to house and street to street. Even then the steep citadel-rock, held by Hasdrubal and the remnant of the garrison, remained; to clear the approaches, Scipio ordered the city to be set on fire and the ruins to be leveled. The garrison at last capitulated, and life was granted to the survivors, a bare tenth part of the former population. Hasdrubal, to whose gluttony and bragging incapacity the fall of Carthage was in no small measure due, gained the boon of life for which he prayed Scipio on his knees; but his wife scorned to survive her city's destruction, and plunged with her children into the flames of a burning temple. Despite the protests of Scipio, the senate ordered the consul to raze Carthage to the ground, to pass the plow over its site, and to curse the ground forever. Where the industrious Phoenicians had bustled and trafficked for five hundred years, Roman slaves henceforth pastured the herds of their distant masters. Scipio, however, whom nature had destined for a nobler part than that of an executioner, gazed with horror on his own work, and instead of the joy of victory, the victor himself was haunted by a presentiment of the retribution that would inevitably follow such a misdeed. The Carthaginian territory as possessed by the city in its last days became a Roman province under the name of Africa, and the boundaries of the enlarged Numidian kingdom were clearly defined. Utica was the capital of the new province, and thither Roman merchants flocked to turn to account the new acquisition.

About the same time Macedonia also experienced the common fate. The four small confederacies into which Roman wisdom had parceled out the ancient kingdom soon showed how impracticable

such an arrangement was. A pretender, calling himself Philip, the
son of Perseus, was accepted as king by the Macedonian nation, but
was crushed in 148 B.C.   Macedonia was now converted into a Roman province, and covered much the same area as had formerly
been subject to Macedonian sway.

In Greece itself all Roman efforts at conciliation failed, and at
last, despite the warnings of the Roman envoys, the Achaean
league declared war against Sparta about 146 B.C.   This action,

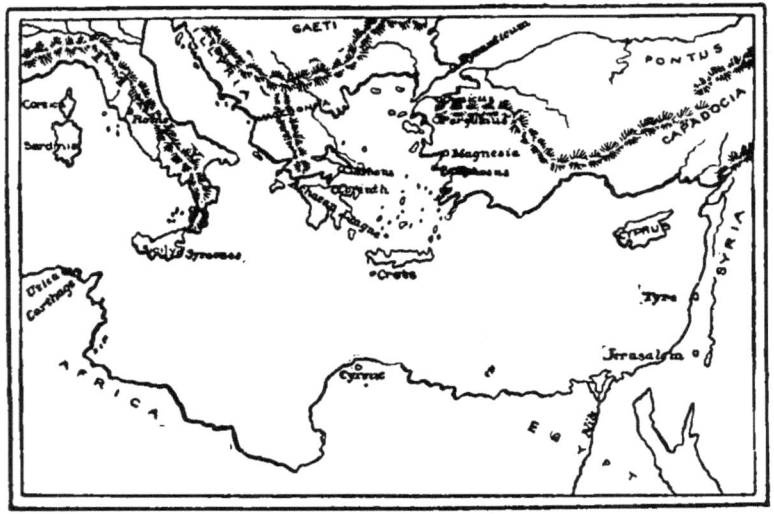

combined with the insulting attitude of the Greeks towards Rome,
caused the senate to send Lucius Mummius to crush the pretensions
of Critolaus, the Achaean strategus.   A battle at Leucopetra was
utterly disastrous to the Achaeans, and was followed by the conversion of Greece into the province of Achaia.   On the whole,
Mummius seems to have acted with justice and moderation in his
administration of Greek affairs; but the Roman senate showed a
hideous severity in the destruction of Corinth, the first commercial
city in Greece, and the last precious ornament of a land once so rich
in cities.   Doubtless this barbarous act was due to the political influence of the Roman merchants, who gladly seized the opportunity
to rid themselves of a commercial rival.

In Asia Minor the bequest of Pergamus to the Romans by the

last of the Attalids, in 133 B.C., gave Rome a new province, though she had to vindicate her right by the sword, as Aristonicus, a natural son of one of the former kings of Pergamus, succeeded for a time in making good his claim to the throne. Most of the small states and cities in western Asia remained unchanged, but both Cappadocia and Pontus received some additional territory on the dissolution of the Attalid kingdom. Roman authority in Syria and Egypt became weaker and weaker, owing to the negligent and spasmodic manner in which the senate attempted to settle the various disputes that arose. Many causes had combined to destroy the once huge empire of Asia: the battle of Magnesia had wrested western Asia from the Great King; the two Cappadocias and the two Armenias had become independent kingdoms; lastly, Antiochus Epiphanes (175-164 B.C.) had adopted the course, equally foolish and fatal, of introducing Roman and Greek ideas both in manners and religion throughout his dominions. This step, enforced as it was by religious persecution and plundering of temples, drove the Jews to revolt in 167 B.C., and the successful issue of their rebellion was mainly due to the brave and prudent conduct of the house of the Maccabees.

A still more important result of the folly of Antiochus was the founding of the Parthian kingdom, the outcome of a reaction on the part of the native religion and manners against Hellenism. Mithradates I. (175-133 B.C.) laid the foundations of this empire by his successes over the Bactrian kingdom, and in all the countries west of the great desert. Aided by the internal dissolution of the kingdom of the Seleucidae, from which Persia, Babylonia, and Media were forever severed, this new empire reached from the Oxus and the Hindu Khush to the Tigris and the desert of Arabia. The foundations of its strength rested not merely on the revival of the wild physical forces of the East, on the bow and arrow and the whirlwind rush of the cavalry of the desert, but far more on the revival of the national customs and national religion; on the old Iranian language, the order of the Magi and the worship of Mithra. From the founding of the Parthian empire dates the ebb of that great Hellenic movement which had reached its height under Alexander the Great. The East once more reasserted itself, and re-entered the world of politics: the world had again two masters. Thus the Roman senate sacrificed the first essential result of the policy of Alexander, and thereby paved the way for that retrograde movement whose last offshoots ended in the Alhambra of Granada and in the great Mosque of Constantinople.

If we glance at the maritime relations of this period, we find that practically no naval power existed. Rome had no fleet, and her maritime police, once so effective, ceased to control the piracy everywhere prevalent. A check no doubt was kept on the buccaneers of the Adriatic and Tyrrhene seas; but Crete and Cilicia became the recognized home of organized bands of pirates. The Roman government merely looked on, and the Roman merchants kept up a friendly traffic with the pirate captains, who furnished them with that marketable commodity—slaves.

We have now reviewed Rome's position in and dealings with the outer world. The problem of governing this new empire was not wholly misunderstood, though it was by no means solved. Showing themselves often stern masters where leniency was needed, and lenient where sternness was required, the Romans governed from one day to another with feeble and selfish hands, merely transacting the current business of the hour. Senators had learned to despise the old maxim that office was its own reward, and that such office was a burden and duty rather than a privilege and benefit, and we find that foreign powers constantly bribed influential senators by enormous gifts. The Roman fleet was allowed to go to ruin; the decay of the old military spirit and prestige was no less marked. The better classes had begun to disappear from the army, and officers for the Spanish wars were found with great difficulty. In truth the Roman senate had solved the problem of acquiring the sovereignty of the world, but had broken down under the more difficult task of its government.

PART III

THE REVOLUTION PERIOD. 133-78 B.C.

Chapter XVIII

THE REFORMS OF THE GRACCHI. 133-121 B.C.

WE have now reached the epoch in Roman history forever rendered famous by the revolutionary reforms of Tiberius and Gaius Gracchus. It is our duty to trace the causes which called for those reforms, and to form some judgment both of the measures and their authors. In the preceding chapter we have sketched the evils underlying the outward calm which pervaded the whole Roman empire for a full generation after the battle of Pydna. Cato's question as to the future of Rome, when she no longer had a state of fear, had a profound significance now. The younger generation of aristocrats thought no more of foreign foes, but of maintaining and, if possible, of increasing the privileges they had usurped. The various measures of the opposition—the institution of a standing senatorial commission to try the complaints of provincials touching the extortion of Roman governors; the introduction of the vote by ballot in the burgess-assemblies, the exclusion, a little later, of the senators from the equestrian centuries,—failed entirely to emancipate the electors from aristocratic influence, and to restore to the comitia the power and independence they had once possessed. The Romans lacked what alone compensates for the evils of party life, the free and common movement of the masses to some definite aim. Politics were, as a rule, merely partisanship for individuals, not for great principles, and the people arrayed itself now on the side of this aristocratic coterie, now on the side of that. Hence sprang that despicable canvassing of the mob by an aspirant for public office; hence, too, those demagogic cries for reform and attacks on eminent persons to catch the popular ear; hence, again, arose the necessity for providing costly popular amusements, the long-recognized duty of any candidate for the consulship. A still graver evil was the miserable position which the government, by thus cringing for the favor of the mob, was forced to occupy towards the governed. The burgesses became used to the dangerous idea that they were exempt from all direct taxation, and they were no longer forced to enter the hateful military service across the sea. The two factions, which now became known by the names of Optimates and Populares, fought alike for shadows, being completely destitute of political morality and political ideas. It would have been better for Rome had the Optimates substituted hereditary rotation for election by the burgesses, or had the Populares developed a real democratic government.

The crisis with which the Roman revolution opened arose from the old evil, the land question. The warfare which had for centuries been waged between the small farmer and the capitalist had at last produced the most disastrous results; and as formerly the farmer had been ruined by the chain of debt, so now he was crushed by the competition with transmarine and slave-grown corn. The ultimate result was in both cases the same: Italian farms sank in value; small holdings became merged in large estates; agriculture gave place to stock-raising and the growing of olives and vines; and, finally, free labor was supplanted in Italy, as in the provinces, by that of slaves. The new and huge system of slavery now introduced owed its rise to the all-powerful capitalist. In earlier days captives taken in war and the hereditary transmission of slavery had sufficed, but this new system of servitude was, just like that of America, based on the methodically pursued hunting of man. The " negroland " of that period was western Asia, and the Cretan and Cilician corsairs, the professional slave-hunters and slave-dealers, robbed the coasts of Syria and the Greek islands. Their example was imitated by the Roman revenue-farmers, who instituted similar human hunts to such an extent that they well-nigh depopulated certain provinces. At the great slave-market at Delos it is said that as many as ten thousand slaves were disembarked in the morning and sold before the evening of the same day. Every financial arrangement, every speculation, every trade, was carried on by means of slaves. Pastoral husbandry, now so common, was almost entirely performed by armed and often mounted slaves. But far worse than any previous form of slavery was the plantation system proper—the cultivation of fields by chained gangs, who worked under overseers and were locked up together at night in the common laborers' prison. This system, introduced from the East into Carthage and thence into Sicily, was developed in that island earlier and more fully than in any other part of the Roman dominions. In fact, for the present, Italy was still substantially free from this worst form of slave husbandry, though the Roman government was soon aroused to the danger which the system developed elsewhere.

It requires but little imagination to picture the hideous sufferings of the slaves themselves, far exceeding the sum of all negro misery. Slave wars and slave insurrections now became frequent, not only in the provinces, but in Italy itself, though, as was natural, it was in Sicily that the evil results of slavery were most conspicuous. At Enna the slaves rose *en masse,* murdered their masters, and crowned a Syrian juggler as king. His general Achaeus, a Greek slave, traversed the island, and united under his standard both slaves and free laborers. Agrigentum was seized by another band, under Cleon, a Cilician slave; and the united forces utterly defeated the pretor Lucius Hypsaeus, and reduced the whole island under their sway. It was not until three successive consuls and armies had been dispatched from Rome (134-132 B.C.) that the servile war was ended by the capture of Tauromenium and Enna, the latter stronghold being reduced by famine rather than by Roman arms, after a siege of two years. Such results were due partly to the lax control of the Roman police system as worked by the senate and its officials in the provinces, partly to the disinclination of the government to disoblige Italian planters, to whom revolted slaves were often surrendered for punishment.

The real remedy for these evils doubtless was to be found, not in the severe repression of such revolts, but in the elevation, by the government, of free labor, a natural consequence of which would be the restriction of the slave proletariate. But the difficulty of this measure was beyond the capacity of the senate. In the first social crisis the landholder had been forced by law to employ a number of free laborers in proportion to the number of his slaves. Now the government caused a Punic treatise on agriculture to be translated for the use of Italian speculators, the solitary instance of a literary undertaking suggested by the senate! The same wisdom was shown in the matter of colonization. It was quite clear that the only real remedy against an agricultural proletariate consisted in a comprehensive and regular system of emigration. Hitherto the constant assignations of land and the establishment of new farm allotments had proved a fairly effective remedy for the evil. But after the founding of Luna in 177 B.C., no further assignations took place for a long time, for the simple reason that no new territory was acquired in Italy, with the exception of the unattractive

Ligurian valleys. Therefore there was no other land for distribution except the leased or occupied domain land, with which the aristocracy was as loath to part now as it had been three hundred years before. For political reasons it was deemed impossible to distribute the land in the provinces: Italy was to remain the ruling country, and the wall of partition between the Italian masters and the provincial servants was not to be broken down. The result was inevitable—the ruin of the farmer-class in Italy. Even as early as 134 B.C. not a free farmer existed in Etruria, where the old native aristocracy combined with the Roman capitalist; and in the very capital one could hear it said that the beasts had their lairs but the burgesses had nothing left but air and sunshine, and that the so-called masters of the world had no longer a clod they could call their own. The census list supplies a sufficient commentary. From the close of the war with Hannibal down to 159 B.C. the numbers of the burgesses steadily rose, owing to the distributions of the domain land; while from 159 to 131 B.C. they declined from 324,000 to 319,000—an alarming result for a period of profound peace at home and abroad.

The urgent need of reform in the government was patent to every eye. When laying down the censorship in 142 B.C., Scipio Aemilianus called on the gods to deign to preserve the state, whereas all his predecessors had prayed for increased glory to Rome. This expressed the feeling of the experienced and conservative citizens of the state. But, where Scipio despaired, Tiberius Sempronius Gracchus, a youth unmarked by any achievement, dared to hope. His father had been the true model of a Roman aristocrat, and had given proof of his noble and generous feelings both as consul and censor, but, above all, had by his strict integrity and humane governorship of the province of the Ebro not only rendered service to his country, but also endeared himself to the subject Spaniards. His famous mother, Cornelia, was the daughter of the conqueror of Zama, and had been given in marriage to Gracchus in return for his generous intervention on behalf of his political opponent, Scipio, when a petty and miserable charge had been got up against the Scipionic house. Thus Tiberius, who had taken part in the storming of Carthage under his cousin and brother-in-law, Scipio Aemilianus, had been brought up in all the political ideas and social and intellectual refinement of the Scipionic circle. Nor were he and his brother Gaius the only members of that circle who felt that far-reaching reforms must be instituted at once. Appius Claudius, consul in 143 B.C. and censor in 136 B.C., the father-in-law of Tiberius, censured the Scipionic circle for their desertion of the state with bitter vehemence; the pontifex maximus, Publius Crassus Mucianus, father-in-law of Gaius Gracchus, the revered warrior Quintus Metellus, and other men of note were known to favor the cause of reform. Tiberius brooded over the lofty ideals of statesmanship which he had imbibed in the atmosphere around him, and public placards often summoned the grandson of Africanus to think of the poor people and of the deliverance of Italy. He was elected tribune in 134 B.C., at a time when one of the consuls had met with disaster in his attempt to quell the rebellion of the Sicilian slaves, and when a small Spanish town had defied for months the efforts of Scipio Aemilianus. Not only had Tiberius the support and counsel of his father-in-law, but he also hoped for the influence of the new consul, Publius Mucius Scaevola, the founder of scientific jurisprudence in Rome, and a man whose abstention from party conflict gave his opinion the greater weight.

At the outset Tiberius proposed what was in a certain sense but the renewal of the Licinio-Sextian law of 367 B.C. Under it all the state lands held and enjoyed without remuneration were to be resumed on behalf of the state, with the restriction that each occupier should reserve for himself three hundred acres and for each son one hundred and fifty acres (so as, however, not to exceed a total of six hundred acres) in permanent and guaranteed possession; moreover, compensation was to be given to an ejected occupier for any improvements executed by him. The domain land thus resumed was to be broken up into lots of eighteen acres, and to be distributed among burgesses and Italian allies on permanent lease at a moderate rent, and the new holders were bound to use the land for agriculture. A board or "college" of three men, regarded as ordinary state magistrates and annually elected by the people, was intrusted with the work of confiscation and distribution; and later the same board had the difficult and important task of determining what was domain land and what private property.

This permanent executive, the absence of which had chiefly caused the Licinian rogations to remain in abeyance, was the special point of difference between the Sempronian and the older proposals. War was thus declared against the great landholders, whose organ now, as three centuries ago, was the senate. The old plan was adopted of silencing Tiberius. His colleague Marcus Octavius interposed his veto when the measure was about to be put to the vote; Gracchus replied by suspending all public business and administration of justice. He again brought his law to the vote, and Octavius again vetoed it. Gracchus, now feeling that all constitutional means were exhausted, began a revolution by proposing to the burgesses that they should vote whether he or Octavius should retire from office. Such deposition was impossible according to the Roman constitution, but Gracchus persevered, and was, of course, backed up by the almost unanimous vote of the assembled multitude. He then had his opponent removed from the tribunes' bench, and amid great rejoicing the law was carried.

The first three commissioners elected were Tiberius Gracchus, his brother, and his father-in-law Appius. Such a family selection only irritated the aristocratic party still more, and the strife was carried into every district where the commissioners' task lay. Gracchus' very life was in danger, and he appeared in public with a retinue of three thousand men—a step possibly necessary, but the cause of bitter words from senators as well disposed to him as Metellus. He clearly saw that he was a lost man unless he continued indispensable to the people, and that his only course lay in forming fresh plans and introducing still wider reforms. So he proposed that the treasures of Pergamus, which had just been bequeathed to Rome, should be divided among the new landholders for the purchase of the necessary farming implements and stock. What his other proposals were we do not know, but it is certain that he was well aware that reëlection to the tribunate could alone secure his safety. At the next meeting of the tribes to elect tribunes, the aristocratic party opposed its veto with the effect that the assembly broke up on the first and second days without accomplishing its object, though on both occasions the first divisions voted for Gracchus. To attain his object at the second meeting of the tribes Gracchus had resorted to every art, and even employed force to expel his opponents; they, in their turn, spread abroad that he had deposed all the other tribunes and was aiming at sole power. On the assembling of the senate the consul Scaevola refused the urgent request for the death of Tiberius, whereupon Publius Scipio Nasica, at the head of an aristocratic following armed with legs of benches and clubs, began the civil bloodshed. Tiberius was struck down on the slope of the capitol, and his body, with the corpses of three

THE GRACCHI

hundred adherents, was thrown into the Tiber. Such a day had never before been seen in Rome. The more moderate aristocrats had not only to acquiesce in, but even to defend, the deed of blood, as was the case with Publius Scaevola and even Scipio Aemilianus, and official sanction was given to the assertion that Gracchus had aimed at the crown.

It remains for us to form some judgment touching events so momentous. In the first place, the appointment of an official commission, though a sign of the unhealthy state of things, was a judicious and necessary step. In the second place the distribution of the domain lands was not in itself a question affecting the existing constitution or the government of the aristocracy; nor, seeing that the state was admitted to be the owner of the occupied land, was it a violation of rights. But, inasmuch as many of these lands had been in private hereditary possession for as long as three centuries, the state's proprietorship in the soil had virtually lost its character of private right and become extinct. Therefore, though legally defensible, the resumption of these lands by the state was regarded as an ejection of the great landholders for the benefit of the agricultural proletariate. Still, strong as the objections to such a course might be, the fact remains that no other plan seemed capable of checking the extinction of the farmer-class in Italy. But, whatever view wise men took of the aims of Tiberius Gracchus, none could approve of his method. He practically began a revolution with regard to the spirit of the constitution when he submitted his agrarian proposals to the people, and it was a revolution with regard to the letter, when he destroyed for all time the tribunician veto, by which the senate rid itself of interference with its government, by the unconstitutional deposition of his colleague. Yet even this was not the moral and political mistake of Gracchus; for a revolutionist may be at the same time a sagacious and praiseworthy statesman. The essential defects of the Gracchan revolution lay in the nature of the burgess assemblies at that time. The sovereign assembly of Rome was what it would be in England, if, instead of sending representatives, the electors of England were to meet together in Parliament. Not only was the assembly a chance conglomeration of men assembled in the capital, incapable of intelligent action and agitated by every interest and passion, and, therefore, as a rule, ready to accept and ratify the decree of the proposing magistrate, but it was also, in no small degree, under the influence of the opinion of the street. Although the contiones, or meetings of the street populace, had legally no power, and consisted of the lowest rabble, of Egyptians, Jews, street boys, and slaves, yet the opinion of the masses, evinced by the loud shouts of approval or disapproval, began to be a power in Rome. It was bad enough that the demoralized and disorganized comitia should be made use of for the elections and legislation; but when they were allowed to interfere with the government, and when the senate lost the instrument to prevent such interferences—when they could decree themselves lands, and when a single person by his influence with the proletariate could thus play the part of ruler and dictate to the senate—then Rome had reached the end of popular freedom and had arrived, not at democracy, but at monarchy. The very fact that Tiberius Gracchus never harbored the thought of deposing the senate and making himself sole ruler, but was the victim of events which irresistibly urged him into the career of demagogue tyrant, was only a fresh ground of charge against him rather than a justification. The infamous butchery which slew him condemns the aristocratic party, and has cast a halo of martyrdom round his name—a glory undeserved both in the opinion of his mother and of Scipio Aemilianus.

Though Tiberius was dead, his two works, the land distribution and the revolution, survived their author. Indeed, the moderate party in the senate, headed by Metellus and Scaevola, in combination with the adherents of Scipio, gained the upper hand, and the land commission, composed now of Gaius Gracchus, Marcus Flaccus, and Gaius Carbo, continued its work. The census furnishes the strongest evidence that the distribution of the domain lands went on very vigorously, an increase of 76,000 burgesses being noted in six years, from 131-125 B.C. But the commissioners, in their ardor, overreached themselves. They attacked that part of the lands which had been assigned by decrees to Italian communities, or which had been occupied with or without permission by Latin burgesses. The senate could not disregard the complaints of those communities who were already smarting under other wrongs, and the Latins appealed for protection to the most prominent man in Rome, Scipio Aemilianus. Through his influence the people in 129 B.C. decreed that the commissioners' jurisdiction should be suspended, and that the consuls should decide what were domain lands and what private property. Thus practically the land distribution ceased, and the reform party were bitterly indignant at Scipio's intervention. Shortly afterwards Scipio was found dead in his bed, murdered, no doubt, by some assassin, at the instigation of the Gracchan party. The matter was hushed up as far as possible, both parties in the state being glad to let it rest; but all men of moderate views were horrified at so atrocious a crime.

The revolution still went on under the leadership of the orator Carbo, Flaccus, and Gaius Gracchus. The chief object of the revolutionary party was to revive the allotment commission, and to this end they proposed to confer the rights of citizenship on the Italian allies. Marcus Pennus, tribune in 126 B.C., and member of the aristocratic party, carried his proposal that all non-burgesses should leave the city. Flaccus, consul in 125 B.C., made a counter-proposal that every ally should take the vote of the comitia on the subject of his request to be entitled to Roman citizenship. But Carbo had deserted the popular party and joined the aristocrats, and Gaius Gracchus was away as questor in Sardinia; so Flaccus's proposal found no support, and he left Rome to take command against the Celts. Still, his action bore fruit in the revolt of Fregellae, at that time the second city in Italy and the mouthpiece of the Latin colonies. This was the first instance, for one hundred and fifty years, of a serious insurrection in Italy against Rome, without the instigation of foreign powers. But before it spread Fregellae was surprised and seriously punished by the loss of its walls and all its privileges, in 124 B.C. The democratic party was regarded as implicated in the revolt of Fregellae, and Gaius Gracchus, who had returned from Sardinia, was tried, but acquitted. He now threw down the gauntlet, and by being elected tribune in 123 B.C. declared open war upon the aristocracy.

Gaius resembled his brother only in his dislike for vulgar pleasures and pursuits, in his culture and personal bravery. He was decidedly his superior in talent, character, and passion. His ability as a statesman was evinced in his clearness and self-possession, in his grasp of details and practical powers. His lovable nature was proved by the devotion of his intimate friends. Disciplined by suffering, he masked the terrible energy of his nature and the bitter indignation he felt against the aristocracy by a compulsory reserve. At times, indeed, his passion mastered him, and caused his brilliant oratory to become confused and faltering; but he was one of the greatest speakers Rome ever saw. He had none of the sentimental good-nature of his brother; fully and firmly resolved, he entered on the career of revolution with vengeance as his goal and aim. To attain this end he counted not too great the price of his own fall and the ruin of the state. His mother's creed, that the country should at all cost be saved, was nobler, but posterity has been right in rather lamenting than blaming the course taken by her son.

The proposals now made by Gracchus were nothing less than a new constitution, the foundation-stone of which rested upon the legal right of the same man to be elected tribune for two or more years in succession. This having been carried, the next object was to attach the multitude of the capital to the holder of the tribunate. This was first of all effected by distributions of corn. Gaius enacted that every burgess, on personal application, should receive a monthly allowance of $1\frac{1}{4}$ bushels at the extremely low rate of 24 cents a bushel. This measure would both attract into the capital the whole mass of the burgess proletariate, and would make them dependent on the tribune, and supply him with a bodyguard and a firm majority in the comitia. Though thus securing his position in Rome, he did not neglect to legislate for the existing social evils. His agrarian law only revived that of his brother, and he did not proceed any further in the distribution of domain land. But by establishing colonies at Tarentum and Capua, he rendered that land, which had been let on lease by the state and had been exempt from distribution, liable to be divided; and no doubt he intended these colonies to aid in defending the revolution to which they owed their existence. He also opened a new outlet for the Italian proletariate by sending six thousand colonists chosen from Italian allies as well as from Roman citizens—to the site of Carthage. Further, Gracchus attempted to restrict capital punishment as far as possible, by withdrawing the cognizance of such crimes as poisoning and murder from the popular assemblies and intrusting it to permanent judicial commissions. These tribunals could only sentence a man to exile, and their sentence could not be appealed from, nor could they, like the tribunals of the people, be broken up by the intercession of a tribune.

In order to work the ruin of the aristocracy, Gracchus took advantage of the already existing elements favorable to a rupture in that body. The aristocracy of the rich consisted of two classes, the governing senatorial families whose capital was invested in land, and the wealthy merchants and speculators, who conducted all the money transactions of the empire, and who had gradually risen to take their place by the side of the older aristocracy. At the present time the latter class was generally known as the equestrian order, which title had gradually come to be used of all who possessed an estate of at least twenty thousand dollars, and as such were liable to cavalry service. Already senators had been marked off from this body by a law passed in 129 B.C., but many members of senatorial families, not yet members of the senate, were included in the equites. The natural antipathy between the aristocrats of blood and those of wealth was adroitly increased by Gracchus, until the equestrian order ranged itself on his side. Partly by conferring on them various insignia, but still more by offering them the revenues of Asia and the jury courts, Gracchus won over the class of material interests. Hitherto the direct taxes of each province had been farmed by the provincials themselves, and thus the Roman publicani had been kept at a distance. Gracchus now enacted that Asia should be burdened with the heaviest taxes, both direct and indirect, and that these taxes should be put up for auction in Rome; he thus excluded the provincials from participation, and gave the capitalists an opening for the farming of these various taxes, of which they did not fail to avail themselves.

Having thus opened up a gold mine for the merchant princes, Gracchus gave them a sphere for public action in the jury courts. Most processes, alike civil and criminal, were up to this time decided by single jurymen or by commissioners, whether permanent or extraordinary, and in both cases the members had been exclusively taken from the senate. Gracchus now transferred the functions of jurymen, both in strictly civil processes and in the various commissions, to the equestrian order, and directed a new list of judices to be made out annually from all persons of equestrian rating. The result of these measures was that not only was the moneyed class united into a compact and privileged order on the solid basis of material interests, but that also, as a judicial and controlling power, it was almost on a footing of equality with the ruling aristocracy. All the old antipathies found expression in the sentences of the new jurymen, and the senator, on his return from governing a province, had no longer to pass the scrutiny of his brother peers, but of merchants and bankers.

For the complete overthrow of the senate, Gracchus not only

had to deprive it of the substance of its powers by legislative changes, but also to ruin the existing aristocracy by more personal and less permanent measures. He did both. For not only did he deprive the senate of administrative power by settling questions by comitial laws, dictated as a rule by the tribune, but also by taking the business of the state into his own hands. He had meddled with the state finances by his distributions of corn; with the domain lands by sending out colonies, not at the decree of the senate, but of the people; with the provincial administration by overturning the provincial constitution of Asia and substituting his own for that of the senate. The marvelous activity Gracchus showed in all his new functions quite threw into the shade the lax administration of the senate, and began to make it clear to the people that one vigorous man could control the business of the state better than a college of effete aristocrats. Still more vigorous was his interference with the jurisdiction of the senate. He forbade their appointing any extraordinary commission of high treason, such as had tried his brother's adherents, and he even planned to reinforce the senate by three hundred new members, to be elected by the comitia from the equestrian order.

Such was the political constitution projected and carried by Gaius Gracchus, as tribune, in 123 and 122 B.C., without any serious resistance or recourse to force. It is clear that he did not wish to place the Roman Republic on a new democratic basis, but that he wished to abolish it and introduce in its stead an absolute despotism, in the form of an unlimited tribuneship for life. Nor can he be blamed for it; as, though an absolute monarchy is a great misfortune for a nation, it is a less misfortune than an absolute oligarchy. Besides this, he was fired with the passion for a speedy vengeance, and was in fact a political incendiary,—the author not only of the one hundred years' revolution, which dates from him, but the founder of that terrible urban proletariate which, utterly demoralized by corn largesses and the flattery of the classes above it, and at the same time conscious of its power, lay like an incubus for five hundred years on the Roman commonwealth, and only perished with it.

Many of the fundamental maxims of Roman monarchy may be traced to Gracchus. He first laid down that all the land of subject communities was to be regarded as the private property of the state—a maxim first applied to vindicate the right of the state to

THE GRACCHI

tax the land and then to send out colonies to it, which later became a fundamental principle of law under the empire. He invented the tactics by which his successors broke down the governing aristocracy, and substituted strict and judicious administration for the previous misgovernment. He first opened the way to a reconciliation between Rome and the provinces, and his attempt to rebuild Carthage and to give an opportunity for Italian emigration to the provinces was the first link in the chain of that beneficial course of action. Right and wrong, fortune and misfortune, were so inextricably blended in this singular man and in this marvelous political constellation, that it may well beseem history in this case— though it beseems her but seldom—to reserve her judgment.

Having thus established his new constitution, Gracchus turned to the task of enfranchising the Italian allies, which had been proposed and rejected in 125 B.C. But a considerable section of the mob, thinking that their own interests would be seriously injured by a new influx of men to share the profits they were enjoying, combined with the senate in rejecting the proposal, made by Gracchus in 122 B. C., that the Latins should receive the full franchise. This encouraged the senate to work his ruin. Another tribune, Marcus Livius Drusus, was put forward to outbid him for the popular favor by offering the proletariate more than he had done. Those who had received land under the Gracchan laws were to be freed from their rent, and twelve new Italian colonies were to be founded. Gracchus was away at the time in Africa, founding the Carthaginian colony, and the incapacity of his lieutenant, Marcus Flaccus, made all easy for his opponents. The people ratified the Livian laws as readily as they had the Sempronian, and then declined to reëlect Gracchus, when he stood for the third time for office. On December 10, 122 B.C., therefore, he ceased to be tribune and so lay exposed to the vengeance of the enemies he had made.

The first attack was directed against the most unpopular measure of Gracchus, the restoration of Carthage. National superstition was invoked, and the senate proposed a law to prevent the planting of the colony. Gracchus, attended by an armed crowd of partisans, appeared on the day of voting at the Capitol, to procure the rejection of the law. The sight of his armed adherents, and the intense excitement which prevailed, could hardly have failed to result in a collision between the two sides. A tumult broke out, in which a lictor attending the consul was killed, but a heavy rain dispersed the people for the time. Next day the consul, Lucius Opimius, a personal enemy of Gracchus, took vigorous measures to put down the insurrection, and the Gracchan party, under the command of Flaccus, took refuge on the Aventine, where they entrenched themselves. Gracchus was averse to resistance, but Flaccus hoped to come to a compromise with his foes. The aristocrats rejected all his proposals, and ordered an attack on the Aventine. The defenders of the mount were speedily dispersed, and Flaccus was killed after vainly seeking concealment. Gracchus was persuaded to fly, but sprained his foot in the attempt. The devotion of two of his attendants, who sacrificed their lives to give him time to escape, enabled him and his slave to cross the Tiber. Here, in a grove, both he and his slave were found dead. The Gracchan party was hunted down by prosecutions, and three thousand are said to have been strangled in prison. The memory of the Gracchi was officially proscribed, and Cornelia was forbidden to put on mourning for the death of her son; but, despite the precautions of the police, the common people continued to pay a religious veneration to the spots where the two leaders of the revolution had perished.

Chapter XIX

THE RULE OF THE RESTORATION. 121-101 B.C.

GRACCHUS had fallen, and with him the structure he had reared; nor was there anyone left fit to take the lead of the Gracchan party. But, though the aristocracy once more ruled, it was the rule of a restoration, which is always in itself a revolution; and in this case it was not so much the old government as the old governor that was restored. The senate practically continued to govern with the constitution of the Gracchi, though no doubt resolved to purge it in due time from the elements hostile to its own order. The distributions of grain, the taxation of Asia, and the new arrangements as to jurymen and tribunals remained as before; nay, the senate exceeded Gracchus in the homage it paid to the mercantile class, and, more especially, to the proletariate. But the noble scheme of Gracchus to introduce legal equality, first between the Roman burgesses and Italy, and then between Italy and the provinces, and also his attempt to solve the social question by a comprehensive system of emigration, were alike disregarded by the aristocrats. They still held fast to the principle that Italy ought to remain the ruling land, and Rome the ruling city in Italy. The colony of Narbo, founded in 118 B.C., was the sole exception to the success of the government in preventing assignations of land outside Italy. So also the Italian colonies of Gracchus were canceled, and, where already planted, were again broken up; those who had received domain lands, not by virtue of being members of a colony, retained their possessions. With regard to those domain lands, which were still held by the right of occupation, and from which to a great extent the thirty-six thousand new allotments promised by Drusus were to have been formed, it was resolved to maintain the rights of the present occupiers, so as to preclude the possibility of future distribution.

The allotment commission was abolished in 119 B.C., and a fixed rent imposed on the occupants of the domain land, the proceeds of which went to benefit the populace of the capital.

The final step was taken in 111 B.C., when the occupied domain land was converted into the rent-free private property of the former occupants. It was added that in future domain land was not to be occupied at all, but was either to be leased or lie open as public pasture; thus too late the injurious character of the occupation system was officially recognized, when the state had lost almost all its domain lands. The aristocracy thus converted all the occupied lands they still held into private property, and pacified the Italian allies by preserving their rights with regard to the Latin domain land, though they did not actually confer it upon them.

But practically the restored government was powerless in the presence of the dread forces evoked by Gracchus. The proletariate of the capital continued to have a recognized claim to being kept by largesses of corn; and the attempt by the consul Quintus Caepio in 106 B.C., to transfer the courts back again to the senatorial order, resulted in failure. The miserable condition of the senate at this period is only too apparent: its rule rested on the same basis as that of Gracchus, and its strength lay only in its league with the city rabble or with the mercantile order; confronted with either, it was powerless. It sat on the vacated throne with an evil conscience and divided hopes, indignant at the institutions of the state which it ruled, and yet incapable of even systematically assailing them, vacillating in all its conduct except where its own material advantage prompted decision, a picture of faithlessness towards its own as well as the opposite party, of inward inconsistency, of the most pitiful impotence, of the meanest selfishness—an unsurpassed ideal of misrule. Moral and intellectual decay had fallen upon the whole nation, and especially on the upper classes. The aristocracy returned to power with the curse of restoration upon it, and it returned neither wiser nor better. Incompetency marked alike its leaders in the world of politics and on the field of battle. Social ruin spread apace; small farm-holders quickly disappeared; and in 100 B.C. it was said that among the whole burgesses there were scarce two thousand wealthy families. Slave insurrections became almost annual in Italy, the most serious of which was in the territory of Thurii, headed by a Roman knight named Titus Vettius, whom his debts had driven to take this step in 104 B.C. Piracy was practiced in the Mediterranean by the magisterial and mercantile classes of Rome as well as by professional freebooters. At last the government was forced to dispatch a fleet, in 102 B.C., and occupy stations on the coast of Cilicia, the main seat of the pirates, and this was the first step to the establishment of the province of Cilicia; but piracy flourished in spite of these precautions.

Throughout the provinces slaves constantly rose in insurrection; and the most terrible tumults occurred, as usual, in Sicily, which swarmed with slaves brought from Asia Minor to work on the plantations. Practically, too, the free natives were little better than slaves, and many had become enrolled as such. Publius Nerva, the governor of Sicily, in 104 B.C. was ordered by the senate to hold a court at Syracuse, and to investigate the cases of those who applied for freedom. Numbers were declared free, and, in alarm, the planters succeeded in causing Nerva to suspend the court and to order the rest of the applicants to return to their former masters. This set ablaze the smoldering embers of revolt. A band of slaves defeated part of the garrison at Enna, and thus supplied themselves with arms; they placed a slave at their head with the title of King Tryphon. The open country between Enna and Leontini was overrun by their forces, and they defeated a hastily-collected force of militia under the Roman governor with ridiculous ease.

On the west coast a still more serious revolt arose under the leadership of Athenion, who had been a robber captain in Cilicia, and was alike versed in military tactics and in the superstitious arts so necessary for gaining a hold on vulgar minds. He avoided jealous quarrels by submitting to King Tryphon, and the two ruled all the flat country in Sicily and laid siege to many towns, Messana itself being all but captured by Athenion. Rome was at that time engaged with the war against the Cimbri, but in 103 B.C. it sent a large force under Lucullus, who gained a victory, but did not follow it up. Nor was his successor Servilius any more fortunate; and, on the death of Tryphon, Athenion, in 102 B.C., stood sole ruler of the greater part of the island. In 101 B.C. Manius Aquillius, who had gained distinction in the war with the Teutones, arrived, and, after two years of hard struggles, quelled the revolt and killed Athenion, thus terminating the war after five years.

A clear proof of the gross incompetency of the senate is furnished by the origin and conduct of this second Sicilian slave war. If we turn our eyes to Africa, this is still more clearly proved by the fourteen years' insurrection and usurpation successfully achieved by Jugurtha. Numidia included the greatest portion of the territory held by Carthage in its days of prosperity, as well as several old Phoenician cities, and thus embraced the largest and the best part of the rich seaboard of northern Africa. This kingdom was now ruled over by Adherbal, grandson of Massinissa, and his illegitimate cousin, Jugurtha, who had secured the assassination of another heir, and was constantly intriguing against Adherbal. Civil war arose between the two in 118 B.C., in which all Numidia took part. Jugurtha was victorious, and seized the whole kingdom, while Adherbal escaped and made his complaints in person at Rome. Jugurtha's envoys, however, bribed the senators, and, notwithstanding the disgust of the leading men in Rome, the senate divided the kingdom equally between the two, and sent Lucius Opimius to arrange the division. An unfair distribution gave Jugurtha far the best half of the kingdom. But, not content, he tried to provoke Adherbal to war, and, finding this impossible, made war upon him, and laid siege to Cirta, which was defended more vigorously by the resident Italians than by Adherbal's troops. In answer to the latter's complaints, the senate sent a commission of inexperienced youths, whose demands Jugurtha contemptuously rejected. At last, when matters were getting desperate at Cirta, Rome sent another commission, headed by the chief man of the aristocracy, Marcus Aemilius Scaurus; but the conference at Utica ended without any result. In the end, Cirta capitulated, and Jugurtha put all the males, whether Italian or African, to the sword, in 112 B.C. This was too much for the people in Italy; a storm broke out against the government, headed by Gaius Memmius, tribune designate for the next year, and war was declared against Jugurtha. A Roman army was sent to Africa, and Bocchus, the father-in-law of Jugurtha and king of Mauretania, took the Roman side, but he neglected to bribe the Roman commanders, and so his alliance fell through. Jugurtha, on the other hand, more wisely made free use of the treasures left by Massinissa, and gained a peace on most favorable terms, being merely condemned to pay a moderate fine and give up his war elephants. On this the storm again broke out in Rome; all men now knew that even Scaurus, who was serving in Africa, was amenable to bribes, and Gaius Memmius pressed for the appearance of Jugurtha to answer the charges made against him. The senate yielded, and granted a safe conduct to Jugurtha; but his gold was as powerful as ever, and the colleague of Memmius interposed his veto, when the latter addressed his first question to the king. Endless discussions took place in the senate as to the validity of the peace, and Massiva, a grandson of Massinissa, living in Rome, was induced to claim the throne of Numidia. He was at once assassinated by Bomilcar, one of Jugurtha's confidants. This new outrage caused the senate to cancel the peace and dismiss Jugurtha from the city, at the beginning of 110 B.C. War was resumed under the command of the consul Spurius Albinus; but, owing to the utterly demoralized state of the African army, and, possibly, to the gold of Jugurtha, Albinus could effect nothing. His brother, however, in 109 B.C., rashly conceived the plan of storming the town of Suthul, where Jugurtha kept his treasures. The attack failed, and the Roman general pursued the troops of Jugurtha, who purposely decoyed him into the desert. In a night attack the Roman army was utterly routed, and the terms dictated by Jugurtha were accepted, which involved the passing of the Romans under the yoke, the evacuation of Numidia, and the renewal of the canceled peace.

On news of this peace the fury of the popular party, allied for the time with the mercantile classes at Rome, swept away by public prosecutions many of the highest aristocrats. The second treaty of peace was canceled, and Quintus Metellus, an aristocrat inaccessible to bribes and experienced in war, had the conduct of the campaign in Africa. Gaius Marius accompanied him as one of his lieutenants.

Metellus speedily reorganized the army in Africa, and in 108 B.C. led it over the Numidian frontier. He returned an evasive answer to Jugurtha's proposals for peace, and tried to end the war by having Jugurtha assassinated. Failing in this, he destroyed the Numidian army in battle and occupied most of the country, but his object was not gained, and the Roman army had to retire into winter quarters. The capture of Jugurtha was all-important to the speedy conclusion of the war. Vaga, one of the Numidian cities occupied by the Romans, revolted early in 107 B.C., and put to death the whole Roman garrison; and, although Metellus surprised the town and gave it over to martial law, such a revolt sufficiently indicated the difficulty of the Roman enterprise.

In 107 B.C. the war in the desert went on, but Jugurtha nowhere withstood the Romans; now here, now there, he was perpetually appearing and then vanishing from the scene. Metellus took Thala, a city situated on the edge of the great desert and only to be reached with great difficulty, where Jugurtha had placed his treasures, children, and the flower of his troops. But Jugurtha escaped with his chest, and, though Numidia was virtually in the hands of the Romans, the war only seemed to extend over a wider area.

Metellus had now to resign the command to his lieutenant, Marius. The latter had gained his consulship, in spite of the sneers of Metellus and the whole aristocratic party, by appealing to the credulity of the Roman mob and by misleading them with the most unfair and absurd misrepresentations of the conduct by Metellus of the African war. He succeeded to the command in 106 B.C. In spite of his boast that he would deliver Jugurtha bound hand and foot, he seemed to abandon all hope of his capture, and turned his attention to storming towns and strongholds, though without accomplishing many results. Most of the glory of the war fell to his lieutenant, Sulla, who manifested his bravery and adroitness conspicuously in the negotiations between Marius and Bocchus, and at last induced the latter, with whom Jugurtha had taken refuge, to surrender his son-in-law to the Romans. By an act of treachery Jugurtha was given up to Sulla, and thus the war which had lasted for seven years came to an end. Jugurtha was brought to Rome on January 1, 104 B.C., and perished in the old tullianum in the Capitol, which the Numidian king grimly termed the bath of ice.

There can be little doubt that Marius cuts but a sorry figure, when contrasted with either his predecessor, Metellus, or his still more brilliant officer, Sulla. The fatal consequences produced by the praise lavished on both these men at the expense of Marius bore bitter fruit in succeeding history.

Contrary to the usual policy, Numidia was not converted into a province, probably because a standing army would have been necessary to protect its frontier. The most westerly district was annexed to the kingdom of Bocchus, and the kingdom of Numidia was handed over to the last surviving grandson of Massinissa, a man feeble alike in mind and body. But politically the results of the Jugurthine war were more important. It had made clear to all, not only the utter baseness and venality of the restored senatorial government, but also the complete nullity of the opposition.

It was not possible to govern worse than the restoration governed from 117 to 109 B.C.; it was not possible to be more defenseless and forlorn than was the senate in 109 B.C.; had there been in Rome a real opposition, that is to say, a party which wished and urged a fundamental alteration of the constitution, it must at least have made an attempt to overturn the restored senate; but no such attempt took place. The so-called popular party, as such, neither could nor would govern, and the only two possible forms of government were a despotism or an oligarchy. The appearance of Marius on the scene indicated clearly the danger which threatened the oligarchy. Probably he was unaware of the real significance of his action when he canvassed the people for the supreme command in Africa; but there was evidently an end of the restored aristocratic government when the comitia began to make generals, or when every popular officer could legally nominate himself as general. As might be expected, the new element introduced into politics was the part played by military men. It could now be foreseen that the new despot would not be a statesman like Gaius Gracchus, but a soldier like Gaius Marius. The contemporary reorganization of the military system—which Marius introduced when, in forming his army destined for Africa, he disregarded the property qualification and allowed even the poorest burgess to enter the legion as a volunteer —may have been projected by its author on purely military grounds; but it was none the less a momentous political event, that the army was no longer, as formerly, composed of those who had much, no longer even, as in the most recent times, composed of those who had something, to lose, but became gradually converted into a host of people who had nothing but their arms and what the generals bestowed on them. The aristocracy ruled in 104 B.C. as absolutely as in 134 B.C.; but the signs of the impending catastrophe had multiplied, and on the political horizon the sword had begun to appear by the side of the crown.

Let us now for awhile turn our attention outside Rome and its political crisis, and consider what was taking place to the north of Italy. Behind the mighty mountain screen nations were moving uneasily to and fro, and reminding the Graeco-Roman world that it was not the sole possessor of the earth. In the country between the Alps and Pyrenees Rome found her chief mainstay in the powerful city of Massilia, whose mercantile and political connections extended in all directions. In that region the Romans now proceeded to attack the various Ligurian and Celtic tribes, and after a series of campaigns succeeded in bringing them into subjection. The result of these wars was the creation of the province of Narbo, between the Alps and the Pyrenees, Narbo being the seat of the governor of this province, in which several Roman settlements were formed at Aquae Sextiae and elsewhere. The policy which gave rise to this new field for colonization was checked by the death of Gaius Gracchus, but the mercantile class at Rome proved strong enough to protect the colony of Narbo from the narrower policy of the restored optimates.

A similar problem had to be solved in the northeast of Italy, but there Rome contented herself with taking the strong town of Delmium, and subduing the Dalmatians, in 155 B.C. The conversion of Macedonia into a province in 146 B.C., and the acquisition of the Thracian Chersonese in 133 B.C., brought Rome into close relations with the various tribes of the northeast, but also gave her the double basis of the Po valley and the province of Macedonia, from which she could now advance in earnest towards the Rhine and Danube. Of the various Celtic tribes in these regions, the Helvetii, who occupied both banks of the Upper Rhine, were the most powerful; near them were the Boii, settled in Bavaria and Bohemia. To the southeast came the Taurisci, next to whom were the Iapydes, partly Illyrian, partly Celtic; while in the interior the powerful and cruel Celtic tribe of the Scordisci roamed hither and thither, leaving a path marked by crime and bloodshed.

Although Roman expeditions against Alpine tribes were frequent, no adequate scheme of conquest was attempted, so as to create a barrier strong enough to ward off the constant inroads of barbarism. Marcus Aemilius Scaurus was the first to cross the eastern Alps, in 115 B.C., and to compel the Taurisci to a friendly alliance with Rome; the first Roman general to reach the Danube was Marcus Livius Drusus, in 112 B.C.; and, two years later, Marcus Minucius utterly defeated the Scordisci and reduced them to harmless insignificance.

But these victories only brought upon the scene a still more terrible foe in the Cimbri, or "champions." Whence this people really came and the causes of their migration are matters of which we cannot be certain. That they were in the main of German race, as were their brothers-in-arms, the Teutones, is shown by the existence of two small tribes of the same name, left behind, probably, in their primitive seats—the Cimbri in Denmark and the Teutones in the northeast of Germany, near the Baltic; and by the judgment of Caesar, who first showed the difference between Celts and Germans, and who includes the Cimbri among the Germans. This classification is further borne out by their names and the account given of their physical appearance and habits.

No doubt a number of Celts joined these hordes, and thus men of Celtic name directed their armies, and the Celtic tongue was spoken among them. The invasion was not one of mere plunder, but that of a whole nation seeking a new home, with their wives and children drawn along in wagons, which served as houses and means of locomotion. Their army was accompanied by priestesses —a truly Germanic custom. They came like lightning, like lightning they vanished; and in that dull age no observer traced this marvelous meteor. Thus the first Germanic movement that came in contact with civilization passed away unnoticed till it was too late to have any accurate knowledge of it. Owing to Roman attacks on the Danubian Celts, the Cimbri broke through the barrier which had prevented their advance, and reached the passes of the Carnian Alps in 113 B.C., where the consul Gnaeus Papirius Carbo was posted to meet them, not far from Aquileia. He ordered them to evacuate the territory of the Taurisci, and they complied and followed his guides into an ambush. But the betrayed utterly worsted the betrayer, and then they turned westward and reached the west bank of the Rhine and passed over the Jura. There, some years after the defeat of Carbo, they again threatened Roman territory. In 109 B.C. Marcus Junius Silanus appeared with an army in southern Gaul, and replied to the Cimbrian request for land to settle in by an attack; he was completely defeated.

The Cimbri now occupied themselves with subduing the neighboring Celtic cantons, and for a time left the Romans unmolested. But, fired by the example of the Cimbri, the Helvetii rose, under their leader Divico, and sought new and more fertile settlements in western Gaul. The consul Longinus, with most of his army, was decoyed by the Helvetii into an ambush, and fell fighting, in 107 B.C. Then for a time all was quiet, but in 105 B.C., under their king Boiorix, the Cimbri again moved onward, this time with the serious purpose of invading Italy.

Their first assault fell on Marcus Aurelius Scaurus, whose corps was easily overthrown. Then, owing to the foolish discord between the two Roman commanders, Gnaeus Maximus and the proconsul Caepio, and through the rash haste of the latter, the battle of Arausio (Orange), on the left bank of the Rhone, took place. Both Roman armies were utterly annihilated. Such a calamity materially and morally far surpassed the day of Cannae. Allia and the burning of Rome recurred to men's minds, and every Italian capable of bearing arms was bound by oath not to leave Italy. But, happily for Rome, the Cimbri turned upon the Arverni, and then set out to the Pyrenees.

As after the African defeats, so now, the storm of popular indignation at Rome fell upon individuals, not on the rotten system of senatorial government. Quintus Caepio barely escaped with his life. Gaius Marius was now, in defiance of the law, nominated as consul, and given the chief command not merely for one year, but was reinvested with the consulship for five years in succession, from 104 to 100 B.C. The traces of this unconstitutional step remained visible for all time.

Owing to the disappearance of the Cimbri from the stage, Marius had time to reduce revolted tribes and to reassure the wavering. At last the wave of invasion, having broken itself on the resistance of the brave Celtiberians, flowed back over the Pyrenees. Near Rouen the Cimbri received reinforcements from the Helvetii, and were also joined by their kinsmen, the Teutones, and now resolved to invade Italy. But for some reason they broke up again into two hosts, one of which, the Cimbri, was to recross the Rhine and invade Italy by way of the Rhaetian Alps, while the other, the Teutones, together with some of the bravest Cimbrian troops, was to descend into Italy by way of Roman Gaul and the western passes of the Alps.

In 102 B.C. the latter host attacked the camp of Marius at the confluence of the Isère and Rhone, for three days, but in vain; they then marched onward to Italy, occupying six days in defiling past the Roman camp. Marius followed them to the district of Aquae Sextiae, and defeated the rear guard. On the third day after this success Marius drew up his army on a hill; the barbarians rushed up with hot impatience. For a long while the struggle was terrible, but, owing to the heat of the sun and a false alarm raised in the rear by Roman camp boys, the barbarian ranks broke and were utterly cut to pieces.

The Cimbri, meanwhile, owing to a panic which seized the army of the consul Quintus Lutatius Catulus, had passed the Alps and reached the plain between the Po and the Alps in the summer of 102 B.C., when their brethren were annihilated at Aquae Sextiae. Fortunately for Rome, they remained in this rich land for the winter, and thus gave the Romans time to prepare for the coming struggle. Marius, having refused a triumph for his first victory, returned in the spring and crossed the Po with his army. On the invitation of the Cimbri he named the Raudine plain as the place for battle. There, in a dense morning mist, the Celtic cavalry of the barbarians was driven back on to the infantry; and thus taken by surprise and thrown into disorder, the whole Cimbrian host fell an easy victim. Thus the battle of Vercellae, in 101 B.C., ended the dreaded invasion of these Germanic peoples. Marius was justly regarded as the conqueror of the Cimbri, although Catulus, a polished art-critic and member of the aristocracy, had overthrown the center of the Cimbrian hosts and captured thirty-one standards, while Marius took but two. But the victory of Vercellae was only rendered possible by that of Aquae Sextiae. With the victories of Marius were associated hopes of the overthrow of the detested government. Could it be that the rough farmer of Arpinum was destined to be the avenger of Gracchus, and to continue the revolution which he had begun?

Chapter XX

MARIUS AS REVOLUTIONIST AND DRUSUS AS REFORMER. 100-91 B. C.

SUCH were the fears and hopes that moved the people in the capital on the news of the final overthrow of the Germanic invaders. These hopes were raised afresh when the saviour of Rome himself returned, late in 101 B.C., by far the first man in Rome, and yet a mere tyro in politics. Born in 155 B. C., Gaius Marius had, as a poor day-laborer's son, schooled his frame to bear hunger and thirst, cold and heat. His early training had fitted him to rise rapidly from the ranks and to gain distinction, first as a mere soldier, and then as governor of Further Spain. His subsequent military career in Africa and Gaul has been already described. Success in speculation had given him wealth, and a union with a daughter of the ancient Julian gens had given him powerful connections. But he never rid himself of the taint of his plebeian origin. No one was ever so popular with the masses, either before or after, both on account of his thorough honesty and disinterestedness, and of his boorish uncouthness.

The time had now come to test the power of the rustic soldier to realize the expectations of the people, and to justify the extravagant joy manifested at his return. The newly organized army might prove a formidable weapon in his hand, though the day was hardly yet come for the sword to achieve what it afterwards did in the world of politics. His military revolution was as follows: Before his time the old Servian constitution had undergone considerable relaxation; and the minimum census, which bound a man to serve in the army, had been lowered from $215 to $85. The cavalry was still drawn from the wealthiest and the light-armed troops from the poorest citizens, but the arrangement of the infantry of the line in the three divisions of hastati, principes, and triarii was no longer determined by property, but by duration of service. Moreover, the Italian allies had long taken part in the military service. Still, the primitive organization was in the main the basis of the Roman military system, and it was no longer suited to the altered circumstances of the state. The better classes held aloof more and more from service, and the middle class of both Romans and Italians was fast disappearing; while the allies and subjects outside Italy, as well as the Italian proletariate, were available to fill up the gaps thus caused. The cavalry formed of the wealthiest burgesses had acted as a guard of honor in the Jugurthine war, and thenceforth it ceases to appear. In ordinary circumstances it was a very difficult task to fill up the legions with properly qualified persons; in times of emergency, as after the battle of Arausio, it was impossible. Already the cavalry, as a rule, came from Thrace and Africa, while the light Ligurian infantry and Balearic slingers were employed in daily increasing numbers. Moreover, owing to the dearth of properly qualified citizens, non-qualified and poorer men pressed into the service, nor could it be hard to find plenty of volunteers for so lucrative a profession. Thus it was a necessary result of the social and political changes that the old system of the burgess levy should give place to that of contingents and enlistments, that the cavalry and light troops should mainly consist of subject contingents, and that every free-born citizen should be admitted to the line service, as was, in fact, first allowed by Marius in 107 B.C.

Marius also abolished all the old aristocratic distinctions, whether of definite rank and place or of standards and equipments, which had hitherto obtained among the four divisions of the army. All were uniformly trained under the new method of drill devised by Publius Rufus, consul in 105 B.C., and borrowed from the gladiatorial schools; and thus the infantry of the line were reduced to a common level. The thirty maniples, or companies, of the legion were now replaced by ten cohorts, each cohort having its own standard and being formed of six or five sections of one hundred men apiece. The light infantry were suppressed, but the numbers of the legion were raised from 4200 to 6000 men. Although the custom of fighting in three divisions was retained, yet the general could distribute his cohorts in the three lines as he thought fit. The old four standards of the wolf, the ox with a man's head, the horse, the boar, gave place to the new standard of the silver eagle, given by Marius to the legion as a whole. Thus all the old civic and aristocratic distinctions were abolished, and all future distinctions were purely military. The pretorian cohort, or bodyguard of the general, owed its existence to a pure accident. In the Numantine

war Scipio Aemilianus had been obliged, owing to the insufficiency
and unruly nature of the soldiers with which he was supplied, to
form out of volunteers a band of five hundred men, into which he
afterwards admitted his ablest soldiers. This cohort had the duty
of serving at the pretorium, or headquarters, and was exempt from
encamping and entrenching service, and enjoyed higher pay and
greater prestige.

This revolution in the military system probably saved the state,
in a military point of view, from destruction, but it involved a complete political revolution, the effects of which time alone could
develop. The republican constitution was essentially based on the
view that the citizen was also a soldier, and that the soldier was,
above all, a citizen; it was at an end so soon as a soldier class was
formed. Under the new system of drill, the military service became
gradually a profession. The admission, though at first restricted,
of the proletariate to the service speedily took effect, the more so as
the general had a right to reward the successful soldier and give
him a share in the spoil. To the burgess in old times the service
had always been a burden and duty, but little alleviated by the
rewards it might give him. To the proletarian this was far from
the case. All his hopes, both of pay, rewards, and citizenship, lay
in his success in war and in his general; thus the camp became his
only home and hope. Marius defended his action in giving Roman
citizenship to two Italian cohorts on the Raudine plain, by saying
that amid the din of battle he could not distinguish the voice of the
laws. So, if once the interest of the general and army concurred
in producing unconstitutional demands, it was unlikely that any law
would be of much avail amid the clashing of arms.

They had now the standing army, the soldier class, the bodyguard; as in the civil constitution, so also in the military, all the
pillars of the future monarchy were already in existence; the monarch alone was wanting. When the twelve eagles circled round the
Palatine hill, they ushered in the kings; the new eagle which Gaius
Marius bestowed on the legions proclaimed the advent of the
emperors.

Marius, in the eyes of the populace, who still mourned the
death of Gaius Gracchus, was the one man capable alike from his
military and political position of averting the ruin of the state,
and of substituting in the place of the effete oligarchy a new and
vigorous administration. It remains for us to see how he realized

the expectations so confidently formed of him. Two methods of operation were apparently open to him: one, to overthrow the oligarchy by means of the army; the other, to follow the example of Gracchus and effect his object in a constitutional manner. The first plan, perhaps, he never entertained, relying on his immense popularity and on the support of his discharged soldiers, but still more on the weakness of his opponents, whose downfall he probably thought could be more easily compassed than proved to be the case. Moreover, the army was still in a state of transition, and as yet ill adapted for effecting a *coup d'état,* and at the beginning of this crisis the use of such an instrument might well have recoiled upon the user. Having therefore discharged his army, Marius depended for further action upon the leaders of the popular party, which now once more sprang into active existence. This party had much deteriorated during the interval between Gaius Gracchus and Marius; much of the enthusiasm, faith, and purity of aim had been rubbed off in the years of confusion and turmoil; and the popular leaders were, for the most part, either political novices, or men who had nothing to lose in respect of property, influence, or even honor, and who, from personal motives of malice or a wish to attract notice, busied themselves with inflicting annoyance and damage on the government. To the first class belonged Gaius Memmius and the noted orator, Lucius Crassus; to the second, and these were the most notable leaders, belonged Gaius Glaucia, the Roman Hyperbolus, as Cicero called him, and his better and abler colleague, Lucius Appuleius Saturninus. The latter, owing to a personal slight at the senate's hands, had joined the ranks of the opposition. As tribune of the people in 103 B.C. he excited a popular indignation by his public speeches touching the briberies practiced in Rome by the envoys of Mithradates, and also by his invectives against Quintus Metellus, when he was a candidate for the censorship in 102 B.C. Moreover, he had carried the election of Marius as consul for 102 B.C. in the teeth of a fierce opposition. His violence and unscrupulousness marred his very considerable powers both as a politician and orator, but he was the most prominent and dreaded enemy of the senate. He and Glaucia now entered into partnership with Marius, and it was agreed that the latter should become a candidate for his sixth consulship, Saturninus for a second tribunate, and Glaucia for the pretorship, for the year 100 B.C., in order to carry out the intended revolution.

Despite all the opposition of the senate, they succeeded in effecting their object—partly by craft, partly by violence. The laws of Saturninus, known as the Appuleian, revived the chief objects of Gaius Gracchus. Marius was called upon to conduct the assignations of land which had been promised his soldiers, firstly in Africa, and then in all provincial land, and even in that beyond the Alps, which was still occupied by independent Celtic tribes. As the Italian allies were to receive these assignations together with Roman burgesses, this was practically a first step to placing them on an equality with Romans; and thus not only the extensive schemes of transalpine and transmarine colonization, as sketched by Gaius Gracchus, were revived, but also his project of gradually giving first the Italians and then all Roman subjects the same political privileges. For this work of land distribution it was, doubtless, necessary that Marius should have his consulship annually renewed, and thus practically be king of Rome. The main difference between his case and that of Gracchus was that he occupied a military as well as civil position. Following the example of Gracchus, Marius and his confederates made advances to the equites and the proletariate. They extended the powers of the former as jurymen, and gave them greater control over the extortions of provincial magistrates; while to the latter they now sold grain at the merely nominal price of three cents instead of twenty-four cents a bushel. Still their real power lay in the discharged Marian soldiers, and this fact lent a strong military color to their attempt at a revolution.

In spite of the vehement opposition of the aristocrats by means of tribunician veto, the invocation of portents, and the armed interference of the urban questor Quintus Caepio, the Appuleian laws were ratified. This was partly due to the firmness of Saturninus, and still more to the appearance of the dreaded soldiers of Marius. Quintus Metellus, rather than take the oath which bound every senator to observe the new laws, went into exile, but that was only a gain to his opponents. When, however, the plans came to be executed, it was soon clear that a politically incapable general, and a violent street demagogue could not long be allies. In the first place, Marius, from his utter incapacity as a statesman, was unable either to keep his own party in check or to gain over his opponents. The wealthy classes had no liking for Saturninus and his street riots; nay, the equites had skirmishes with his armed bands, and he was only with difficulty elected tribune in 100 B.C. Thus this powerful body began to side with the aristocracy when they saw that Marius was practically the tool of his more violent associates.

But the attitude of Marius not only alienated those who should have been his most powerful supporters, but, what was more important, caused Saturninus and Glaucia to lose all trust in him. His refusal to go the lengths that they went, his negotiations with his own party and the senate at one and the same time, his reservation when he swore as a senator to observe the Appuleian laws, "so far as they were really valid," soon caused a total rupture between himself and the most violent democrats. But Saturninus and Glaucia had gone too far to recede; they now resolved to grasp the sovereignty for themselves. They arranged that the former should again seek the tribuneship, the latter the consulship, for which he was not legally eligible till two years had elapsed. For the latter office Gaius Memmius was the government candidate; he was suddenly murdered. Hereupon the senate called upon the consul Marius to interfere; he complied, and a hasty levy of young men was drawn up in array, while the senators appeared armed in the Forum, led by Marcus Scaurus. The democrats saw their danger, and set free all the slaves in prison; and on December 10, 100 B.C., a great battle took place in the market-place, the first ever fought within the walls of the capital. It ended in the utter overthrow of the popular party. Saturninus and Glaucia were put to death with many others, so that there perished on one day four Roman magistrates, a pretor, questor, and two tribunes, together with a number of other notable men, in some cases of good family. The victory of the government was complete. Not only were its noisiest opponents dead, but the one man who might have proved really dangerous had publicly and completely effaced himself; and, what was perhaps still more important, the two chief elements of the opposition—the capitalists and the proletariate—emerged from the struggle bitter enemies.

Thus the force of circumstances, and, still more, the incapacity of Marius, had completely destroyed the fabric reared by Gaius Gracchus. Pitiful, indeed, was the position of the great general; he retired to the East so as not to witness the return of his rival Metellus. When he came back to Rome his counsel was not sought, and the continuance of profound peace rendered vain his hopes that the time would come when his strong arm would be needed.

But his superstitious soul ever kept in mind the oracular promise of
seven consulships, and, though in the eyes of all insignificant and
harmless, he brooded over his schemes of vengeance, and in moody
sullenness bided his time.   In addition to this, the current of popular
feeling now set in strongly against the remnants of the party left
behind by Saturninus.   The tribunals of the equites condemned
with the utmost severity everyone who professed the views of the
Populares; nay, they even assailed men on the ground of injuries
years old against the aristocrats.   Moreover, abroad the Roman
arms were everywhere successful.   In Spain a serious rising was
quelled by the consuls, in the years 98-93 B.C.   In the East, too,
much greater energy was displayed than had been shown for many
years.   At home the government was more popular and secure
than it had ever been since the restoration.   The laws of Saturninus
were, of course, canceled, and the transmarine colonies of Marius
dwindled down to a small settlement in Corsica.

In 98 B.C. the two consuls passed a law which made an interval
of seven days between the introduction and passing of a bill obligatory, and forbade the combination in a single proposal of several
enactments differing in their nature.   Thus the government was
protected from being taken by surprise by new laws, and some
restriction was placed on the initiative power in legislation.

It was clear that the Gracchan constitution, which had rested
on the union of the multitude and the moneyed aristocracy, was
on the eve of perishing, and that the hour had come to reëstablish
the governing oligarchy in undisputed possession of political power.
All depended on the recovery by the senate of the nomination of
jurymen; for of late the governors had administered the provinces,
not for the senate, but for the order of capitalists and merchants.
The latter fiercely resisted all attempts to wrest their power from
them; and even Quintus Mucius Scaevola, one of the most eminent
jurists and most noble-minded men of the time, was rewarded
for his stern repression of all crime, and for his scrupulous justice
in administering the province of Asia, by seeing his legate, Publius
Rufus, brought to trial before the equites on the most absurd charge
of maladministration.   Rufus refused to submit to the moneyed
lords, and was condemned and had his property confiscated.   He
retired to the province which he was accused of plundering, and
was there welcomed with every honor by all men, and there spent the
rest of his life.   Soon after, Marcus Scaurus, seventy years of age,

and for twenty years the chief of the senate, was tried for unjust extortions; and it was evident that neither nobility of descent, blamelessness of life, nor age itself were any screen against the wildest charges preferred by men who made a regular profession of reckless accusation. The very commission touching exactions became the scourge instead of the shield of the provincials; the vilest scoundrel, provided that he satisfied the claims of his fellow-robbers, went unpunished; while those who trusted to their innocence, and attempted to do their duty by the provinces they governed, were found guilty by the juries whom they neglected to bribe.

Marcus Livius Drusus, tribune in 91 B.C., son of the overthrower of Gaius Gracchus, a conservative of the conservatives, the proudest and noblest of the aristocrats, vehemently earnest, pure of life, and an object of respect to the humblest citizen, felt that the time had come to attack the equestrian jury courts. He was aided by Marcus Scaurus and Lucius Crassus, the famous orator; but against him were not only the consul Lucius Philippus and the reckless Quintus Scaepio, but also the more corrupt and cowardly mass of the aristocracy, who, sooner than lose all chance of plunder, were quite content to share the spoils of the provinces with the equites. Drusus proposed to take away the functions of jurymen from the equestrian order, and to restore them to the senate, and to add three hundred new members to the senate, in order to enable it to meet its increased obligations. Moreover, a special criminal commission was to be appointed to try all jurymen who had been or should be guilty of taking bribes. But he also had a wide and well-considered scheme of reform. He proposed to increase the largesses of corn and to cover the increased expense by the permanent issue of copper-plated by the side of the silvered denarii; to reserve all the still undistributed arable land of Italy, and the best part of Sicily, for the settlement of burgess colonists; lastly, he bound himself to give the Italian allies the Roman franchise.

There is a marked similarity of means and aims in the cases of Drusus and Gaius Gracchus; both relied on the proletariate, and both had practically the same measures of reform in view. The great difference was as to who should be the governing power in the state; in all other points the best men of both political parties had much in common, widely different as often were the processes of reasoning by which they arrived at such views.

In order to carry his laws, Drusus wisely kept in the background his proposal touching the Italian franchise, and embodied all his other measures in one law; thus he caused those interested in largesses of corn and distributions of land to also carry the proposal touching the transference of the jury courts. He was stoutly opposed, especially by the consul Philippus, whom he caused to be imprisoned. Though the Livian laws were carried, the consul summoned the senate to reject them. On its refusal, Philippus declared he would seek another state council, and seemed to meditate a *coup d'état.* Many of the senate now began to waver, and their fears were still further aroused by the sudden death of Lucius Crassus in September, 91 B.C. Gradually the connections of Drusus with the Italians became known, and a furious cry of high treason was raised. The opposition grew more powerful, and the senate at last issued a decree canceling the Livian laws on the ground of informality. Drusus refused to interpose his veto, and thus the senate once more became subject to the yoke of the capitalists.

Shortly after Drusus perished by the hand of an assassin, who escaped undetected; nor was the crime investigated. Thus the same end which swept away the democratic reformers was the fate of the Gracchus of the aristocracy. The weakness of the aristocracy frustrated reform, even when the attempt came from their own ranks.

Chapter XXI

THE REVOLT OF ALL ITALY. 91-87 B.C.

JUST as the failure of the previous attempt of Flaccus, in 125 B.C., to confer the citizenship on the Italians was followed by the revolt of Fregellae, so the despair of the subjects of Rome after the death of Drusus broke forth in a revolt of all Italy.

The Italian allies had two inducements to revolt; they wished to obtain the enjoyment of certain privileges; they wished also to free themselves from many disabilities and wrongs. The voting power was perhaps the chief, but by no means the only, privilege which they sought. There were others, such as immunity from taxation and flogging. On the other hand, they were subject to vexation and oppression in many forms from which Roman citizens were exempt. The rigor of martial law, largely modified for the burgess soldiers, remained unsoftened for them. Italian officers of any rank might be condemned and executed by sentence of court-martial, while the meanest burgess-soldier could appeal to the civil courts at Rome. The contingent furnished by the allies to the army was disproportionate to their number, and the disproportion was increasing. In civil matters the general superintendence of the Roman government over the dependent communities was extended till the allies were at the mercy of the caprice of any Roman magistrate. At Teanum Sidicinum the chief magistrate had been scourged by order of the Roman consul for supposed remissness in gratifying a whim of the consul's wife. In the Latin colony of Venusia a free peasant was whipped to death for a laugh at the passing litter of a young Roman holding no office. Incidents like these must have been frequent; and all non-citizens, from Latins downward, became united by the bond of a common oppression. Since the completion of the Roman conquests the Roman citizenship had become the one thing worth having; it alone would give protection from tyranny and a status in the world; for the Roman empire by this time embraced all civilization, and to be outside the Roman state was to be outside the world.

The privilege was thus more valuable than it had ever been before; but it was also becoming more and more difficult to acquire. The tendency of the body of Roman citizens was to close their ranks. The practice of bestowing the franchise on whole communities had ceased; the right of individuals to acquire it by residence at Rome was curtailed; and in 126 B.C. all non-burgesses were expelled from the city by decree of the senate.

It might have been thought that the senate and the conservative party objected, not to the demands of the Italians, but to the revolutionary schemes of those by whom these demands were supported; but in 95 B.C. the deliberate policy of the oligarchy was made clear by a consular law which prohibited under penalties any non-burgess from laying claim to the franchise. With Drusus hope arose once more for the Italians; Drusus accomplished nothing but his own destruction, and now no resource was left but an appeal to arms.

The chief difficulty with which rebellions always have to contend is want of organization. They have to contend against an established government completely equipped and organized, and to create their own organization during the course of the struggle. The Italian peoples were not entirely unprepared in this respect. In the first place, a secret league had been formed in connection with the attempt of Drusus, with members of all the most important Italian towns, bound by oath to be faithful to each other and to the common cause. Again, each allied town furnished a contingent to the Roman army, and these trained troops formed a valuable nucleus for the allied army. Thirdly, there were the old Roman confederacies of the various Italian peoples—of the Marsians, Paelignians, and others,—which had of course lost all political significance after the conquest by Rome, but which still existed for purposes of common sacrifice.

The revolt broke out prematurely at Asculum in Picenum, where all the resident Romans were massacred. The flame spread rapidly through all central and southern Italy. The Marsians were the first to declare war, and round them gathered the Paeligni, the Marrucini, the Frentani, and the Vestini, while the Samnites were the center of the southern group of peoples, from the Liris to Apulia and Calabria.

On the other hand, the Romans had many adherents where the richer classes were influential. Thus the whole of Umbria and Etruria, where the middle class had entirely disappeared, remained faithful; so also many isolated communities in insurgent districts, such as Pinna in the Vestini. Lastly, many of the most favored of the allied communities, such as Nola, Nuceria, and Neapolis in Campania, and Rhegium; and Latin colonies, such as Alba and Aesernia, refused to rise. The strength of the revolt was in the middle classes and the small farmers; the moneyed and aristocratic classes held with Rome.

After the first blood had been shed at Asculum the insurgents still made an attempt at negotiation: they offered even now to lay down their arms if Rome would grant them the citizenship. Instead of complying, the Roman government instituted a commission, on the proposal of the tribune Varius, to investigate the conspiracy set on foot in connection with the agitation of Drusus. The result was the banishment of many members of the moderate senatorial party who were favorable to compromise. Great preparations were made for the struggle. Officers of all parties, including both Sulla and Marius, offered themselves to the government. The largesses of corn were curtailed in order to husband supplies; and all business, except military preparations, was at a standstill.

The Italians on their side were preparing not merely to secede from Rome, but to crush her and form a new state. Corfinium, a town on the Paeligni, was to be the head of the new government, under the new name· of Italica. All burgesses of insurgent communities were declared citizens of Italica. A new forum and senate-house were made, a senate, consuls, and pretors appointed. The Latin and Samnite languages were placed on an equality as the official tongues; and the imitation of the Roman constitution was carried out in the minutest details. The most important feature of the new organization is this—that Italica, like Rome, was to remain merely a governing city-state. The Italians, like Rome itself, were unable to rise above the conception of the Greek πόλις, or city-state. No idea occurred to them of any means, such as modern representative institutions, by which a vast population could be welded into a united nation.

Their plan of campaign was settled for the Romans by the character and extent of the revolt. They had to relieve the many fortresses which held out for them in various parts of the insurgent districts, and they had to combat a numerous enemy at widely distant points. Accordingly, two consular armies were formed to meet the forces of the two Italian consuls, the one acting in the northern group of insurgent states, the other in the southern. The operations of the first year of the war, 90 B.C., were distinctly unfavorable to Rome, especially in the south, where several important towns were lost, the Roman armies defeated, and most of the country occupied by the Italians. In central Italy the course of events was less disastrous, but many communities in Umbria and Etruria soon declared for the allies.

The change in popular feeling at Rome due to these reverses was shown by the repeal of the Varian commission which had sent into exile many prominent men of the party favorable to concession. About the same time a policy of compromise was adopted. The *Lex Julia* of the consul Lucius Julius Caesar at the end of 90 B.C. granted the citizenship to all Italian communities which had not declared against Rome. The *Lex Plautia Papiria* a short time later granted the citizenship to all allies who presented themselves before a Roman magistrate within sixty days.

At the same time the effect of these concessions was largely nullified by the restriction which allowed the new citizens to be enrolled in eight only of the thirty-five tribes. These laws applied to all Italy south of the Po, while the Celts between the Po and the Alps were invested with the inferior privileges which had hitherto belonged to Latin towns. The aim of these measures was to secure the loyalty of the allies who had hitherto remained faithful, and to draw over deserters from the enemy. But they by no means constituted a complete capitulation; only so much of the existing political institutions had been pulled down as seemed necessary to arrest the progress of the conflagration.

In the second year of the war the tide began to turn. The alliance of her enemies was gradually weakening before the Roman concessions, and by the end of the year the war was over, except in the southern part of the peninsula. There the last organized forces of the insurgents were being put down by Sulla, the only Roman general who had added conspicuously to his laurels in this Social War.

While events were progressing favorably to Rome during the second year, the internal condition of the city was becoming more and more critical. At the end of 89 B.C. it had become necessary to declare war against Mithradates, and Rome was by no means prepared. The treasury was exhausted; no new army could be raised, but that of Sulla was destined to embark as soon as it could safely be spared; money was raised by the sale of unoccupied sites within the city.   In Rome and in Italy all classes were seething with discontent.   The Varian prosecutions had embittered the strife between the moderate and the extreme parties.   The former was dissatisfied with the concessions already made to the Italians; the Italians themselves were dissatisfied with an enfranchisement which limited their influence to eight tribes—a limitation all the more galling that it found a precedent in the restriction of the freedmen to four tribes.   The revolted communities who had been subdued were in the position of *dediticii*—that is, in the eye of the law they were prisoners of war, absolutely at the mercy of their conquerors; they were not yet admitted to the citizenship, and they had forfeited their ancient treaties; where these treaties had been restored they had been made revocable at the will of the Roman people.   It was desirable to recall the men exiled by the Varian commission, who included many of the best men of the senatorial order; but the canceling of a legal verdict by a decree of the people was seen to be a most undesirable precedent.   Lastly, Marius was thirsting for fresh command to recover his lost influence, and was ready to go to any length to accomplish his purpose.

To all these elements of disorder must be added the decay of military discipline and an economic crisis.   The social war had necessitated the enrollment of every available man in the army, and had carried party spirit into the ranks.   The result was an appalling slackness of discipline, and more than one Roman division had put its commander to death and escaped all punishment.

At the same time the old cry of the oppression of capital was heard again.   Debtors unable to pay the interest on their loans had applied to the urban pretor Asellio for time to realize on their property, and were trying to get the obsolete laws against usury enforced.   Asellio sanctioned actions to recover interest under these laws, and was murdered by the offended creditors under the leadership of the tribune Lucius Cassius.   The debtors now clamored for *novae tabulae*—the canceling of all existing debts.

At this critical point the tribune Publius Sulpicius Rufus came forward with three laws.   He proposed that every senator that owed more than four hundred dollars should be expelled from the senate; that those who had been exiled by the Varian commission should be recalled; and that the new burgesses and the freedmen should be distributed among all the tribes.

Sulpicius was no revolutionary; by these laws he attempted simply to carry out the traditional policy of the moderate senatorial party, of the party of Crassus and Drusus. During the early period of his office he had been a supporter of constitutional forms, had opposed the recall of the Varian exiles, and had vehemently resisted an attempt of Gaius Caesar to stand for the consulship before he had been pretor. Nor was the tendency of his proposals toward revolution. The first was necessary on account of the venality of the senate and the dependence of the poorer senators upon their richer colleagues. The second was necessary if there was to be a moderate party at all. The third, so far as it concerned the allies, was merely a measure of justice, and necessary to render the Roman concessions a reality; and the admission of the freedmen into all the tribes would extend the influence of a class largely dependent on the great aristocratic houses. But though the proposals of Sulpicius need not have alarmed the senate, he became exasperated by opposition, kept a hired bodyguard in his pay, and carried on the struggle with great violence.

The proposals were strongly resisted by the senate; and the consuls Sulla and Pompeius Rufus suspended all popular assemblies on pretense of extraordinary religious observances. Sulpicius replied by a violent tumult. The consuls then yielded, and the proposals became law. But Sulpicius could not yet feel secure; Sulla had departed to the army in Campania, and Sulpicius feared lest he might lead his legions to overthrow the recent laws. Accordingly a fourth *Lex Sulpicia* was brought forward, and by decree of the people the supreme command against Mithradates was transferred from Sulla to Marius.

On the arrival of two tribunes from Rome to take over the command of the army, Sulla refused to submit. The command had been conferred upon him legally and constitutionally; he knew that he could count upon the devotion of the legions, and he had no scruple about using force against his country. He laid the matter before the troops, and hinted to them that Marius would raise a fresh army for service in the East. The superior officers held aloof, but the common soldiers tore the tribunes in pieces, and clamored to be led to the city. Sulla availed himself of their enthusiasm, and for the first time a Roman army was led against Rome. The city was reached by forced marches, and troops posted at the bridge over the Tiber and at the gates; the sacred boundary was crossed by two legions in battle array. Stones were thrown from the roofs, but Sulla brandished a blazing torch and threatened to fire the city, and the legions steadily advanced. The forces of Marius and Sulpicius were overcome; when they summoned the slaves to arms not more than three appeared, and in a few hours Sulla was master of Rome.

Sulla's first step was to declare the Sulpician laws null and void; his next, to proscribe Sulpicius and twelve of his most strenuous adherents. Sulpicius was captured at Laurentum, and put to death, and his head was exposed in the Forum before the rostra. The adventures of Marius are well known. After escaping successively the cavalry of Sulla, the magistrates of Minturnae, and the treachery of the Numidian king, he found a temporary rest in a small island off the coast of Tunis.

The legislation which Sulla now undertook aimed at relieving the debtors and strengthening the power of the senate. His chief measures were: A law fixing the maximum of interest; schemes for a number of new colonies; the addition of three hundred new senators to restore the reduced numbers of the senate; the revival of the old Servian arrangement for voting in the comitia centuriata by giving nearly one-half the votes to the first class alone, consisting of those who possessed an estate of five thousand dollars or more; and the restoration of the full probouleutic power of the senate. No proposal could henceforth be submitted to the people unless it had first been approved by the senate.

Formally these laws of Sulla appeared revolutionary in the extreme. The proscription of Sulpicius and his adherents was a violation of the sacred laws of appeal. The initiative in legislation was taken from the magistrates and given to the senate, which had legally no privilege but that of giving advice. The old voting arrangements in the centuries, now revolutionized by Sulla, had existed unchanged for a century and a half. But in substance these changes contained little which violated the spirit of the constitution. In occupying Rome and in proscribing the adherents of Sulpicius, Sulla merely accepted actual facts and repelled violence with violence. The extension of the power of the senate was but giving legal sanction to a power which it had always exercised until recent times by means of the tribunician or augural veto; and the later practice, according to which any magistrate proposed a law to the tribes without previous deliberation in the senate, was already seen to be fraught with great inconvenience and danger. The measures with regard to interest and colonization show that Sulla was not indifferent to the wrongs of the poorer classes, and they were proposed by him after the victory, and of his own free will. Lastly, it is important to remember not only what he changed, but what he left unchanged. The principal foundations of the Gracchan constitution, the corn largesses, and the equestrian jury courts were left untouched.

Meanwhile affairs in the East grew more threatening every day, and Sulla could no longer postpone his departure. He endeavored to insure the permanence of his measures by procuring the election of consuls favorable to the restored government, and by transferring the army of the north from the doubtful Strabo to his own devoted friend, Quintus Rufus.

But one of the new consuls was Cinna, a most determined opponent of Sulla, and Rufus had no sooner taken over his command than he was murdered by the soldiers, and Strabo resumed the leadership. Sulla himself, on the expiration of his consulship, was summoned to appear on his defense before the people.

Notwithstanding these ominous incidents, Sulla merely exacted an oath from the consuls to maintain the existing constitution, and immediately embarked for the East early in 87 B.C.

Chapter XXII

THE MITHRADATIC WAR. 88-84 B.C.

EVER since the beginning of the revolution under Tiberius Gracchus Rome had been too much occupied with her internal affairs to bestow much attention upon the provinces. During this period important changes had taken place in the East. The two kingdoms of Armenia, which dated their existence from the war with Antiochus, had been united under Tigranes, originally king of the northeastern portion; and to him the title of Great King and the titular supremacy of Asia now passed. Phrygia became, in the time of Gaius Gracchus, an independent kingdom in connection with the Roman province of Asia; but otherwise Asia remained unchanged, except for the oppression of the Roman tax farmers, which was ever growing more merciless and more intolerable.

The ruler of the kingdom of Pontus was, at that time, Mithradates VI., surnamed Eupator. After the death of his father he became a fugitive and a wanderer for seven years. Eastern legend ascribed to him a stature more than human, strength and swiftness surpassing that of all other men, and a constitution inured alike to any fatigue or excess. He collected Greek and Persian antiquities and works of art, and kept Greek poets and philosophers in his train.

As a ruler he does not rise beyond the ordinary Eastern sultan. What really distinguishes him is his boundless activity and energy. He extended the limits of his dominions in every direction, founded a new empire on the northern shores of the Black Sea, and, alone among the princes of the East, was able seriously to contend with the Roman power.

His ancestral dominion was Pontus, or Cappadocia, on the Black Sea, between Bithynia on the west and Armenia on the east. It was a rich and fertile country, producing large quantities of grain and fruit, but almost entirely destitute of towns properly so called, though there were numerous fortresses where the peasants might take refuge, and where the king's treasure was deposited. The real basis of his wealth and power lay in the flourishing Greek seaports of Trapezus, Amisus, and Sinope.

Instead of developing the resources of his dominions, Mithradates devoted himself to extending them.   After conquering the district of Colchis, east of Pontus, he proceeded to extend his sway over the region north of the Black Sea, the modern Crimea.   The Greek cities here had long groaned under the exactions and blackmail extorted by the Sythian and Sarmatian tribes of the interior, the ancestors of the modern Cossacks, and they were glad to be delivered by the arms of Mithradates, and to acknowledge his supremacy.   The new kingdom, based, like Pontus, on a number of Greek cities, was called the Bosporus.   It embraced the peninsula

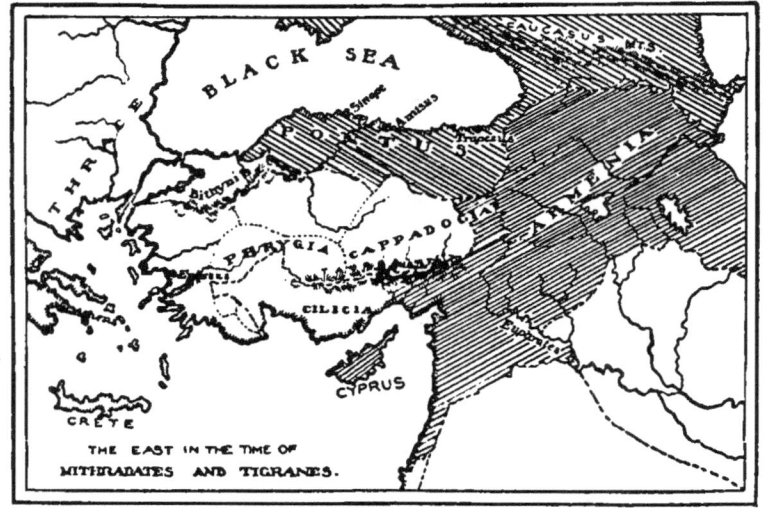

THE EAST IN THE TIME OF MITHRADATES AND TIGRANES.

and the opposite coast, and paid an annual tribute of two hundred talents ($244,000), besides enormous quantities of grain, to the king.   The barbarian tribes acknowledged some sort of dependence upon Mithradates, and supplied a valuable recruiting ground.   At the same time Lesser Armenia was annexed to Pontus. Mithradates gave his daughter in marriage to Tigranes, king of Greater Armenia, and it was by his help that Tigranes established his supremacy in Asia.

The king now turned his attention to Paphlagonia and Cappadocia, and it was his conduct with regard to these countries which made Roman interference at length inevitable.   Paphlagonia was claimed by Mithradates as having been left to his father by will.   He gained over the king of Bithynia by allowing him to occupy the western half of the kingdom. Cappadocia had once been united with Pontus, and after the murder of the Cappadocian king Ariarathes, and of his young son, the reunion was practically accomplished. Nominally the country was ruled by a pseudo-Ariarathes, actually by Gordius, a Cappadocian instrument of Mithradates.

The Roman senate had been entirely passive during all these aggressions. The reunion of Cappadocia at last aroused them to energy. Paphlagonia was declared independent, and Mithradates was commanded to evacuate Cappadocia. No army was sent to enforce these decrees, but the energy of Sulla, the governor of Cilicia, compelled Mithradates to submit at all points. The Cappadocian Ariobarzanes was elected king by the people. Sulla marched to the Euphrates, and gained great fame by a conference in which, as representative of Rome, he arranged the relations between Tigranes and the Parthians in 92 B.C.

This was the first time that the Romans came into contact with the great nation with which they were destined to dispute the sovereignty of the world. Thus the *status quo* in the East was restored.

But Sulla had no sooner retired than turmoil once more broke out, and Mithradates, with the help of his son-in-law, Tigranes, renewed his intrigues and sought once more to extend his kingdom. The Roman commissioner in Asia at this time, Manius Aquillius, knowing there was little hope for tranquillity in these regions so long as Mithradates's power was not checked, determined to bring matters to a head by stirring up Nicomedes, the king of Bithynia, against him. Accordingly Nicomedes invaded Pontus and closed the Bosporus with his ships. Mithradates contented himself with appealing to the Romans. He was ordered, in any case, to refrain from war against Nicomedes. Then the king's decision was taken. His son Ariobarzanes was ordered to invade Cappadocia in 89 B.C., and envoys were sent to the Roman envoys to demand their ultimatum. War now ensued as a matter of course.

Mithradates made the most energetic preparations: he obtained a promise from Tigranes of an auxiliary army; to the Greeks he presented himself, like Philip of Macedon, as a deliverer from an alien yoke; and he had hopes of the revolt of Numidia and Syria, of risings in Thrace and Macedonia. The Mediterranean swarmed with Pontic privateers: a foreign corps, composed chiefly of Italian refugees, was formed in Asia, armed and equipped in the Roman fashion. The king's infantry is said to have amounted to 250,000 and his cavalry to 40,000, while his fleet numbered 400 vessels.

For the Romans the moment was most unfavorable. The Italian insurrection was yet unsubdued, and it was impossible for a Roman army from Italy to arrive, at earliest, till the summer of 88 B.C. Besides the native levies there was but a small Roman force in Asia; but the Roman officers hoped to protect the Roman province and maintain their present positions. The Bithynian fleet still blockaded the Bosporus.

The war began in 88 B.C., and the first operations were all in favor of Mithradates. He defeated the Bithynians and captured their military chest. The Roman officers were everywhere worsted, and had to shut themselves up in fortified towns. To conciliate the inhabitants, all Asiatic prisoners were immediately dismissed by the king. The whole country to the Maeander was in his hands. The only hope of the Romans was in Sulla, and now news arrived of the Sulpician revolution and of Sulla's march upon Rome. The Asiatics everywhere sided with Mithradates; the Roman officers, Quintus Oppius and Aquillius, were delivered into his hands. In the hour of conquest the savagery of the king broke forth in a stupendous crime. Orders were issued from Ephesus that on one and the same day all Italians, bond and free, should be put to death. Severe penalties were threatened against any who should shelter the proscribed, and while one-half of their property was to go to the royal treasury, the other half was given over to the murderers. The orders were strictly carried out, and by the smallest computation eighty thousand persons perished in the massacre. The act was one of brutal and impolitic revenge. By striking not merely at Romans, but at all Italians, the king alienated his most important allies.

The new conquests were now organized. Pergamus became the new capital, the old Pontus was given over to the sons of Mithradates, and the other provinces of Asia Minor became Pontic satrapies. All arrears of taxes were forgiven, and exemption from all taxes for five years was promised. Besides the petty ruler of Paphlagonia, the only communities still adhering to Rome were the city leagues of Caria and Lycia and the cities of Rhodes and of Magnesia on the Maeander, which successfully withstood all attempts to reduce them.

The king now determined to carry the war into Europe and to occupy Hellas. His fleet overran the Aegean Sea, all the islands were occupied, and the mainland was soon attacked. At Athens, Aristion, a philosopher by trade, persuaded the people to renounce Roman rule; the Piraeus became a Pontic harbor; and the other free states—Achaia, Boeotia, Laconia—followed the example of Athens.

The position of the Roman government was critical: three armies were required to keep down Rome, Italy, and Asia; only one, that of Sulla, was available. Sulla had to choose between these three tasks. He chose Asia, and in the spring of 87 B.C. he landed in Epirus—but with only thirty thousand men: he was without a single ship and his treasury was empty. But his action was none the less vigorous; as soon as his proposals for peace on the basis of the *status quo* before the war were rejected, he advanced into Boeotia, defeated the Pontic generals, and quickly possessed himself of the whole of the mainland except Athens and the Piraeus, which he failed to carry by assault. He then established camps at Eleusis and Megara, and proceeded to besiege the city and port of Athens. The siege of Athens was long and tedious. The Pontic relieving army was overthrown under the walls of the city; but abundant supplies arrived at the Piraeus by sea, and considerable quantities even reached Athens. The winter passed without result: all the Roman assaults on the Piraeus were repulsed and the siege was turned into a blockade. Athens at length made overtures of surrender; but when there was delay in accepting Sulla's terms the city was captured by escalade. It was plundered and the ringleaders of the insurrection executed; but the Athenians were allowed to retain their liberty and their possessions, including Delos, just presented to them by Mithradates. Thus once more was Athens " saved by its illustrious dead."

The Piraeus still held out, and a fleet became imperatively necessary to prevent supplies from entering by sea. Lucullus had been dispatched to raise ships, but the Egyptian court refused his request for aid. Sulla was compelled to confiscate the temple treasures to supply his needs, and compensated the gods by devoting to them one-half of the territory of Thebes. The worst blow was the news of the democratic revolution at Rome, and the transference of the Eastern command from Sulla to Flaccus.

From these difficulties Sulla was extricated by the rashness of

Mithradates, who forbade his generals to act on the defensive, and ordered them to crush Sulla at once. An army of over 100,000 men, under Taxiles, arrived at Thermopylae; Archelaus evacuated the Piraeus and joined the main army. In the plain of the Cephissus the great battle of Chaeronea was fought. The Pontic forces were three times as numerous as the Roman, and were especially superior in cavalry, but after a stubbornly contested conflict the forces of Mithradates were defeated, the Pontic camp was captured, and the remnant of the army pursued to the Euripus.

The effect of the victory was slight—partly for want of a fleet, partly because of the approach of Flaccus, who was now in Thessaly. For some days the two Roman armies were encamped opposite to each other; but the soldiers of Flaccus began to desert, and he turned northwards, intending to march through Thrace to Asia. Sulla, from whatever motives, remained at Athens for the winter.

In the spring of the next year a second Pontic army reached Boeotia by way of Euboea, where it was joined by the relics of the army of Archelaus; the latter general was suspected of treason by his master, and the most peremptory orders were given to fight a decisive battle. The armies met in the same plain of the Cephissus —near Orchomenus. The Pontic cavalry caused the Roman line to waver by the fury of its charges; but Sulla rallied his soldiers in person,—the horse were driven back and the defeat of the infantry was then an easy task. The Pontic camp was stormed on the next day; the army was almost annihilated. The Boeotian communities were severely punished for their defection, many being almost totally destroyed. The way was now open through Macedonia and Thrace; Philippi and Abdera were occupied, and the winter, 85-84 B.C., was consumed by Sulla in preparing a fleet for the next year's campaign in Asia.

During the course of the war in Europe circumstances had greatly changed in Asia Minor. The hopes with which the Asiatic communities had hailed their deliverer were bitterly disappointed: the Roman whips were as nothing to the Pontic scorpions, and even the long-suffering Asiatics were driven to revolt. The most anarchical decrees were issued by the new sovereign, giving independence to the revolting communities, full remission of debts to debtors, lands to the poor, and liberty to slaves. All manner of outrage and violence was the consequence. The most important mercantile cities, Smyrna, Ephesus, Sardes, revolted from the king. At

Adramyttium the whole of the senate were put to death by his orders. The Chians, suspected of disloyalty, were first heavily fined, and then deported to the coast of Colchis. A massacre of Celtic chiefs in Asia was planned and carried out, in order to convert Galatia into a Pontic province. But those who escaped raised the powerful Celtic tribes and expelled the Pontic governor.

At the same time the king was hard pressed by the Romans on sea and land. Lucullus had at length succeeded in raising a considerable fleet, and had wrested several islands from the enemy. The army of Flaccus had reached Chalcedon in 86 B.C., but a mutiny had deposed Flaccus and placed Fimbria in command, and the new general had defeated the younger Mithradates and dislodged the king himself from Pergamus; and it was only through the refusal of the Optimate Lucullus to coöperate with the democrat Fimbria that Mithradates was enabled to escape to Mitylene. Thus, by the end of 85 B.C., Europe was entirely lost to Mithradates; and of Asia Minor the greater part was in revolt or occupied by the Romans. The fleet of Lucullus fought two successful engagements off the Trojan coast, and, when joined by the fresh vessels equipped by Sulla in Thessaly, completely commanded the Hellespont.

Mithradates now opened negotiations for peace. He applied to both Sulla and Fimbria, but he knew well that it was Sulla with whom he had really to reckon. The king offered Sulla his aid against the democratic party at Rome in return for the cession of Asia to himself. But Sulla refused to cede one foot of ground, and would take nothing but the following terms: Restoration of all the king's conquests, both continental and insular; surrender of prisoners and deserters, and of the Pontic fleet; pay and provisions for the army, and a war indemnity of three thousand talents ($3,360,000); the Chians to be restored to their homes, and the Macedonian refugees, friendly to Rome, to be allowed to return.

These negotiations were carried on at Delium, but Archelaus could not at first persuade his master to agree. Sulla meanwhile proceeded to settle Macedonian affairs, and set out with fleet and army for the Hellespont. At last Mithradates was brought to consent. But Sulla's march was still continued; he crossed the Hellespont, and at Dardanus concluded peace, orally, with Mithradates. At length he encamped close to Fimbria, at Thyatira, near Pergamus. Fimbria's troops refused to attack the Sullan army, and an attempt to assassinate Sulla failed. When Sulla refused a conference, Fimbria gave up all for lost and fell upon his sword; the main body of the troops joined Sulla, while those who were most deeply compromised repaired to Mithradates.

The settlement of Asia was now proceeded with. Two legions were left under command of Lucius Licinius Murena, and their interference was, in some cases, necessary to enforce the Sullan regulations. The most important of these were as follows: The revolutionary decrees of Mithradates were canceled; the most prominent adherents of the king and the authors of the massacre of the Italians were put to death; the arrears of tithes and customs for the last five years were exacted, together with a war indemnity of twenty thousand talents ($24,400,000); the few faithful communities—Rhodes, the province of Lycia, Magnesia on the Maeander—were rewarded, and compensation was made to the Chians and to the people of Ilium for the exceptional cruelty with which they had been treated.

During the winter of 84-83 B.C. Sulla allowed his troops to enjoy luxurious winter quarters in Asia, and in the spring transferred them across the Aegean and the Adriatic to Brundisium.

Chapter XXIII

THE DEMOCRATIC REVOLUTION AND ITS OVER-
THROW BY SULLA. 87-82 B. C.

THE departure of Sulla left Italy full of the discontented elements from which revolution might be expected to arise. The Italian revolt still smoldered dangerously in many quarters, and the principal army was in the hands of a general whose loyalty to the senate was doubtful. The capitalists had suffered greatly through the severe financial crisis. The insurgents who had laid down their arms since the expiration of the sixty days appointed by the *Lex Plautia Papiria* were in the position of subjects entirely destitute of rights. The new citizens and the freedmen were exasperated by the canceling of the Sulpician laws; while the large class of those who adhered to the men outlawed by Sulla after the revolution of Sulpicius were bent on obtaining the recall of their banished friends.

So far as the malcontents had a common aim, they were united upon this last point of the recall of the exiles; but the movement was mainly one of pure discontent, and had no distinct political object. Its aimlessness is shown by the character of the person chosen to lead it—Lucius Cornelius Cinna. He was unknown except as an officer in the social war; he had no political aim but that of vulgar selfishness, and is said to have been bought over by the party of Marius merely because the restriction of the power of tribunes made it necessary for the conspirators to have a consul as their instrument. There were abler men in the second rank of the conspiracy —Gnaeus Papirius Carbo, a powerful popular orator, and Quintus Sertorius, a man of the highest ability and integrity.

Immediately on Sulla's departure in 87 B.C. the conspirators took action. Cinna, supported by the majority of the tribunes, proposed two laws: the reënactment of the Sulpician law permitting the enrollment of the freedmen and the new citizens in any of the tribes; and that the Sulpician exiles should be recalled and restored to their rights.

On the day of voting both sides appeared in arms. The senatorial tribunes vetoed the new law. When swords were drawn the bands of the other consul, Octavius, cleared the Forum, and committed the most frightful atrocities on the assembled multitude. Ten thousand persons are said to have been slain. There was no legal means of proceeding against the conspirators, but a prophet opportunely gave out that the banishment of Cinna and of six tribunes was necessary for the peace of the country, and a decree of outlawry was accordingly passed by the senate against these persons. Lucius Cornelius Merula was chosen consul in place of Cinna.

But the senate omitted to expel the new exiles from Italy, and they appeared in Tibur, in Praeneste, and in all the new burgess communities of Latium and Campania, asking money and arms for the common cause. The army besieging Nola, a city still held by the Italian insurgents, induced partly by their own democratic leanings, partly by the bribes of the exiles, made common cause with Cinna, and furnished a valuable nucleus for the recruits who soon flocked in. Cinna now moved towards Rome, and was soon joined by fresh forces from the north. Marius and the refugees of the previous year had landed in Etruria with a body of five hundred horse. He now ordered the ergastula, or prisons in which the slaves were confined at night, to be broken open; and soon gathered round him a force of six thousand men; he also contrived to collect a force of forty ships, with which he intercepted the corn supply of Rome. He placed himself at the disposal of Cinna, though the wiser leaders, like Sertorius, saw the imprudence of associating themselves with so dangerous a man.

The democratic forces gathered round the city, and the senate appealed to Strabo for protection. He pitched his camp at the Colline Gate, but refrained from battle, and allowed the insurgents to invest the city. A decree was now passed conferring the franchise on all the Italian allies who had forfeited their old treaties. This was meant to gratify one large and important class of malcontents, but the concession did not produce more than ten thousand men. Negotiations were opened with the Samnites, in order to make the troops of Metellus in that quarter available for the defense of the city; but the Samnite terms were too humiliating, and when Metellus marched to Rome, leaving behind him a small division, the latter was at once attacked and defeated. Moreover, Cinna and Marius granted all that the Samnites required and were reinforced by a Samnite contingent.

The insurgents were already in possession of the sea, and the land communications were soon cut off by the capture of Ariminum, which shut off the supplies of food and men expected from the region of the Po; they also held Antium, Lanuvium, and Aricia, which closed all approaches from the south. At the same time a terrible pestilence broke out among the troops of the city, by which seventeen thousand men perished. After the sudden death of Strabo his troops were incorporated with those of Octavius, but their temper was such that the consul dared not fight. The Optimates were at variance with each other: Octavius opposed all concession, while Metellus was in favor of compromise. The soldiers first besought Metellus to take over the command, then, on his refusal, deserted in large numbers. At length the government was compelled to think of surrender. Envoys were sent to Cinna, but, while the negotiations dragged on, Cinna moved close up to the city gates, and desertions became so common that the senate was reduced to unconditional surrender. Cinna promised, at the entreaty of the senate, to abstain from bloodshed; but Marius kept an ominous silence.

Marius scoffingly refused to set foot in the city until his sentence of exile had been revoked; and a hurried assembly was held in the Forum, and the necessary decree passed. The old man at length entered, and the work of bloodshed began. The gates were closed and the slaughter was uninterrupted for five days, but for months afterwards individuals who had escaped at first were put to death. Gnaeus Octavius was the first victim; others of the illustrious slain were Lucius Caesar, consul in 90 B.C., and the victor of Acerrae; Marcus Antonius, the first pleader of his time, Lucius Merula, Cinna's successor; and Quintus Catulus, Marius' colleague in the Cimbrian wars. The fury of Marius amounted to madness; he could scarce be restrained from hunting out the bitterest of his enemies and slaying them with his own hand; he forbade the burial of the bodies, and had the corpse of Gaius Caesar stabbed afresh at the tomb of Quintus Varius. The man who presented to him, as he sat at table, the head of Antonius was publicly embraced. His own associates were appalled at his frenzy, but none had the courage or the power to oppose him, and he was even elected consul with Cinna for the following year. He lived to enter upon his seventh consulship; the few remaining days of his life were passed in a delirium, which ended in a burning fever. He expired on January 13, 86 B.C. He died in full possession of what he called power and honor, and in his bed, but Nemesis assumes various shapes, and does not always requite blood with blood. Was there no sort of retaliation in the fact that Rome and Italy now breathed more freely on the news of the death of the famous deliverer of the people, than at the tidings of the battle on the Raudine plain?

With the death of Marius the massacre ceased, though there were individual instances of murder. Thus Fimbria attempted to kill the revered pontifex maximus, Quintus Scaevola, whom even Marius had spared; but Sertorius secured the public tranquillity by calling together the Marian slaves, to the number of four thousand, and having them cut down by his Celtic troops.

During the next three years Cinna enjoyed a power as absolute and despotic as any ever exercised by the tyrant of a Greek city. He was consul each year, and nominated himself and his colleague without going through the form of consulting the people. During this period he gave no sign of any definite political plan or aim; no attempt was made to reorganize the constitution and to place the new government on a firm basis. Only the reactionary measures of Sulla were annulled, and a few laws passed as the exigencies of the moment demanded.

The law of Sulpicius, granting to the new burgesses and to the freedmen equality with the old citizens, was revived and confirmed by the senate, and censors were appointed to distribute the Italians among the thirty-five tribes. It was at this time probably that the restrictions on the largesses of corn, introduced on the outbreak of the social war, were removed. The old design of Gracchus for the colonization of Capua was carried out. All debts were reduced to one-fourth of their nominal amount.

No steps were taken to secure the support of either senate or equites, or to regulate the position of the Samnites, who, though nominally Roman citizens, were really Rome's bitterest enemies, and whose one aim was still their country's independence. The real strength of the government lay in the new citizens, with whose privileges its existence appeared bound up; while many of the old citizens acquiesced, because they saw that a restoration of the Sullan constitution meant a fresh reign of terror under the opposite party.

Most of the provinces adhered to the oligarchy. Quintus

Metellus and the young Marcus Crassus attempted to hold Africa for the same party, but were compelled to submit to the revolutionary governor. Most of the senatorial refugees fled to Macedonia, which was to some extent in Sulla's power. Sulla, like many of the refugees, was outlawed and deprived of his command; but the government took no adequate steps to enforce its decrees, so that Sulla was enabled to finish his work in the East without serious opposition. In 84 B.C. he addressed a letter to the senate, announcing his return to Italy. He promised to respect the rights of the new burgesses, and that the inevitable punishment should fall, not on the rank and file, but on the leaders of the revolution. On the arrival of this letter, Cinna hastily set out for Ancona, intending to cross the Adriatic, but his troops mutinied and he himself was killed. His colleague, Carbo, abandoned the idea of carrying war into Greece, and went into winter quarters at Ariminum. Meanwhile the moderate party had tried to bring about a compromise, but without success. Sulla's envoys were not admitted into the city, and he was summoned to lay down his arms. For the year 83 B.C. consular elections were once more held: the choice fell upon Lucius Scipio and Gaius Norbanus—neither of them men of capacity. The delay caused by Sulla's crossing into Asia was utilized at Rome in making energetic preparations for war, and 100,000 men are said to have been under arms at Sulla's landing.

Against this force Sulla had barely forty thousand men, all of them veterans, it is true, and devoted heart and soul to their leader, and to him alone. But still Sulla saw that these numbers would be powerless against a united Italy, and he took measures to gain over the strength of the nation—the mass of respectable men who desired nothing but peace and quiet, and the new burgesses who feared for their new privileges. Accordingly he offered unconditional pardon to all who would break off from the revolutionary government; he made the most binding declarations to maintain the privileges of the new citizens, and caused his soldiers to swear singly to welcome all Italians as friends and fellow-citizens.

In the spring of 83 B.C. Sulla landed at Brundisium without opposition; the town opened its gates to him, and all Apulia followed its example. Many members of the oligarchical party, like Quintus Metellus and Marcus Crassus, and some deserters from the democratic ranks, repaired to Sulla's camp, but brought no appreciable increase to his numbers.

By far the most important accession was that of the young Gnaeus Pompeius, by whose exertions the district of Picenum was induced to declare for Sulla. Pompeius had made his peace with the revolution, but the part which his father, Strabo, had played against Cinna was not forgotten: an indictment, charging him to give up the booty said to have been embezzled by his father at Asculum, threatened his ruin, from which he was only saved by the protection of Carbo. As soon as Sulla landed in Italy, Pompeius repaired to Picenum, raised the oligarchical standard at Auximum, and gathered round him a force of three legions, with which he skillfully effected a junction with Sulla in Apulia. Sulla received him with great honor, and rebuked the slackness of the rest of his partisans by greeting the young commander with the title of Imperator.

Thus reinforced, Sulla advanced into Campania; the army of Norbanus was at Capua, that of Scipio was advancing along the Via Appia from Rome. But before its arrival Norbanus had been crushed, and the remnants of his army were blockaded in Capua and Neapolis. Sulla hurried to Teanum, where Scipio was posted, and made proposals for peace; an armistice was concluded, and a personal conference took place between the two generals, while the soldiers of the two armies mingled as they pleased. An agreement was almost concluded, and envoys were sent to procure the opinion of Norbanus at Capua; but the negotiations, after all, fell through, and Scipio denounced the armistice. Sulla hereupon maintained that the agreement had already been actually concluded. The imprudence of allowing the common soldiers to fraternize was now forcibly demonstrated, and Scipio's soldiers passed over to Sulla in a body. The consul was required to resign his office, and was escorted to a place of safety. Sulla and Metellus took up winter quarters in Campania, and maintained the blockade of Capua.

Thus the first campaign had ended in the submission of Apulia, Picenum, and Campania, and the discomfiture of both consular armies. The Italian communities already began to negotiate with Sulla, and had their rights secured to them by separate formal treaties. Sulla boasted that in the next year he would march into Rome and overthrow the revolutionary government.

The government made the greatest preparations for the next campaign. The consuls were Carbo and the younger Marius; Sertorius was sent to raise new levies in Etruria; the gold and silver in the temples was melted down; new divisions came from Umbria and the Po. But, most important of all, the most strenuous exertions were made in Samnium and Lucania. It was well understood that Sulla would not, like the Cinnan government, acquiesce in the independence of these districts, and they made ready for a renewal of their old struggle against the hated Latin race.

For the campaign of 82 B.C. the army of the Optimates was divided: Metellus, resting on Picenum, advanced towards upper Italy; the main body, with Sulla, marched straight upon Rome. Near Signia he came upon the enemy under Marius, who retired to Sacriportus and drew up his line of battle. The issue was not long doubtful, and was made certain by the desertion of one of the divisions of Marius. By this battle the capital was lost, and Marius sent orders to the pretor Lucius Brutus Damasippus to evacuate it, after putting to death all the notable men of the other party. Among the victims of this latest massacre were the pontifex maximus, Quintus Scaevola, who had so narrowly escaped the vengeance of Fimbria. Sulla left behind Quintus Ofella to blockade Praeneste, into which Marius had thrown himself, and pushed on to Rome, which offered no resistance; he then hurried on to Etruria.

In the north the campaign resulted in the complete overthrow of the Marian party, and the Sullans then concentrated all their forces for the capture of Praeneste, where the young Marius had taken refuge. A large force of Samnites and Lucanians, which, with reinforcements, is said to have amounted to 70,000 men, hurried from the south to the relief of the city, but, finding that he was too late to rescue the remnants of the democratic party shut up in Praeneste, the Samnite general, Pontius of Telesia, in his desperation, resolved to throw himself upon Rome, which was but one day's march distant. From a military point of view the step was ruinous; even if successful the democratic army must be crushed at Rome, wedged in between the armies of Sulla and of Metellus. But the measure was dictated, not by policy, but by revenge; it was the last outbreak of revolutionary fury and of Samnite hatred.

On November 1 Pontius, with the Lucanian general Lamponius, and the democratic commanders Damasippus and Carrinas, encamped close to the Colline Gate. The force which sallied from the city was scattered like chaff, and the citizens gave way to despair. But before morning a body of horse appeared, which

proved to be Sulla's advanced guard under Balbus, and before noon
Sulla arrived in person. He had set out immediately on hearing of
the departure of the Samnites, and, in spite of his forced march,
immediately drew up his army in line, and ordered the attack. The
battle lasted the whole night through, and into the following morning. The left wing, under Sulla, was driven back, and the battle
was reported to be lost; but the right wing, under Crassus, routed
its opponents and pursued them to Antemnae, and gradually the
left wing likewise gained ground. The defection of a division of
three thousand of the enemy decided the issue, and Rome was
saved. The insurgents were all but extirpated. The three or four
thousand prisoners who were taken—including Damasippus, Carrinas, and Pontius—were, on the third day after the battle, massacred by Sulla's orders, in the Campus Martius.

Praeneste surrendered on the news of this disaster, and the
leaders put themselves to death. Of the twelve thousand prisoners,
all the Roman senators, all the Samnites, and most of the Prae-
nestines were slaughtered, and the town was given up to pillage.
Capua was voluntarily surrendered, but other towns made the
most obstinate resistance. Nola was not evacuated till the year
80 B.C. As to Samnium, Sulla declared that the very name ought
to be extirpated; he invaded the country, and made it a waste, as it
has remained to this day. In Etruria a long resistance was offered
by some towns. Volaterrae stood a siege of nearly three years,
and the garrison was massacred after a free departure had been
granted to it.

Of the provinces there still remained Sicily, Spain, and Africa
to be subdued. Gnaeus Pompeius was sent to Sicily with six legions in 82 B.C., and the island was immediately evacuated by the
governor Perpenna. Pompeius then proceeded to Africa, in 80
B.C., where he defeated the forces of the governor Lucius Domitius
Ahenobarbus, and Hiarbas, the usurping king of Numidia, and captured their camp. Hiempsal was restored to the kingdom of Numidia, and various Gaetulian tribes, hitherto independent, were
made subject to him. In forty days the war in Africa was at an
end. In Spain Sertorius was too weak to resist the Sullan officers,
and on his departure both provinces willingly submitted.

At the close of the African campaign Pompeius had been
ordered to break up his army—a command at which both general
and soldiers were discontented. Pompeius desired a triumph, though

as an extraordinary officer he had no legal claim to the honor. Sulla, however, yielded to his wish, and Pompeius could boast of having been the first Roman who had enjoyed a triumph before he was a senator. It was now that Pompeius was saluted by Sulla by the surname of Magnus.

In the East there had been no cessation of warfare; the carrying out of Sulla's regulations had in many cases to be accomplished by force; and fresh difficulties had arisen with Mithradates. The king was preparing an expedition into his Bosporan kingdom; and Murena, the governor of Asia, perhaps fearing lest the preparations were really directed against Rome, had crossed the Pontic frontier. Mithradates complained to the Roman government; and Sulla had sent envoys to dissuade the governor, who nevertheless continued his advance. Mithradates now resolved to repel him by force, and Murena was driven over the frontier with great loss in 82 B.C.

Peace was now renewed with Mithradates, and at last the ten years of war and insurrection which had convulsed the whole Roman world were at end.

Chapter XXIV

THE SULLAN CONSTITUTION. 81-78 B. C.

THE problem which lay before Sulla after his victories was vast beyond conception—it was the reconstruction of a whole state in ruins. About the time when the first pitched battle was fought between Romans and Romans, in the night of July 6, 83 B.C., the venerable temple which had been erected by the kings, dedicated by the youthful republic, and spared by the storms of five hundred years,—the temple of the Roman Jupiter in the Capitol,—perished in the flames. It was no augury; but it was an image of the state of the Roman Constitution. That, too, lay in ruins, and needed reconstruction. The mass of the aristocratic party had no idea of the magnitude of the task. They imagined that now, when the revolution had been suppressed, it would be enough to return to the old lines, taking precautions against similar outbreaks in future. Hence it was that Sulla chose his instruments, with the exception of Quintus Metellus, from the moderate party, or from the deserters from the democratic camp— Lucius Flaccus, Lucius Philippus, Quintus Ofella, Gnaeus Pompeius. Sulla was quite in earnest about restoring the old constitution; but he alone saw the enormous difficulties of restoration. He saw clearly that comprehensive concession and energetic repression were alike necessary. He also saw that the senate would mutilate every measure of either kind, and that it was necessary to accomplish the work by his own hand, without check or hindrance. At the same time, even Sulla was far from grasping the whole truth about the condition of the empire; otherwise he must have given up the work in despair. In fact, the constitution was past reconstruction; the ancient polity had broken down irretrievably; economic causes had corrupted or destroyed every class in the state—aristocracy, middle class, and lower class; and where no class in the state remained sound, absolute rule by the authority and intelligence of a single man alone remained possible. But not for another generation was this truth to be brought home in all its remorseless fatality.

The authority with which Sulla was at present provided was the purely military proconsulship.   It was necessary that he should be endowed with an office which should preserve as far as possible constitutional forms, and yet be powerful enough to coerce both friends and foes.   Sulla accordingly requested the senate to place the regulation of the state in the hands of a single man with unlimited powers, and intimated that he considered himself qualified for the task.   The senate directed the interrex Lucius Valerius Flaccus to propose a law to the people, conferring upon Sulla the "dictatorship for the making of laws and the regulation of the commonwealth," and approving, retrospectively, of all his acts as consul or proconsul.   His office was unlimited in point of time, and included absolute power to dispose of the lives and property of the citizens and of the state lands.   He might alter the boundaries of the city, of Italy, or of the empire; dissolve or establish communities in Italy; regulate the provinces and dependencies; confer the imperium on whom he pleased, and nominate proconsuls and propretors.   Lastly he might regulate the state by new laws.   The new office took its name from the old dictatorship, obsolete since the Hannibalian war.   The boundlessness of its power recalled that of the old decemvirs, but in reality it was nothing but the monarchy. The protector of the oligarchic constitution had himself to come forward as a tyrant, in order to avert the ever-impending tyrannies. There was no little of defeat in this last victory of the oligarchy.

The work of punishment was first taken in hand.   Sulla was not of a vindictive temperament,—even after his landing in Italy he had shown himself ready to forget and forgive,—but the democrats had used their last moments of power to set on foot fresh massacres, and henceforth Sulla showed no mercy.   He immediately outlawed all civil and military officers who had taken part in favor of the revolution after the convention with Scipio, and any other citizens who had actively aided the cause.   A reward of $2500 was offered to the murderer of any of these outlaws; sheltering them was forbidden under the severest penalties; their property was forfeited to the state, their children and grandchildren excluded from a political career; and this confiscation was also extended to the property of those who had fallen during the war.   Sulla caused a list of the proscribed to be posted up, and fixed upon June 1, 81 B.C., as the day for closing it.   It was said at last to have amounted to 4700 names.

The fury of the persecution fell primarily upon the Marians. The tomb of Marius himself was broken open, and his ashes scattered. His nephew was executed with torments at the tomb of Catulus. Of the leaders of the first rank few remained; but other classes suffered severely. Sixteen hundred equites who had speculated in the Marian confiscations were upon the list, and the professional accusers were largely represented. The heads of the slain were publicly piled at the junction of the Vicus Jugarius with the Forum. Bands of soldiers ravaged all Italy to earn the rewards of murder, and many, even of the oligarchy, fell victims to private revenge.

In the disposal of the confiscated property the greatest abuses prevailed. Sulla himself, and his immediate dependents and connections, bought largely, and had the purchase-money wholly or partially remitted. If there was any difference between the Marian and the Sullan reign of terror, it was that Marius murdered to satisfy his personal vengeance, while Sulla showed no personal feeling, but regarded the work almost as a political necessity.

With regard to the new citizens, the general rule was laid down that every citizen of an Italian community was *ipso facto* a citizen of Rome; all distinctions between citizens and allies—between citizens old and new—were abolished. But the freedmen were restricted, as before, to their old four tribes. There were, however, exceptions to the general rule; particular communities were punished, or, less frequently, rewarded. For instance, Brundisium obtained exemption from customs; but of the guilty communities many had to pay fines, to raze their walls, or to forfeit a part or the whole of their lands. Praeneste and Spoletium, Florentia, Faesulae, Arretium, Volaterrae, all fell under the last penalty. The dispossessed burgesses were placed in the position of Latins of the lowest class, with the additional hardship that they were attached to no particular community, but were without either home or city.

The lands thus confiscated were mainly utilized in settling the soldiers of the victorious army, mostly in Etruria, Latium, and Campania; and in many cases, as in the Gracchan colonies, the settlers were attached to existing communities. The number of allotments is stated at 120,000. This arrangement was made by Sulla with varied objects. Firstly, he redeemed the pledge given to his soldiers; secondly, he carried out the idea of the moderate conservative party of strengthening the class of small proprietors in Italy—an idea which he had attempted to realize in 88 B.C.   To accomplish this object the settlers were forbidden to sell their allotments.   Lastly, and this was no doubt the strongest reason, the new colonists formed standing garrisons, as it were, for the support of the restored constitution; and for this reason, where they were attached to an old community, as at Pompeii, the new citizens were not amalgamated with the old, but formed a separate body within the same enclosing wall.   Very similar in its aim was the object of another act of Sulla's—the manumission of a body of ten thousand of the slaves of the proscribed, who formed a bodyguard in support of the oligarchy and a garrison for the capital.

Sulla now destroyed at one blow the constitution so carefully built up by Caius Gracchus, and restored in all its plenitude the rule of the senate.   Gracchus had bribed the mob of the capital into quiescence by introducing free distributions of corn; these were now completely abolished.   Gracchus had organized the order of equestrians, and tried to give them a definite place in the constitution by introducing the system of farming the taxes of the provinces, by intrusting to them the functions of jurymen, and by assigning them a special place in the theater at popular festivals.   Sulla abolished the farming system, and converted the former taxes into fixed tributes; the jurymen were now taken from the senatorial order alone, and the equites were deprived of their seats of honor in the theater and relegated to the ordinary benches.   The senate was henceforth to be the only privileged order.

In order to fill up the fearfully reduced numbers of the senate, probably also with the intention of permanently increasing the number of its members, three hundred new senators were nominated by the tribes from men of equestrian census—chiefly from the younger men of the senatorial houses, and from Sullan officers whom the late events had brought into prominence.   At the same time the mode of admission to the senate was changed.   Hitherto men had entered the senate either by summons from the censors or by holding one of the curule magistracies—the consulship, the pretorship, or the edileship: the tribunate and questorship gave no right to a seat, but the choice of the censors was generally directed towards men who had held these offices.   The censorial functions of appointing to the senate and of deleting from its roll were now set aside; the senatorial seat was taken from the ediles and given to the questors, who were now raised from eight to twenty in number.   Several important results followed from these regulations.   In the first place, the abolition of the censorial deletion made the senator irremovable.   Secondly, the number of members was considerably increased: hitherto the average number had probably been something below 300; in Cicero's time a full meeting consisted of 417 members.   Thirdly, as both the new extraordinarily nominated senators and the augmented body of questors were nominated by the comitia tributa, the senate was now thoroughly based on popular election.

The comitia tributa remained, as before, formally sovereign; but the initiative of the senate in all legislation was solemnly enacted.   This was sufficient to exclude the people from interference in administration, or in criminal jurisdiction, and the voice of the people was confined practically to giving assent to alterations in the constitution.

The right of the people to elect magistrates in the comitia centuriata was not interfered with by Sulla, nor did he even attempt, as in 88 B.C., to restore the old Servian voting arrangements; but the election to the priestly offices was entirely taken from the tribes, and the right of coöptation restored to the sacerdotal colleges. At the same time various restrictions were imposed or confirmed afresh with regard to the qualifications for office.   The limit of age for holding each office was strictly enforced; and the first step in the gradation of offices was in future to be the questorship instead of the edileship, so that the questorship was now the necessary step to the pretorship, and the pretorship to the consulship. Two years at least must elapse between the holding of any office and of the next above it; while a ten-years' interval was required before reëlection to the same office.

The senate was originally, and was still in theory, a council, from which the magistrates might seek advice; but it had gradually acquired the right, not merely of advising, but of controlling the magistrates.   It was Sulla's aim to consolidate this power, and, accordingly, all magistracies emerged from his hands with diminished rights.

The heaviest blow fell upon the tribunate, an office naturally most independent of the senate.   The original right of the tribunes to veto the official acts of magistrates, and the further right to fine and punish all who disregarded their veto, were still left to them; but the abuse of the right of intercession was punished by a heavy fine. At the same time the power and influence of these magistrates were heavily fettered by two ordinances, which forbade them to consult the people or submit laws to them without permission from the senate; and made the holding of the tribunate a bar to the holding of any curule magistracy.

The power of the consuls and pretors was restricted by the complete separation of their civil and military functions,—an arrangement for which the practice of recent times had formed a precedent. Hitherto there had devolved upon the two chief magistrates, besides the proper consular functions, all official duties for which no special magistrates were appointed. The administration of justice in the capital, and the government of the four transmarine provinces, Sicily, Sardinia, and the two Spains, were provided for by the six pretorships, and with these functions the consuls had nothing to do. There remained the non-judicial business of the capital, and the military command in the continental possessions. At times, when these eight magistrates did not suffice, and when there were extraordinary commands to be provided for, there were two usual expedients : a particular military command was prolonged after its term had expired, or non-military functions were combined; as, for instance—the two judicial departments at Rome might be managed by one pretor instead of two, or the duties of the consul in the capital might be performed by the *practor urbanus,* and so one magistrate set at liberty for extraordinary duties. But in such cases the senate merely defined the sphere and function of the extraordinary office; the particular person who was to fill it was left to the magistrates themselves to decide by agreement or by lot.

Within the last century six new official departments had been created—the governorships of the five new provinces—Macedonia, Africa, Asia, Narbo, Cilicia—and the presidency of the court of extortions; and yet the number of magistrates had not been increased. The senate preferred to fill up vacancies by prolonging the term of office; for this prolongation might be granted or refused, and thus the senate kept a hold over the magistrates. Usually those magistrates who during their year of office were confined to the city were appointed for a second year to a transmarine command.

This expedient of prolongation was seized upon by Sulla as

the basis for a complete separation between the political authority of the magistrate over Roman citizens and his military authority over non-citizens. The consulship and pretorship were in future uniformly extended for a second year; the first year was devoted to civil, the second to military functions. Moreover, as the Roman citizen body now embraced all Italy south of the Rubicon, the military jurisdiction of the magistrate did not extend south of that river, and it was a fundamental principle of the constitution that there should ordinarily be no troops and no commandant within that district.

The pretors were now increased from six to eight; and according to the new arrangement the ten chief magistrates devoted themselves in the first year of their office to the business of the capital; the two consuls to government and administration; two pretors to the administration of civil law—the other six to the administration of the newly organized criminal justice. During the second year they were invested with the command of the ten chief governorships, Italian Gaul having been added to the list of provinces.

The effect of these regulations was very largely to increase the power of the senate over the magistrates. In the first place, all offices, whether at home or abroad, were for the future strictly limited to one year, whereas in former times the same man had held the same office for two or even more years. Secondly, by the arrangement as to military commands, no one could in future be, as Marius had been, both commander-in-chief and supreme civil magistrate. Thirdly, the whole military power became, formally at least, dependent on the senate; the people chose the consuls and pretors, but it was the senate that conferred on them the military authority by prolonging their term of office for a second year as proconsuls or propretors.

The censorship was not formally abolished, but its chief functions were taken from it. The new arrangement as to the questorship provided for the filling up of the senate, and the register for purposes of taxation and military service was unnecessary now that Italy was tax free, and the army was raised by enlistment; there remained only the financial functions, which were in future to be performed by the consuls.

The finances of the state were largely affected by three of Sulla's acts: the first, the conversion of the Asiatic taxes into a fixed tribute, certainly produced no gain to the state, though the tax-payers were greatly benefited: but the resumption of the Campanian domain lands to the state, and the abolition of the corn largesses, secured an ample revenue for the future.

But the most important and enduring part of Sulla's work was the reform of the criminal law.

As Sulla found it the judicial system was threefold. The whole citizen body formed a court of appeal from sentences of the magistrate affecting the life of a citizen. Then there was the ordinary procedure for all cases civil or criminal, except treason. In these cases, one of the two pretors investigated the general character of the case, and determined the law under which it was to be tried; he then nominated a single judge, who decided the case on the lines laid down by the pretor. Thirdly, there was the extraordinary procedure applicable to particular cases or groups of cases of importance, whether civil or criminal. For such cases, not a single judge, but a special body of judges or jurymen, was appointed by a special law. Such were the special tribunals appointed in 110 B.C. for the investigation of the alleged treason in connection with Numidian affairs, and in 103 B.C. with regard to the treason of the Roman generals in Gaul, in 105 B.C. Such also were the standing commissions for the investigation of special crimes, the earliest of which was the court of extortions, to try governors of provinces, established in 149 B.C., and the so-called spear-court for dealing with cases with regard to inheritances. Special provision was made for the presidency of each of these courts, in the law constituting them—to some a pretor was assigned, to others an ex-edile or an ex-pretor.

The reforms introduced by Sulla were also threefold. First, he largely increased the number of standing commissions or jury courts. Henceforth there were at least eight of these, called respectively the commissions on exaction, treason, injuries to person or honor, murder, election, bribery, fraud, embezzlement, and adultery. By these reforms the judicial power, both of the citizen body and of the ordinary courts, was curtailed, since the crime of treason was withdrawn from the jurisdiction of the former, and many of the most serious crimes from that of the latter.

Secondly, the presidents of these new courts were six of the pretors and other specially appointed officers. The power to appoint special commissions for special cases of course still remained.

Thirdly, the jurymen (judices) were in future drawn, not from the equites, but from the senate. The constitution of the spear-court remained unchanged.

The political aim of these measures was, of course, to exclude the equites from any share in the government; but they also constituted a most valuable system of legal reform. From this time dates the distinction, hitherto unknown, between civil and criminal causes; the former were now such as came before a single judge, the latter such as came before a jury. Moreover, Sulla's legislation may be regarded as forming the first Roman code since the Twelve Tables, and the first criminal code which had ever been issued at all. Among other noteworthy results of Sulla's arrangements was that capital punishment fell into abeyance; for the whole body of citizens could alone pronounce sentence of death, and the cognizance of cases of high treason was now withdrawn from it, and given to a special commission, which could sentence neither to death nor imprisonment. It may be added that new sumptuary laws were enacted, to restrain luxury at funerals and banquets, so that the law now attempted to perform what had formerly been the functions of the censors.

To the Sullan period, though perhaps not to Sulla, belongs an important development of the municipal system of Italy. Hitherto the government of Italy had been completely centralized in Rome; but from this period dates a great advance in the direction of local self-government by each particular community. Antiquity was certainly as little able to dovetail the city into the state as to develop of itself representative government and other great principles of our modern state life; but it carried its political development up to those limits at which it outgrows and bursts its assigned dimensions, and this was the case especially with Rome, which in every respect stands on the line of separation between the old and the new intellectual worlds. The social war was a sufficiently striking proof that the old Roman polity was outgrown, and the subsequent arrangements were a great stride in the advance from the city-state to the nation.

Before the social war the dependent communities were either allowed to keep their municipal constitution by being formally declared sovereign independent states of non-citizens, or, if they obtained the franchise, they were deprived of all local municipal rights, so that even the administration of justice and the charge of building devolved upon the Roman pretors and censors. The utmost concession ever made was that the most urgent law cases might be settled on the spot by a deputy nominated from Rome. After the social war, when all Italy became one civic community by the extension of the franchise, it was necessary to form smaller communities within the larger; it was impossible that the local affairs of all Italy should be settled by the magistrates of the city of Rome. These new communities were formed very much on the model of Rome; there were the same institutions, but with different names, and names such as implied inferiority to the institutions of the capital. There was a citizen-assembly, which passed laws and chose the local magistrates, and a council of one hundred members representing the Roman senate. The duumviri corresponded to the Roman consuls; two questors managed the local funds, and there were the local colleges of pontifices and augurs.

The imperial authority of Rome, however, existed side by side with the municipal constitution. Taxation might be imposed or public buildings set on foot by the Roman authorities as well as by those of the town; and in event of collision the town, of course, gave way. It is probable that in judicial matters a formal division of functions was made to avoid the extreme inconvenience of a collision of authority. The more important cases, both civil and criminal, would probably be reserved for the Roman authorities, while minor suits, or such as were most urgent, were decided on the spot.

Such was the constitution which Sulla now presented to the Roman state. He had used the power which he had gained by the sword to introduce really valuable reforms, and to compel all classes in the state, and especially the soldiery, to submit once more to civil authority. The mass of the community, if they did not welcome the Sullan arrangements, at any rate acquiesced in them without open opposition. But not so the military officers. The two most trusted lieutenants of Sulla, Gnaeus Pompeius and Quintus Ofella, were the first to rebel. The former had resisted the command of the senate to disband his army, and had only been conciliated by the concession of the honor of a triumph. The latter, in defiance of the new ordinance, became a candidate for the consulship without passing through the inferior magistracies. In his case no leniency was shown. Sulla had him cut down in the Forum, and then explained to the assembled citizens his reasons for the act.

On the completion of his work Sulla abdicated the extraordinary office conferred on him by the Valerian law. Although endowed with absolute power, he had, in the case of many of his enactments, consulted the people or the senate. Consuls had been elected for 81 B.C.; and for the next year Sulla himself was consul with Quintus Metellus, retaining the regency, but without exercising it for the time. For 79 B.C. the elections were left entirely free, and early in that year he resigned the regency, dismissed his lictors, and invited any citizen who wished to call him to account to speak.

The family to which Sulla belonged had remained for many generations in comparative obscurity, and his character at first gave no promise of an extraordinary career. In person he was blue-eyed and of a fair complexion, with piercing eyes. His tastes made him incline to a life of cultivated luxury, sometimes descending to debauchery. He was a pleasant companion in city or in camp, and even in the days of the regency would unbend after the business of the day. One of the most curious traits in his character was a vein of cynicism, which showed itself in the playful but dangerous irony of many of his acts. Thus he ordered a donation from the spoil of the proscribed to be given to a wretched author who had written a panegyric upon him, upon condition of never singing his praises again. When he seized the treasures of the Greek temples he declared that the man could never fail whose chest was replenished by the gods themselves. He displayed great vigor both of body and mind; even in his last years he was devoted to the chase, and after the conquest of Athens he could remember to bring with him the writings of Aristotle to Rome. In religion he followed the general tendency of the age towards unbelief and superstition. He flattered himself that he was the chosen favorite of the gods, and believed that he held intercourse with them in dreams and omens. When at the summit of his power he formally adopted the surname of Felix, and used it from that time forward.

Sulla's brilliant career seemed to come to him rather by caprice of fortune than by any seeking of his. He passed, like the ordinary aristocrat, through the usual routine of office; and in 107 B.C. the questorship under Marius in Africa fell to his lot. He soon made himself master of the military art, and, after the close of the Jugurthine war, performed the task of organizing supplies for the Roman army in the war with the Cimbri. During his pretorship,

93 B.C., the first Roman victory over Mithradates and the first treaty with the Parthians took place. He took a prominent part in the social war, and, as consul, suppressed the Sulpician revolution with startling energy. Wherever Sulla and Marius had come into competition the result had always been loss of renown to the elder general and increase of reputation to the younger; and the revolution of 88 B.C., which ended in the outlawry and flight of Marius, gave to Sulla the most important position within the empire. Then came the Mithradatic war and the Cinnan revolution—and it was Sulla who crushed the enemies of Rome abroad and put down anarchy at home. Now absolute autocrat of the state, he abolished the Gracchan constitution which had fettered the oligarchy for forty years, and compelled all orders and classes to yield a common obedience to the law; he established the oligarchy with all the stability that laws and constitution can give, and provided it with a bodyguard and an army. He was one of the few generals who never lost a battle, nor in his political career was he ever compelled to retrace a single step.

There is nothing original in the character of Sulla's constitution; and the reason is to be found in the very nature of his work. His task was to restore, not to create: the germ at least of every one of his institutions existed before; they had grown up out of the previous régime, and were merely regulated and fixed by Sulla. But his constitution could not last, because of the worthlessness of the aristocracy. Sulla might erect a fortress, but could not create a garrison. The gratitude of posterity is due to the man who, in the course of his hopeless task, carried out such admirable isolated reforms as those of the Asiatic revenue system and of criminal justice.

The short remainder of his life was passed in the strictest retirement; in a little more than a year he died, at the age of sixty, in full vigor of body and mind. Immediately after his death voices were raised in opposition to the proposal of a public burial; but his memory was still too fresh, and he was honored with, perhaps, the grandest funeral procession Italy had ever seen.

Chapter XXV

ECONOMIC CONDITION OF THE EMPIRE DURING THE REVOLUTION PERIOD. 133-78 B. C.

THE general tendency and result of the revolution period are evident from the history of the time and from the legislation of Sulla. The financial condition of the empire is worth more particular attention, and will furnish valuable evidence on many points with regard to the social and political relations of the time.

The revenues paid into the state treasury may be divided into two classes: those received from Italy and those contributed by the various provinces.

With regard to the former, the land-tax, with minor imposts upon Italians, had for some time been in abeyance; so that from the peninsula, including Cisalpine Gaul, the Roman exchequer drew nothing but the produce of the state lands, chiefly those in Campania, and of the gold mines in the North; customs dues on goods imported for trading purposes; and taxes levied on the manumission of slaves.

The provinces furnished two sources of revenue to the government, the proceeds from state lands and the returns from taxation. The state lands comprised the territory belonging to cities destroyed by martial law, such as Leontini, Carthage, and Corinth; and domain lands which had belonged to former rulers dispossessed by the Romans, such as the lands of the kings of Macedonia, Pergamus, Cyrene, and the mines in Spain. All such property was leased, like the state lands in Italy, by the state to tenants, and the rents formed a large part of the public revenue.

Within the bounds of the empire there were some states, like the kingdoms of Numidia and Cappadocia, which were recognized as fully sovereign and independent; there were others, like Rhodes, Massilia, and Gades, which enjoyed a free and equal alliance by special treaty with Rome. Both classes were exempt from ordinary taxation, and were merely bound to supply ships and men at their own expense in time of war. Besides these there were a few scattered cities, like Narbo, on which the Roman franchise had been specially conferred; and others, such as Centuripa in Sicily, which were specially exempted from taxation; but with these four exceptions the whole extent of the empire contributed to the Roman exchequer by a regular system of taxation which fell under three principal heads:

First, the decumae and scriptura. The former was a tenth of the produce of arable land; the latter, a corresponding tax upon pasture land. Of these kinds were the taxes levied in the fertile islands of Sicily and Sardinia.

Second, the stipendium, or tributum—*i. e.*, a fixed sum paid annually by a community to the Roman exchequer, amounting, for Macedonia, to about $120,000 of our money; for Gyaros, a small island near Andros, to about $31. This tax was usually lower than that paid by the community to its former rulers before the Roman conquest: the amount was fixed by the Roman authorities, while the magistrates of each community were responsible for collecting and paying over the amount to the Roman treasury.

Third, the customs. The Romans recognized the right of each community to levy its own customs at its own ports and frontiers, and made no attempt to set up a general tariff for the whole empire. Dues were levied by the Romans themselves at all the ports of Italy; most of the subject communities in the same way levied dues on their own frontiers, which would have to be paid even by Roman citizens, unless special exemption was secured by treaty. But in the provinces proper, like Sicily and Asia, where the Roman state was sole ruler and sovereign, the customs, of course, went into the imperial coffers. The amount raised was five per cent. on all imports or exports in Sicily, and two and a half in Asia. The customs, like the decumae and scriptura, were invariably leased to tax farmers.

These, with the unimportant item of tolls from roads, bridges, canals, etc., were the only regular taxes imposed upon the provincials by the Roman government. But they are far from representing the full amount of the burdens borne by the provinces.

In the first place, the expenses of collection were large; so that the amount paid by the contributors was much greater than that received by the government. Collection by middlemen is well known to be the most expensive system of all; and at Rome the lettings were so large that only a few capitalists could undertake them, and consequently the competition was small, and the profits of the lessees large.

Secondly, there were the military requisitions in time of war, frequently, also, in time of peace. Legally, all transport pay and provisions for the soldiers were provided by the Roman government; the provincial communities had only to furnish housing, wood, hay, and such things. But in time of war the governor demanded from them grain, ships, money, or anything he required; and though such requisitions were considered as advances to be made good by the government, yet practically they became a serious burden. This is proved by frequent laws restricting requisitions, fixing their maximum amount and the rate of compensation. At extraordinary times of course requisitions assumed the form of punishment, as when Sulla compelled the subjects of Asia to give fortyfold pay to every common soldier among them, and seventy-five fold to every centurion.

Thirdly, there were all kinds of extortions, legal or illegal, for which the Roman official had ample opportunity. The right of requisition, the free quartering of soldiers and of the clerks and lictors and innumerable officials in the train of a Roman governor, gave him sufficient pretext for amassing a princely fortune. The existence of a standing commission for the trial of such offenses shows their frequency.

Lastly, it must be remembered that Rome undertook the military expenses only of her subjects: all other burdens—the maintenance of roads and buildings, the pay of fleets and of the local contingent to the Roman army—were supported by the subject community, and must have formed a considerable addition to their taxation. For instance, in Judea the Jews paid a tenth to their native princes in addition to the temple tribute and to their payments to Rome.

The general conclusion at which we must arrive with regard to provincial taxation is, that, though moderate in theory, it must have been extremely oppressive in practice.

The revenues of the empire were devoted either to military or administrative purposes. Roman taxation, like the tribute paid to Athens by her subject allies, was in the main meant to defray the expense of the military system alone. Hence its comparatively small amount, $10,275,000—only two-thirds of the annual revenue of the king of Egypt. Hence, too, it may be guessed that the surplus revenue after payment of expenses was small, and that provinces like the Spains and Macedonia, which required a large garrison, cost more than they yielded. Still, in the times before the revolution, the surplus was large enough to defray the expenses of public buildings and to form a reserve fund. But the old principle, that the Roman hegemony should not be treated as a privilege from which profit might be derived, was infringed upon in the latter portion of this period in several ways: the customs in conquered territories were appropriated by Rome, and the mode of levying them was oppressive. By Gaius Gracchus Roman citizenship was treated as a privilege conferring a right to a certain amount of corn; and to provide the money for these largesses the soil of Asia was declared to belong absolutely to the Roman state, and was taxed accordingly.

The earlier portion of this epoch was an era of vast public undertakings. A new road was made, in 132 B.C., from Capua to the Straits of Sicily—branching from the great road which led from Rome through Capua to Tarentum and Brundisium. The coast road on the east was completed by extension southward to Brundisium and northward to Aquileia. About Rome itself, the Mulvian bridge over the Tiber was rebuilt of stone. In north Italy the Via Postumia was constructed in 148 B.C., from Genua to Aquileia through Placentia, Cremona, and Verona, thus connecting the two seas. Gaius Gracchus provided for the maintenance of the roads by assigning pieces of ground by the side of them to which was attached the duty of keeping them in repair.

To the same period belong the great provincial highways: the Via Domitia, connecting Italy with Spain; the Via Egnatia and the Via Gabinia, connecting the ports of the east coast of the Adriatic with the interior. The draining of the Pomptine marshes was undertaken in 160 B.C. The two ancient aqueducts were thoroughly repaired, and two new ones, the Marcia and the Calida, constructed. Not only were these stupendous works carried out, but paid for in cash; the Marcian aqueduct, which cost $10,000,000, was paid for in three years. Nor did these costly undertakings prevent the accumulation of a reserve, which at the very beginning of the period amounted to $4,300,000.

At the same time, it must be said that, even in the early part of this epoch, before the revolution, other duties of the government at least as imperative as these were entirely neglected. Brigands infested the frontier countries, and even the valley of the Po. There was no Roman fleet, and the vessels raised by the provincials were not numerous enough to check piracy, much less to carry on a naval war. The traffic of Rome had still to depend upon the old wooden Janiculan bridge over the Tiber, and the roadstead of Ostia was allowed to become blocked with sand.

But from the time of the revolution the picture is far worse. Public works were at a standstill; either because the corn largesses drained the treasury, or because the oligarchy were bent upon accumulating a large reserve fund in self-defense. This reserve is said to have reached its highest point in 91 B.C. The social war was the first severe strain to which the Roman state had been subjected since the Hannibalic war. During the latter the reserve was not touched till the tenth year, when the resources of taxation were exhausted; the social war was supported from the first from the reserve, and when this was exhausted the government preferred to sell the public sites in the city to imposing a tax upon the citizens.

In agriculture the forces previously at work are visible during this period in increased activity, and already produced startling results. The smaller holdings were absorbed by the large estates, as the sun absorbs the drops of rain. The senatorial government rather favored than opposed this process, which the opposition constantly endeavored to counteract. The two Gracchi gave 80,000 new farmers to Italy, and Sulla settled 120,000 of his veterans on the land, but the process still went on; the small farms were constantly being absorbed, while the creation of new farmers was only intermittent. In the provinces the same evils existed, and not the slightest attempt was made to check them; while they were attended with this additional disadvantage, that the rents were of course sent out of the country to Italy.

In trade and commerce there is little but inactivity to record; the Romans destroyed the industries of Corinth, and created nothing in their place. Building was, perhaps, an exception to the general stagnation, but produced little benefit to the commonwealth, as only slave labor was employed.

Commerce was exclusively in the hands of the Romans, and the political ascendency of Rome was unscrupulously used to favor this monopoly. Usury was one of the most lucrative of trades; for instance, the indemnity imposed by Sulla upon the province of

Asia was advanced by the Roman capitalists, and swelled in fourteen years to six times the original amount; public buildings, works of art, even their children, had to be sold by the unfortunate communities to meet their claims. Next in importance to money dealing came the export of wine and oil from Italy to all parts of the Mediterranean, and the import of all kinds of articles of luxury. The importation of slaves was enormous, especially from Syria and Asia Minor. The chief emporia for the reception of imports were Ostia and Puteoli, which traded chiefly with Alexandria and the cities of Syria, in the valuable commodities of the East.

Thus, side by side with the political oligarchy of senatorial families, there was a financial oligarchy of capitalists. These men absorbed the rents of the soil of Italy, and of the richest parts of the provinces; the usury and the commerce of the whole empire were in their hands, and even of the state revenue itself they drew a considerable share by their profits as lessees. Their influence in the state is clearly seen in the destruction of Corinth and Carthage, the commercial rivals of Rome; and it is to be remembered that their wealth was based, not upon sound economic principles, but upon the political supremacy of Rome; hence every political crisis was attended by a financial crisis.

One important result of the commercial monopoly of Rome was an interchange of population, greatly to the disadvantage of the Roman state. Everywhere in the provinces there were large numbers of Italians temporarily settled, mostly for commercial reasons. We have seen that 80,000 Italians perished in a single day in Asia Minor and 20,000 in Delos. Again, the population of Italy suffered enormous diminution during the social wars, when 300,000 persons are said to have perished. In return for the loss of these citizens, Italy received vast numbers of provincials, chiefly Oriental Greeks, who acted as physicians, schoolmasters, and priests, or who came to her ports as traders and mariners; while the proportion of slaves to freemen was continually increasing. The servile insurrections, the appeals to slaves, in times of disturbance, to take up arms against their masters, are plain enough signs of the times. If we conceive of England with its lords, its squires, above all its city, but with its freeholders and farmers converted into proletarians and its laborers and sailors converted into slaves, we shall gain an approximate image of the population of the Italian peninsula in those days.

Socially, no less than politically or financially, the period is one
of decadence, and is marked by growing extravagance and frivolity.
Enjoyment lost all freshness and spontaneity, and became a labor-
ious and pedantic study.   Animal hunts and gladiatorial games became the chief feature in the public festivals.   Huge sums were
expended at every great funeral on public games—Marcus Aemilius
Lepidus left strict injunctions to his children to avoid empty show,
and not to spend more at his obsequies than 1,000,000 asses
($51,000).   Houses and gardens reached fabulous prices; gambling
and extravagance in dress were fashionable foibles; but the favorite
mode of expenditure was on the luxuries of the table.

Every villa along the coast had its tanks for securing a constant
supply of fish.   At the best entertainments, not whole birds, but
only the most delicate portions, were served up, and the guests were
expected merely to taste of the multitude of dishes presented to them.
There were sumptuary laws totally prohibiting certain delicacies,
regulating the price of meals and the amount of plate, but of all the
Roman nobles, only three are said to have kept these laws, and that
on account of regard for the principles of Stoic philosophy, not for
the law.   A century earlier few houses contained any silver plate
beyond the traditional salt dish, but in Sulla's time there were 150
silver dishes at Rome of 100 lbs. weight.   Some of it was of
such exquisite workmanship as to be valued at eighteen times
its weight of metal, and Lucius Crassus gave $5,250 for a pair of
silver cups.

Perhaps the most significant mark of the corruption of the age
is the frequency of divorce and the general aversion to marriage.
Even Metellus Macedonicus, censor in 131 B.C., a man renowned
for his honorable domestic life, urged the duty of marriage upon
his fellow-citizens in the following terms: " If we could, citizens,
we should indeed all keep clear of this burden.   But as nature has
so arranged it that we cannot either live comfortably with wives or
live at all without them, it is proper to have regard rather to the
permanent weal than to our own brief comfort."   These facts are
important, for it is only by trying to realize the ignoble private life
of the time that we can comprehend the political corruption which
prevailed.   There were exceptions, especially among the rural
towns, but immorality was the rule.   One of the censors of
92 B.C. publicly reproached his colleague with having shed tears
over the death of a favorite fish; the other retaliated on the

former that he had buried three wives and shed tears over none of them.

In 161 B.C. an orator in the Forum gave the following descrip-tion of the senatorial jurymen: "They play hazard, delicately per-fumed, surrounded by their mistresses. As the afternoon advances they summon the servant and bid him make inquiries at the comi-tium, what has occurred in the Forum, who has spoken in favor of or against the new project of law, what tribes have voted for and what against it. At length they go themselves to the judgment seat, just early enough not to bring the process down on their own neck.

"Reluctantly they come to the tribunal and give audience to the parties. Those who are concerned bring forward their cause. The juryman orders the witness to come forward; he himself goes aside. When he returns, he declares that he has heard everything, and asks for the documents. He looks into the writings—he can hardly keep his eyes open for wine. When he thereupon withdraws to consider his sentence, he says to his boon companions, ' What concern have I with these tiresome people? Why should we not rather go to drink a cup of mulse mixed with Greek wine, and accompany it with a fat fieldfare, and a good fish—a veritable pike from the Tiber island?'" All this was, no doubt, very ridiculous; but was it not a very serious matter that such things were subjects of ridicule?

Governors accused of tyrannous maladministration of their provinces found it a simple thing to bribe their judges, and all the more as these latter knew that corresponding charges might at any time be brought against themselves. Indeed, indictments such as the young Julius Caesar's against Dolabella for extortion in Mace-donia were frequent, but only represented the means adopted by ambitious young Romans to call attention to themselves. Seem-ingly the most noble denunciation had this ulterior motive, and, while almost invariably resultless to the oppressed province, served the orator's purpose. It was commonly estimated that three years of office would adequately provide, first for the private fortune of the governor, second for the satisfaction of his host of followers, and lastly for the bribing of the judges and the purchase of his own acquittal.

Statesmen and generals alike were notoriously venal, moved by cupidity and ambition. No arts were considered too base that served their purpose. It is true there were noble exceptions, but the rankness of the times was frankly admitted and attempts to check the progress of corruption by censorial power and law were practically all in vain. Thus was Rome sapped by the very wealth added by her conquests, and the empire weakened by the abuse of her extended power. It could be said that the misery of her subject states was greater in time of peace under the corrupt rule of Roman governors than it had been under the ordinary misfortunes of war.

PART IV

FALL OF THE REPUBLIC AND ESTABLISH-ING OF THE MONARCHY. 78-44 B.C.

Chapter XXVI

THE RULE OF THE SULLAN RESTORATION. 78-70 B.C.

SULLA'S arrangements had been acquiesced in by all the chief classes in the state, and on his death his constitution had nothing to fear from any organized body of opponents. There was, however, a large but heterogeneous body of malcontents opposed to the present condition of things for varied reasons.

This opposition was made up of widely different classes. There were the jurists, who considered the Sullan laws unconstitutional, and the moderate senators, who desired to compromise with the democratic party; there were the democrats themselves, who aimed at the restoration of the tribunate, and the disfranchised, who wished to recover or obtain political influence; there were the poor, who had been deprived of their free corn, and the proscribed, who demanded back their confiscated property; and there were the equestrian capitalists, whose chances for gain had been curtailed by the restoration of senatorial privileges. To all these classes one more remains to be added—the men of ambition and the men of ruined fortunes. The latter included alike the aristocratic lords, who had lost their patrimony by riotous living, and the Sullan colonists, who refused to settle down to a life of husbandry and were eager for fresh spoil. The former included men, outside the senatorial circle, who were eager to force their way into office by popular favor; and men of more daring ambition, who might perhaps emulate Gaius Gracchus.

It is most necessary, for the understanding of the history of the following years, that all these elements of opposition should be fully grasped; and it may be well here to recall to mind the two great and constant difficulties of the Roman government—the difficulty of controlling its military governors in the provinces; and the difficulty of managing the masses of slaves and freedmen in the capital, without either police or troops at its disposal.

It was, perhaps, the greatest misfortune of all that there was everywhere at this period a dearth of political leaders. The man-

agement of parties was in the hands of political clubs, a system
which had existed for centuries at Rome, but which was now seen
in its worst and most aggravated form.   These clubs, as common
among the rabble as among the aristocrats, controlled the whole
political life of the city through organized bribery and intimidation.
Such a system of faction and corruption, however, was not one likely
to produce statesmen, however much it might add to the bitterness
and violence of personal and political struggles.

Among the men prominent in the political life of the day, three
alone are worthy of consideration.   The first is Gnaeus Pompeius,
born in 106 B.C.   He had raised troops and fought for Sulla in the
second civil war, and had enjoyed the titles of imperator and tri-
umphator before his age permitted him to stand for any office.
Already he began to be known by the title of Magnus.   He was
an able soldier, but no genius; cautious to timidity, and averse to
strike till he had established an immense superiority over his opponent.   In culture, as well as in integrity of character, he was at least
up to the level of the time; he was a good neighbor, a good husband
and father.   His temperament was kind and humane; and he was
the first to depart from the custom of putting to death captive kings
and generals after a triumph.   Yet he sent a divorce to the wife
whom he loved, at the command of Sulla, because she belonged to
an outlawed family.   For politics he had little aptitude.   He was
awkward and stiff in public; easily managed by his freedmen and
clients; eager for power, but affecting to despise it.   His relations
to the parties of the time were peculiar.   Though a Sullan officer,
he was opposed to Sulla personally.   Nor was he in sympathy with
the senatorial government; for his family was not yet fully established among the aristocracy, and Pompeius himself had once been
a Cinnan adherent.   He had no political sagacity, and little political
courage.   He might have had a definite and respectable position
had he contented himself with being the general of the senate—
the office for which he was from the beginning destined.   With this
he was not content, and so he fell into the fatal plight of wishing
to be something else than he could be.   He was constantly aspiring
to a special position in the state, and when it offered itself, he could
not make up his mind to occupy it.   Constantly tormented by an ambition which was frightened at its own aims, his deeply agitated life
passed joylessly away in a perpetual inward contradiction.

Marcus Crassus was famed for his boundless activity, especially in the acquisition of wealth; he was contractor, builder, banker, and usurer, and carried on numerous other trades through his freedmen. Unlike Pompeius, he was unscrupulous in the means he employed. He was proved to have committed a forgery in the matter of the Sullan proscription lists; he did not refuse a legacy because the will which gave it him was known to be forged; and he allowed his bailiffs to dislodge the small farmers adjoining his estates by force and by fraud. He soon became the richest man in Rome; and at his death, after expending enormous sums, he was still worth $8,500,000. But his wealth was only a means to the gratification of his ambition; he extended his connection by every possible means; he could salute every burgess of the capital by name; never refused his services as an advocate, and, though without any gift of oratory, overcame all obstacles by his pertinacity in speaking. He advanced money on loan to influential men without distinction of party, and thus acquired a power which none dared to provoke. His ambition knew no bounds; while he stood alone the crown of Rome was beyond his grasp, but it was not impossible that, with the aid of a suitable partner, he might attain to supremacy in the state.

In the ranks of the democrats the revolution had made such havoc that scarcely a man of note survived. Of the rising generation. Gaius Julius Caesar was now only twenty-four years of age, but was already perhaps the third most important man in Rome. His family connections naturally inclined him towards the democratic party; for his father's sister had been the wife of Marius, and his own wife was the daughter of Cinna; while his early career had so far been one of opposition to the senatorial rule. He had refused to divorce his wife at the bidding of Sulla, and with difficulty escaped proscription at the intercession of his relatives. But Caesar could only be the hope of the future, and the actual leadership of the democratic party fell for the present into other hands.

Scarcely was Sulla dead when the democratic party began to attack his work. Their candidate, Lepidus, was elected consul for the year 78 B.C., and at once proposed the renewal of the corn distribution and a restoration of the confiscated lands. At the same time, portions of the party in Etruria raised the standard of revolt and attempted to resume their estates by force. The two consuls were sent to suppress the rising, but Lepidus turned his arms against the government. He was finally defeated and driven out of Italy by Pompeius, and most of his forces joined Sertorius in Spain.

Spain was now the only province of the empire where opposition to the senate still existed. Sertorius had appeared in that province again in 80 B.C., and soon built up a power that it taxed all the resources of the Roman government for eight years to subdue. Even then the government could find no means to overthrow him but the assassin's dagger. He was a man of tender, sensitive nature, and at the same time of the most chivalrous courage, and in the revolutionary war his military talent and his genius for organization presented a striking contrast to the incapacity of the other democratic leaders. His Spanish followers called him the New Hannibal, and indeed his adroitness and versatility, in politics and in war, savor far more of the Phoenician than of the Roman genius. He was careful always to act as Roman governor of the province; and he began to organize the country in the same spirit. He formed the chief men of the exiles into a senate to conduct affairs and to nominate magistrates. The officers of the army were exclusively Roman; to the Spaniards he was the Roman governor who levied troops by virtue of his office. At the same time he endeavored to attach the provincials to Rome and to himself. The strictest discipline was maintained in the army, and the inhabitants were relieved from all fear of outrage on the part of the soldiers. The tribute of the province was reduced, and the soldiers were made to build winter barracks for themselves, to avoid the necessity of quartering them on the inhabitants. The children of the noble Spaniards were educated in an academy at Osca, where they learned to speak Latin and Greek, and adopted the Roman dress—the first attempt to Romanize the provinces by Romanizing the provincials themselves.

For eight years Sertorius maintained himself in Spain against every army and every general sent out against him. He defeated the able Metellus and confined him to a few coast towns, and even Pompeius, who had demanded and received from the senate the Spanish command, with extraordinary powers, was more than once defeated, though he gradually drove the rebel back into the interior and forced him to confine himself mostly to guerrilla warfare.

The losses of the state in men and treasure during all this time are difficult to estimate: not only were the Spanish revenues lost, but vast sums had annually to be sent for the support of the army in Spain. The province itself was devastated; whole communities had frequently perished, and the towns which adhered to Rome had countless hardships to endure. Gaul suffered scarcely less from the constant requisitions of men and money, and from the burden of providing winter quarters. Generals and soldiers were alike dissatisfied; the former because victory was difficult and of a kind that brought no fame; the latter because the booty was poor, and even their pay irregular. At the same time the government was contending against its enemies all over the Mediterranean, on the sea, in Macedonia and in Asia Minor; while Sertorius was already in open league with the pirates, and was negotiating with Mithradates on the basis of mutual assistance.

But the odds in the contest were too great for Sertorius to withstand indefinitely. The whole insurrection rested for success on his genius alone and the love the Spanish people bore him. Knowing this, the Romans set a price on his head, promising, it is said, one hundred thousand dollars to any man who would kill him. A conspiracy was formed against him by his own lieutenants, and in 72 B.C. he was treacherously stabbed at a banquet to which they had invited him. After this the rebellion quickly died out, and at the close of the following year Pompeius returned to Italy with his victorious army.

The Sullan constitution had thus survived the dangers which beset it on the death of its author. It remains to be seen how the senate fulfilled the duties of government during its new lease of power. In order to do this, it is necessary to go back a little, and to review the condition of other parts of the empire during the last years of Sulla's regency and the first years after his death in 78 B.C. The condition of Spain had thrown all other questions into the shade; but there were other serious dangers threatening—especially from Thrace and Macedonia, from the East, and from the pirates of the Mediterranean.

In Thrace and the adjacent regions there was warfare for the space of twelve years, the result of which was that the pirates of the Dalmatian coast and the tribes between Macedonia and the Danube were subdued, while Thrace became a portion of the province of Macedonia.

The most important feature in the history of the East, during the years succeeding the settlement of Sulla, was the rapid increase of the power and territory of Tigranes, king of Armenia, and son-in-law of Mithradates. Hardly had Sulla left Asia before the king began to extend his dominions at the expense of the Parthians, to the south, and of the kingdoms of Asia Minor to the west. Upper

Mesopotamia, Cappadocia, eastern Cilicia, and upper Syria were reduced, and it was the evident aim of Tigranes to become supreme monarch of the East.   The Romans, anxious to avoid a conflict, did not at first interfere with these conquests.   Even Mithradates was allowed to strengthen himself until he was again dangerous. He had felt that a rupture with Rome could only be a question of time, and so, finally taking advantage of the Sertorian war in Spain, he overran Asia Minor in 75 and 74 B.C.   Fortunately the Romans had in the consul Lucullus one of the ablest generals the state had produced, and, though he had but a small force under his command, he soon recovered Asia and drove Mithradates to take refuge with the king of Armenia.   The latter had in the beginning held aloof from the war, but he now refused to deliver up his father-in-law, and Lucullus marched against him in 69 B.C.   In a short and brilliant campaign Tigranes was driven from his capital and immense quantities of booty were secured, enough to pay all the expenses of the campaign and to furnish a present of one hundred and sixty-five dollars to each soldier.   But again the incapacity of the home government was seen in the conduct of affairs at this critical period. Lucullus was a cold, unbending man and a strict disciplinarian, and his troops hated him accordingly.   Many of them had come out to the East with Flaccus and Fimbria, in 86 B.C., and now demanded their discharge.   Their insubordination was encouraged by the knowledge that their general was in disfavor with the ruling powers at Rome.   Lucullus, whose honesty was above reproach, had protected the natives of the province of Asia from the usury of the Roman capitalists, and these all clamored for his recall.   The senate accordingly refused reinforcements and sent out a new governor to supersede him.   He was obliged to retire west of the Euphrates, his army quickly broke up, and Tigranes and Mithradates once more recovered their kingdoms, 67 B.C.   Thus, after nearly eight years of war in the East, the Romans were exactly in the same position as at the beginning.

The remissness of the senatorial government is, however, most strikingly seen in the extraordinary growth of piracy.   The whole Mediterranean was infested with corsairs, so that all traffic by sea was at an end.   The import of corn into Italy ceased, while the cornfields of the provinces could find no vent for their produce. Romans of rank were carried off for the sake of the ransom paid for their liberation; merchants, and even troops, put off their voyages till the winter season, preferring the risk of storm and tempest to that of capture. Worst of all were the outrages on the islands and coast towns of Asia Minor, which were either sacked or compelled to purchase safety by the payment of large sums. All the rich temples of this region were plundered, and even towns one or two days' march from the coast were no longer safe.

The pirates of this day were no longer mere freebooters or slave-catchers, but formed a regular state, with an organization, a home of their own, and at least the germs of a political league. They called themselves Cilicians, but drew their recruits from all sources—discharged mercenaries, citizens of destroyed communities, soldiers from the Sertorian or Fimbrian armies, the refugees of all vanquished parties. The motto of the new state was vengeance upon civil society; its members were bound together by a strong sense of fellowship—by a determination to be true to each other, and by loyalty to their chosen chiefs. They regarded their plunder as military spoil, and as in the case of capture they were sure of the cross, they too claimed the right of executing their prisoners. Their ships were small, open, and swift—mostly light " myoparones "—and they sailed in squadrons under regularly appointed admirals. Their home was the whole Mediterranean, but their special haunts, where they kept their plunder and their wives, were Crete and the southern coast of Asia Minor. Here the native leagues were weak, and the Roman station was inadequate for the guardianship of the whole coast, while the Armenian king troubled himself little about the sea. In the prevailing weakness of the legitimate governments of the time the pirates gained a body of client states among the Greek maritime cities, which made treaties and carried on an extensive trade with them. The town of Side in Pamphylia, for instance, allowed them to build ships on its quays and to sell their captures in its market. The pirate state even formed alliances with Mithradates and with the Roman emigrants; it fought battles with the fleets of Sulla, and some of its princes reigned over many coast towns.

Evidently the Romans had shamefully neglected all the duties of maritime police. Instead of keeping up a fleet to guard the whole sea, they left each province and each client state to defend itself as it could. Though the provincials paid tribute to the Romans for their defense, there was no Italian fleet. The government depended on ships furnished by the maritime towns at the expense of the provinces, which were even called upon to contribute to the ransom of Roman captives of rank. In 79 B.C. one of the consuls, Publius Servilius, defeated the pirate fleet and destroyed the pirate towns on the south coast of Asia Minor, including Olympus and Phaselis, which belonged to the prince Zenicetes. He next led an army over the Taurus, captured Isaura, and subdued the Isaurians in the northwest of rough Cilicia. His campaigns lasted for three years, and were not without fruit; but, naturally, the main body of the pirates simply betook itself to other regions—especially Crete. Nothing but the establishment of a strong maritime police could meet the case, and this the Romans would not undertake.

In 74 B.C. they did intrust the clearance of the seas to a single admiral in supreme command. But such appointments were managed by the political clubs: and the choice fell upon the pretor Marcus Antonius, who was quite unfit for the post. Moreover, the government did not furnish supplies and money adequate for the purpose, so that the requisitions of the admiral were more burdensome to the provincials than were the pirates themselves. The expedition came to nothing: the Roman fleet was defeated off Cydonia by the pirates and the Cretans combined; Antonius died in Crete in 71 B.C., and the government fell back upon the old system of leaving each state to protect itself.

The defeat of Cydonia roused even the degenerate Romans of that day from their lethargy; yet the bribes of the Cretan envoys would probably have bought off Roman vengeance had not the senate decreed that the loans to the envoys from Roman bankers at exorbitant interest were not recoverable—thus incapacitating itself for bribery. The most humiliating terms were now offered to the Cretans, and on their rejection Quintus Metellus, the proconsul, appeared, in 68 B.C., in Cretan waters. A battle was fought under the walls of Cydonia, which the Romans with difficulty won, but the siege of the towns lasted for two years. With the conquest of Crete the last spot of free Greek soil passed under the power of the Romans.

Metellus assumed the surname of Creticus, as Servilius had become Isauricus; but the power of the pirates in the Mediterranean was never higher than now. The coast towns paid taxes for defense to the Roman governor and blackmail to the pirates at the same time; the admiral of the Cilician army was carried off, as well as two pretors with all their retinue and insignia; the Roman fleet, equipped to clear the seas, was destroyed by the pirates in the port of Ostia itself: and so things went on, from bad to worse, until Pompeius put an end to the pest in 67 B.C.

The rule of the restored oligarchy in Macedonia, in the East, and on the sea has thus been reviewed; we have now to see how it fulfilled its duties within the confines of Italy.

Politically and economically slavery was the curse of all ancient states, and it is to be remembered that, where this institution exists, the richer and more prosperous the state, the greater the proportion of slaves to the free population becomes. There had already been serious servile wars, and the evil had grown with the growth of the plantation system, but the decade after the death of Sulla was the golden age of buccaneers by sea and land. Violence of all kinds was rife in the less populated parts of Italy, but the crime of abduction of men and seizure of estates was peculiarly dangerous to the state. For it was frequently perpetrated by the overseers and slaves of great landowners, who did not disdain to keep what their officious subordinates had thus acquired for them; and, of course, bands of slaves and proletarians were ready enough to learn their lesson, and to carry on the business of plunder on their own account. Thus Italy was full of inflammable material, and a spark was not long wanting to set it ablaze.

In 73 B.C. a number of gladiators broke out from one of the training schools of Capua, and took up a position on Mount Vesuvius, under the leadership of two Celtic slaves, Crixus and Oenomaus, and of Spartacus, a Thracian of noble, perhaps even of royal, lineage. At first only seventy-four in number, they quickly increased, until aid had to be sought from Rome to repel them. A hastily collected army of three thousand men blockaded the mountain, but when attacked by the robbers it at once fled. This success of course increased the number of the insurgents, and the pretor Varinius found them encamped like a regular army in the plain.

The Roman militia soon became sorely weakened by disease, and undermined by cowardice and insubordination. The greater number refused to obey the order to attack, and when at length Varinius advanced, the enemy had retreated southward out of his reach. He followed, but was disastrously defeated in Lucania. The robber band soon rose to the number of forty thousand men; Campania was overrun, and many strong towns were stormed.

The slaves naturally showed no more mercy to their captives than was shown to themselves by their masters; they crucified their prisoners, and with grim humor compelled them to slaughter each other in gladiatorial combat.

In the year 72 B.C. both consuls were sent against the slaves. The Celtic band under Crixus, which had separated from the rest, was destroyed at Mount Garganus in Apulia, but Spartacus won victory after victory in the north, and overcame both consuls and every Roman commander who opposed him. Still the insurgents remained a mere band of robbers, roaming aimlessly in search of plunder, and all the efforts of Spartacus to restrain the mad orgies of his followers and to induce them to carry on a systematic war were in vain. Nor was the band united in itself, but separated into two parts, the one consisting of half-Greek barbarians, the other of Celts and Germans. It is said that Spartacus wished after his victories to cross the Alps, and lead his followers to their old homes, but was unable to persuade them, and that he then turned south to blockade Rome, which again was too arduous an enterprise to suit the wishes of slaves.

The supreme command was now intrusted by the Roman government to Marcus Crassus, the pretor. He raised an army of eight legions, and restored discipline by killing every tenth man of the first division which ran away. Spartacus was defeated and marched south to Rhegium, where he attempted to throw a corps into Sicily, but without success. Crassus followed, and made his troops build a wall across the whole peninsula of Bruttium: but Spartacus broke through, and in 71 B.C. appeared again in Lucania. But their own disunion and arrogance were more fatal to the robbers than the Roman armies. Once more the Celts and Germans broke off from the rest, and though after a narrow escape they once more pitched their camp for safety near that of Spartacus, Crassus managed to compel them to a separate engagement, and slaughtered the whole body. Spartacus even now gained a slight success over the Roman vanguard, but his men compelled him to lead them into Apulia and to fight a decisive battle. Crassus gained a dearly bought victory, and being joined by the troops of Pompeius from Spain, he hunted out the refugees in every part of southern Italy: six thousand crucified slaves lined the road from Capua to Rome.

If the events of the ten years after the death of Sulla are

viewed as a whole, what must be the judgment on the senatorial government? The most striking fact about all the movements of that period is, that though none of them—neither the insurrection of Lepidus, nor the Sertorian war, nor the wars in Asia and Macedonia—any more than the risings of the pirates and of the slaves, constituted a really great and serious danger, yet they were allowed to grow by neglect into struggles in which the very existence of the empire was at stake. It was no credit to Rome that the two most celebrated generals of the government party had, during a struggle of eight years, marked by more defeats than victories, failed to master the insurgent chief Sertorius and his Spanish guerrillas; and that it was only the dagger of his friends that decided the Sertorian war in favor of the legitimate government. As to the slaves, it was far less an honor to have conquered them than a disgrace to have been pitted against them in equal strife for years. Spartacus, too, as well as Hannibal, had traversed Italy with an army from the Po to the Sicilian straits, beaten both consuls, and threatened Rome with blockade. The enterprise which it required the greatest general of antiquity to undertake against the Rome of former days, could be undertaken against the Rome of the present by a daring captain of banditti.

The external wars produced a result less unsatisfactory, but quite disproportionate to the expenditure of money and men. The Romans were driven from the sea, and in Asia, in spite of the genius of Lucullus, the result was tantamount to defeat. And though, to some extent, every class in the Roman state is responsible for this deplorable state of affairs, as every rotten stone in the building helps to bring about the ruin of the whole, yet, in great part, it can be distinctly traced to the mismanagement of the governing body. For instance, the failure of the Asiatic war was due to the remissness of the government in abandoning their client states in the first instance, and to their neglect to support their general after the war had begun; while the power of the pirates was due to the culpable reluctance of the government to deal with the evil in the comprehensive manner by which alone it could be met. To sum up, the material benefits which a state exists to confer—security of frontier, undisturbed peaceful intercourse, legal protection, and regulated administration—began, all of them, to vanish for the whole of the nations united in the Roman state; the gods of blessing seemed all of them to have ascended to Olympus, and to

have left the miserable earth at the mercy of official or volunteer
plunderers and tormentors. Nor was this decay of the state felt as
a public misfortune by such only as had political rights and public
spirit; the insurrection of the proletariate, and the prevalence of
brigandage and piracy carried the sense of this decay into the re-
motest valley and the humblest hut of Italy, and made everyone who
pursued trade or commerce, or who bought even a bushel of wheat,
feel it as a personal calamity.

Chapter XXVII

FALL OF THE OLIGARCHY—RULE OF POMPEIUS
70-63 B.C.

THE new government had survived the danger of external war and of insurrection in Italy. We have now to consider its relations with parties in Rome during the same decade of years. With characteristic want of energy it had not even completed the half-finished arrangements of Sulla. The lands destined by him for distribution had not been parceled out; even domain lands were again occupied in the old arbitrary fashion which prevailed before the Gracchan reforms. Whatever in the new constitution was inconvenient to the optimates was ignored, such as the disfranchisement of particular communities and the prohibition against conjoining the new farms.

Still the Gracchan constitution remained formally abolished, and it was the aim of the democratic party to restore it in its main features, so the old watchwords were heard again—the corn largesses, the tribunician power, and the reform of the senatorial tribunals. The government consented, in the year of Sulla's death (78 B.C.), to a limited revival of the corn distributions, and in 73 B.C. a new corn law regulated the purchases of Sicilian grain for this purpose.

The agitation regarding the tribunician power was begun as early as 76 B.C., and continued in later years, though without result. But for the reform of the tribunals the cry was louder and the need more pressing. The crime of extortion had become habitual, and the condemnation of any man of influence could scarcely be obtained. Not only was there a fellow-feeling with the accused on the part of the senatorial jurymen, many of whom had either been guilty or hoped some day to be guilty of a similar offense, but the sale of the votes of the jurymen had become an established custom. A specially flagrant case might provoke an outcry for the time, but, generally speaking, bribery was so universal that the commission as to extortions might be regarded as an institution for taxing the

senators returning from the provinces for the benefit of their col-
leagues that remained at home.	Even Roman citizens in the
provinces, unless senators or equites, were no longer safe from the
rods and axes of the Roman magistrates.	The opposition did not
fail to avail itself of this state of things; for the prosecution of a
powerful opponent in the law courts was the only weapon left to it.
So Caesar prosecuted Gnaeus Dolabella and Gaius Antonius, and
Cicero made himself famous by his indictment of Verres; while
the whole party loudly demanded the restoration of the tribunician power and of the equestrian tribunals, and the renewal
of the censorship as the only means of purifying the governing
board.

With all this no progress was made; the restoration of corn
distributions had conciliated the mob of the capital, and the senate
could afford to be resolute on the other points.	Some slight con-
cession was made with regard to the exiles of the insurrection of
Lepidus; and the influence of Gaius Cotta, leader of the moderate
reform party in the senate, abolished the provision which forbade
the tribunes of the plebs to stand for other magistracies; but the
other restrictions remained, and neither party was satisfied.

The present condition of affairs, so happy for the government,
was completely changed by the return of Pompeius from Spain in
71 B.C.	Pompeius belonged to the optimates, but he was very little
at home in his own party.	He had ambition above that of the
ordinary aristocrat, and could not be content with passing through
the regular routine of office, with nothing before him but a luxuri-
ous and indolent retirement.	Yet this was all that his own party
could offer.	The command in the Mithradatic war, which he
ardently desired, he knew the senate would never give him.	The
interests of the oligarchy could not permit him to add fresh laurels
to those he had already gained in Africa and Europe; they dared
not intrust the Eastern command to any but the most approved and
stanchest aristocrat.	And there were other grounds of dissension.
It was only with reluctance that the senate had conferred upon him
the Spanish command; while, in return, the general accused the
government of neglecting the Spanish armies and endangering the
expedition.	Moreover, he demanded for himself a triumph and
the consulship, and for his soldiers assignations of land.	But
Pompeius had never filled any of the subordinate magistracies, and
therefore could not legally be consul.	Nor could he triumph, for,

in spite of his extraordinary commands, he had never been invested with the ordinary supreme power. There were but two courses open to him: he could either make his demands openly at the head of his army and intimidate the senate into compliance, or he could ally himself with the democrats. The timid nature of Pompeius and his want of political adroitness inclined him to the latter course; he thus gained for himself able political adjutants like Gaius Caesar, while the forlorn democratic party were only too glad of the alliance—they knew that the government could refuse no demand presented by so formidable a combination.

There was still one man whose influence, though it might not be able-to give victory to either side, was yet considerable. This was Marcus Crassus, who was at the head of the army with which he had crushed the servile rising, and who, moreover, was the richest man in Rome, and had great influence in the political clubs. He, like Pompeius, was a Sullan, but had personal aims, quite outside the ordinary constitutional routine. He chose the safer course of joining the coalition, and was welcomed by the democrats, who were not unpleased to find in him a possible counterpoise to the now all-powerful Pompeius. This, the first coalition, took place in the summer of 71 B.C. The terms were simple. The generals adopted the democratic programme, while they were to have the consulship for the following year. Pompeius, in addition, was to get his triumph and the allotments promised to his soldiers, and Crassus the honor of a solemn entrance into the capital. The senate had nothing to oppose to the coalition, for Metellus had already disbanded his troops. They granted the necessary dispensations, and Pompeius gave formal adherence to the democratic proposals in an assembly of the people.

The Sullan constitution was now speedily abolished. Pompeius himself, as consul, introduced a law restoring to the tribunes all their old prerogatives, especially the right of initiating legislation. The law-courts were reformed, probably with the consent of the moderate senatorial party, for the senators were not altogether excluded from the roll of jurymen, who in future were to be composed one-third of senators, two-thirds of equestrians; but, of the latter, one-half must have filled the office of district presidents. As these officers were elected by the tribes, one-third of the jurymen were now indirectly elective. The farming system was reintroduced for the taxes of the Asiatic province; this, of course, was to conciliate the capitalists at the expense of the provincials. Finally, the censorship was restored—probably without the earlier limitation which restricted the term of office to eighteen months.   The constitution of Sulla had been based on a monopoly of power by the senate, and on the political annihilation of every other class in the state; but under the new arrangement the senate was held in check by fear of the censors and of the equestrian jurymen. The tribunes of the people could propose new laws and overturn any existing arrangements at will, while the moneyed classes, as farmers of the revenue and as judges of the provincial governors, again raised their heads beside the senate. The further aims of the democrats were not for the present attained.

Meanwhile the armies of the two generals still lay before the walls of Rome, and the danger was great lest Pompeius should yield to the temptation of making himself absolute master of the city and of the empire. The coalition had only one bond of union—the desire to destroy the Sullan constitution; that work being now accomplished, the combination was in reality dissolved. Crassus had throughout played an inferior part, and his terror became so great that he began to make advances to the senate and to attempt to gain over the mob by immense largesses. But Pompeius really lacked the courage to take a decisive step; he wished to be master of Rome and loyal citizen at the same time. The adroit leaders of the democratic party plied him with flatteries, urged him to surpass his former services to the state by a still greater victory, and to banish the fearful specter of civil war. Crassus was induced to make the first overtures for disbandment, and at length the great general yielded, and the troops dispersed. The Mithradatic war appeared now at an end, and as Pompeius would not accept a province he retired at the expiry of his consulship wholly from public affairs.

During the next few years the condition of parties was very much what it had been before the time of Sulla. The direction of affairs lay with the senate, while the constitution through which it governed was pervaded by a hostile spirit. The democrats were impotent without a leader, and the chief feature of the period is the increase of the influence of the capitalist party, which, though courted by both sides, on the whole drew closer to the senate. Their influence is seen in the law of the year 67 B.C., which restored to them the fourteen special benches in the theater and in the fact that the senate withdrew, at their instance, the administration of Asia from Lucius Lucullus.

But the course of the war in the East soon brought about a change. All the conquests there were lost, and the sea was given up to the undisputed sway of the pirates. The democrats eagerly seized the opportunity of settling accounts with the senate, and Pompeius saw once more before him an opportunity of gratifying his ambition. Accordingly, in 67 B.C., two projects of law were introduced in the assembly of the tribes at his instigation. The first measure decreed the discharge of the soldiers in the East who had served their term, and the substitution of Glabrio, one of the consuls of the year, for Lucullus in the command. The second proposed a comprehensive plan for clearing the seas of pirates.

The terms of the proposal are extraordinary, and require close attention. First, a generalissimo was to be appointed by the senate from the consulars, to hold supreme command over the whole Mediterranean and over all the coasts for fifty miles inland, concurrently with the ordinary governors, for three years. Second, he might select from the men of senatorial rank twenty-five lieutenants with pretorian powers, and two treasurers with questorian power. Third, he might raise an army of 120,000 infantry and 7000 cavalry, and a fleet of 500 ships, and for this purpose might dispose absolutely of all the resources of the provinces. Besides this, a large sum of money and a considerable force of men and ships were at once handed over to him.

By the introduction of this law the government was practically taken out of the hands of the senate; it was the final collapse of the oligarchic rule. But it was more than this—it was practically the institution of an unlimited dictatorship.

Like all extraordinary commands, this new office no doubt required the confirmation of the people; but it was an undoubted prerogative of the senate to define the sphere of every command, and, in fact, to control and limit it in all ways. The people had hitherto interfered only on the proposition of the senate, or at any rate of a magistrate himself qualified for the office of general. Even during the Jugurthan war, when the command was transferred to Marius by popular vote, it was only to Marius as consul for the year. But now a private man was to be invested by the tribes with extraordinary authority, and the sphere of his office was defined by themselves. The new commander was empowered to confer pretorian powers—that is, the highest military and civil authority —upon adjutants chosen by himself, though hitherto such authority could only be conferred with the coöperation of the burgesses; while the office of general, which was usually conferred for one year only, with strict limitations as to forces and supplies, was now committed almost without reserve to one man, who could draw upon the whole resources of the state.

Thus at one stroke the government was taken out of the hands of the senate, and the fortunes of the empire committed for the next three years to a dictator. The step, no doubt, was in accordance with the wishes of Pompeius, for it would naturally lead in the end to the command against Mithradates, and it gave him an extraordinary position in the state without violating constitutional forms. Still, it was probably due immediately to the instigation of his bold adherents, in particular of Aulus Gabinius, the tribune, who proposed the law, who grasped the situation more completely than Pompeius himself, and took the decision out of his hands. The senate and the moneyed aristocracy alike were furious, while the democrats, though they could not but dislike a bill which threatened to annihilate all parties, dared not break with their ally; accordingly, Caesar and Lucius Quinctius supported the measure. The scarcity of corn, and the rumors as to the conduct of Lucullus were enough to secure the support of the multitude.

On the day of the voting, the Forum and even the roofs of the buildings around were covered with men. All the colleagues of Gabinius had promised to veto the measure; but only one, Lucius Trebellius, had the courage to keep his pledge. Gabinius immediately proposed to deal with him as Tiberius Gracchus had dealt with Octavius, but after seventeen tribes had voted, Trebellius withdrew his veto. All was now lost; attempts were made to secure the appointment of two generals instead of one, and to have the twenty-five lieutenant-generals elected by the tribes, but the bill passed without alteration.

Pompeius and Glabrio immediately set out. The success of Pompeius was rapid and complete; indeed, such was the confidence in his powers that the price of grain had fallen to the ordinary rate as soon as the law was passed. But in Asia the condition of affairs passed from bad to worse; Glabrio, instead of taking command of the forces, contented himself with fomenting the discontent of the soldiers against Lucullus, who, of course, was powerless. It seemed the most natural course to appoint Pompeius to the Asiatic command, which he was known to ardently desire. But no party in the state was willing to increase his already enormous authority. At this juncture, Gaius Manilius, a tribune, who was without influence in either party, wishing to force himself into the favor of the great general, brought forward, in 66 B.C., a proposal to recall Glabrio from Pontus and Bithynia, and Marcius Rex from Cilicia, and to confer both their offices—apparently without limit of time— together with free authority to conclude peace and alliance, upon the proconsul of the seas and coasts. The proposal was repugnant to every party, and yet was passed almost unanimously. The democrats concealed their fears, and openly supported it; the moderate optimates declared themselves on the same side; they saw that resistance was hopeless, and that their best policy was to try to bind Pompeius to the senate. Marcus Cicero made his first political speech in support of it, and the only opposition was from the strict aristocratic party headed by Quintus Catulus. Thus, by the action of an irresponsible demagogue, Pompeius, in addition to his former powers, obtained command of the most important Eastern provinces, and the conduct of a war of which no man could foresee the end. Never since Rome stood had such power been united in the hands of a single man.

The two laws of Gabinius and Manilius terminate the struggle between the senate and the popular party, which was begun sixty-seven years before by Tiberius Gracchus. The first breach in the existing constitution was made when the veto of Octavius was disregarded by Tiberius Gracchus; and the last bulwark of senatorial rule fell in like manner with the withdrawal of Trebellius. But the struggle, which was begun by men of high ideals and of noble personal character, was brought to a close by venal and intriguing demagogues. And the contrast was but an indication of the change which the whole state had undergone; everything—law, military discipline, life and manners—had changed. A comparison between the Gracchan ideal and its later realization could only provoke a painful smile.

But the end of the first struggle was but the beginning of a second—of a new struggle between the allies who had overthrown their common enemy the senate, between the democratic civil opposition and the military power. The exceptional position of Pompeius was incompatible with a republican constitution: he was not general, but regent of the empire. If at the close of his Eastern campaign he should stretch forth his arm and seize the crown, who was to prevent him? " Soon," exclaimed Catulus, " it would be necessary once more to flee to the rocks of the Capitol, in order to save liberty." It was not the fault of the prophet that the storm came not, as he expected, from the East, but that, on the contrary, fate, fulfilling his words more literally than he himself anticipated, brought on a destroying tempest a few years later from Gaul.

Pompeius began the work of subjugating the pirates by dividing the whole field of operations into thirteen districts, each of which was assigned to a lieutenant, who equipped vessels, searched the coast, and captured the ships of the freebooters. He himself, with the best of his ships, swept the Sicilian, African, and Sardinian waters, while his lieutenants dealt with the coasts of Spain and Gaul. Within forty days the western Mediterranean was free, and the dearth at Rome relieved. The general now repaired, with sixty of his vessels, to Lycia and Cilicia. The pirates everywhere disappeared from the sea on his approach, and many even of the mountain strongholds of Lycia accepted the terms offered to them, and opened their gates. But the Cilicians, after placing their families and their treasures in their strongholds, awaited the Romans, with a large fleet, off the western frontier of Cilicia. Pompeius gained a complete victory, landed and subdued the strongholds, and in forty-nine days after his first appearance in the Eastern seas brought the war to a close. The whole affair was, of course, rather an energetic and skillful police-raid than a victorious war; but the rapidity of the achievement was astounding, and made a great impression on the public mind. Thirteen hundred pirate vessels are said to have been destroyed; ten thousand pirates perished, and more than twenty thousand were captured, while numerous captive Romans, among them Publius Clodius, regained their liberty. Pompeius caused a fleet to be maintained to protect the Asiatic coasts, and on his return to Rome persuaded the senate to take similar measures for Italy; and though there were subsequent expeditions in 58 B.C. and in 55 B.C., piracy never regained its old predominance in the Mediterranean.

As soon as Pompeius was invested by the Manilian law with the command he had so long desired, he began strenuously to prepare for his new campaign. At the outset a great piece of good fortune befell him. A son of the great king Tigranes, who bore the same name as his father, rebelled, and took refuge at the Parthian court, and by his influence determined that power to adhere to the Roman side and to renew with Pompeius the agreement formed with Lucullus to accept the Euphrates as the boundary of the two empires. At the same time the great king suspected Mithradates of secretly encouraging his rebellious son, and the good understanding between the two monarchs was disturbed. Meanwhile Pompeius completed his preparations, and collected a force of from 40,000 to 50,000 men, many of whom were discharged Fimbrian veterans who had enlisted again as volunteers.

In the spring of 66 B.C. Pompeius took over the command of the legions from Lucullus, and the war that followed was an easy one. The power both of Mithradates and of Tigranes had already been broken by Lucullus, and it now required only an energetic commander, backed with the necessary resources in troops and supplies, to deal the final blows. The old king of Pontus saw his army quickly destroyed, and fled to his Bosporan kingdom, north of the Black Sea. From there he planned to lead a force up the valley of the Danube, collect the various tribes on his way, and invade Italy from the north. But his favorite son, Pharnaces, in hopes of currying favor with the Romans, led an insurrection against him, and, seeing that all was lost, Mithradates committed suicide, to avoid falling into his enemies' hands. Thus ended, in 63 B.C., the career of Rome's most potent enemy in the East.

Meantime, Pompeius had turned his attention to Tigranes, and settled matters with that monarch, who was resolved to purchase peace at any price. He was compelled to pay a fine of seven million dollars, besides making a present of nine dollars to each of the Roman soldiers, and forced to surrender all his conquests to Rome, becoming once more merely the petty king of Armenia.

After arranging the affairs of Armenia and Pontus, Pompeius, in the summer of 64 B.C., set out to regulate the affairs of Syria. The Syrian provinces were now in the hands of three powers—the Bedouins, the Jews, and the Nabataeans. The Bedouins, who were masters of northern Syria, had their home in the desert which stretches from the peninsula of Arabia up to the Euphrates, where they lived under their emirs, the most noted of whom were Abgarus and Sampsiceramus. The Jews, under Jannaeus Alexander, who died 79 B.C., had extended their dominion southward to the Egyptian frontier, and northward to the Lake of Gennesareth, including a considerable stretch of coast. Their further expansion was checked by internal dissension between the Pharisees and the Sadducees. Their fierce religious and political contentions broke out with violence after the death of Jannaeus, and a civil war ensued, in which the Pharisees supported one of his sons, Hyrcanus, and the Sadducees another, Aristobulus, a strong and able prince. These divisions gave an opportunity to the Nabataeans, who were settled in the region of Petra, to obtain a footing in southern Syria. At the invitation of the Pharisees, the Nabataean king Aretas advanced with a large force and besieged Aristobulus in Jerusalem.

To put an end to the anarchy, Pompeius resolved to annex Syria, and in the person of Antiochus Asiaticus, who had been acknowledged by the senate and by Lucullus, the house of Seleucus was ejected from the throne it had held for two hundred and fifty years. At the same time Pompeius advanced with his army into the province, and enforced his regulations, where necessary, by arms. The Jews alone refused to obey, and when Aristobulus, after much hesitation, resolved to submit, the more fanatical portion of his army would not comply with his orders, and sustained a siege of three months on the steep temple rock. The Nabataeans still remained. King Aretas retired from Judaea, but retained the city of Damascus, and would not acknowledge the supremacy of Rome. The expedition against him was intrusted to Marcus Scaurus; it obtained only trifling successes, but ultimately Aretas was persuaded to purchase for a sum of money a guarantee for all his possessions, including Damascus, from the Roman governor.

In his settlement with the Parthians, Pompeius was true to the old Roman policy of favoring the humbled foe at the expense of the powerful ally. The province of Corduene, which was claimed by both Phraates, the Parthian king, and Tigranes, was occupied by Roman troops for the latter. What was most serious of all was the fact that the Romans did not respect the agreement by which the Euphrates was fixed as the boundary. Oruros, a point between Nisbis and the Tigris, and 220 miles east of the Euphrates, was fixed as the limit of the Roman dominion. When, in 64 B.C., Phraates declared war upon Tigranes on the question of the frontier, it seemed certain that he had resolved to defy the power of Rome, but he yielded and acquiesced in the Roman award.

Thus the work begun by Lucullus was completed by Pompeius. The system of protectorates had been exchanged for that of direct sovereignty over the more important dependent territories—Bithynia, Pontus, and Syria; while to the indirect dominion of Rome were added Armenia and the district of the Caucasus, and the kingdom of the Cimmerian Bosporus.

From the new territories four new provinces were formed: Bithynia with Pontus; Cilicia, which was an enlargement of the old province of that name, and which now embraced Pamphylia and Isauria; Syria; Crete. The government of the mass of countries now added to the empire probably remained substantially as before, only Rome stepped into the place of the former monarchs; and the new dominion included a number of kingdoms, princedoms, and lordships of various kinds, all in different relations of dependence upon Rome. Such were the kingdoms of Cappadocia and Commagene; the tetrarchies ruled by Deiotarus and Bogodiatarus; the territories of the high priest of the mother of the gods at Pessinus, and of the two high priests of the goddess Ma, in Comana. There were also leagues, like that of the twenty-three Lycian cities, whose independence was secured by charter.

Both Lucullus and Pompeius did everything in their power to protect and extend the urban communities in the East. They were centers of Romanization, of the civilization of trade and commerce as opposed to the Oriental military despotism. Cyzicus, Heraclea, Sinope, and Amisus, all received a number of new inhabitants and extensions of territory, and everything was done to repair the devastation they had suffered in the late war. Many of the captured pirates were settled in the desolated cities of Plain Cilicia, especially at Soli; and many new towns were founded in Pontus and Cappadocia, the most famous of which were Nicopolis in Pontus, Megalopolis on the Cappadocian frontier, and Ziela. In fact nearly the whole of the domain land of these provinces must have been used for these settlements. At the same time many existing cities obtained an extension of rights: autonomy was conferred upon Antioch on the Orontes, upon Selucia in Pieria, upon Gaza, Mitylene, and Phanagoria.

Pompeius had done good work for Rome, but he had not performed miracles, and had done nothing to call forth the absurd exaggerations of his triumph or the fulsome adulation of his adherents. His triumphal inscriptions enumerated twelve millions of people as subjugated, 1538 cities and strongholds taken, while his conquests were made to extend from the Sea of Azov to the Caspian and to the Red Sea, not one of which he had ever seen. Coins were struck in his honor, exhibiting the globe itself surrounded by triple laurels plucked from three continents, and surmounted by the golden chaplet which was conferred upon him by the citizens. On the other hand, there were voices which affirmed that he had only worn the laurels which another had plucked, and that the honors belonged of right to Lucullus. What really deserves praise in the conduct of Pompeius is his rare self-restraint. The most brilliant undertakings against the Bosporus, or the Parthians, or Egypt, offered themselves on all sides, but he had resisted all temptations, and had turned to the less glorious task of regulating the territories already acquired. But his conduct towards the Parthians deserves grave censure; he might have made war upon them, but when once he had decided against this course he should have loyally observed the agreement to regard the Euphrates as the boundary, instead of, by his silly perfidy, sowing seeds of hatred which were to bear bitter fruit for Rome at a later time.

The financial gain to Rome from the arrangements of Pompeius was immense, and her revenues were raised by one-half. And if the exhaustion of Asia was severe, and if both Pompeius and Lucullus brought home large private fortunes, the blame falls rather upon the government at home and on the system by which the provinces were regularly plundered for the benefit of Rome than upon the generals themselves.

After the departure of Pompeius peace was on the whole maintained in the East; but the governors of Cilicia had constantly to fight against mountain tribes, and those of Syria against the tribes of the desert. There were also dangerous revolts among the Jews, which were with difficulty suppressed by the able governor of Syria, Aulus Gabinius, and after which the Jews were subjected to a specially heavy taxation.

Egypt, with its dependency of Cyprus, now remained the only independent state in the East. It had indeed been formally bequeathed to Rome, but was still governed by its own kings, who were themselves controlled by the royal guard which frequently appointed or deposed its rulers. The isolation of Egypt, surrounded as it is by the desert and the sea, and its great resources, which gave its rulers a revenue almost equal to that of Rome even after its recent augmentation, made the oligarchy unwilling to intrust the annexation of the kingdom to any one man. Propositions were frequently made at Rome for its incorporation of the empire, particularly by the democratic party, but the Egyptian ruler succeeded always in purchasing a respite by heavy bribes. Cyprus was annexed by decree of the people in 58 B.C., and the measure was carried out by Cato without the interference of an army. But in 59 B.C. Ptolemy Auletes purchased his recognition from the masters of Rome—it is said for the sum of six thousand talents ($7,300,000). On account of the oppression which the payment of this money brought upon the people of Egypt the king was chased from his throne, but after the conference of Luca, in 56 B.C., and on the promise of a further sum of twelve million dollars, Aulus Gabinius was ordered to restore him. Victory was secured by a decisive battle on the Nile, and Ptolemy once more sat on the throne. The sum promised could not possibly be paid in full, though the last penny was exacted from the miserable inhabitants. At the same time the pretorians were replaced by a force of regular Roman infantry, with Celtic and German cavalry.

Chapter XXVIII

PARTY STRUGGLES IN ROME—POMPEIUS, CAESAR AND
CRASSUS. 65-58 B.C.

AFTER the departure of Pompeius the optimates remained
nominally in possession of the government; that is, they
commanded the elections and the consulate. But the consulship was no longer of primary consequence in the face of the
new military power; and the best of the aristocrats—men like
Quintus Metellus Pius and Lucius Lucullus—retired from the lists
and devoted themselves to the elegant luxury of their private life.
The younger men either followed their example or turned to court
the favor of the new masters of the state.

There was one exception—Marcus Porcius Cato. Born in 95
B.C., he was now about thirty years of age. He was by nature a
man of great courage and firmness, and of the strictest integrity,
but dull of intellect and destitute of imagination or passion. The
two influences which molded his character were Stoicism, the principles of which he adopted with the greatest ardor, and the example
of his great-grandfather, the famous censor. Like him, he went
about the capital rebuking the sins of the times, a living model of
the *prisca virtus* of the good old days—the Don Quixote of the
aristocracy. In a corrupt and cowardly age his courage and integrity gave him an influence which was warranted neither by his age
nor his capacity, and he soon became the recognized champion of
the optimates. He did good work in the region of finance, checking the details of the public budget and waging constant war with
the farmers of the taxes; but he had none of the higher qualities of
a statesman; he failed completely, if indeed he ever tried, to grasp
the political situation. All his policy consisted in steadfastly opposing everyone who appeared to deviate from the traditional aristocratic creed.

During the next few years the activity of the democrats showed
itself in two ways: by attacks upon individuals of the senatorial
party, and upon the abuses of which the senate was guilty; and by

efforts to complete the realization of the democratic ideas which had been in the air ever since the time of the Gracchi.

Among the senatorial abuses against which measures were passed were the acceptance of bribes from foreign envoys; the granting of dispensations from the laws in particular cases; and the pretor's frequent failure to adminster justice according to the rules he laid down on entering office. Various senators were prosecuted for malfeasance, and the strength of the popular party was seen in 63 B.C. in the election of Gaius Caesar to the supreme pontificate against two of the leading aristocrats.

At the same time the democratic restoration was pressed on. The election of pontiffs and augurs by the tribes was restored in 63 B.C. An agitation was begun for the complete restoration of the corn laws. The criminal jurisdiction of the comitia was restored. The Transpadani were taken under the protection of the populares, and an agitation was set on foot for conferring upon them the full franchise, just as Gracchus had supported the enfranchisement of the Latins. Finally, the long proscribed heroes and martyrs of the democracy were rehabilitated in the public memory, and Gaius Marius's memory was restored to public honor through the audacity of his nephew, Gaius Caesar. The latter had dared to display the features of his uncle, in spite of prohibitions, at the burial of the widow of Marius in 68 B.C., and now the emblems of victory erected by Marius and thrown down by Sulla were restored to their old places in the Capitol.

Such were the successes of the democrats, but, after all, they did not amount to much. In their contest with the aristocracy the democrats had conquered, and it was but natural that they should insult the prostrate foe. But they knew that the real reckoning was to come,—not with the vanquished oligarchy, but with the too-powerful ally by whose aid they had conquered. Their schemes were directed ostensibly against the optimates, but really against Pompeius. If direct proofs of this are few, it is because both the present and the succeeding age had an interest in throwing a veil over the events of this period; but such proofs are not wanting. It is stated by Sallust that the Gabinian and Manilian laws inflicted a grievous blow on the democracy. Again, the Servilian rogation was directed against Pompeius, as is clear from the character of the bill itself, and from the statements of Sallust and Cicero. Finally, the more than suspicious attitude of Caesar and Crassus towards the

Catilinarian conspiracies is proof enough in itself. The object of the democratic party during the years 67-63 B.C. was to possess themselves of the reins of government by securing the return of one or more members of the conspiracy for the consulship, and then to intrust one of their leaders with the conquest of Egypt, or some such commission, which would give an opportunity for raising a military power capable of counterbalancing that of Pompeius.

The first object of the democratic leaders was the overthrow of the existing government by means of an insurrection in which they would not themselves appear. Materials for such a conspiracy existed in abundance in the capital. There were the slaves; there was the herd of free paupers who lived by the corn distributions and who were always ready for any scheme which promised anarchy and license. Again, there were numbers of young men of rank, ruined in fortunes, ruined in body and mind by a life of fashionable debauchery, who sighed openly for a return of the times of Cinna and for release from their burden of debt. Among them two men were marked out as leaders by their superior ability—Gnaeus Piso and Lucius Catilina. The latter, in spite of a dissoluteness conspicuous even in that dissolute age, had courage, military talent, and a certain criminal energy which gave him an ascendency over other men. He had been one of Sulla's executioners, and had hunted down the proscribed at the head of a band of Celts; but he had now a special quarrel with the aristocracy because they had opposed his candidature for the consulship. A secret league was formed, numbering more than four hundred members and including associates in all the urban districts of Italy.

In December, 66 B.C., the two consuls-elect for 65 B.C. were rendered ineligible for office by conviction for electoral bribery. They immediately joined the association, and it was determined to procure the consulship for them by force. Accordingly on January 1, 65 B.C., the senate house was to be assailed and the new consuls were to be killed; Crassus was to be invested with the dictatorship, Caesar with the mastership of the horse. But the signal was never given and the plot was foiled. A similar plan for February 5 was also a failure, and the secret became known. Guards were assigned to the new consuls, and Piso was got rid of by a mission to Hither Spain with pretorian powers; but farther the government dared not go.

For the present no further attempt was made by the conspirators; but in 64 B.C. Pompeius was in Syria, and approaching the conclusion of his task; and it was therefore resolved to set up as candidates for the consulship of 63 B.C. Catilina and Gaius Antonius —an ex-Sullan and an ex-senator, who was willing to lend himself to the conspiracy. The plan was to seize the children of Pompeius, and to arm in Italy and in the provinces against him. Piso was to raise troops in Hither Spain; and to secure communications with him negotiations were entered into with the Transpadani and with several Celtic tribes.

The optimates had no one of their own order who possessed the requisite courage and influence to defeat the democratic candidates; they therefore supported Marcus Cicero, who as yet belonged properly to no political party, but was always a supporter of the party of material interests. The result was the election of Cicero and Antonius, and for the moment the conspiracy was checked. A little before this Piso had been put to death by his escort in Spain; and now Cicero gained over Antonius by voluntarily giving up to him the lucrative governorship of Macedonia, instead of insisting on his privilege of having the provinces determined by lot.

Meanwhile the settlement of Syria proceeded rapidly, and it was more than probable that Pompeius would soon advance into Egypt. Caesar's attempt to get the settlement of Egypt intrusted to himself was foiled. A bold stroke was imperatively necessary, and as soon as the new tribunes entered on their office the Servilian rogation was brought forward. The nominal object of this bill was the founding of colonies in Italy; the Campanian domain land was to be parceled out, and other land was to be acquired by purchase. The money necessary for this purpose was to be provided in various ways, and the execution of the measure was to be intrusted to decemviri armed with special jurisdiction and with the imperium, who were to remain in office for five years, and to choose two hundred subordinate officers from the equestrian ranks. All candidates were to announce themselves personally, and only seventeen tribes were to vote.

The real object of the bill was to create a power which might counterbalance that of Pompeius; but it pleased no class; the mob preferred to subsist on the corn largesses rather than by tilling the soil; the masses of the democrats were afraid to offend Pompeius, and the measure was withdrawn by its author, January 1, 63 B.C.

Catilina now determined to strike a decisive blow. All through

the summer preparations for civil war went on. Faesulae was to
be the headquarters of the insurrection—thither arms and money
were sent, and troops were raised by Gaius Manlius, an old Sullan
captain. The Transpadani seemed ready to rise; bodies of slaves
were ready for insurrection in the Bruttian land, on the east coast,
and in Capua. The plan of the conspirators was to put to death
the presiding consul and the rival candidates on the day of the consular elections for 62 B.C. (October 20), and to carry the election of
Catilina.

But on the day fixed Cicero denounced the conspiracy in full
senate; and Catilina did not deny the accusation. On the 21st the
senate invested the consuls with the exceptional powers usual in
such crises. On the 28th, to which day the elections had been postponed, Cicero appeared in the Campus Martius with an armed bodyguard, and the plots of the conspirators again failed.

But on the 27th the standard of insurrection had been raised
by Manlius at Faesulae, and proclamations had been issued demanding the liberation of debtors from their burdens, and the reform of
the law of insolvency, which still, in some cases, permitted the
enslavement of the debtor. But the rising was isolated. The government had time to call out the general levy, and to send officers
to various regions of Italy in order to suppress the insurrection in
detail. Meantime the gladiatorial slaves were ejected from the
capital, and patrols were kept in the streets to prevent incendiarism.

Catilina was in a difficult position. The outbreak in the city,
which should have been simultaneous with the rising at Faesulae,
had miscarried. He could hardly remain longer in Rome, and yet
there was no one among his associates who could be trusted to carry
out his design with courage and capacity, or who could command
sufficient influence to induce the conspirators in the city to strike an
effective blow at once. So he remained, brazening out the situation
with the most audacious insolence. The spies of the government
had made their way into the circle of the conspirators, and kept it
informed of every detail of the plot. An attempt to surprise
Praeneste failed. On the night of November 6 a conference was
held, and in accordance with the resolution passed by those who met,
an attempt was made early in the morning to murder the consul
Cicero. But the man selected found the guard round his house
reinforced—the consul was already aware of the result of the conference.

On the 8th Cicero convoked the senate and acquainted them with the events of the last few days. Catilina could not obtain a hearing, and departed at once for Etruria. The government declared Catilina, Manlius, and such of their followers who should not lay down their arms by a certain day to be outlaws, and called out new levies, which, with incredible folly, were placed under the command of Antonius.

It had been arranged, before Catilina's departure, that Cethegus should make another attempt to kill Cicero in the night, and that Gabinius and Statilius should set fire to the city in twelve places. Meanwhile Catilina was to advance toward Rome. But now that their leader was gone the conspirators seemed incapable of action, though the government took no measures against them.

At last the decisive moment came. Lentulus had entered into relations with the deputies of the Allobroges—a Celtic canton, which was deeply in debt—and had given them letters to carry to his associates. On the night of December 2 the envoys were seized as they were leaving the city—probably in accordance with a preconceived plan; and from their evidence and from the documents they carried full details of the plot were furnished to Cicero. Some of the conspirators saved themselves by flight; but Lentulus, Cethegus, Gabinius, and Statilius were arrested. The evidence was laid before the senate; the prisoners and other witnesses were heard; and other proofs, such as deposits of arms in the houses of the conspirators and threatening expressions used by them, were afterwards procured. The most important documents were published, to convince the public of the facts of the plot.

The plans of the conspirators were now made bare, and their leaders arrested. In a well-ordered commonwealth there would have been an end of the matter. The military and the legal tribunals would have done the rest. But the government of Rome was so disorganized that for the moment the most difficult question for settlement was the custody of the prisoners. These had been given into the keeping of certain eminent private men—two of whom were Caesar and Crassus—who were responsible for their safety. But the freedmen of the prisoners were stirring; the air was full of rumors of schemes for liberating them by force; Rome was full of desperadoes, and the government had no efficient force of military or of police at its disposal. Finally, Catilina was near enough to attempt a *coup de main*. Accordingly the idea was suggested of executing the prisoners at once. By the constitution of Rome no citizen could be put to death except by sentence of the whole body of citizens, and as such sentences had fallen into disuse, capital punishment was now no longer carried out. Cicero shrank from the step; he convoked the senate and left to it the decision, although it had even less title to act than the consul, and therefore could not possibly relieve him of the responsibility. All the consulars and the great majority of the senate had already declared for the execution, when Caesar, in a speech full of covert threats, violently opposed the proposal; and probably the limits of the law would have been observed had not Cato, by throwing suspicion upon those who were for milder measures, and by throwing the waverers into fresh alarm, secured a majority for the immediate execution of the prisoners. On the night of December 5 they were conducted under strong guards to the Tullianum, a dungeon at the foot of the Capitol, and there put to death.

Never perhaps had a commonwealth more lamentably declared itself bankrupt than did Rome through this resolution to put to death in all haste a few political prisoners, who were no doubt culpable according to the laws, but who had not forfeited life; because, forsooth, the security of prisons was not to be trusted, and there was no sufficient police.

There still remained the insurrection in Etruria. Catilina had now under him nearly ten thousand men, of whom scarcely more than a fourth were armed. On the news of the failure at Rome, the mass of them dispersed, and the remnant of desperate men determined to cut their way through the passes of the Apennines into Gaul. But on their arrival at the foot of the mountains near Pistoria they were confronted by the troops of Quintus Metellus, who had come up from Ravenna and Ariminum. In their rear was Antonius, and there was nothing left but to throw themselves upon his army. The battle took place in a narrow rocky valley where superiority of numbers was of small avail, and there the conspirators, with Catilina at their head, fell almost to the last man.

The plot was suppressed; but the blow had fallen, not merely on the conspirators themselves, but on the whole democratic party. If the complicity of the democratic leaders, Caesar and Crassus, is not an ascertained fact, they are at any rate open to the gravest suspicion. That they were accused of complicity by Catulus, and that Caesar spoke and voted against the judicial murder of the prisoners, is of course no proof; but there are other facts of greater weight. Crassus and Caesar supported the candidature of Catilina for the consulship. When Caesar, in 64 B.C., indicted the Sullan executioners for murder he allowed Catilina alone to be acquitted. In his revelations to the senate, Cicero did not indeed include the names of Caesar and Crassus; but it is known that he erased the names of many "innocent persons," and in later years he named Caesar as among the accomplices. The fact that Gabinius and Statilius were intrusted to the custody of Crassus and Caesar is probably to be explained by the wish of the government to place them in a dilemma. If they allowed the prisoners to escape they would be regarded as accessories; if they detained them they would incur the hatred and vengeance of their fellow-conspirators. After the arrest of Lentulus a messenger from him to Catilina was arrested and brought before the senate; but when, in his evidence, he mentioned Crassus as having commissioned him, he was interrupted, his whole statement was canceled at the suggestion of Cicero, and he was committed to prison until he should confess who had suborned him. The senate were clearly afraid to allow the revelations to go beyond a certain limit. The general public were less scrupulous, and Caesar narrowly escaped with his life when he left the senate on December 5. When Caesar had made himself head of the state he was in close alliance with Publius Sittius, the only surviving Catilinarian, the leader of Mauretanian banditti. The facts that the government offered no serious hindrance to the conspiracy until the last moment; that the chief conspirator was allowed to depart unmolested; that the troops sent against the insurrection were put under the command of Antonius, who had been deeply concerned in the plot,—all point to the suspicion that there were powerful men behind the scenes, who threw their protection over the conspiracy while they kept in the background themselves.

That the evidence is not more abundant is no matter for surprise. The government was too weak to provoke the democratic party à outrance; and, after the failure of the plot, the democratic leaders naturally made every effort to conceal their participation in it; and when Caesar had got the upper hand the veil was only drawn all the more closely over the darker years of his life.

The close of this period found the democratic party at its lowest ebb. By its alliance with anarchists and murderers it had alienated, not only the party of material interests, but even the city mob who, although having no objection to a street riot, found it inconvenient to have their houses set on fire over their heads. The popular leaders felt the hopelessness of their position. Crassus prepared to carry his family and his riches to a safe refuge in the East; and even Caesar declared, in 63 B.C., as he left his home on the morning of the election for the office of pontifex maximus, that, if he failed in this, too, he would never cross the threshold again.

The one question that agitated men's minds as the time approached for the return of Pompeius from the East was what attitude the victorious general would take toward the two parties in the state. His eyes were fully opened by recent events to the folly and weakness, if not the treachery, of his former allies, and his interests now appeared identical with those of the optimates. If the latter were not wholly blind to their own interests, they would see to it that his legitimate demands were acceded to, and thus secure the final overthrow of the democrats. It was evident that the present form of government was a failure, and that but one alternative remained—the rule of a single man. But it remained to be seen whether that man should come to power as the representative of the aristocracy or of the common people.

In the autumn of 63 B.C. Quintus Metellus Nepos arrived in the capital from the camp of Pompeius, and got himself elected tribune with the avowed purpose of procuring for Pompeius the command against Catilina by special decree, and afterwards the consulship for 61 B.C. Everything depended upon the reception which parties at Rome might give to these proposals. It must be remembered that, whatever cause Pompeius might have to be discontented with the conduct of Caesar and his partisans, no open rupture had taken place. The coalition of 70 B.C. was still formally in existence. The democracy still treated Pompeius with the greatest outward respect, and this very year had granted him, spontaneously and by special decree, unprecedented honors. At the same time nothing had occurred to bridge over the chasm which the coalition had created between Pompeius and the optimates. The senate had decreed him no exceptional honors, and two of its most influential members, Lucullus and Metellus, were his bitterest personal enemies. Lastly, the aristocracy were at present under the guidance of the uncompromising pedant Cato, while the democracy were led by the most supple master of intrigue—Caesar. Accordingly the aristocracy at once showed their hostility to the proposals of Metellus, and Cato had himself elected tribune expressly for the purpose of thwarting him. But the democrats were more pliant, and it was soon evident that they had come to a cordial understanding with the general's emissary. Metellus and his master both adopted the democratic view of the illegal executions, and the first act of Caesar's pretorship was to call Catulus to account for the moneys alleged to have been embezzled by him in rebuilding the Capitoline temple, and to transfer the superintendence of the works to Pompeius. By this stroke Caesar brought to light a disgraceful abuse of public money, and threw odium upon the aristocracy in the person of one of its most distinguished members; while Pompeius would be delighted at the prospect of engraving his name upon the proudest spot in the capital of the Roman state.

On the day of voting Cato and another of the tribunes put their veto upon the proposals of Metellus, who disregarded it. There were conflicts of the armed bands of both sides, which terminated in favor of the government. The senate followed up the victory by suspending Metellus and Caesar from their offices. Metellus immediately departed for the camp of Pompeius; and when Caesar disregarded the decree of suspension against himself the senate had ultimately to revoke it.

Nothing could have been more favorable to the interests of Pompeius than these late events. After the illegal executions of the Catilinarians, and the acts of violence against Metellus, he could appear at once as the defender of the " two palladia of Roman liberty "—the right of appeal and the inviolability of the tribunate— and as the champion of the party of order against the Catilinarian band. But his courage was unequal to the emergency; he lingered in Asia during the winter of 63-62 B.C., and thus gave the senate time to crush the insurrection in Italy, and deprived himself of a valid pretext for keeping his legions together. In the autumn of 62 B.C. he landed at Brundisium, and, disbanding his army, proceeded to Rome with a small escort. On his arrival in the city in 61 B.C. he found himself in a position of complete isolation; he was feared by the democrats, hated by the aristocracy, and distrusted by the wealthy class.

He at once demanded for himself a second consulship, the confirmation of all his acts in the East, and the fulfillment of the promise he had made to his soldiers to furnish them with lands. But each of these demands was met with the most determined opposition. From the senate, led by Lucullus, Metellus, and Cato, there was no hope of obtaining dispensation from the Sullan law as to reëlection. As to the arrangements of Pompeius in the East, Lucullus carried a resolution that they should be voted upon separately, thus opening a door for endless annoyances and defeats.

His promise of lands to his soldiers was indeed ratified, but not executed, and no steps were taken to provide the necessary funds and lands. When the general turned from the senate to the people, the democrats, though they offered no opposition, did nothing to assist him, and when the proposal for the grant of lands was submitted to the tribes, it was defeated, early in 60 B.C. To such straits was he reduced that he had to court the favor of the multitude by causing a proposal to be introduced for abolishing the Italian tolls; but he had none of the qualifications of a demagogue, and merely damaged his reputation without gaining his ends.

From this disagreeable position Pompeius was rescued by the sagacity and address of Caesar, who saw in the necessities of Pompeius the opportunity of the democratic party. Ever since the return of Pompeius, Caesar had grown rapidly in influence and weight. He had been pretor in 62 B.C., and, in 61, governor of Further Spain, where he utilized his position to free himself from his debts and to lay the foundation of the military position he desired for himself. Returning in 60 B.C., he readily relinquished his claim to a triumph, in order to enter the city in time to stand for the consulship. At last the democracy seemed on the eve of realizing its hopes, and of seeing one of its own leaders invested with the consulship and a province where he might build up a military position strong enough to make it independent of external allies. But it was quite possible that the aristocracy might be strong enough to defeat the candidature of Caesar, as it had defeated that of Catilina; and again, the consulship was not enough; an extraordinary command, secured to him for several years, was necessary for the fulfillment of his purpose. Without allies such a command could not be hoped for; and allies were found where they had been found ten years before, in Pompeius and in Crassus, and in the rich equestrian class. Such a treaty was suicide on the part of Pompeius, for he owed his strength entirely to his position as the only leader who could rely on a military force; but he had drifted into a situation so awkward that he was glad to be released from

PARTY STRUGGLES 289

it on any terms. The capitalists were at the moment all the more inclined to join the coalition because of the severity with which they were being treated with regard to their tax leases by the senate, at the instigation of Cato.

The bargain was struck in the summer of 60 B.C. Caesar was promised the consulship and a governorship afterwards; Pompeius, the ratification of his arrangements in the East, and land for his soldiers; Crassus received no definite equivalent, but the capitalists were promised a remission of part of the money they had undertaken to pay for the lease of the Asiatic taxes. The parties to the coalition were the same as in 70 B.C., but their relative positions were entirely changed. Then the democracy was a faction without a head; now it was a strong party with leaders of its own, and could demand for itself, not merely concessions to democratic traditions, such as the restoration of the tribunician power, but office and authority, the consulship, and the supreme military command, while it conceded nothing material to its allies.

In spite of all the opposition of the senate the plans of the coalition were carried out in their entirety. Caesar was easily elected consul for 59 B.C., and at once proceeded to fulfill his obligations to Pompeius by carrying an agrarian law. All remaining Italian domain land, which meant practically the territory of Capua, was to be given up to allotments, and other estates in Italy were to be purchased out of the revenues of the new Eastern provinces. The allotments were to be small, and to be given to poor burgesses, fathers of three children. The soldiers were simply recommended to the commission, and thus the principle of giving rewards of land for military service was not asserted. The execution of the bill was to be intrusted to a commission of twenty.

Caesar had thus loyally fulfilled his obligations to Pompeius, and the most important question now to be considered was his own future position. The senate had already selected for the year of his proconsulship two provinces where nothing but the work of peaceful administration could be expected; but it was determined by the confederates that Caesar should be invested by decree of the people with a special command resembling that lately held by Pompeius. Accordingly the tribune Vatinius submitted to the tribes a proposal which was at once adopted. By it Caesar obtained the governorship of Cisalpine Gaul, and the supreme command of the three legions stationed there, for five years, with the rank of propretor for his adjutants. His jurisdiction extended southward as far as the Rubicon, and included Luca and Ravenna. Subsequently the province of Narbo was added by the senate, on the motion of Pompeius. Since no troops could be stationed in Italy, it was evident that such a command as Caesar's dominated both Italy and Rome. The coalition had succeeded; it was master of the state. It kept its adherents in good humor by the most lavish exhibitions of games and shows, and kept the exchequer filled by selling charters and privileges to subject communities and princes: for instance, the king of Egypt at last obtained recognition by decree of the people, in return for a large sum. The permanence of the present arrangement was assured by securing the return of Aulus Gabinius and Lucius Piso for the consulship of the ensuing year. Pompeius watched over Italy while he executed the agrarian law, and Caesar's legions in north Italy were a guarantee against all opposition, Caesar and Pompeius were at present kept united by community of interest, and the personal bonds between them were cemented by the marriage of Pompeius with Julia, the only daughter of Caesar.

The aristocracy were in despair. "On all sides," wrote one of them, "we are checkmated; we have already, through fear of death or of banishment, despaired of ' freedom '; everyone sighs, no one ventures to speak." Nevertheless Caesar had hardly laid down his consulship when it was proposed, in the senate, to annul the Julian laws; there were clearly some among the optimates who would not be content with the policy of sighing and silence. The regents determined to make examples of some of the most determined of their opponents, and to drive them into exile. An infamous attempt was made to involve the heads of the aristocracy in a charge of conspiring to murder Pompeius on the evidence of a worthless informer named Vettius; but the scheme was too hollow, and the whole matter was allowed to drop.

Ultimately they were content with a few isolated victims. Cato openly proclaimed his conviction that the Julian laws were null and void, and to get rid of him he was intrusted by special decree with the regulation of the municipal affairs of Byzantium, and with the annexation of the kingdom of Cyprus. Cicero was abandoned to the vengeance of the thorough-going democrats, who could not leave unpunished the judicial murder of December 5. And so the tribune Publius Clodius, his bitter private enemy, proposed to the tribes a resolution declaring the execution of a citizen without trial a crime punishable with banishment. Both this decree and that relating to Cato were passed without opposition, and, though the majority of the senate put on mourning, and Cicero besought Pompeius on his knees for mercy, he had to go into exile even before the passing of the law. Cato accepted his commission, and set out for the East; and Caesar could now safely leave Italy, to face the heavy task he had imposed on himself in Gaul.

Chapter XXIX

IT has been too generally assumed that Caesar regarded Gaul merely as a parade ground on which to exercise himself and his troops for the impending war; but though the conquest of Gaul was undoubtedly for him a means to an end, yet it was much more. It is the special privilege of a statesman of genius that his means themselves are ends in their turn. Caesar needed, no doubt, for his party aims a military power, but he did not conquer Gaul as a partisan. It was necessary that Italy should be protected by a barrier against the ever-threatening invasions of the Germans; and it was also necessary, now that Italy had become too narrow for its population, that a fresh field of expansion should be provided elsewhere. The Roman state remained a chaotic mass of countries which required to be thoroughly occupied, and to have their boundaries fixed and defined: the senate had done little or nothing to carry out this great work; it was only when the democracy assumed the reins in 67 B.C. and in 66 B.C. that the Roman sovereignty over the Mediterranean was restored, and the dominion in the East consolidated by the annexation of Pontus and Syria. Now that the democracy and its leaders were supreme, another and even more important section of the work was at last taken in hand.

Something had been accomplished by Caesar towards the subjugation of the West during his governorship in Spain in 61 B.C.: the Lusitanians and Gallaeci were subdued, the tribute of the subjects reduced, and their financial affairs regulated.

The term Gallia has been applied, since the age of Augustus, to the country bounded by the Pyrenees, the Rhine, the Atlantic Ocean, and the Mediterranean. The Roman province which had been constituted for sixty years, and which corresponded pretty nearly to the modern Languedoc, Dauphiné, and Provence, had seldom been in a state of peace. Pompeius had had to fight his way through the insurgent tribes in order to reach Spain in 77 B.C.; while the connection of the Allobroges with the Catilinarian conspiracy is but one indication of the perpetual ferment in which the more remote cantons lived. Still the bounds of the province were not extended, Lugdunum Convenarum, Tolosa, Vienna, and Genava remained the most remote Roman townships towards the west and north.

But the importance of Gallia was continually increasing; its glorious climate, the fertility of the soil, the commercial routes stretching northward as far as Britain, the easy communication with Italy, the civilization and luxury which were to be found in the

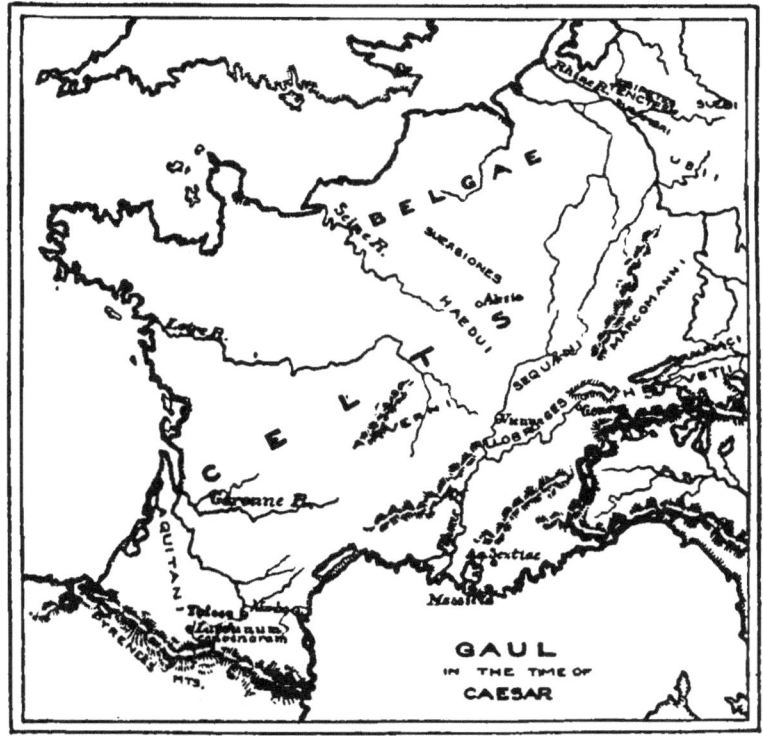

GAUL
IN THE TIME OF
CAESAR

city of Massilia, all combined to make Gallia the most attractive of the Roman provinces. Ten years before Caesar's arrival it was swarming with Roman burgesses and merchants, with Roman farmers and graziers, while a large proportion of the land was owned by Roman nobles, who lived in Italy and cultivated their estates by means of stewards.

This region had for a long time been under the influence of Hellenism, spreading from the great Greek colony of Massilia; and even in the Roman period Greek physicians and rhetoricians were employed in the Gallic cantons; but, as elsewhere, Hellenism was superseded by the mixed Latino-Greek culture. The Celtic and Ligurian populations gradually lost their nationality, were compelled to exchange the sword for the plow, which they were forced to use in the service of a foreign master, and they attested by many insurrections the hardness of the bondage into which they had fallen.   But the towns flourished and grew; Aquae Sextiae, Narbo, and, above all, Massilia, might be mentioned in comparison with the most prosperous Italian towns.

But as soon as the Roman frontier was crossed Roman influence practically ceased.   North of the Cevennes the great Celtic race was found in all its native freedom.   The great body of this people had settled in modern France, in the western districts of Germany and Switzerland, and in the south of England; but there were Celts in modern Austria and Spain, though cut off from their kinsmen by the barriers of the Alps and the Pyrenees.   Little can be known of the development of this great people; we have to be content with a mere outline of their culture and political condition in the time of Caesar.

The population of Gaul appears to have been comparatively dense.   From the numbers of the Belgic levy against Caesar it may be computed that in those regions the proportion was about 200 persons to the square mile—about the same rate which holds at present for Wales; in the canton of the Helvetii it was about 245: hence in the more cultivated districts of the Haedui and Arverni it was probably higher.   Agriculture was no doubt known in Gaul, and a kind of beer was made from the barley which was grown there.   But the pursuit was despised, and, even in the south, was held unbecoming for a free Celt.   Pastoral husbandry was much more esteemed.   The Romans availed themselves of the Celtic breed of cattle, and of the skill of Celtic slaves in the raising of animals; Gallic oxen and ponies were much used, and in the northern districts the raising of cattle was almost universal.   In the northeast, between the sea and the Rhine, dense woods covered the ground, and on the plains of Flanders and Lorraine the Menapian and Treverian shepherd fed his half-wild swine in the impenetrable oak forests.   In Britain there was hardly any agriculture, and the culture of the olive and the vine did not extend beyond the Cevennes.

The Gauls lived mainly in open villages, of which the Helvetii alone had four hundred, besides many single homesteads. But there were also walled towns, of which the walls were an admirable combination of timber and stone, while the buildings were wholly of wood. There were twelve such towns among the Helvetii, and the same number among the Suessiones. But in the northern parts morasses and forests, and in Britain a sort of wooden abatis, were the only protection in time of war.

Roads and bridges were numerous, and the number and character of the largest rivers—the Rhone, Garonne, Loire, and Seine—made river intercourse easy and profitable. In maritime affairs the Gauls had attained no inconsiderable skill, and in one respect had surpassed the nations of the Mediterranean. They were the first nation that regularly navigated the Atlantic, and the tribes which bordered on the ocean employed sailing vessels, with leathern sails and iron anchor-chains, not only for commerce, but for war; while the war vessels of the Phoenicians, Greeks, and Romans were all, up to this time, propelled by oars, and used the sail only as an occasional aid; their trading vessels alone were sailers properly so-called. In the Channel the Gauls, still and for long afterwards, employed a sort of leather-covered skiff.

There was considerable commercial intercourse between even the most northern Celtic regions and the Roman province. The people of modern Brittany brought tin from the mines of Cornwall, and carried it by river or by land to Narbo and Massilia. Among the tribes at the mouth of the Rhine fishing and the collection of birds' eggs was an important industry. The tolls levied on rivers and at maritime ports play a large part in the finance of certain cantons.

In manufactures, working in metals was the only important known industry pursued: the copper implements even now discovered in tombs, and the gold coins of the Arverni, attest the skill of the Gallic workmen; and they are even said to have taught the Romans the arts of tinning and silvering. Naturally the art of mining went hand in hand with the working of metals. There were extensive iron mines on the Loire, and the art of mining was adapted in those regions to the purposes of war. The Romans believed that Gaul was very rich in gold, but the idea is negatived by the small amount of gold discovered in tombs, and probably arose from the fables of travelers. Still the streams flowing from the Alps and Pyrenees may then have yielded sufficient produce to

have made the search for gold profitable through the employment
of slave labor.

The taste of the Celtic workmen was not equal to their me-
chanical skill.   The ornaments they produced were gaudy and
parti-colored, and their coins invariably imitate two or three Greek
dies.   But the art of poetry was highly valued, and was intimately
connected with religion.   Science and philosophy existed, though in
subordination to theology.   The knowledge of writing was general
among the priests.

Among the Celts the town had, as in the East, merely mercantile and strategic—not political—importance.   The Greeks and
Romans had lived, in early times, in cantons, each clan by itself;
they had villages in which they bought and sold, and strong places
whither they fled for refuge in case of invasion.   But very soon the
tower of refuge grew into a town, and became the head and center
of the clan, and the seat of law and justice.   Among the Celts,
however, this development never took place; they remained a mere
collection of clans, and never took the step by which the clan becomes a state with a fixed center of government.

The constitution of the clan canton was based upon three
elements, the prince, the council of elders, and the body of freemen
capable of bearing arms.   The supreme authority rested with the
general assembly, by which, in important matters, the prince was
bound.   The council was often numerous, sometimes reaching the
number of six hundred, but had not more power than the Roman
senate in the regal period.   In some southern clans—the Arverni,
Haedui, Sequani, and Helvetii—a revolution had taken place, before the time of Caesar, which had overthrown the power
of the kings and set up that of the senate in its place.   In all
cases their towns, even when walled, were destitute of political
importance.

The dominant feature in all Celtic commonwealths is the high
nobility—a class the existence of which is almost incompatible with
that of a flourishing urban life.   This nobility consisted for the most
part of members of royal, or formerly royal, families.   It monopo-
lized all power in the state, financial, warlike, or political.   The
nobles forced the common freemen to surrender their freedom first
as debtors and then as slaves.   They maintained large bodies of
mounted retainers, and by their means defied the government and
broke up the commonwealth.   These retainers sometimes reached

the number of ten thousand, besides the bondmen and debtors, who were equally dependent. Moreover, the leading families in different states were connected by marriage and by treaty, and were together stronger than any single clan. The community could no longer maintain peace or protect individuals: only those who were clients of some powerful noble enjoyed security.

The general assembly lost its importance; the monarchy usually succumbed to the nobility, and the king was superseded by the vergobretus, or judgment-dealer, who, like the Roman consul, held office for a year. So far as the canton held together it was led by the council, which was governed by the heads of the aristocracy.

Like the Greeks in the Persian wars, the Transalpine Gauls seem to have become conscious of their unity as a nation only in their wars with Rome. The combination of the whole Celtic nobility was favorable to the development of the idea, and there were many who were willing to sacrifice the independence of the canton or of the nobility to purchase the independence of the nation. The universal popularity of the opposition to Caesar is attested by the telegraphic rapidity with which news was carried throughout the length and breadth of Gaul.

But though politically divided, the Gauls had long been held together by the bond of a close religious union. The corporation of Druids embraced the British islands and all Gaul, perhaps even other Celtic countries. It possessed a special head, elected by the priests themselves; schools, in which its traditions were transmitted; special privileges, such as exemption from taxation and military service; and held annual councils near Chartres. Such a priesthood, strengthened by the blind devotion of the people, could not but possess considerable political power: in monarchical cantons it conducted the government in case of an interregnum; it excluded individuals or states from religious and therefore also from civil society; it decided important suits, especially with regard to boundaries and inheritance; it had an extensive criminal jurisdiction, and even claimed the right of deciding on war or peace. The Gauls were not much removed from an ecclesiastical state with its pope and councils, its immunities, interdicts, and spiritual courts; only this ecclesiastical state did not, like that of recent times, exist apart from the nation, but was on the contrary preëminently national.

But though the priests and nobility constituted a certain union of the clans, their class interests were too strong to allow this union to become really national. The only attempt at political union was the system of hegemony among the cantons; a stronger clan induced or compelled a weaker to become subordinate to it. The stronger had control of all external relations for both, while the weaker was obliged to render military service, and sometimes to pay tribute. Thus a series of leagues arose—like that among the Belgae, in the northeast, under the Suessiones; that in southern and central Gaul, under the Arverni; and that of the maritime cantons in the north and west.

The union in these confederacies was of the loosest kind. The league was represented in peace by the federal diet, and in war by the general. Contests for the hegemony went on in every league and the rivalry spread into every dependent clan, and into every village and house, just as the rivalry between Athens and Sparta split up every independent community in Greece.

In a country where knighthood was the predominant social feature, the strength of the army was naturally the cavalry; war-chariots were also used among the Belgae and in Britain. When the general levy was called out, every man who could keep his seat on horseback took up arms, and, when attacking an enemy whom they despised, they swore, man by man, in the true spirit of chivalry, to charge at least twice through the enemy's line. There were also hired free-lances, who displayed in its extremest form the spirit of utter indifference to their own lives and to those of others which such a mode of life produces. They would often, we are told, fight for life and death at a banquet for sport, and even sell themselves to be killed for a fixed sum of money or a number of casks of wine.

Besides the mounted force there was the levy *en masse* of infantry. Their arms were still a large shield and a long thrusting spear. There is no trace of military organization or of tactical subdivisions; each canton fought *en masse,* without other arrangement. The baggage was carried in wagons, which were used as a barricade at night. The infantry of certain cantons, such as the Nervii, was more efficient; but the Nervii had no cavalry, and were, perhaps, an immigrant German tribe. Caesar's estimate of the Celtic infantry is made plain enough by the fact that, after the first battle, he never employed them in conjunction with Roman troops.

Undoubtedly the Celts of Transalpine Gaul, as they appeared in Caesar's time, had advanced as compared with their kinsmen who had come into contact with the Romans a century and a half previously in the valley of the Po. The militia had been replaced by the cavalry as the preponderating arm. Open villages had been replaced by walled towns. Articles found in the tombs of Lombardy are certainly inferior to those found in northern Gaul. Lastly, the sense of nationality, which scarcely appears in the battles fought south of the Alps, is seen with striking force in the struggle against Caesar.

Many aspects of Celtic civilization are interesting as approaching nearly to modern culture—its sailing vessels, its knighthood, its ecclesiastical constitution, its attempts to build the nation, not on the city, but on the tribe; but a general view of the whole, so far as the materials exist for it, suggests the thought that the Celtic nation had reached its culminating point of development. It was unable to produce from its own resources either a national art or a national state, and attained at most to a national theology and a peculiar order of nobility. Thus the original simple valor was no more, while the higher military courage, based on morality and organization, appears but in a very stunted form. Again, the coarser features of barbarism were gone: faithful retainers were no longer sacrificed at the death of their chief, but human sacrifices remained; torture, inadmissible in the case of a free man, was still inflicted upon free women or upon slaves. The Celts had lost the advantages which especially belong to the primitive epoch of nations, but had not acquired those which civilization brings with it when it intimately and thoroughly pervades a people.

The Celts had long ceased to press on the Iberian tribes, and the country between the Pyrenees and Garonne was occupied by the Aquitani, a number of tribes of Iberian descent. The Roman arms and the Roman culture had already made great inroads upon the Celtic nation. The latter was now cut off by the Roman province from Italy, Spain, and the Mediterranean. Trade and commerce had already paved the way for conquest north of the Roman bounds. Wine especially, which the Gauls drank undiluted, was greatly prized, and Italian horses were imported. Roman burgesses were already in possession of land in cantons north of the frontier, and the Roman language was by no means unknown in free Gaul.

But the strongest pressure came from the Germans on the north and east: a fresh stock from the cradle of peoples in the East, which made room for itself by the side of its elder brethren with youthful vigor, although also with youthful rudeness. The German tribes nearest the Rhine—the Usipetes, Tencteri, Sugambri, and Ubii— were by this time partly civilized and inhabited fixed territories; but in the interior agriculture was of small importance; even the names of the various tribes were unknown to the Celts, who called them by the general appellation of Suebi (wanderers), and Marcomanni (border warriors). Before this period the Celts had been driven over the Rhine; the Boii, who were once in Bavaria and Bohemia, were harmless wanderers, and the region of the Black Forest, formerly possessed by the Helvetii, was a desert, or occupied by Germans. Nor had the intruders stopped at the Rhine; certain tribes, among whom were the Aduatuci and the Tungri, perhaps also the Nervii and the Treveri, had formed settlements west of the river, and exacted hostages and tribute from the neighboring Gauls. Thus free Gaul was threatened at once by two powerful nations, and was at the same time torn by internal dissensions. How should a nation, which could name no day like those of Marathon and Salamis, of Aricia and the Raudine field,—a nation which, even in its time of vigor, had made no attempt to destroy Massilia by a united effort—now, when evening had come, defend itself against so formidable foes?

The internal condition of Gaul readily became mixed up with its external relations. The Romans, from their first interference, had availed themselves of the perpetual contests for the hegemony, by which every canton was torn asunder; they had supported the Haedui in their rivalry with the Arverni for predominance in the south, had reduced to subjection the Allobroges and many of the client cantons of the Arverni, and got the hegemony transferred from the latter to the Haedui. But the power of Rome was not the only foreign force which might be invoked. The Sequani in central Gaul, who were at the head of the anti-Roman faction, had availed themselves of the remissness of the senatorial government to make an attempt to destroy Roman influence and to humble their rivals, the Haedui.

A dispute arose between the two tribes as to tolls on the river Saone, which separated the two cantons; and about the year 71 B.C. the German prince Ariovistus crossed the Rhine at the head of fifteen thousand men in support of the Sequani. After a long war the Haedui were reduced, in 61 B.C., to conclude a most unfavorable peace, by which they became tributary to the Sequani, and swore never to invoke the intervention of Rome. The Romans talked of assisting the Haedui, and even issued orders to that effect to the governors of Gaul; but nothing was done, and Ariovistus was even enrolled upon the list of friends of the Roman people. The result of this inaction was that numerous bands of Germans continued to cross the Rhine, and that Ariovistus determined to extend his power over the whole of Gaul. The Celts were treated as a conquered nation; even his friends, the Sequani, were forced to cede a third of their territory to make room for his followers, and a second third was soon demanded for the tribe of the Harudes.

But the invasion of Ariovistus was not the only movement in progress. The Usipetes and Tencteri, on the right bank of the Rhine, hard pressed by Suebian hordes, had set out to find new settlements lower down the Rhine. Suebian bands gathered opposite the canton of the Treveri. Lastly, the Helvetii, the most easterly of the Celtic cantons, in modern Switzerland, formed the desperate resolution of evacuating their own territory, in order to find a more spacious and less exposed habitation west of the Jura mountains, hoping at the same time to acquire the hegemony of central Gaul. The Rauraci, in southern Alsace, and the remnant of the homeless Boii were induced to make common cause with the Helvetii. If their scheme were carried out, their original settlement would, of course, fall to the German invader. From the source of the Rhine to the Atlantic Ocean the German tribes were in motion; the whole line of the Rhine was threatened by them. It was a moment like that when the Alamanni and the Franks threw themselves on the falling empire of the Caesars; and even now there seemed on the eve of being carried into effect against the Celts that very movement which was successful, five hundred years afterwards, against the Romans.

It was at this moment that Caesar entered upon his province, in 58 B.C. He was now governor of both the Gauls, including Istria and Dalmatia; his office was secured to him for five years, and it was extended, in 55 B.C., for five years more; he had the right of nominating ten lieutenants and (at any rate, according to his own interpretation of his powers) to fill up his legions or form new ones

from the population of his provinces. His army consisted of four
veteran legions, the seventh, eighth, ninth, and tenth, in all about
24,000 men, besides auxiliaries; he had some Spanish cavalry, and
archers and slingers from Numidia, Crete, and the Balearic isles.
His staff contained several able officers, such as Publius Crassus,
son of Caesar's old political ally, and Titus Labienus. Caesar had
not received definite instructions; to one who was discerning and
courageous these were implied in the circumstances with which he
had to deal. The negligence of the senate had to be retrieved, and,
first of all, the stream of German invasion had to be checked.

The invasion of the Helvetii had just begun; they had burned
their towns and villages to make return impossible, and had gathered to the number of 380,000 souls at the Lacus Lemannus, near
Geneva.   They attempted first to cross the Rhone and proceed
through Roman territory to the shores of the Atlantic, where they
had determined to settle. Caesar prevented this movement, and
following them north into the territory of the Haedui there inflicted
on them such a defeat that the remnant submitted and returned to
their old homes.

The attention of Caesar was next drawn to the middle Rhine,
where the German leader Ariovistus had established himself in
Gallic territory and was levying heavy tribute on the tribes of that
region.   They appealed to the Roman governor, and after fruitless
negotiations Caesar marched against the Germans and in a severe
battle destroyed their entire army.   Only a few besides their king
Ariovistus escaped.   The line of the Rhine was won by this battle.
Caesar might have expelled the Germans who had already settled
themselves on the left bank, but preferring, as everywhere, conquered foes to doubtful friends, he allowed them to remain, and
intrusted them with the defense of the Rhine against their countrymen.

The consequences of this one campaign were great and lasting.
It was now finally determined that the whole of Gaul should be
under Roman sway, and that the Rhine should be the boundary of
the empire against the Germans.   People felt that now another
spirit and another arm had begun to guide the destinies of
Rome.

After the first campaign all central Gaul submitted to the
Romans, while the middle and upper Rhine were rendered safe from
German incursions.   But the northern cantons were not affected by

the blow; moreover, close relations subsisted between them and the Germans over the Rhine, while at the mouth of the river Germanic tribes were making ready to cross. Accordingly, in the spring of 57 B.C., Caesar set out with eight legions against the Belgic cantons. He made an alliance with one of these, the Remi, and succeeded in attacking and defeating the other Belgic tribes in detail. Then turning east he destroyed the entire army of the Nervii in modern Hainault, and sold the Aduatuci for slaves *en masse*.

The next year was occupied with the subjection of the Aremorican cantons in the west. Publius Crassus had been sent to them in the autumn of 57 B.C., and had induced the powerful Veneti to submit. But they soon repented, and during the winter detained as hostages the Roman officers who came to levy grain among them. The whole coast from the Rhine to Loire rose against Rome, and the leaders were calculating on the rise of the Belgae and on aid from Britain and from the Germans.

Caesar sent Labienus with the cavalry to the Rhine, and Q. Titurius Sabinus to Normandy, while the main attack was directed against the Veneti by land and sea. Decimus Brutus hastily formed a fleet of ships, which he levied from the maritime cantons, or caused to be built on the Loire, while Caesar advanced with the best of his infantry. But the Romans encountered the greatest difficulties in the campaign. The ships of the Veneti carried off the goods and inhabitants of each town as soon as it was about to fall into Caesar's hands, and when Brutus's fleet appeared it could at first make no headway against the enemy's, on account of the size and strength of their sailing vessels. Finally by a happy inspiration the Romans managed to cut down the sails of the Venetian vessels with sickles bound to the end of long poles, and their ships, being unprovided with oars, were then boarded and captured. After this the whole coast submitted, and the Veneti were sold into slavery as an example to the other Gauls.

Communications with Gaul had hitherto been carried on by the road over the western Alps, laid out by Pompeius in 77 B.C. Now that central Gaul was open to intercourse with Italy, a shorter route crossing the Alps in a northerly direction was required. Accordingly, in 57 B.C. Servius Galba was sent to occupy Octodurum and to subdue the neighboring tribes, in order to secure the merchant route over the St. Bernard and along the lake of Geneva. In 56

B.C. Publius Crassus was sent into Aquitania with the similar object of conquering the Iberian tribes there, and, though opposed by contingents from beyond the Pyrenees led by officers trained in the Sertorian wars, he succeeded in reducing all the country between the Garonne and the Pyrenees.

The pacification of Gaul, so far as it could be effected by the sword, was now accomplished; but the work of defending the country from the Germans was still unfinished. During the winter peoples of this nation to the number of 430,000 crossed the Rhine into Gaul, and in 55 B.C. Caesar marched against them and cut them to pieces. He then crossed to the east side of the river and ravaged the country, but returned after a stay of eighteen days.

The remainder of the season was occupied with an expedition into Britain, which furnished, if not armed assistance, at any rate a safe asylum to the patriots of the continent. Publius Crassus had already, in 57 B.C., crossed to the Scilly islands, and in the summer of 55 B.C. Caesar himself crossed, in the narrowest part of the Channel, with two legions. The coast was covered with multitudes of the enemy, and the war chariots moved on as fast by land as the Roman galleys by sea; and it was only with great difficulty, and under cover of the missiles thrown from the ships of war, that a landing was effected. Some villages submitted, but soon the natives appeared from the interior and threatened the camp; a storm severely damaged the fleet, and as soon as the necessary repairs were accomplished the Romans returned to Gaul.

During the winter of 55 B.C. a fleet of eight hundred sail was fitted out, and in the spring Caesar sailed a second time to Britain, with five legions and two thousand cavalry. The landing was unopposed; but a second time the fleet was nearly destroyed by the storms, and while the Romans repaired the disaster the British tribes made preparations for defense. The resistance was headed by Cassivellaunus, who ruled in what is now Middlesex and the surrounding counties. He dismissed the general levy, retaining only the war chariots, with which he dogged Caesar's footsteps, threatening his communications and devastating the country through which he was about to pass. The Thames was crossed, but an attack by the men of Kent upon the fleet warned Caesar of the danger to which he was constantly subject, and the storming of a huge abatis where the cattle of the country were collected was an

CAESAR IN GAUL

exploit considerable enough to afford an excuse for retreat.   Cassivellaunus promised hostages and tribute, probably with no intention of giving either, and Caesar recrossed into Gaul.   His immediate object—of "rousing the islanders from their haughty security"—seems certainly to have been attained.

The subjection of Gaul was now complete, while both Britons and Germans had been impressed with a sense of the power of Rome; but many circumstances combined to make the Celtic nation restive under its yoke.   They were ashamed when they had to confess that a nation numbering a million armed men had been subdued by fifty thousand Romans.   Central Gaul and the Belgian confederacy had submitted almost without striking a blow; but the heroic resistance of the Veneti and of the Britons incited the patriotic Celts to make another attempt to recover their freedom. Even in 54 B.C., the Treveri had absented themselves from the general diet, and Caesar had carried with him into Britain their foremost men as hostages; and when the Haeduan Dumnorix refused to embark, he was pursued and cut down by Caesar's orders.   His death created a deep impression all through the ranks of the Celtic nobility; every man felt that the fate of Dumnorix might be his own.

The winter of 54-53 B.C. found the Roman legions quartered in northern Gaul and wrapped.in a sense of complete security.   But suddenly the people arose on their conquerors and, under the leadership of Ambiorix, king of the Eburones, began a simultaneous attack on.the scattered posts.   One division of troops under Quintus Sabinus was annihilated and another under Quintus Cicero would have met the same fate but for the opportune arrival of Caesar with a relieving force.   The Gallic army was again defeated and the various tribes soon scattered to their homes.   After taking a terrible vengeance on the Eburones and making another short incursion into Germany as punishment for aid given the insurgents, Caesar crossed the Alps at the end of 53 B.C. to watch the daily increasing complications of the capital.

But for once Caesar had miscalculated.   The fire was smothered, but not extinguished.   The position of affairs was most favorable for revolt.   Caesar was at a distance on the other side of the Alps, while his army was encamped on the Seine.   The Roman troops might be surrounded and the province overrun before he could appear, even if affairs in Italy did not prevent his return.   The signal was given at Cenabum (Orléans), and all the Romans there were massacred. Everywhere the patriots were astir. Even the Arverni, the stanchest supporters of the Romans in all Gaul, were brought to join the insurrection, after a revolution which overthrew the government of the common council and made Vercingetorix, the leader of the Arvernian patriots, king. The latter soon became for the Celts what Cassivellaunus had been for the Britons. It was felt that he, if any man, was to save the nation. The insurrection spread in the west from the Garonne to the Loire, and Vercingetorix was everywhere recognized as commander-in-chief. Long before he was expected, however, Caesar reappeared to direct his troops; but the summer of 52 B.C. saw the severest fighting that the Romans had yet known in Gaul. The whole country was roused and many advised a retreat over the Cevennes into the old province. Vercingetorix ordered the country to be laid waste, and it seemed impossible either to bring on a general engagement or even to procure supplies for the Roman troops. The Gauls burned their own towns, saving only those capable of defense, and in these they defied their enemy. Finally Caesar succeeded in blockading Vercingetorix in a strongly fortified position at Alesia, and it became evident that here the fate of the country was to be decided.

At the moment when the Roman lines were on the point of completion, Vercingetorix dismissed all his cavalry with orders to rouse the whole nation for the relief of the city. The miserable inhabitants were turned out of the town, and perished of hunger between the lines of either side. At last the huge host of the relieving army appeared—in number amounting to 250,000 infantry and 8000 cavalry. But Caesar had prepared himself to be besieged, and his rear was protected by a strong line of entrenchments. A determined assault was made upon the Romans from without and from within; and on the second day the Celts succeeded, at a point where the lines ran over the slope of a hill, in filling up the trenches and hurling the defenders from the ramparts. Labienus threw himself with four legions upon the enemy. It was the crisis of the struggle, and the assailants were gradually forced back, while squadrons of cavalry attacked them in the rear and completed the rout.

The fate of Alesia and of the Celtic nation was decided. The army dispersed, and the king was, by his own consent, delivered up to the Romans for punishment, in order to avert as far as possible destruction from the nation, by bringing it upon his own head. Mounted on his steed and in full armor the king of the Arvernians appeared before the Roman proconsul, and rode round his tribunal; then he surrendered his horse and arms, and sat down in silence on the steps at Caesar's feet.　Five years afterwards he was led in Caesar's triumph, and beheaded at the foot of the Capitol.　As after a day of gloom the sun breaks through the clouds at its setting, so destiny bestows on nations that are going down a last great man.　Thus Hannibal stands at the close of the Phoenician history, and Vercingetorix at the close of the Celtic. They were not able to save the nations to which they belonged from a foreign yoke, but they spared them the last remaining disgrace, an inglorious fall.

The whole ancient world presents no more genuine knight than Vercingetorix, whether as regards his essential character or his outward appearance.　But man ought not to be a mere knight, and least of all the statesman.　It was the knight, not the hero, who disdained to escape from Alesia, when he alone was of more consequence to the nation than a hundred thousand ordinary brave men.　It was the knight, not the hero, who gave himself up as a sacrifice, when the only thing gained by the sacrifice was that the nation publicly dishonored itself, and with equal cowardice and absurdity employed its last breath in proclaiming that its great historical death-struggle was a crime against its oppressor.　How very different was the conduct of Hannibal in similar positions! It is impossible to part from the noble king of the Arverni without a feeling of historical and human sympathy; but it is characteristic of the Celtic nation, that its greatest man was after all merely a knight.

After the fall of Alesia no united effort was made to continue the insurrection; the league fell to pieces, and every clan made what terms it could with the conqueror.　Caesar was anxious for many reasons to bring the war to a close, and the easy temperament of the Gauls met him halfway.　Where there was a strong Roman party, as among the Haedui and Arverni, the cantons obtained a complete restoration of their former relations with Rome, and their captives were released without ransom, while those of the other clans became the slaves of the legionaries.　But not a few cantons refused to make submission, until the Roman troops appeared within their borders. Such expeditions were undertaken in the winter and in the following summer against the Bituriges and Carnutes, the Bellovaci and other Belgic cantons. The Bellovacian king Correus offered a brave resistance, but was at last slain in a skirmish. On the Loire strong bands assembled which required a considerable Roman force to defeat them. The last remnant of opposition was at Uxellodunum on the Lot, where Drappes and Lucterius, the brave adjutant of Vercingetorix, shut themselves up. The town was taken only after Caesar had appeared in person, and the spring from which the garrison derived water had been diverted. The whole garrison were dismissed to their homes after their hands had been cut off.

Thus Gaul was finally subdued after eight years' war. Hardly a year later the Roman troops had to be withdrawn, owing to the outbreak of civil war; yet the Celts did not rise against the foreign yoke, and Gaul was the only part of the Roman empire where there was no fighting against Caesar. Later disturbances, like the rising of the Bellovaci in 46 B.C., were easily dealt with by the local governors. This state of peace was, it is true, purchased to a large extent by allowing the more distant districts to withdraw themselves *de facto* from the Roman allegiance; but however unfinished the building of Caesar may have been, its foundations remained firm and unshaken.

For the present the newly acquired provinces were united with the province of Narbo, but when Caesar gave up this governorship, in 46 B.C., two new governorships, of Gaul proper and Belgica, were formed. The individual cantons of course lost their independence, and paid to Rome a fixed tribute which they levied themselves. The total was two million dollars, but masses of gold from the treasures of temples and of rich men also flowed to Rome to such an extent that, as compared with silver, gold fell twenty-five per cent.

Existing arrangements were everywhere allowed to remain as far as possible; the hereditary kingships, the feudal oligarchies, even the system of clientship by which one canton was dependent on another still existed. Caesar's sole object was to arrange matters in the interest of Rome, and to bring into power the men favorably disposed to Roman rule. Cantons where the Roman party was strong and trustworthy, such as the Remi, the Lingones, and the Haedui, received the right of alliance which gave them much

CAESAR IN GAUL

greater communal freedom, and were invested with the hegemony over other cantons. The national worship and its priests were preserved as much as possible.

At the same time Caesar did what he could to stimulate the Romanization of Gaul. A number of Celts of rank were admitted to Roman citizenship—perhaps into the Roman senate; Latin was made the official language in several cantons; and while smaller money might be coined by the local authorities for local circulation, this might only be done in conformity with the Roman standard, and the coinage of gold and of denarii was reserved for the Roman magistrates alone. Hereafter the organization of the cantons approached more nearly to the Italian urban constitution, and both the common councils and the chief towns became of far greater importance than hitherto. If Caesar did little in the way of founding colonies—only two settlements can be traced to him, that of Noviodunum and that of the Boii—it was because circumstances did not allow him to exchange the sword for the plow. No one probably saw more clearly than himself the military and political advantages of establishing a series of Transalpine colonies as bases of support for the new center of civilization.

Gaul as a nation had ceased to exist; it was absorbed in a politically superior nationality. The course of the war was significant enough of the character of the nation: at the outset only single districts, and those German or half German, offered energetic resistance; and when foreign rule was established, the attempts to shake it off were either without plan or were the work of certain prominent nobles, and with the death or capture of an Indutiomarus or a Vercingetorix the struggle was at an end.

But the ruin of the Celtic nation was not the most important result of Caesar's wars. Nothing but the insight and energy of Caesar prevented Gaul from being overrun by the Germans, in whom the Roman statesman saw the rivals and antagonists of the Graeco-Roman world. By his conquests and organization he gained time for the West to acquire that culture which the East had already assumed: but for him the great migration of peoples which took place five hundred years later would have taken place under Ariovistus. Had it so happened, our civilization would hardly have stood in any more intimate relation to the Romano-Greek than to the Indian and Assyrian culture. That there is a bridge connecting the past glory of Hellas and Rome with the prouder fabric of modern history; that western Europe is Romanic and Germanic Europe classic; that the names of Themistocles and Scipio have to us a very different sound from those of Asoka and Salmanassar; that Homer and Sophocles are not merely like the Vedas and Kalidasa attractive to the literary botanist, but bloom for us in our own garden—all this is the work of Caesar; and while the creation of his great predecessor in the East has been almost wholly reduced to ruin by the tempests of the Middle Ages, the structure of Caesar has outlasted those thousands of years which have changed religion and polity for the human race and even shifted the center of civilization itself, and it stands erect for what we may term perpetuity.

Chapter XXX

THE JOINT RULE OF POMPEIUS AND CAESAR
57-52 B.C.

OF the three joint rulers, Pompeius, Caesar and Crassus, the first-named was the foremost in the eyes of the Roman world. Nor is this surprising, for Pompeius was undoubtedly the first general of his time, while Caesar, so far as he was known, was only a dexterous party leader. In the eyes of the multitude he was to Pompeius what Flavius and Afranius had been—a useful instrument for political purposes. And if the position of Pompeius under the Gabinian law was compared with that of Caesar under the Vatinian, the comparison was to the advantage of the former; for Pompeius had almost the whole resources of the state under his control, and ruled nearly the whole empire, while Caesar had only certain fixed sums and four legions, and ruled two provinces. Caesar, again, was to resign his command after five years, while Pompeius had fixed his own time for retirement.

But Pompeius attempted a task beyond his powers when he undertook to rule the capital—a problem always infinitely difficult, because there was no armed force at the disposal of the government, whatever it might be. The result was complete anarchy: after Caesar's departure the coalition still ruled doubtless the destinies of the world, but not the streets of the capital. The senate felt its impotence, and attempted no show of authority; Pompeius shut himself up and sulked in silence; the sound portion of the citizens, who had at heart freedom and order, kept rigorously aloof from politics. But for the rabble of all sorts, high and low, it was a time of carnival; demagogism became a trade, which accordingly did not lack its professional insignia—the threadbare mantle, the shaggy beard, the long streaming hair, the deep bass voice.

Greeks and Jews, freedmen and slaves, were the most regular attendants at the popular assemblies, and often only a minority of those voting consisted of burgesses legally constituted. The real rulers of Rome were the armed bands, raised by adventurers out of gladiatorial slaves and blackguards of all sorts. These bands had hitherto been usually under the control of the popular leaders, but now all discipline was at an end, and the leaders of the bands fought either for the democracy, for the senate, or for Crassus: Clodius had fought at different times for all three.

The most noted of these street leaders was Publius Clodius, whom the regents had already made use of against Cato and Cicero. During his tribunate he had exerted all his great talent, energy, and influence to promote an ultra-democratic policy: he gave the citizens corn gratis; prohibited the obstruction of the comitia by religious formalities; reëstablished the street-clubs, which constituted a complete organization of the whole proletariate of the city according to streets; and set the seal of divine favor upon his doings by erecting a grand Temple of Liberty on the Palatine.

The position of Pompeius was soon seriously compromised: Clodius opposed him in a trifling matter about the sending back of a captive Armenian prince, and the quarrel became a serious feud. Pompeius revenged himself by allowing the return of Cicero, the bitter enemy of Clodius. But the real battleground was in the streets, and here, though Pompeius had his own hired gangs, Clodius was usually victorious. To complete the spectacle, both parties in the quarrel courted the favor of the senate; Pompeius pleased it by recalling Cicero, Clodius by declaring the Julian laws null and void. Naturally no positive result came from this political witches' revel—it was quite aimless; demagogism was a mere makeshift in the interregnum between republic and monarchy. It had not even the effect of kindling the desire for a strong government based on military power; for those citizens likely to be affected in this way lived mostly away from Rome, and were not touched by the anarchy which prevailed there; and besides, they had already been thoroughly converted to the cause of authority by the Catilinarian attempts. The only important result of all this confusion was the painful position of Pompeius, which must have had considerable influence upon his future conduct.

Far more important than the change in the relations of Pompeius with Clodius was his altered position with regard to Caesar. While Pompeius had failed to fulfill the functions assigned to him, Caesar had been brilliantly successful: he had crushed the threatening German invasion, and in two years had carried the Roman arms to the Rhine and the Channel. Already, in 57 B.C., the senate had voted him the usual honors in far richer measure than had ever been accorded to Pompeius. Caesar was now the hero of the day, master of the most powerful Roman army; while Pompeius was merely an ex-general who had once been famous. No rupture had taken place, but it was evident that the alliance must be at an end ' when the relative position of the parties was reversed. At any rate Pompeius found it necessary to abandon his attitude of haughty reserve, and to come forward and attempt to gain for himself a command which would again put him on equal terms with Caesar. To do this he must be able to control the machinery of government: but by his awkward quarrel with Clodius he had lost command of the streets, and therefore could not count on carrying his point in the popular assembly; and at the same time it was doubtful whether after his long inaction even the senate was sufficiently under his influence to grant what he wished.

The opposition to the regents had been growing in strength and importance, and they were powerless to check it; in consequence, a change occurred in the position of the senate, which found itself largely increased in importance. The marriage alliance of Caesar and Pompeius, and the banishments of Cato and of Cicero, suggested unpleasantly to the public mind the decrees and alliances of monarchs, and men began to perceive that it was no modification of the republican constitution which was at stake, but the existence of the republic itself. Many of the best men who had hitherto belonged to the popular party now passed over to the other side. The " three dynasts," the " three-headed monster," were phrases in everybody's mouth. Even the masses began to waver: Caesar's consular orations were listened to without a sound; at the theater no applause greeted his entrance, and his tools and associates were publicly hissed. The rulers hinted to the equites that their opposition might cost them their new special seats in the theater, and that the commons might lose their free corn. Caesar's wealth was employed in every direction to gain adherents; no one, unless hopelessly lost, was refused assistance in distress, and the enormous buildings set on foot by Caesar and Pompeius brought gain to great numbers of men in every position. But corruption could touch only a comparatively small number, and every day brought proofs of the strong attachment of the people to the existing constitution and of their hatred of monarchy. Under representative institutions the popular discontent would have found an outlet at the elections, but

under the existing circumstances the only course left for the supporters of the republic was to range themselves under the banner of
the senate. Thus, for the moment, the senate rested on a firmer
support than it had enjoyed for years; it began to bestir itself
again. With its approval and support a proposal was submitted
to the people, permitting the return of Cicero. An unusual
number of good citizens, especially from the country towns,
attended on the day of voting, August 4, 57 B.C., and the journey
of the orator from Brundisium to Rome was made the occasion of
a brilliant demonstration in favor of the senate and the constitution.
Pompeius was helpless, and his helplessness disarmed the party in
the senate favorable to the regents. Had the senate possessed a
leader their cause might even yet have won; they might have canceled the extraordinary powers as unconstitutional, and summoned
all the republicans of Italy to arm against the tyrants. But the necessary leader was wanting, and the aristocracy were too indolent
to take so simple and bold a resolution. They preferred to side
with Pompeius against Caesar, in the hope that a rupture between
the two was inevitable; and to settle matters with Pompeius, after
victory, might be expected to be no very difficult matter.

It seemed natural that an alliance between Pompeius and the
republicans should be formed, but the matter was brought to a test
when, in the autumn of 57 B.C., Pompeius came before the senate
with a proposal to intrust him with extraordinary official power.
His proposal was based upon the price of corn in the capital, which
had again reached an oppressive height, owing to the continuance of
piracy and the negligence of the government in supervising the
supply. He wished to be intrusted with the superintendence of all
matters relating to corn supply throughout the whole empire, and
for this purpose to be invested with unlimited control over the state
treasure, with an army and fleet, and with powers superior to those
of the ordinary governor in every province; and to this command
he hoped that the conduct of the impending Egyptian war would
naturally be added. The senate accepted the proposal in principle
with outward obsequiousness, but made alterations which seriously
curtailed the general's authority. Pompeius obtained no unlimited
power, but merely certain large sums and fifteen adjutants for the
purpose of organizing due supplies for the capital, and, in all matters relating to grain supply only, full proconsular power throughout
the empire for five years. The decree of the senate was ratified

by the people. The regent had missed his object, but he had obtained definite employment and an excuse for leaving the capital, and the supply of corn was soon in a more satisfactory condition. Still, without troops his proconsular authority was only a shadow, and he got a second proposal made in the senate, conferring upon him the charge of restoring the expelled king of Egypt, if necessary by force of arms. But the senate grew less and less compliant; it was discovered in the Sibylline books that it was impious to send a Roman army to Egypt. Pompeius was ready to accept the mission even without an army, but the senate refused to risk so valuable a life, and ultimately resolved, in 56 B.C., not to interfere at all.

These rebuffs of Pompeius were, of course, regarded as defeats of the regents generally, and the tide of opposition rose higher and higher. The elections for 56 B.C. had gone only very partially according to the wishes of the triumvirate, and for the consulship of 55 B.C. Lucius Domitius Ahenobarbus announced himself as a candidate with the avowed object of actively opposing them. The senate solemnly deliberated over an opinion which was furnished by certain Etruscan soothsayers of repute, that the whole power over the army and treasure threatened to pass to one ruler, and that the state would lose its freedom. But they soon went on to a more practical declaration of war. As early as December, 57 B.C., the opinion had been expressed in the senate that the laws of Caesar's consulship, especially the law about the domain land of Capua, must be cancelled; and in April, 56 B.C., Cicero moved that the Capuan law should be taken into consideration on May 1. Domitius soon afterwards declared that he intended as consul to propose to the burgesses the immediate recall of Caesar; and in this manner the nobility threw down the gauntlet to the regents.

The triumvirs had no time to lose. Crassus immediately started north to confer with Caesar, whom he found at Ravenna; at Luca they were joined by Pompeius, who had left Rome ostensibly on business connected with the supply of grain. The most noted adherents of the rulers, such as Metellus Nepos, proconsul of Hither Spain, and Appius Claudius, propretor of Sardinia, followed them. A hundred and twenty lictors and two hundred senators were counted at the conference; it was almost a rival senate of the monarchy as opposed to the other senate of the republic. The decisive voice lay with Caesar, and he used it to reëstablish the joint rule on a firmer basis, with a more equal distribution of power. The

most important governorships after Gaul, namely the two Spains
and Syria, were assigned, the former to Pompeius, the latter to
Crassus, and were to be secured by decree of the people for five
years. Caesar was to have his own office prolonged for another
five years, from 54 B.C. to the close of 49 B.C.; and to be allowed
to increase his legions to ten, and to charge the pay of his arbitrarily
levied troops on the state chest. Pompeius and Crassus were to hold
the consulship for 55 B.C., before departing for their provinces, and
Caesar was to be consul in 48 B.C., after the termination of his command. The military support necessary for the regulation of the
capital was to be supplied by raising legions for the Spanish and
Syrian armies, and keeping them in Italy as long as should seem
convenient. Minor details were easily settled by Caesar's magic
influence; Pompeius and Crassus were reconciled to each other,
and even Clodius was induced to give no further annoyance to
Pompeius.

The reasons which induced Caesar to concede to his rival so
powerful a position—a position which he had refused him in 60 B.C.,
when the league was formed—can only be conjectured. It was not
that necessity compelled him, for Pompeius was a powerless sup-
pliant at Caesar's feet; and even if, in case of a rupture, he had
joined the optimates, the alliance would not have been so formidable
as to demand so heavy a price to prevent it. Probably Caesar was
not yet prepared for civil war; but in any case the decision of
peace or war rested, not with Pompeius, but with the opposition.
Possibly purely personal motives may have contributed; Caesar
was not the man to be disloyal to his allies, and he may have hesitated to break the heart of his beloved daughter, who was sincerely
attached to her husband. In his soul there was room for much
besides the statesman. But the main reason was undoubtedly the
consideration of Gaul. If Caesar's object was to become king of
Rome as soon as possible, it was a grave blunder to give up his
present enormous superiority over his rivals, and especially to put
Pompeius in a position to settle matters independently with the
senate. But Caesar's was no vulgar ambition; the conquest of
Gaul was an enterprise on which depended the external security
and internal reorganization of the empire; it was necessary for
the repression of German invasions, and necessary to furnish new
soil for Italian civilization. But Caesar's Gallic conquests hindered
far more than they helped him on the way to the throne, and it

yielded him bitter fruit that he postponed the revolution from 56 to 48 B.C.

The aristocracy did not make good its gage. They had taken up arms only to lay them down as soon as the adversary merely put his hand to the sheath. Nothing more was heard about discussion of the Julian laws in the senate; the legions raised by Caesar were charged on the public chest, and the attempts to take from him one or both of his provinces decisively failed. Cicero was among the first to repent, and applied to himself epithets more appropriate than flattering.[1] The troops for Syria did indeed depart, but the legions for Spain were dismissed on furlough, and Pompeius remained with them in Italy. At the same time the regents acted deliberately in such a manner as to withdraw from the senate what had hitherto been its especial function—the management of military matters and of foreign affairs. The arrangements made at Luca with regard to the provinces of Gaul, Spain, and Syria were submitted to and approved by the people. The regents lent and borrowed troops from each other without authority. The Transpadani were apparently treated by Caesar as full burgesses of Rome, though they had legally only Latin rights. Caesar organized his conquests and founded colonies, such as Novum Comum, without the consent of the senate. The Thracian, Egyptian, and Parthian wars were conducted by the generals in command without consulting or even reporting to the senate.

The majority of the senate submitted humbly enough to necessity. Cicero was now completely in the service of the regents. His brother was an officer in Caesar's army, in some measure as a hostage. Cicero himself was compelled to accept an office under Pompeius, on pretense of which he might be banished at any moment; and he submitted to be relieved from his pecuniary embarrassments by loans from Caesar and by an appointment to the joint overseership of the vast building operations in the capital. Many prominent members of the nobility were kept subservient by similar methods; but there remained a certain section which could be neither intimidated nor cajoled. The foremost of these was Cato, who ceaselessly, at the peril of his life, offered the most determined opposition in senate-house and Forum. The regents did not molest him and his followers; strong measures would have made them martyrs, and, after all, their activity was unavailing. But though

---

[1] "Me asinum germanum fuisse" (*Ad Att.*, iv. 5. 3).

destitute of important results, their action fostered and gave the watchword to the widespread discontent which fermented in secret: and they were often able to draw the majority in the senate, which secretly sympathized with them, into isolated decrees against its masters and their adherents. Thus Gabinius was refused a public thanksgiving in 56 B.C.; Piso was recalled from his province; and the senate wore mourning when the tribune Gaius Cato hindered the elections of 55 B.C. as long as the republican consul Marcellinus remained in office. But the great fact was unaltered—the regents were supreme. "No one," says a contemporary writer, "is of the slightest account except the three; the regents are all-powerful, and they take care that no one shall remain in doubt about it; the whole state is virtually transformed, and obeys the dictators."

The opposition, powerless in the field of government, could not nevertheless be dislodged from certain departments of state which had considerable political influence—the elections of magistrates, and the jury courts. The former, which belong properly to the government of the state, were, under the present *régime*, when the government was really wielded by extraordinary magistrates, unimportant; the ordinary magistrates themselves were ciphers, and the elections sank into mere demonstrations. The regents spared no pains to gain the victory even here: the lists of candidates for some years was settled at Luca; large sums were expended upon elections, and numbers of soldiers were sent on furlough from the armies of Caesar and Pompeius to vote at Rome. But the result was only partial success. For 55 B.C. Pompeius and Crassus were elected only by open violence and after the most scandalous scenes. For 54 B.C. Domitius was elected consul and Cato pretor; while the candidates of the regents were convicted of the most shameful corruption in the elections for 53 B.C., and were abandoned by their principals. These defeats may be accounted for partly by the wide discontent at the rule of the triumvirate; mainly by the elaborately organized system of political clubs which were entirely controlled by the nobility.

The jury courts gave even greater trouble and annoyance. As at present composed the senatorial party was influential in them, but the middle class was predominant; and the fact that in 55 B.C. Pompeius proposed a high-rated census for jurymen shows that the strength of the opposition was in the middle class, and that the capitalists were more easy to manage. A constant warfare of prosecution was waged against the adherents of the rulers, the accusers being generally the younger and more fiery members of the nobility. Still, even here, where the regents chose to insist, the courts dared not refuse to comply. Vatinius, the best hated of all Caesar's personal adherents, was acquitted in all the processes against him. But Pompeius did not know so well how to protect his clients, and Gabinius was sent into banishment in 54 B.C., for extortions in the provinces; and even where unsuccessful, impeachments by such masters of sarcasm and dialectics as Gaius Licinius Calvus and Gaius Assinius Pollio did not miss their mark.

Still less controllable was the power of literature, which throughout these years is pervaded by a tone of the bitterest opposition. The orations of the accusers in the law courts were regularly published as political pamphlets; the youth of the aristocracy and of the middle class in the country towns kept up a constant fire of pamphlets and epigrams; and the senator's son, Gaius Licinius Calvus, fought side by side with Marcus Furius Bibaculus of Cremona, and Quintus Valerius Catullus of Verona. The literature of the time is full of sarcasms against the " great Caesar," " the unique general," the affectionate father-in-law and son-in-law who ransack the globe to enrich their dissolute favorites. Caesar saw that such opposition could not be checked by word of command; he tried rather to gain over by his personal influence the more eminent authors. Cicero was treated respectfully, out of regard for his literary reputation; and Catullus, in spite of his sarcasms, was treated with the most flattering distinction. The commentaries on the Gallic wars were intended partly to meet the enemy on their own ground, and to set forth to the public the necessity and constitutional propriety of Caesar's operations.

The opposition became more and more troublesome, and the regents at length determined to take stronger measures. It was resolved to introduce a temporary dictatorship. At the close of 54 B.C. the dictatorship was demanded in the senate; but Pompeius himself still shrank from openly asking it. Even when the elections for 53 B.C. led to the most scandalous scenes, and had to be postponed for a full year beyond the time fixed, he still hesitated to speak the decisive word, and might long have hesitated but for circumstances which forced his hand. For the consulship of 52 B.C. Titus Annius Milo came forward in opposition to the candidates of the regents, who were both personally connected with Pompeius.

Milo was the great rival of Clodius in the game of the streets, the
Hector to the Achilles of Clodius.   As Clodius was on the side of
the regents, Milo was of course for the republic; and Cato and his
friends supported his candidature in return.   In a chance skirmish
between the rival bands on the Appian Way, not far from the capital, Clodius was wounded and carried into a neighboring house,
from which he was afterwards dragged to be murdered by Milo's
orders.   The adherents of the triumvirs saw here an opportunity
for thwarting the candidature of Milo, and carrying the dictatorship of Pompeius.   The bloody corpse was exposed in the Forum,
speeches were made, and a riot broke forth.   The mob set fire to
the senate-house, and then besieged the residence of Milo till they
were repulsed by his band.   They then saluted Pompeius as dictator and his candidates as consuls; and when the interrex, Marcus
Lepidus, refused to hold the elections at once, he was blockaded in
his house for five days.   Pompeius certainly desired the dictatorship, but he would not take it at the hands of a mob.   He brought
up troops to put down the anarchy in the city, and then demanded
the dictatorship from the senate.   To escape the name of dictator,
this body, on the motion of Cato and Bibulus, perpetrated a double
absurdity, and appointed the proconsul Pompeius " consul without
colleague." [2]

Pompeius at once proceeded energetically to use his powers
against the republican party in their strongholds, the electioneering
clubs, and the jury courts.

The existing election laws were repeated and enforced; and a
special law, which prescribed increased penalties for electioneering
intrigues, was endowed with retrospective force as far back as 70
B.C.   The governorships were to be conferred on the consuls and
pretors, not as heretofore, immediately on their retirement from
office, but after an interval of five years.   The years which must
elapse before this arrangement could be brought into action were
to be provided for by special decrees of the senate from time to
time—a course which put the provinces for the next few years at
the disposal of the person or persons whose influence might be
supreme in the senate.   The liberty of the law courts was curtailed
by limiting the number of advocates and the time of speaking
allowed to each; and the custom of bringing forward *laudatores*

---

[2] Consul means colleague, and a consul who is at the same time a proconsul
is at once an actual consul and a consul's substitute.

as witnesses to character was prohibited.   The senate decreed that the country was in danger, owing to the disturbances connected with the affair on the Appian Way, and accordingly a commission was appointed by a special law to inquire into all offenses connected with the affray, the members being nominated by Pompeius.   At the same time all the men capable of service in Italy were called to arms, and made to swear allegiance to Pompeius; troops were stationed at the Capitol, and the place where the trial respecting the murder of Clodius was going on was surrounded by soldiers.

By these measures opposition was checked, but not, of course, destroyed.   The reins were drawn tighter and the republican party was humbled.   Milo was condemned by the jurymen, and Cato's candidature for the consulship frustrated.   But many mischances occurred through the maladroitness of Pompeius; he was attempting an impossible task—to play at once the parts of impartial restorer of law and order and of party chief.   Thus he allowed many subordinate persons belonging to the republican party to be acquitted by the commission, and looked on in silence while every man who had taken part for Clodius—that is for the regents—in the late riots was condemned.   At the same time he violated his own laws by appearing as a *laudator* for his friend Plancus, and by protecting from condemnation several persons specially connected with himself, such as Metellus Scipio.   Still, the regents were on the whole satisfied, and the public acquiesced, even to celebrating the recovery of Pompeius from a serious illness with demonstrations of joy.   On August 1, 52 B.C., Pompeius laid down his special command and chose Metellus Scipio as his colleague.

Chapter XXXI

CRASSUS AND THE RUPTURE BETWEEN POMPEIUS AND CAESAR. 54-49 B.C.

FOR years Marcus Crassus had been reckoned one of the regents of Rome without any claim to be so considered. But after the conference at Luca his position was changed: Caesar had allowed the consulship and the governorship of Syria to be assigned to him, in order to counterbalance the great concessions he found it advisable to make to Pompeius; and at the close of his consulship Crassus had an opportunity, as governor of Syria, of attaining, through the Parthian war, the position acquired by Caesar in Gaul. Avarice and ambition combined to inspire him, at the age of sixty, with all the ardor of youth. He arrived in Syria early in 54 B.C., having left Rome even before the close of his consulship, eager to add the riches of the East to those of the West, and to achieve military glory as rapidly as Caesar and with as little trouble as Pompeius.

The Parthian war had already begun. Pompeius had not respected his engagements with regard to the frontier, and had wrested provinces from the empire to confer them upon Armenia. Accordingly, after the death of King Phraates, his son Mithradates declared war upon Armenia. This was, of course, a declaration of war against Rome, and Gabinius, the governor of Syria, soon led his troops across the Euphrates. But meantime Mithradates had been dethroned by the grandees of the empire with the vizier at their head, and Orodes now reigned in his stead. Mithradates took refuge with the Romans; but at this juncture Gabinius was ordered by the regents to restore the king of Egypt to Alexandria by force of arms, and he had to give up the Parthian war for the present. But he induced Mithradates to make war on his own account, and the prince was supported by the cities of Seleucia and Babylon. Soon afterwards, however, Seleucia was captured by storm, Babylon was reduced to surrender, and Mithradates was captured and put to death. Gabinius, who had finished the Egyptian campaign, was on the eve of resuming operations against the Parthians when Crassus arrived in Syria and relieved him of the command.

Crassus spent the summer of 54 B.C. in levying troops and contributions, and in making an extensive reconnaissance. The Euphrates was crossed and a victory won at Ichnae; garrisons were placed in several of the neighboring towns, and then the troops returned to Syria. This reconnaissance determined the Romans to march against the Parthians straight across the Mesopotamian desert, rather than by the circuitous route through Armenia; for the numerous Greek and half-Greek towns in the region of the Tigris and Euphrates were found ready at once to shake off the Parthian yoke.

Next year, 53 B.C., the Euphrates was again crossed, and after some deliberation it was decided to march across the desert to the Tigris rather than down the Euphrates to Seleucia, where the two rivers are but a few miles apart. The Roman army consisted of seven legions, four thousand cavalry, and four thousand slingers and archers. For many days they marched, and no enemy appeared. At length, not far from the River Balissus, some horsemen of the enemy were descried in the distance. The Arab prince Abgarus of Edessa, who had been loud in his protestations of loyalty, and who had been mainly instrumental in determining Crassus to adopt the desert route, was sent out to reconnoiter. The enemy disappeared, followed by Abgarus and his men; and after a long interval it was resolved to advance, in the hope of coming upon the enemy. The river was crossed and the army was led rapidly forward, when suddenly the drums of the Parthians were heard, their silken gold-embroidered banners were seen waving, and their helmets and coats of mail blazing in the sun; and by the side of the Parthian vizier stood Abgarus and his Bedouins.

The Romans saw at once the net in which they were ensnared. The whole Parthian army consisted of cavalry; the vizier had seen that no Oriental infantry could cope with that of Rome, and had dispensed with the army altogether. The mass of his troops were mounted archers, while the line was formed of heavy cavalry, armed with long thrusting lances, and protected—man and horse—by armor formed of leather or of metal plates. The Roman infantry were quite unable to bring such an enemy to a close engagement, and, even if they had been able, these ironclad hosts would probably have been more than a match for them. In the

desert every advantage was on the side of the enemy and none on
that of the Romans. The strength of the Roman system of warfare
lay in the close order in which the legions fought, and in the custom
of forming entrenched camps, which made every encampment a
fortification. But the close order now only served to make them an
easier mark for their enemies' missiles, and in the desert ditches
and ramparts could often hardly be formed. It is curious that the
irresistible superiority of the Roman infantry led the enemies of
Rome at about the same time, in widely different parts of the world,
to meet it, and meet it successfully, by the same means—by the use
of cavalry and missiles. The Parthian vizier was only carrying
out on a larger scale, and under infinitely more favorable conditions, what had been completely successful under Cassivelaunus in
Britain, and partially successful under Vercingetorix in Gaul.

Under such conditions the first battle between Romans and
Parthians was fought in the desert, about thirty miles south of
Carrhae. The Roman archers, who began the attack, were driven
back; the legions, which were in their usual close order, were soon
outflanked and overwhelmed by the archers of the enemy. In
order that they might not be completely surrounded, Publius
Crassus, the same who had served with such distinction under
Caesar in Gaul, advanced with a select corps of cavalry, archers,
and infantry. The Parthians retreated, hotly pursued, but when
completely out of sight of the main army of the Romans the heavy
cavalry made a stand and soon completely surrounded the band of
Crassus. All the valor of the Romans and of their leader was in
vain; they were driven to a slight eminence, where their destruction was completed. Crassus and many of his officers put themselves to death; out of the whole number of six thousand only five
hundred were taken prisoners; not one was able to escape. Meanwhile the main army was left comparatively unmolested, but when
it advanced to discover the fate of the detached corps the head of
the young Crassus was displayed on a pole before his father's eyes,
and the terrible onslaught was at the same time renewed. Night
alone put an end to the slaughter. Fortunately the Parthians retired from the field to bivouac; and the Romans seized the opportunity to retreat to Carrhae. They left the wounded and the
stragglers—said to have been four thousand in number—on the
field, and as the Parthians stayed to massacre these, and the inhabitants of Carrhae marched forth in haste to succor the fugitives,

the remnant of the army was saved from destruction. But the Romans, either from want of provisions or from the precipitation of Crassus, soon set out from Carrhae and marched towards the Armenian mountains. Marching by night and resting by day the main body arrived at Sinnaca, within a day's march of safety. There the vizier came to offer peace and friendship, and to propose a conference between the two generals. The offer was accepted and terms were discussed; a richly caparisoned horse was produced—a present from the king to Crassus, and as the servants of the vizier crowded to assist the Roman general to mount, the suspicion arose among the Roman officers that it was a design to seize the person of their leader. Octavius snatched a sword from a Parthian and stabbed the groom. In the tumult which followed all the Roman officers were killed, Crassus refused to survive as a prisoner, and the whole Roman force left behind in the camp was either captured or dispersed. Only one small body, which had broken off from the main force, and some straggling bands found their way back to Syria. Ten thousand Roman prisoners were settled in the oasis of Merv; one-half of the whole force had perished.

This disaster to the Roman arms seemed likely to shake the very foundations of the Roman power in the East. Armenia became completely dependent upon Parthia, and the Hellenic cities were again enslaved. More than this, the Parthians prepared to cross the Euphrates and to dislodge the Romans from Syria. But, fortunately for Rome, the leaders on each side had changed. The vizier was executed by the Sultan Orodes, and the command of the invading army given to the young Prince Pacorus, while the *ad interim* command of Syria was assumed by the able questor Gaius Cassius. For two years the Parthians sent only flying bands, which were easily repulsed. Owing to the negligence of the Roman government the great Parthian invasion, which came at last in 51 B.C., found nothing to oppose it but two weak legions which Cassius had formed from the remains of the army of Crassus, and which could, of course, do nothing to oppose the advance. However, under an ordinary general the Parthians were no more formidable than any other Oriental army; and though the Syrian command soon devolved upon the incapable Bibulus, nothing was effected by the invaders, and Pacorus soon came to an agreement with the Roman commander, and turned his arms against his father Orodes instead.

It is an ominous sign of the times that the national disasters of Carrhae and Sinnaca attracted almost less attention at Rome than the pitiful brawl upon the Appian Way. But it is hardly wonderful; the breach between the regents was now becoming imminent. Like the boat of the ancient Greek mariners' tale, the vessel of the Roman community now found itself, as it were, between two rocks swimming towards each other; expecting every moment the crash of collision, those whom it was bearing, tortured by nameless anguish gazed into the eddying surge that rose higher and higher and were benumbed; and while every slightest movement there attracted a thousand eyes, not one ventured to give a glance to the right or left.

After the conference at Luca it seemed that the division of power was made on a basis sufficiently firm to ensure its endurance, provided that both parties were disposed to act in good faith. This was the case with Caesar, at any rate during the interval necessary for the completion of his Gallic conquests; but probably Pompeius was never even provisionally in earnest about the collegiate scheme. Still, though he never meant to acknowledge Caesar's equality with himself, the idea of breaking with him formed itself but slowly in his mind. In 54 B.C. the death of Julia, followed closely by that of her child, destroyed the personal bond between the rivals; and when Pompeius refused Caesar's overtures for fresh marriage connections, and himself married the daughter of Quintus Metellus Scipio, the breach had unmistakably begun. Still the political alliance remained, and Pompeius, after the disaster of Aduatuca in 54 B.C., lent Caesar one of his Italian legions, while Caesar gave his consent and support to the dictatorship of Pompeius. But as soon as the latter found himself in a position completely outweighing in influence that of Caesar, and when all the men of military age in Italy had tendered their military oath to himself personally, it became clear that he had made up his mind to a rupture. The proceedings of the dictatorship told largely against the partisans of Caesar. This might have been accident; but when Pompeius selected for his colleague in office his dependent Metellus Scipio instead of Caesar, still more when he got his governorship of the two Spains prolonged for five years more, and a large sum of money assigned to him for the payment of troops, without procuring similar arrangements for Caesar, it was impossible to mistake his intention. Lastly, the new regulations as to the holding of governorships had the ulterior object of procuring Caesar's premature recall. No moment could have been more unfavorable to Caesar. In June, 53 B.C., the death of Crassus occurred—and Crassus had always been the closest ally of Caesar, and a bitter personal enemy of Pompeius. A few months later the Gallic insurrection broke out with renewed violence, and for the first time Caesar had to encounter an equal opponent in Vercingetorix. Pompeius was dictator of Rome and master of the senate; what might have occurred if, instead of intriguing obscurely against Caesar, he had boldly recalled him from Gaul?

The impending struggle was, of course, not between republic and monarchy, but between Pompeius and Caesar for the crown of Rome. Nevertheless, each of the rivals found it convenient to adopt one of the old party battle cries; neither dared to alienate from himself the mass of respectable conservative citizens, who desired the continuance of the republic, by openly aiming at monarchy. Caesar, of course, inscribed upon his banner, " The people and democratic progress." He had been from the outset an earnest democrat, and the monarchy meant to him something which differed in little but name from the Gracchan government of the people. To Caesar this subterfuge brought little advantage, except that he thus escaped the necessity of directly employing the name of king. But Pompeius, who, of course, proclaimed himself the champion of the aristocracy and of the legitimate constitution, gained besides a large and influential body of allies. In the first place, he rallied round him the whole republican party, and the majority, or, at any rate, the soundest part of the burgesses of Italy. Secondly, what was no mean advantage for so awkward a politician, it relieved him of the difficulty of finding a plausible pretext for provoking the war. His new allies would be willing enough to provoke a conflict with Caesar, and to intrust the conduct of the war to Pompeius, who would then come forward, in obedience to the general wish, as the protector of the constitution against the designs of anarchists and monarchists—as the regularly appointed general of the senate against the imperator of the streets.

Thus the republican party became once more a factor in the politics of Rome, owing to the rupture between the rulers. The heart and core of the republican opposition was the small circle of the followers of Cato, who were resolved to enter on the struggle against monarchy under any circumstances. The mass of the aristocracy, though averse to monarchy, desired, above all things, peace, and could not be counted on for decisive action. Hence Cato's only hope lay in a coalition with one of the regents. In alliance with Pompeius he might compel the timid majority to declare war; and though Pompeius was not in earnest in his fidelity to the constitution, yet the war would train a really republican army and republican generals, and it would be, at any rate, easier to settle matters with Pompeius after victory than with Caesar. The *rapprochement* between the general and the senate was made easy by the events of the dictatorship. Pompeius had refused to accept the office except from the senate; he had shown unrelenting severity against disorder of every kind, and surprising indulgence towards Cato and his followers; while, on the other hand, it was directly from the hands of Cato and Bibulus that Pompeius received the undivided consulship. An outward and visible sign that the alliance was already practically concluded was given, when, for the consulship of 51 B.C., one of Cato's pronounced adherents, Claudius Marcellus, was elected, evidently with the concurrence of the regent.

Caesar was kept constantly informed of all that happened at Rome, and formed his plans accordingly. He had doubtless long determined to take for himself, if necessary by force of arms, the supreme power after the conclusion of his Gallic wars; but he wished earnestly to avoid the deep disorganization which civil war must produce in a state; and even if civil war could not be avoided, no time could be more unfavorable for it than the present, when the insurrection in Gaul was at its height, and when the constitutional party was dominant in Italy. If he became, according to the arrangement at Luca, consul for the year 48 B.C., he might confidently reckon on outmaneuvering his awkward and vacillating rival, and with the compliant majority in the senate at his disposal, might either reorganize the state by peaceful means or at least enter upon the war with far greater prospects of success. Meanwhile he armed, certainly, and raised his legions during the winter of 52-51 B.C. to the number of eleven. But at the same time he publicly approved of all Pompeius's acts as dictator, and took no steps when he saw the alliance gradually formed between his rival and the aristocracy, only adhering immovably to the one demand, that the consulship for 48 B.C. should be granted him, according to the agreement.

It was upon this demand that the diplomatic war between

Caesar and the senate began, and it is important to grasp fully and accurately the exact point in dispute.

If there should be any interval between the day on which Caesar resigned his Gallic command and the day on which he entered upon his consulship, he would be liable during that interval to criminal impeachment, which, according to Roman law, was allowable only against a man not in office; and in that case it was extremely probable that he would meet the same fate as Milo, and be compelled to go into exile. Was it necessary that there should be such an interval? According to the usual mode of reckoning, a provincial command began in theory on March 1, of the magistrate's year of office in Rome, so that Caesar's Gallic command theoretically began on March 1, 59 B.C., the year of his consulship, and the ten years for which it was secured to him would expire on the last day of February, 49 B.C. Accordingly there would be an interval of ten months between the end of the Gallic command and the beginning of the consulship. Caesar's opponents aimed, both directly and indirectly, at preventing him from retaining his provinces during this interval.

Firstly, according to the old custom, Caesar's successor would have been appointed from among the magistrates for the year 49 B.C., and could not, therefore, have taken over the command until the beginning of 48 B.C.; and by the same old custom Caesar would have had the right to the command for the remaining ten months of the year 49 B.C., pending the arrival of his successor. But by the new regulation, made specially for this purpose during the dictatorship of Pompeius in 52 B.C., the senate might immediately fill up any legally vacant governorship, and Caesar might therefore be relieved of his command on March 1, 49 B.C.

Secondly, even without this special regulation passed for the purpose, the senate had a very simple means of compelling Caesar to leave his command before entering upon his consulship. The law required every candidate for the consulship to appear in person before the presiding magistrate, and to enter his name upon the official list before the election; that is, about half a year before entering on office. It was probably assumed at Luca that Caesar should be exempted from this regulation, as was often done with regard to particular candidates. At any rate, during the dictatorship of Pompeius in 52 B.C., Caesar's appearance in person was dispensed with by a tribunician law; but when the new election ordinance was passed, the obligation to appear in person was repeated in general terms, and no exemption in Caesar's case was mentioned. Caesar complained, and an exempting clause was interpolated by Pompeius, but not confirmed by the people, and was therefore legally of no effect. The whole matter is a good example of Pompeius's tortuous methods. Where he might have simply kept by the law, he had preferred first to make a spontaneous concession, then to recall it, and lastly to palliate this recall in a manner most illegal. The remaining events of the outbreak of the civil war may be viewed in three separate stages: the discussion at the beginning of 51 B.C., the discussions of the year 50 B.C., and Caesar's ultimatum.

In accordance with custom, the governorships of the year 49 B.C., which were to be filled by consuls, would be deliberated upon in the beginning of 51 B.C. On this occasion the consul Marcus Marcellus proposed that the two provinces of Caesar should be handed over on March 1, 49 B.C., to the two consuls who were to hold governorships for that year. The long repressed torrent of indignation against Caesar burst forth. The followers of Cato demanded that the exemption of Caesar from appearing to announce his name in person should be held invalid; that the soldiers of his legions who had served their time should be at once discharged; and that the bestowal by him of burgess-rights and the establishment of colonies in upper Italy should be considered null and void. Marcellus, in accordance with this last proposal, caused a local senator of the Caesarian colony of Comum to be scourged as a non-burgess.

On the other side, the supporters of Caesar affirmed that both equity and the condition of affairs in Gaul required that Caesar should be allowed to hold his command and his consulship simultaneously; they pointed out that Pompeius had in time past combined the Spanish provinces and the consulship, and was even now in possession of proconsular power for the purpose of the supply of grain, of the Spanish governorships, and of the supreme command in Italy. The timid majority in the senate prevented any resolution being taken for months. Pompeius at last declared on the whole in favor of the proposal of Marcellus, while hinting at certain concessions which might perhaps be made to Caesar; and ultimately, on September 29, 51 B.C., the nomination of successors was postponed to the last day of February, 50 B.C.

Meanwhile the republicans tried to break up Caesar's army by inducing the veterans to apply for their discharge, and the elections for the next year were thoroughly unfavorable to Caesar. The latter had at length quelled the insurrection in Gaul, and had moved one of his legions to north Italy. War was clearly inevitable, but even now he was willing to make great sacrifices; it was still advisable to keep the legions for some time in Gaul, and he had still perhaps some hope in the strong desire for peace which the majority of the senate entertained. When the senate, at the suggestion of Pompeius, requested each general to furnish a legion for the Parthian war, and when Pompeius at the same time demanded from Caesar the legion lent him some years before, Caesar complied, and the two legions from his army were kept by the government at Capua. For the discussions of 50 B.C. Caesar had succeeded in buying the services of one consul, Lucius Aemilius Paullus, and, above all, one of the tribunes, Gaius Curio, a man of brilliant talents, but of the most profligate character. Caesar paid this man's debts, amounting to $2,875,000, and thenceforth his great gifts of eloquence and energy were exerted for, instead of against, the enemy of the senate.

In March, 50 B.C., when the question of Caesar's successors arose, Curio approved of the decree of the year before superseding Caesar on March 1, 49 B.C., but demanded that it should be extended to Pompeius; he argued that the constitution could be rendered safe only by the removal of all exceptional positions; and at the same time declared that he would prevent any one-sided action against Caesar by his tribunician veto. Caesar at once declared his consent to Curio's proposal, but Pompeius would only reply that Caesar must resign, and that he himself meant soon to do so, though he mentioned no definite term. The decision was delayed for months, but at last Curio's proposal was adopted by 370 votes against 20—all that the extreme republican party could muster. All good citizens rejoiced, and the party of Cato was in despair. The latter had undertaken to force the senate to a declaration of war, and they were bitterly reproached for their failure by Pompeius. As matters stood, Pompeius and Caesar were both recalled by the senate, and while Caesar was ready to comply, Pompeius refused—the champion of the constitution and the aristocracy treated the constitutional decisions of the senate as null! But the extreme republicans were determined to bring matters to a crisis. A rumor arose that Caesar had moved four legions across the Alps, and stationed them at Placentia. This was an act quite within his prerogative, and the rumor was shown to be groundless, and yet the consul Marcus Marcellus proposed, on the strength of it, to give Pompeius orders to march against Caesar. When the senate rejected the proposal, Marcellus, in concert with the two consuls designate for 49 B.C., who were also Catonians, proceeded to Pompeius and requested him, on their own authority, to put himself at the head of the legions at Capua, and to summon the Italian militia to arms. No more informal authorization for the commencement of civil war could be imagined, but it was enough for Pompeius, and he left Rome in December, 50 B.C.

Caesar had fully attained his object of throwing upon his opponents the onus of declaring war, and while himself keeping on legal ground, he had compelled Pompeius to begin the struggle as the general of a revolutionary minority of the senate which overawed the majority. It was now his interest to strike a blow as soon as possible; his opponents were only just beginning to make preparations, and it might be possible to surprise the city undefended, or even to seize all Italy and shut them off from their best resources. Curio represented these considerations strongly to his chief, and Caesar at once sent to hurry on the nearest legion to Ravenna. Meanwhile he sent an ultimatum to Rome, in which he dropped all counterdemands, offered to resign Transalpine Gaul and dismiss eight of his ten legions, if only the senate would allow him either Cisalpine Gaul and Illyria with one legion, or Cisalpine Gaul alone with two—and that not up to his investiture with the consulship, but only till the close of the consular elections for 48 B.C. It may almost be doubted whether Caesar can possibly have been sincere in these proposals; but it is probable that he committed the fault of playing too bold a game, and that if his ultimatum had been accepted he would have made good his word. The ever-available Curio undertook once more to enter the lion's den. January 1, 49 B.C., he delivered his master's letter in a full meeting of the senate. The grave words of Caesar, in which he set forth the imminence of civil war, the general wish for peace, the arrogance of Pompeius, and his own yielding disposition with all the irresistible force of truth; the proposals for a compromise, of a moderation which doubtless surprised his own partisans; the distinct declaration that this was the last time that he should offer his hand for peace—all made the deepest impression. The sentiment of the majority was so doubtful that the consuls would not allow a vote to be taken, even on the proposal of Marcus Marcellus, to defer the determination till the Italian levy could be under arms to protect the senate. The consul Lentulus said openly that he would act on his own authority whatever the senate might decree, and Pompeius let it be known that he would take up the cause of the senate now or never. Thus overawed, the senate decreed that Caesar should, at no distant day, give up Transalpine Gaul to Lucius Domitius Ahenobarbus, and Cisalpine Gaul to Marcus Servilius Novianus, and should dismiss his army, failing which he should be esteemed a traitor. The Caesarian tribunes who tried to veto the decree were menaced with death in the senate-house, and had to fly in slave's clothing from the capital. On January 7, 49 B.C., the senate declared the country in danger, called all citizens to arms, and all magistrates, faithful to the constitution, to place themselves at their head.

Hesitation was now no longer possible for Caesar. He called together the soldiers of the thirteenth legion, which had now arrived at Ravenna, and set before them the whole circumstances. He spoke not to the dregs of the city, but to young men from the towns and villages of northern Italy who were capable of real enthusiasm for liberty, who had received from Caesar the burgess rights which the government had refused them, and whom Caesar's fall would leave once more at the mercy of the fasces. He set before them the thanks which the nobility were preparing for the general and the army which had conquered Gaul, the overawing of the senate by the extreme minority, and the last violation of the tribunate of the people, wrested five hundred years ago by their fathers from the nobility. And when he summoned them, as the general of the popular party, to follow him in the last inevitable struggle against the despised, perfidious aristocracy, not an officer or soldier held back. At the head of his vanguard Caesar crossed the Rubicon, the narrow brook which separated his province from Italy, and which it was forbidden, by the constitution, to the proconsul of Gaul to pass.

Chapter XXXII

THE CIVIL WAR. 49-46 B.C.

BEFORE describing the course of the struggle between the two aspirants to the crown of Rome, it will be well to examine the resources at the disposal of each.

Caesar's authority was wholly unlimited within his own party; in all matters, military and political, the decision lay with him. He had no confederates, only adjutants, who, as a rule, were soldiers trained to obey unconditionally. So, on the outbreak of war, one officer alone, and he the foremost of all, refused him obedience. Titus Labienus had shared with Caesar all his political and military vicissitudes of defeat and victory. In Gaul he had always held an independent command, and had frequently led half the army. As late as the year 50 B.C. Caesar had given to him supreme command in Cisalpine Gaul; but from this very position he entered into a treaty with the other side, and on the outbreak of hostilities went at once to the camp of Pompeius. It was the one great disadvantage on Caesar's side that he had no officers to whom he could intrust a separate command, but this was quite outbalanced by the unity of the supreme leadership—the indispensable condition of success.

The army numbered nine legions—at most fifty thousand men, two-thirds of whom had served in all the campaigns against the Celts. The cavalry consisted of mercenaries from Germany and Noricum, and had been well tried in the war against Vercingetorix. The physical condition of the soldiers was beyond all praise; by the careful selection of recruits and by training they had been brought to a perfection never perhaps surpassed in marching power and in readiness for immediate departure at any moment. Their courage and their *esprit de corps* had been equally developed by Caesar's system of rewards and punishments—a system so perfectly carried out that the preëminence of particular soldiers or divisions was acquiesced in even by their less favored comrades. Their discipline was strict, but not harassing; and while maintained with unrelenting rigor in the presence of the enemy, was relaxed at other times, especially after victory, when even irregularities and outrages of a very questionable kind went unpunished. Mutiny was never pardoned, in either the ringleaders or their dupes. Caesar took care that victory should be associated in the minds of both officers and soldiers with hopes of personal gain; everyone had his share of the spoil, and the most lavish gifts were promised at the triumph. At the same time that unquestioning obedience was exacted from all, yet all were allowed some glimpse at the general's aims and springs of action, so that each might feel that he was doing his part towards the attainment of the common object, and no one could complain that he was treated as a mere instrument. During the long years of warfare a sense of comradeship grew up between soldiers and leader. They were his clients, whose services he was bound to requite, and whose wrongs he was bound to revenge. The result was that Caesar's soldiers were, and knew themselves to be, a match for ten times their number, and that their fidelity to him was unchangeable and unparalleled. With one exception no Roman soldier or officer refused to follow him into the civil war, and the legionaries even determined to give credit for the double pay which Caesar promised them from the beginning of the war, while every subaltern officer equipped and paid a trooper out of his own purse.

Thus Caesar had two requisites for success—unlimited authority and a magnificent and trustworthy army. But his power extended over a very limited space. It was based essentially on the province of upper Italy, which was indeed devoted to him and furnished an ample supply of recruits. But in Italy the mass of the burgesses were all for his opponents, and expected from Caesar only a renewal of the Marian and Cinnan atrocities. His only friends in Italy were the rabble and the ruined of all classes—friends infinitely more dangerous than foes. The newly conquered territory in Gaul could not, of course, be relied on, and in Narbo the constitutional party had many adherents. Among the independent princes Caesar had tried to effect something by gifts and promises, but without important result except in the case of Voctio, king of Noricum, from whom cavalry recruits were obtained.

Caesar thus began the war without other resources than efficient adjutants, a faithful army, and a devoted province. Pompeius, on the other hand, was chief of the Roman commonwealth and

master of all the resources at the disposal of the legitimate government of the empire. But unity of leadership was inconsistent with
the nature of a coalition; and though Pompeius was nominated by
the senate sole generalissimo by land and sea, he could not prevent
the senate itself from exercising the political supremacy, or from
occasionally interfering even in military matters. Twenty years of
antagonism made it impossible for either party of the coalition to
place complete confidence in the other.

In resources Caesar's opponents had an overwhelming superiority. They had exclusive command of the sea, and the disposal
of all ports, ships, and naval material. The two Spains were
specially devoted to Pompeius, and the other provinces had during
recent years been put into safe hands. The client states were all
for Pompeius; many of them had been brought into close personal
relations with him at different times. He had been the companion
in arms of the kings of Numidia and of Mauretania; he had re-
established the kingdoms of Bosporus, Armenia, and Cappadocia,
and created that of Deiotarus. He had caused the rule of the
Lagidae to be reëstablished in Egypt, and even Massilia was
indebted to him for an extension of territory. Moreover, the democratic policy handed down from Gaius Gracchus of uniting the
dependent states and of setting up provincial colonies was dreaded
by the dependent princes, more especially by Juba, king of Numidia,
whose kingdom Curio had lately proposed to annex. Even the
Parthians by the convention between Pacorus and Bibulus were
practically in alliance with the aristocracy.

In Italy, not only the aristocracy, but the capitalists, were
bitterly opposed to Caesar, together with the men of small means,
and the landowners, and generally all classes who had anything
to lose.

The army of Pompeius consisted chiefly of the seven Spanish
legions—troops in every way trustworthy—and of scattered divisions in Syria, Asia, Macedonia, Africa, and Sicily. In Italy
there were the two legions lately given over by Caesar—not more
than seven thousand men, and, of course, of doubtful trustworthi-
ness. There were also three legions remaining from the levies of
54 B.C., and the Italian levy, which had been sworn to allegiance
and then dismissed on furlough. Altogether the Italian troops
which might, within a very short time, be made available amounted
to about sixty thousand men. Cavalry there was none, but a

THE CIVIL WAR 337

nucleus of three hundred men was soon formed by Pompeius, out of the mounted herdsmen of Apulia.

Under such circumstances the war began, early in January, 49 B.C. Caesar had only one legion—five thousand men and three hundred cavalry—at Ravenna, distant by road about 240 miles from Rome. Pompeius had two weak legions—seven thousand infantry and a small force of cavalry—at Luceria, about equally distant from Rome. The remainder of Caesar's troops were either on the Saone and Loire or in Belgica, while Pompeius's reserves were already arriving at their rendezvous. Nevertheless Caesar resolved to assume the offensive: in the spring Pompeius would be able to act with the Spanish troops in Transalpine and with his Italian troops in Cisalpine Gaul; but at the moment he might be disconcerted by the suddenness of the attack.

Accordingly Marcus Antonius pushed forward across the Apennines to Arretium, while Caesar advanced along the coast. The recruiting officers of Pompeius and their recruits fled at the news of his approach; several small successes were gained, and Caesar resolved to advance upon Rome itself, rather than upon the army of Luceria. A panic seized the city when the news arrived; Pompeius decided not to defend it, and the senators and consuls hurried to leave, not even delaying to secure the state treasure. At Teanum Sidicinum new proposals from Caesar were considered, in which he again offered to dismiss his army and hand over his provinces if Pompeius would depart to Spain and if Italy were disarmed. The reply was that if Caesar would at once return to his province the senate would bind itself to procure the fulfillment of his demands. As to the war, Pompeius was ordered to advance with the legions from Luceria into Picenum, and personally to call together the levy of that district, and try to stop the invader.

But Caesar was already in Picenum. Auximum, Camerinum, and Asculum fell into his hands; and such of the recruits as were not dispersed left the district and repaired to Corfinium, where the Marsian and Paelignian levies were to assemble. Here Lucius Domitius Ahenobarbus was in command; and instead of conducting the recruits, who now amounted to fifteen thousand men, to Luceria according to the instructions of Pompeius, he remained where he was, expecting Pompeius to come to his relief. Instead of Pompeius Caesar arrived, now at the head of forty thousand men. Domitius had not the courage to hold the place; neither did he resolve to

surrender it, but rather to escape during the night with his aristocratic officers.   But his dastardly plan was betrayed; the troops
mutinied, arrested their staff, and handed over the town to Caesar.
Thereupon the forces in Alba and in Tarracina laid down their
arms; a third division, of 3500 men, in Sulmo had previously
surrendered.

As soon as Picenum was lost, Pompeius had determined to
abandon Italy, and had set out at once for Brundisium.   Here all
the available troops were assembled, to the number of twenty-five
thousand; part of them were at once conveyed across in the ships;
the remaining ten thousand were besieged by Caesar in Brundisium,
but were skillfully withdrawn by Pompeius before Caesar could
close the harbor.

In two months Caesar had broken up an army of ten legions,
and made himself master of the state chest, of the capital, and of
the whole peninsula of Italy.   But though his resources were thus
largely increased, the military difficulties of the situation were pro-
portionately complicated.   He had now to leave behind a large
garrison in Italy, and to guard against the closing of the seas and
the cutting off of grain supplies by his opponents.   Financial difficulties, too, soon arose, now that Caesar had to feed the population
of the capital while the revenues of the East were still in the
enemy's hands.

The general expectation was that confiscations and proscrip-
tions would be resorted to. Friends and foes saw in Caesar a second
Catilina; and it must be allowed that neither his own antecedents
nor the character of the men who now surrounded him—men of
broken reputation and ruined fortunes like Quintus Hortensius,
Curio, and Marcus Antonius—were reassuring.   But both friends
and foes were soon undeceived; from the beginning of hostilities
the common soldiers were forbidden to enter a town armed and the
people were everywhere protected from injury.   When Corfinium
was surrendered late at night, Caesar postponed the occupation of
the town until the next day, to prevent confusion and outrage in
the darkness.   Everywhere the officers captured were allowed to
carry off their private property, and in his worst financial straits
Caesar preferred borrowing from his friends to levying exactions
from his foes.   The aristocrats indeed, far from being appeased by
Caesar's moderation, were only goaded to more frantic hatred, but
the mass of quiet people, in whose eyes material interests were more

important than politics, were completely gained over. Even the senators who had ventured to remain behind acquiesced in Caesar's rule. His object was fully attained: anarchy, and even the alarm of anarchy, had been kept under—an incalculable gain with regard to the future reorganization of the state. The anarchists, of course, were bitterly disappointed, and showed a spirit which might be expected at some future time to give trouble. The republicans of all shades were neither converted nor disarmed. In their eyes their duty to the constitution absolved them from every other consideration. The less decided members of the party who accepted peace and protection from the monarch were none the more friendly to him in their hearts, and the consciences of the more honorable among them smote them when they thought of other members of the party who had gone into exile rather than compromise their principles. Besides, emigration had become fashionable; it was plebeian to remain and perhaps take a seat in the Caesarian senate of nobodies, instead of emigrating with the Domitii and the Metelli.

Caesar had begun the war as the protector of the overawed senate against the violent minority; but the same inertness which had made it possible for Caesar to prevent strong action on the part of his opponent prevented him from obtaining aid from the senate himself. The first meeting was on April 1, but Caesar could not procure approval of his acts or power to continue the war; he then tried in vain to be named dictator. When he sent men to take possession of the treasure, the tribune Lucius Metellus attempted to protect the state chest with his person, and had to be removed by force. And at length Caesar was obliged to tell the senate that, since it refused him its assistance, he would proceed without it. He appointed Marcus Aemilius Lepidus prefect of the city, and hastened to resume the war.

Pompeius, for whatever reason, had preferred to remain in Greece rather than to go to Spain, where he had able lieutenants, a strong army, and provinces devoted to him. Accordingly Caesar had the option of directing his first attack against Pompeius himself in the East, or against the strong Spanish army under his lieutenant. He had already collected on the lower Rhone nine of his best legions and six thousand cavalry; but his enemies had been active in the same region. Lucius Domitius had induced Massilia to declare against him and to refuse a passage to his troops, and the five best Spanish legions, together with forty thousand Spanish infantry and five thousand cavalry, were on their way, under the command of Afranius and Petreius, to close the passes of the Pyrenees. But Caesar anticipated them, and the line of the Pyrenees was lost to the Pompeians. The latter now established themselves at Ilerda on the right bank of the Sicoris, about twenty miles north of its junction with the Ebro. To the south of the town the mountains approach pretty close to the river; to the north stretches a plain commanded by the town. Connection with the left bank of the Sicoris was maintained by means of a single solid bridge close to the town. The Caesarians were stationed above Ilerda, between the River Sicoris and its tributary, the Cinga, which joins it below the town; but they could not make good their ground between the Pompeian camp and the town, which would have given them command of the stone bridge, and consequently they depended for their communications upon two temporary bridges twenty miles higher up the river. These were swept away by the floods, and the whole army was now cooped up in the narrow space between the two streams.

Famine and disease appeared. A body of reinforcements from Gaul, together with foraging parties on their way back to the camp, to the number of six thousand, were attacked and dispersed under the eyes of the Caesarians on the other side of the river. Had the river been adequately guarded the Pompeians could hardly have failed of success; but the further bank was observed to be unoccupied; Caesar succeeded in restoring the bridges without much difficulty, and provisions again entered the camp in abundance. Soon his superior cavalry scoured the country far and wide, and the most important Spanish communities to the north, some even to the south, of the Ebro passed over to him, while the Pompeians began to feel the want of supplies. They determined to retreat south of the Ebro, but it was necessary first to build a bride of boats over that river. This was done at a point below the mouth of the Sicoris. Caesar sought by all means to detain the enemy, but was unable to do so as long as he had not control of the bridge of Ilerda, since there was no ford. His soldiers worked night and day to draw off the river by canals, so that infantry might wade it, but the Pompeians had finished their bridge over the Ebro before Caesar had completed his canals, and he could only order his cavalry to follow them and harass their rear. But when the legions saw the enemy retreating they called upon the general to lead them on; they entered the river, and though the water reached their shoulders it was crossed in safety. The Pompeians were now within five miles of the mountains which lined the north bank of the Ebro, and would soon be in safety. But, harassed by the enemy's attacks and exhausted with marching, they pitched their camp in the plain; here Caesar's troops overtook them and encamped opposite, and in this position both armies remained for the next day. On the morning of the third day Caesar's infantry set out to turn the position of the Pompeians and bar the way to the Ebro, and, in spite of all the latter could do, they found themselves anticipated. They were now strategically lost, and, in spite of ample opportunity, Caesar refrained from attacking them. The soldiers of the two armies began to fraternize and to discuss terms of surrender, but Petreius cut short the negotiations and began to retreat towards Ilerda, where were a garrison and magazines. Shut in between the Sicoris and the enemy, their difficulties increased at every step: Caesar's cavalry occupied the opposite bank and prevented them from crossing the river to gain the fortress, and at last, on August 2, 49 B.C., the inevitable capitulation took place. Caesar granted to soldiers and officers life, liberty, and property, and did not, as in Italy, compulsorily enroll the captives in his army. The native Spaniards at once returned to their homes, and the Italians were disbanded at the borders of Transalpine and Cisalpine Gaul.

In Farther Spain Varro determined to shut himself up in Gades; but when this town, together with all the most notable places in the province, gave itself up to Caesar, and when even Italica closed its gates against the Pompeian general, he himself resolved to capitulate.

About the same time Massilia surrendered. By sea Caesar's lieutenant, Decimus Brutus—the same who had conquered the Veneti—had defeated with his improvised fleet the far stronger force of the Massiliots. He gained a second victory not long afterwards, over a small squadron of Pompeians under Lucius Nasidius, who had arrived to reinforce the Massilian squadron, and completely shut the besieged from the sea. On land Gaius Trebonius pressed forward the siege with energy; the works were pushed up to the very walls of the city, when the besieged promised to desist from the defense if Trebonius would suspend operations until Caesar arrived. The armistice was granted, but was used by the Massiliots to make a treacherous sally; the struggle was renewed, and the city once more invested. On Caesar's arrival it was reduced to surrender on any terms. Domitius stole away in a boat. The garrison and inhabitants were protected by Caesar from the fury of his legions, but the city, while it retained its freedom and nationality, lost a portion of its territory and privileges.

While Caesar was occupied in Spain his lieutenants had been at work to prevent the other great danger which was imminent, namely, the starvation of Italy. The Pompeians commanded the sea and the corn provinces, Sardinia and Corsica through Marcus Cotta, Sicily through Cato, Africa through Varus and Juba, king of Numidia. Sardinia was quickly recovered for Caesar, by Quintus Valerius; the conquest of Sicily and Africa was intrusted to Curio. He occupied Sicily without a blow, and, leaving two legions in the island, he embarked with the remaining two and with five hundred horse for Africa. He effected a landing, and pitched his camp near Utica : his legions were for the most part composed of men taken over from the enemy, but he knew well how to gain their affections, and at the same time showed himself a capable officer. He was successful in several minor engagements, and at length put to flight the whole forces of Varus, and proceeded to lay siege to Utica. But there came news that King Juba was advancing with all his forces to its relief, and Curio raised the siege and returned to his former camp to wait for reinforcements. Soon afterwards came a second report, that the king had turned back, and was sending on only a moderate corps under Saburra. Curio immediately sent forward his cavalry, which surprised and inflicted much damage upon this body; he then hastened himself to complete their defeat, and succeeded in putting them to flight. But Saburra was not destitute of support. Only five miles distant was the Numidian main force, which was now seen rapidly approaching. The Roman cavalry were by this time dispersed in pursuit, all but a band of two hundred, who with the infantry were completely surrounded in the plain. In vain Curio attempted to cut his way through : the infantry were cut down to a man; only a few of the cavalry escaped. Curio, unable to bear the shame of defeat, fell sword in hand, and on the following day the force in camp near Utica surrendered on receiving news of the disaster.

The expedition had been successful in relieving the most urgent wants of the capital by the occupation of Sicily, but the loss of Curio was irreparable. He was the only one of Caesar's subordinates who had a touch of genius and a certain magnetic power over the minds of men.

It is uncertain what had been Pompeius's plan of campaign for the year 49 B.C. Probably the Spanish army was meant to stand on the defensive until the Macedonian army was ready to march; a junction would then have been effected between the two armies, and a combined attempt made by land and sea to recover Italy. In pursuance probably of some such plan, the admirals of Pompeius in the Adriatic, Marcus Octavius and Lucius Scribonius Libo, attacked Caesar's fleet under Dolabella, destroyed his ships and shut up Gaius Antonius with the two Illyrian legions in the island of Curicta. All attempts to rescue the latter failed, and the majority had to lay down their arms and were incorporated in the Pompeian army. Octavius proceeded to reduce Illyria; most of the towns gave themselves up to him, but the Caesarians maintained themselves obstinately in Salonae and Lissus.

This, the only result obtained by the Pompeian fleet in the year 49 B.C., is miserably small, considering the superiority of the party by sea, and suggests an appalling picture of the discord and mismanagement which prevailed in the ranks of the coalition. The general result of the campaign had been complete success for the Caesarians in one quarter and partial success in another, while the plan of Pompeius had been completely frustrated by the destruction of the Spanish army.

But though nothing was done to obstruct Caesar in the West, no effort was spared to consolidate the power of the republican party in Macedonia. Hither flocked the emigrants from Brundisium, and the refugees from the West: Marcus Cato from Sicily, Lucius Domitius from Massilia, Afranius and Varro from Spain. The senate of the emigration which met at Thessalonica counted nearly two hundred members, including almost all the consulars. Out of scrupulous regard to formal law they called themselves —not the senate, for that could not exist beyond the sacred soil of the city—but "the three hundred," the ancient normal number of senators. The majority indeed were lukewarm, and only obstructed the energy of others by their querulousness and sluggishness; but the violent minority showed no want of activity. With them the indispensable preliminary of any negotiations for peace was the bringing over of Caesar's head; his partisans were held to have forfeited life and property, and it was even proposed to punish every senator who had remained neutral in the struggle or had emigrated without entering the army. Bibulus and Labienus caused all soldiers and officers of Caesar who fell into their hands to be executed, and probably the main reason why no counter-revolution broke out in Italy during Caesar's absence was the fear of the unbridled fury of the extreme section of the aristocracy. Cato alone had the force and the courage to check such proceedings; he got the senate to prohibit the pillage of subject towns and the putting to death of burgesses otherwise than in battle, and confessed that he feared the victory of his own party ever more than their defeat.

The position of Pompeius became more and more disagreeable after the events of the year 49 B.C. All the failures of his lieutenants were visited upon himself, while the newly formed senate took up its abode almost in his headquarters, and impeded his action at every step. There was no man of sufficient mark to put a stop to these preposterous doings; Cato, who alone might have effected something, was jealously kept in the background by Pompeius, and Pompeius himself had not the necessary intellect or decision.

The flower of the troops were the legions brought from Italy, out of which, with recruits, five legions were formed. Two others were on their way from Syria and one from Cilicia, and three more were formed from Romans settled in Crete, Macedonia, and Asia Minor. Finally there were two thousand volunteers, and the contingents of the subjects. The militia of Epirus, Aetolia, and Thrace were called out to guard the coast, and a body of archers and slingers were drawn from Greece and Asia Minor. Of cavalry there was a considerable body formed from the young aristocracy of Rome and from the Apulian slave herdsmen; the rest consisted of contingents from the subjects and clients—Celts from the garrison of Alexandria and from the princes of Galatia, Thracians, Cappadocians, mounted archers from Commagene, Armenians, and Numidians, amounting in all to seven thousand.

The fleet numbered five hundred sail, one-fifth of which were Roman vessels, and the rest from the Greek and Asiatic maritime states. Immense stores of corn and war material were collected at Dyrrachium, and for money the whole Roman and non-Roman population within reach, subjects, senators, and tax farmers, were laid under contribution. The temper of the soldiers was good, but a great part of the army consisted of newly raised troops, and required time for training and discipline.

The design of the commander was to unite his whole force, naval and military, during the winter along the coast of Epirus. The land army moved slowly from its winter quarters at Berrhoea towards Dyrrachium; the Syrian legions were not expected until the spring. The admiral Bibulus was already at Corcyra with 110 ships.

The Pompeians were taking their time, but Caesar was not slow to act. On the conclusion of the western campaign he had ordered the best of his troops to set out immediately for Brundisium, where ships of war and transports were already collected. These unparalleled exertions thinned the ranks of the legions more than their conflicts, and the mutiny of the ninth legion at Placentia showed the dangerous temper of the soldiers; it was mastered by the personal authority of Caesar, and at present the evil spread no further. But at Brundisium only twelve ships of war were found, and the transports were scarcely sufficient to convey a third of the army, which numbered twelve legions and ten thousand cavalry, while the enemy commanded the Adriatic and all the islands and harbors of the opposite coast. Nevertheless, on January 4, 48 B.C., Caesar, with a temerity which is not justified by the success of the immediate enterprise, set sail with six legions and six hundred horse. The Pompeians were not ready to attack, and the first freight was landed in the middle of the Acroceraunian cliffs. The vessels returned to bring over the remainder of the army. Caesar at once began to disperse the Epirote militia, and succeeded in taking Oricum and Apollonia, while Dyrrachium, the arsenal of Pompeius, was in the greatest danger.

But the further course of the campaign did not fulfill the promise of this brilliant beginning. Thirty of Caesar's transports were captured by Bibulus, and destroyed with every living thing on board. The whole coast, from the island of Sason to Corcyra, was closely watched, and for a time even Brundisium was blockaded. Nor was Dyrrachium captured, for Pompeius had hastened his march and secured it in time. Thus Caesar was wedged in among the rocks of Epirus, between the immense fleet of the enemy and a land army twice as strong as his own. Pompeius was in no hurry to attack, but established himself on the right bank of the River Apsus, between Dyrrachium and Apollonia, facing Caesar on the left bank, and awaited the arrival of the Syrian legions which had wintered at Pergamus.

Caesar was rescued from this perilous position by the energy of Marcus Antonius, the commandant of Italy. Again the transport fleet set sail, with four legions and eight hundred horse. The wind fortunately carried it past the galleys of Libo, the Pompeian admiral; but the same wind carried it northward, past the camps of Caesar and Pompeius to Lissus, which still adhered to Caesar, where it was enabled to land only by the most marvelous good fortune. At the moment when the enemy's squadron overtook the ships of Antonius, at the mouth of the harbor, the wind veered and drove them back into the open sea. Pompeius was unable to prevent the junction of Caesar's forces, and now took up a new position on the Genusus, between the River Apsus and Dyrrachium. When he refused to give battle, Caesar succeeded in throwing himself with his best marching troops between the enemy's camp and the town of Dyrrachium, on which it rested; and Pompeius again changed his position, and encamped upon a small plain enclosed between the fork formed by the main chain of the Balkans, which ends at Dyrrachium, and a lateral branch which runs to the sea in a southwesterly direction. His communication with the town was secured by the fleet, and there was therefore no difficulty about supplies, while to Caesar's camp provisions were brought at intervals only by strong detachments sent into the interior, and flesh, barley, and even roots had to be eaten by the legions instead of wheat.

Under these circumstances inaction meant destruction to the Caesarians, and they proceeded to occupy the heights commanding the plain on which Pompeius lay. They invested his army with a chain of posts sixteen miles long, and cut off the rivulets which flowed into the plain, thus hoping to compel him either to fight or to embark. At the same time, as at Alesia, Caesar caused a second, outer line of entrenchments to be formed, to protect himself against attacks from Dyrrachium or from attempts to turn his position. The works advanced amid incessant conflicts, in which the tried valor of the Caesarians had usually the advantage. At one point, for instance, a single cohort maintained itself against four legions for several hours until help arrived. At length the want of fodder and water began to be so severely felt by the Pompeians that it was absolutely necessary for them to strike a decisive blow. The general was informed by some Celtic deserters that the enemy had neglected to secure the beach between his two lines of entrenchments, six hundred feet distant from each other. Pompeius could thus attack from three sides at once. While the inner line was attacked from the camp and the outer line by light-armed troops, conveyed in vessels and landed beyond it, a third division landed in the space between the two lines and attacked in the rear the defenders who were already sufficiently occupied. The entrenchment next the sea was taken, and the second was with difficulty held by Antonius against the advance of the enemy. Soon afterwards Caesar eagerly seized an opportunity of attacking a Pompeian legion, which had become isolated, with the bulk of his infantry; but a valiant resistance was made, and as the ground had been already used for the encampment of several successive divisions, it was much intersected by mounds and ditches. Caesar's right wing and cavalry missed their way; Pompeius, advancing with five legions to the aid of his troops, found the two wings of the enemy separated and one of them isolated. A panic seized the Caesarians; a disorderly flight ensued, and the matter ended with the loss to Caesar of one thousand of his best soldiers. But the results of the day's fighting were more serious than this. Caesar's lines were broken. The cavalry of Pompeius now ranged at will over the adjacent country, and rendered it almost impossible for him to obtain provisions. Gnaeus Pompeius the younger had destroyed his few ships of war which lay at Oricum, and soon afterwards burned the transports at Lissus. Caesar was thus cut off from the sea more than ever, and, in fact, was completely at the mercy of Pompeius.

It was now open to Pompeius to attack or to blockade his enemy, or to cross in person to Italy with the main army and try to recover the peninsula. But he left his opponent to make the first move, and Caesar had no choice. He began immediately to retreat to Apollonia, followed by the enemy, who, however, after four days, had to give up the pursuit. Many voices now advised Pompeius to cross to Italy; but this plan would necessitate the abandonment of the Syrian legions, now in Macedonia under Metellus Scipio; and, besides, he hoped to capture the corps of Calvinus, whom Caesar had detached to encounter Metellus. Calvinus was now on the Via Egnatia at Heraclea Lyncestis, and only learned the condition of things just in time to escape destruction by a quick departure in the direction of Thessaly. Caesar, who had arrived at Apollonia, and had deposited his wounded there, now set out for Thessaly, in order to get beyond the reach of the enemy's fleet.

He crossed the mountain chain between Epirus and Thessaly, effected a junction with Calvinus at Aeginium, near the source of the Peneus, and, after storming and pillaging Gomphi, the first Thessalian town before which he appeared, quickly received the submission of the others.

Thus the victories of Dyrrachium had borne little fruit to the victors. Caesar and Calvinus had escaped pursuit, and stood united and in full security in Thessaly. But the former caution of the Pompeians was succeeded by the most boundless confidence. They regarded the victory as already won, and were resolved at any price to fight with Caesar and crush him at the first opportunity. Cato was left in command at Dyrrachium and in Corcyra. Pompeius and Scipio marched southward and met at Larissa.

Caesar was encamped near Pharsalus, on the left bank of the River Enipeus, which intersects the plain stretching southward from Larissa. Pompeius pitched his camp on the right bank, along the slope of Cynoscephalae. His entire army was assembled, and he had now eleven legions, numbering 47,000 men and 7000 horse, while Caesar was still expecting two legions from Aetolia and Thessaly, and two which were arriving by way of Illyria from Italy; his eight legions did not number more than 22,000 men and his cavalry but 1000 troopers. All military reasons urged Pompeius to fight soon, and the impatience of the emigrants had doubtless more weight than these reasons. The senators considered their triumph secure. Already there was strife about filling up Caesar's pontificate, and houses were hired in the Forum for the next elections. Great indignation was excited when Pompeius hesitated to cross the rivulet which separated the camps. He was only delaying the battle, they alleged, in order to perpetuate his part of Agamemnon and to rule the longer over so many noble lords. The general yielded, and prepared to attack. The battlefield was almost the same as that on which, a hundred and fifty years before, the Romans had laid the foundation of their Eastern dominion. The right of the Pompeians rested on the Enipeus, Caesar's left upon the broken ground in front of the river. The other wings were both out in the plain, and each was covered by cavalry and light troops. The plan of Pompeius was to scatter with his cavalry the weak band of horsemen opposite to him, and then to take Caesar's right wing in the rear. But Caesar, foreseeing the rout of his cavalry, had stationed behind his right flank about two thousand of his best legionaries. As the enemy's cavalry galloped round the line, driving Caesar's horsemen before them, they were met and thrown into confusion by this unexpected infantry attack, and galloped from the field of battle.[1] This unexpected repulse of the cavalry raised the courage of the Caesarians. Their third division which had been held in reserve, advanced all along the line. Pompeius, who had never trusted his infantry, rode at once from the field to the camp. His legions began to waver and to retire over the brook, an operation which was attended with much loss. The day was lost, but the army was substantially intact. Nevertheless, Pompeius lost all hope, and when he saw the troops recrossing the brook he threw from him his general's scarf and rode off by the nearest route to the sea. The army, discouraged and leaderless, found no rest within the camp. They were driven from its shelter, and withdrew to the heights of Crannon and Scotussa. As they attempted to march along the hills and regain Larissa Caesar's troops intercepted their route, and at nightfall cut them off from the only rivulet in the neighborhood. Fifteen thousand of the enemy lay dead or wounded upon the field, while the Caesarians had only two hundred men missing. The next morning twenty thousand men laid down their arms, and of the eleven eagles of the enemy nine were handed over to Caesar. Caesar had on that very day reminded his men that they should not forget the fellow-citizen in the foe; but he found it necessary to use some severity. The common soldiers were incorporated in the army, fines and confiscations were inflicted upon the men of better rank, and the senators and equites of note were with few exceptions beheaded.

The immediate results of this memorable day, August 9, 48 B.C., were soon seen. All who were not willing or not obliged to fight for a lost cause now passed over to Caesar's side. The client communities and princes recalled their contingents. Pharnaces, king of the Bosporus, went so far as to take possession of Phanagoris, which had been declared free by Pompeius, and of Little Armenia, which had been conferred upon Deiotarus. So also many lukewarm members of the aristocracy made their peace

[1] It was in this attack that the well-known direction of Caesar to his troops to strike at the faces of the enemy's horsemen was given. The infantry, acting in an irregular way against cavalry, were not to throw their pila, but to use them as spears, and, to be more effective, were to thrust at the faces of the troopers. It was probably the rough wit of the camp which suggested the idea that the Pompeian cavalry fled for fear of scars on their faces.

with the conqueror. But the flower of the defeated party made no compromise; aristocrats could not come to terms with monarchy. Into whatever abyss of degeneracy the aristocratic rule had now sunk, it had once been a great political system; the sacred fire, by which Italy had been conquered and Hannibal had been vanquished, continued to glow—although somewhat dim and dull—in the Roman nobility as long as that nobility existed, and rendered a cordial understanding between the men of the old *régime* and the new monarchy impossible. Many submitted outwardly, and retired into private life. Marcus Marcellus, who had brought about the rupture with Caesar, retired into voluntary banishment at Lesbos; but in the majority passion overwhelmed reflection. No one grasped the hopelessness of the situation more clearly than Marcus Cato. Convinced from this moment that monarchy was inevitable, he doubted whether the constitutional party ought to continue the struggle. But when he resolved still to fight—not for victory, but for a more honorable fall—he sought to draw no one into the struggle who chose to make his peace. It was, in his eyes, merely senseless and cruel to compel the individual to share the ruin of the republic.

Most of the leading men who escaped from Pharsalus made their way to Corcyra, where a council of war was held, at which Cato, Metellus Scipio, Titus Labienus, Lucius Afranius, and Gnaeus Pompeius the younger were present. But the absence of the commander-in-chief and the internal dissensions prevented the adoption of any common resolution, and it was indeed difficult to say what ought to be done. Macedonia and Greece, Italy and the East, were lost to the coalition. In Egypt there was indeed a large army, but it was soon evident that the court of Alexandria was not to be relied on. In Spain, Pompeian sympathies were very strong, especially in the army, so much so that the Caesarians had to give up the idea of invading Africa from that quarter; in Africa, again, the coalition, or rather King Juba, had been arming unmolested for more than a year; so that in two regions it was still possible for the constitutionalists to prolong the struggle in honorable warfare for some time to come. By sea, too, their power was still considerable, even after the recall of the subject contingents, while Caesar was still almost without a fleet. And there was yet another possibility—that of a Parthian alliance, and of procuring the restoration of the republic at the hands of the common foe.

Meanwhile, Caesar was in hot pursuit of Pompeius. The latter had gone first to Lesbos, where he joined his wife and his younger son Sextus; thence he proceeded to Cilicia and to Cyprus. Fear of the reception he might meet with from his aristocratic allies appears to have decided him to take refuge with the Parthian king, rather than to fly to Corcyra. He was in Cyprus, collecting money and arming a band of slaves, when he heard that Antioch had declared for Caesar and that the Parthian route was no longer open; he thereupon hastened to Egypt, from the resources of which he might hope to reorganize the war.

After the death of Ptolemy Auletes, in 51 B.C., his two children —Cleopatra, aged about sixteen, and Ptolemaeus Dionysius, a boy of ten—had ascended the throne, according to their father's will, as consorts. But the brother, with his guardian Pothinus, had driven Cleopatra from the kingdom, and was lying with the whole Egyptian army at Pelusium, to protect the eastern frontier against her, when Pompeius anchored at the promontory of Casius and asked permission to land. His request was about to be refused when the king's tutor, Theodotus, pointed out that, if rejected, Pompeius would probably use his connections in Egypt to instigate rebellion in the army, and that it would be better to make away with him. Accordingly, on September 28, 48 B.C., Achillas, the royal general, and some of the old soldiers of Pompeius went off in a large barge to Pompeius, whom they invited to come on board in order to be conveyed to land. As he was stepping on shore the military tribune, Lucius Septimius, stabbed him in the back, under the eyes of his wife and son, who had to watch the murder from the deck of their vessel. It was the same day of the same month on which, thirteen years before, he had entered the capital in triumph over Mithradates. He was a good officer, but otherwise a man of mediocre gifts of intellect and of heart. Barely once in a thousand years does there arise among the people a man who is a king not merely in name, but in reality. If this disproportion between semblance and reality has never perhaps been so strongly marked as in Pompeius, the fact may well excite grave reflection that it was precisely he who, in a certain sense, opened the series of Roman monarchs. When Caesar arrived in Alexandria all was over. He turned away in deep agitation when the murderer brought the head of his rival to his ship. How Caesar would have dealt with Pompeius had he been captured alive it is impossible to say. But interest as well as humanity would probably have counseled clemency. The death of Pompeius did not break up the Pompeians, but gave them, in his sons, Gnaeus and Sextus, two leaders, both of whom were young and active, and the second a man of decided capacity. To the newly founded hereditary monarchy the hereditary pretendership attached itself at once like a parasite, and it was very doubtful whether by this change of persons Caesar did not lose more than he gained.

Caesar's immediate object was accomplished; but he landed and proceeded at once to settle matters in Egypt. He was accompanied by 3200 men and 800 cavalry, and, taking up his abode in the royal palace, he began collecting the money he urgently needed, and regulating the Egyptian succession. No war contribution was imposed, and the arrears of the sum stipulated for in 59 B.C. were commuted for a final payment of two million dollars. The brother and sister were ordered to suspend hostilities, and it was decided that they should rule jointly, in accordance with their father's will. The kingdom of Cyprus was given—as the appanage of the second-born of Egypt—to the younger children of Auletes, Arsinoe and Ptolemy the younger.

But a storm was brewing. Alexandria was a cosmopolitan city, hardly inferior to Rome in the number of its population, and far superior in stirring commercial spirit. In the citizens there was a lively national self-importance, which can hardly be called patriotism—a turbulent vein which made them indulge in street riots as heartily as the Parisians of a later day. Pothinus and the boy king were much discontented with Caesar's arrangements, and ostentatiously sent the treasures of the temple and the royal plate to be melted at the mint. Both the piety and the national feeling of the populace were shocked. The Roman army of occupation had become denationalized by its long sojourn in Egypt and by intermarriage with the women of the country; they were indignant at being obliged to suspend their action on the frontier at the bidding of Caesar and his handful of legionaries, and numerous assassinations of his soldiers in the city revealed to Caesar the danger in which he was placed. He contented himself with ordering up reinforcements from Asia, and meantime prosecuted the business in hand. It was a time of rest after toil, and never was there greater gayety in the camp. It was a merry prelude to a grave drama. The Roman army of occupation suddenly appeared in Alexandria, under the leadership of Achillas, and the citizens at once made common cause with the newly arrived soldiers.

Caesar hastily collected his scattered troops, seized the king and his minister, and entrenched himself in the palace and theater. The war fleet, as there was no time to place it in safety, was burned; and the lighthouse island of Pharos was occupied by means of boats. Thus the way was kept cleared for reinforcements. Orders were at once issued to the commandant of Asia Minor and to the nearest subject countries to send troops and ships in all haste. In the streets the insurrection had free course: fighting went on from day to day; but Caesar could not break through to the fresh water lake of Marea, nor could the Alexandrians master the besieged or deprive them of water. The canals from the Nile were spoiled by introducing salt water, but wells dug on the beach furnished a sufficient supply. The besiegers then directed their attention to the sea. The island of Pharos and the mole which connected it with the mainland divided the harbor into a western and an eastern port. The latter, with the island, were in Caesar's power; the former, with the mole, in that of the Alexandrians. The fleet of the latter had been burned, but they equipped a small squadron and attempted, though in vain, to prevent the entrance of transports conveying a legion from Asia Minor. But when, soon after, the besiegers captured the island and compelled Caesar's ships to lie in the open roadstead, his position was indeed perilous. His fleet was compelled to fight repeatedly, and if it should once be defeated he would be completely hemmed in and probably lost. Accordingly he determined to attempt to recover the island. The double attack from the sea and from the harbor was successful, and both the island and the part of the mole nearest it were captured, and henceforward remained in Caesar's hands.

But relief was at hand: Mithradates of Pergamus, who claimed to be a natural son of the old enemy of Rome, arrived with a motley army gathered from all the communities of Cilicia and Syria. He occupied Pelusium, and then marched towards Memphis to avoid the intersected ground of the Delta. At the same time Caesar conveyed part of his troops in ships to the western end of Lake Marea and marched around the lake and along the river to join Mithradates. The junction was effected; and the combined army marched into the Delta, where the young king (who had been released by Caesar in the hope of allaying the insurrection) was posted on rising ground between the Nile and some marshy swamps. Caesar attacked from three sides at once; the camp was taken, and the insurgents were either put to the sword or drowned; among the latter was the young king. The inhabitants met Caesar on his entry in mourning, and with the images of their gods in their hands implored mercy. The conqueror contented himself with granting to the Jews settled in Alexandria the same rights as the Greek population enjoyed, and with substituting for the army of occupation, which nominally obeyed the Egyptian king, a regular Roman garrison of three legions, under a commander nominated by himself, whose birth made it impossible for him to abuse his position—Rufio, the son of a freedman. Cleopatra and her younger brother, Ptolemy, received the crown, under the supremacy of Rome; the princess Arsinoe was carried off to Italy. Cyprus was again added to the Roman province of Cilicia.

The Alexandrian insurrection is unimportant in itself, but it compelled the man on whom the whole empire now depended to leave his proper task for nearly six months. In the meantime accident or the ability of individual officers decided matters everywhere.

In Asia Minor Calvinus had been ordered, on Caesar's departure, to compel Pharnaces to evacuate the territories he had occupied, especially lesser Armenia. But Calvinus was obliged to dispatch to Egypt two out of his three legions, and was defeated by Pharnaces at Nicopolis. When Caesar himself arrived, Pharnaces promised submission, but took no steps to relinquish his conquests, in the hope that Caesar would soon depart. But Caesar broke off negotiations, and advanced against the king's camp at Ziela. A complete victory was gained, and the campaign was over in five days. The Bosporan kingdom was bestowed upon Mithradates of Pergamus. Caesar's own allies in Syria and Asia Minor were richly rewarded, those of Pompeius dismissed, as a rule, with fines and reprimands. But Deiotarus was confined to his hereditary domain, and lesser Armenia was given to Ariobarzanes, king of Cappadocia.

In Illyria there had been warlike operations of some importance while Caesar was in Egypt. The interior swarmed with dispersed Pompeians, and the Dalmatian coast was bitterly hostile to Caesar. But the Caesarian lieutenant, Quintus Cornificius, was able not only to maintain himself, but to defeat Marcus Octavius, the conqueror of Curicta, in several engagements. During the winter Aulus Gabinius arrived to take over the command of Illyria, and soon began a bold expedition into the interior. But his army was swept away; he suffered a disgraceful defeat during his retreat, and soon afterwards died at Salonae. Finally, Vatinius, the governor of Brundisium, defeated the fleet of Octavius with a force extemporized out of ordinary ships provided with beaks, and compelled him to quit those waters.

But the condition of things was most serious in Africa, where the most eminent of the Pompeians had gathered after the defeat of Pharsalus, and had had ample time to reorganize the war on a large scale. The fanaticism of the emigrants had, if possible, increased; they continued to murder their prisoners, and even the officers of Caesar under a flag of truce. King Juba, in whom was combined all the fury of a barbarian and of a partisan, wished even to extirpate the citizens of every community suspected of sympathizing with the enemy, and it was only by the intervention of Cato that Utica itself was saved. It had been no easy task to fill the vacant post of commander-in-chief. Juba, Metellus Scipio, Varus, the governor of the province, all laid claim to it, while the army desired Cato, who was indeed the only man who had the necessary devotion, energy, and authority. But through Cato's own influence the decision fell upon Scipio, as the officer of highest standing; nevertheless it was Cato alone who confronted the insolent claims of King Juba, and made him feel that the Roman nobility came to him, not as suppliants to a protector, but as to a subject from whom they were entitled to demand assistance. With Scipio the king carried his point, that the pay of his troops should be charged on the Roman treasury, and that the province of Africa should be ceded to him in the event of victory.

The senate of the " three hundred " again appeared, and filled up their ranks from the best or wealthiest of the equites. Warlike preparations went forward with great activity. Every man capable of bearing arms was enrolled, and the land was stripped of its cultivators. The infantry numbered fourteen legions, of which four were legions of King Juba armed in the Roman manner. The heavy cavalry, consisting of Celts and Germans who arrived with Labienus, was sixteen hundred strong, to whom must be added Juba's squadron, equipped in the Roman style. The light troops were mostly Numidians, and very numerous, javelin men, and archers mounted or on foot. Lastly there were 120 elephants, and the fleet of fifty-five sail under Varus and Octavius. Money was provided by the self-taxation of the senate, which included many very wealthy men; huge stores were accumulated in the fortresses, while the open towns were denuded of provisions.

An evil star seemed to preside over the African expedition of Caesar. Not only was it delayed by his long absence in Egypt, but the preparatory measures which he set on foot before leaving for Egypt miscarried. From Spain, Quintus Cassius Longinus had been ordered to cross into Africa with four legions, and to advance against Numidia in conjunction with Bogud, king of western Mauretania. But in this army were many native Spaniards, and two of the legions had formerly been Pompeian. Difficulties arose, which were only aggravated by the unwise and tyrannical conduct of the governor. A formal revolt broke out, and was only repressed on the disavowal of Longinus by the respectable Caesarians and on the interference of the governor of the northern province. Gaius Trebonius, who arrived in the autumn of 47 B.C. to supersede Longinus, everywhere received obedience; but meanwhile nothing had been done to hinder the enemy's organizations in Africa.

Still more serious difficulties occurred among the troops collected in southern Italy for the African campaign. The majority of these consisted of the old legions which had "founded Caesar's throne in Gaul, Spain, and Thessaly." They were spoiled by victory and disorganized by their long repose in Italy. The tremendous demands made on them by their general had thinned their ranks to a fearful extent, and had left in the minds of the survivors a secret rancor which only wanted an opportunity to break forth. The only man who had any influence over them had been absent, almost unheard of, for a year; and when orders to embark for Sicily arrived the storm burst. The men refused to obey unless the promised presents were paid to them, and threw stones at the officers sent by Caesar. The mutineers set out in bodies to extort fulfillment of the promises from the general in the capital. Caesar ordered the few soldiers in the city to occupy the gates, and suddenly appeared among the furious bands, demanding to know what they wanted. They exclaimed, "Discharge." Their request was immediately granted. As to the presents promised on the day of triumph, as well as the lands destined for them, though not promised, Caesar added, they might apply to him on the day when he and the other soldiers should triumph; in the triumph itself they could not of course participate, they having been previously discharged.

The men were not prepared for this turn of affairs. They had demanded discharge in order to annex their own conditions to their service if refused. They were ashamed, too, at the fidelity with which the imperator kept his word, even after they had forgotten their allegiance, and at the generosity with which he granted more than he had promised. When they realized that they must appear as mere spectators at the triumph of their comrades, when their general addressed them no longer as "comrades," but as "burgesses" (quirites)—a name which destroyed, as it were, at one blow the whole pride of their past soldierly career—when they felt once more the spell of the man whose presence had for them an irresistible power, they stood for a while mute and undecided, till from all sides a cry arose that the general should once more receive them into favor, and again permit them to be called Caesar's soldiers. After a sufficient amount of entreaty Caesar yielded; but the ringleaders had a third cut off from their triumphal presents. History knows no greater psychological masterpiece, and none that was more completely successful.

Thus again the African campaign was delayed. When Caesar arrived at Lilybaeum the ten legions destined for embarkation had not nearly arrived, and the experienced troops were the farthest distant. However, Caesar sailed on December 25, 47 B.C., with six legions, five of which were newly raised. Storms prevented the enemy's fleet from obstructing their passage, but the same storms scattered Caesar's fleet, and he could not disembark near Hadrumetum more than 3000 men and 150 horsemen. He got possession of the two seaports of Ruspina and Little Leptis, and kept his troops within entrenchments, and ready at a moment's notice to reëmbark if attacked by a superior force. But the remaining ships arrived soon afterwards, and on the following day Caesar made an expedition with three legions into the interior to procure supplies. He was attacked by Labienus, who had nothing but light troops; and the legions were soon surrounded. By deploying his whole line, and by a series of spirited charges, Caesar saved the honor of his arms and made good his retreat; but had not Ruspina been close at hand, the Moorish javelin might have accomplished the same result as the Parthian bow at Carrhae.

Caesar would not again expose his soldiers to such an attack, and remained inactive till his veteran legions should arrive. In the interval he tried to organize some force to counterbalance the

enormous superiority of the enemy in light-armed troops. He
equipped light horsemen and archers from the fleet, and succeeded
in raising against Juba the Gaetulian tribes.   The Mauretanian
kings, Bogud and Bocchus, were Juba's natural rivals, and there
still roamed in these regions a band of Catilinarians under Publius
Sittius of Nuceria, who had eighteen years before become converted
from a bankrupt Italian merchant into a leader of free bands.
Bocchus and Sittius fell upon Numidia, occupied Cirta, and compelled Juba to send a portion of his troops to his southern and western frontiers.   Still Caesar's position was unpleasant enough: his
army was crowded together within a space of six square miles;
corn was supplied by the fleet, but there was great dearth of forage.
If Scipio retired and abandoned the coast towns, he might at least
endlessly protract the war; this plan was advised by Cato, who
offered at the same time to cross into Italy and call the republicans
to arms.   But the decision lay with Scipio, who resolved to continue
the war on the coast.   This blunder was all the more serious because
the army which they opposed to Caesar was in a troublesome temper,
and the strictness of the levy, the exhaustion of the country, and the
devastation of many of the smaller townships had produced a feeling
of exasperation in the region to which the war was transferred.
The African towns declared, wherever they could, for Caesar, and
desertion increased continually in the army.   But Scipio marched
with all his force from Utica, appeared before the towns occupied
by Caesar, and repeatedly offered him battle.   Caesar refused until
all his veteran legions had arrived, when Scipio on his part grew
afraid, and nearly two months passed away in skirmishes and in
efforts to procure supplies.

When Caesar's last reinforcements had arrived he made a lateral movement towards the town of Thapsus, strongly garrisoned
by the enemy.   Scipio now commited the unpardonable blunder of
risking a battle, April 6, 46 B.C., to save the town, on ground which
placed the decision in the hands of the infantry of the line.   He
advanced to a position immediately opposite to Caesar's camp on
the shore, and, at the same time, the garrison of Thapsus prepared
for a sally.   Caesar's campguard sufficed to repulse the latter; and
his legions, forming a correct estimate of the enemy from their want
of precision and from their ill-closed ranks, compelled a trumpeter
to sound for the attack even before the general gave the signal.
The right wing, in advance of the rest of the line, turned the ele-

phants opposed to them back upon the ranks of the enemy; they then broke the left wing of their opponents, and overthrew the whole line. The old camp of the enemy was at a distance, and the new one was not yet ready, so that the defeated army was almost annihilated. The legionaries refused all quarter; they were tired of being hurried from one continent to another in pursuit of an enemy who, though always defeated, was never destroyed. Fifty thousand corpses covered the field of Thapsus, among which were those of several Caesarian officers suspected by the soldiers of sympathy with the enemy. The victorious army numbered no more than fifty dead.

The struggle was over in Africa; Cato convoked the senate at Utica, and asked them to decide whether they would yield or continue their defense. At first the more courageous view seemed likely to prevail, but ultimately it was resolved to yield. Faustus Sulla and Lucius Afranius soon arrived with a body of cavalry and wished to defend the city after slaughtering *en masse* the untrustworthy citizens. Cato indignantly refused; and after checking, as far as he could, by his authority and by largesses, the fury of the soldiery, and after providing the means of flight for those who feared to trust themselves to the mercy of Caesar, he at last held himself released from his command, and, retiring to his chamber, plunged his sword into his breast.

Few of the fugitive leaders escaped: Afranius and Faustus were delivered up to Caesar, and, when he did not order their immediate execution, were cut down by the soldiers. Metellus Scipio was captured by the cruisers of Sittius, and stabbed himself. King Juba, half expecting the issue, had caused a huge funeral pile to be prepared in the market-place of Zama, upon which he proposed to consume himself with all his treasures and the dead bodies of all the citizens. But the latter had no desire to adorn the funeral rites of the African Sardanapalus, and closed their gates when he appeared in company with Marcus Petreius. The king—one of those natures that become savage amid a life of dazzling and insolent enjoyment, and prepare for themselves even out of death an intoxicating feast—resorted with Petreius to one of his country houses, where, after a copious banquet, he challenged Petreius to fight him in single combat. The conqueror of Catilina fell by the hand of the king, and the latter caused himself to be stabbed by one of his slaves. Labienus and Sextus Pompeius fled to Spain, and betook themselves to a piratical warfare by land and sea.

The kingdom of Massinissa was now broken up. The eastern portion was united with the kingdom of Bocchus, and King Bogud was rewarded with considerable gifts. Cirta was handed over to Publius Sittius as a settlement for his half-Roman bands; but this same district, as well as the largest and most fertile part of Numidia, was united as " New Africa ",with the older province of Africa.

The struggle which had lasted for four years thus terminated in the complete victory of the new monarch. The monarchy might no doubt be dated from the moment when Pompeius and Caesar had established their joint rule and overthrown the aristocratic constitution. But it was only the battlefields of Pharsalus and Thapsus that set aside the joint rule, and conferred fixity and formal recognition on the new monarch. Pretenders and conspiracies, even revolutions and restorations, might ensue, but the continuity of the free republic, uninterrupted during five hundred years, was broken through, and monarchy was established as an accomplished fact.

That the constitutional struggle was at an end was proclaimed by Cato when he fell upon his sword at Utica. The republic was dead, the treasure was carried off—why should the sentinels remain? There was more nobility, and, above all, more judgment in the death of Cato than there had been in his life. He was not a great man; he was the ideal of unreflecting republicanism, and this has made him the favorite of all who make it their hobby; but he was the only man who honorably and courageously defended in the last struggle the great system doomed to destruction. Just because the shrewdest lie feels itself inwardly annihilated before the simple truth, and because all the dignity and glory of human nature ultimately depend not on shrewdness, but on honesty, Cato has played a greater part in history than many men far superior to him in intellect. It was a fearfully striking protest of the republic against the monarchy, that the last republican went as the first monarch came—a protest which tore asunder like gossamer all that so-called constitutional character with which Caesar invested his monarchy, and exposed in all its hypocritical falsehood the shibboleth of the reconciliation of all parties, under the egis of which despotism grew up. The unrelenting warfare which the ghost of the legitimate republic waged for centuries—from Cassius and Brutus down to Thrasea and Tacitus, nay, even far later—a warfare of plots and literature, was the legacy which the dying Cato bequeathed to his enemies. Immediately after his death the man was revered as a saint by the party of which in his life he was often the laughing-stock and the scandal. But the greatest of these marks of respect was the involuntary homage which Caesar rendered to him when he made an exception to the

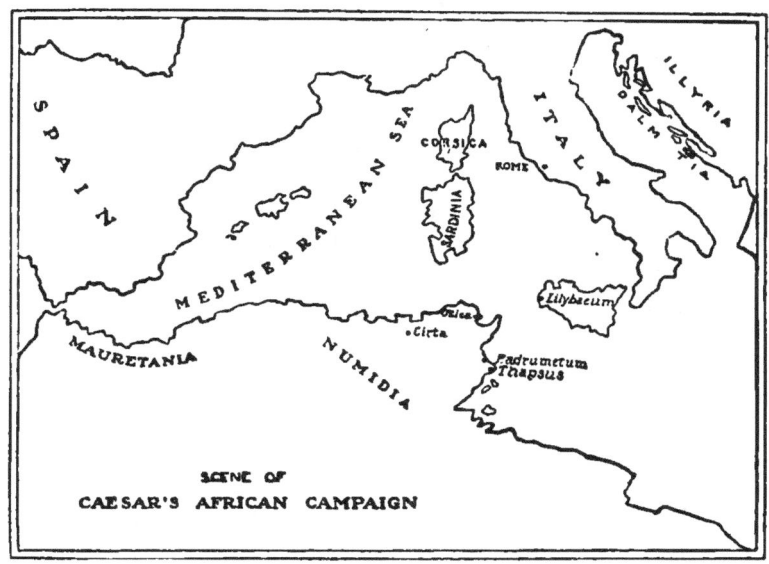

SCENE OF
CAESAR'S AFRICAN CAMPAIGN

contemptuous clemency with which he was wont to treat his opponents, and pursued him even beyond the grave with that energetic hatred which practical statesmen are wont to feel towards antagonists who oppose them in a domain of ideas, which is as dangerous in their view as it lies beyond their reach.

Chapter XXXIII

THE OLD REPUBLIC AND THE NEW MONARCHY
46-44 B.C.

CAESAR was in his fifty-sixth year[1] when the battle of Thapsus made him sole monarch of Rome. He was sprung from one of the oldest noble families of Latium, and traced his lineage back to the heroes of the Iliad and to the kings of Rome; and he spent the years of his boyhood like any other noble youth of the period, in playing with literature and verse-making, in love intrigues and the arts of the toilet, together with another art much studied at that period, that of always borrowing and never paying. But manhood found his vigor both of mind and body unimpaired; in fencing and riding he was a match for any of his soldiers, and the incredible rapidity of his journeys astonished both friend and foe. His power of intuition was remarkable, and displayed itself in the practicability and precision of his orders, even when he had not seen with his own eyes, while his memory never failed him. Although a gentleman, a man of genius, and a monarch, he had still a heart. His love for his mother was deep and lasting, while he was sincerely devoted to his wives, and, above all, to his daughter Julia. His fidelity to his associates was unwavering, and several of them, such as Aulus Hirtius and Gaius Matius, showed their attachment to him after his death. But, above all, Caesar was a realist and a man of sense; his passion was never stronger than he could control. Literature and verse-making occupied him at times, but in his sleepless hours he chose to meditate upon the inflections of Latin nouns and verbs. After the revels of his youth he avoided wine entirely, and though he enjoyed, even when a monarch, the society of women, he allowed them no influence over him. He prided himself upon his personal appearance, and covered the baldness of his later years with the

[1] There is some uncertainty as to the exact year of Caesar's birth. The date has been frequently given as 100 B.C., following the statement of Suetonius and others, but various considerations have led modern writers to conjecture that the true date is 102 B.C. This is the year accepted by Mommsen.

laurel chaplet which he wore in public. It was the result of this cool realism that Caesar possessed the power of living keenly in the present moment, undisturbed by memory or expectation; that he could at any moment apply his whole genius to the most incidental enterprise. To this he owed his marvellous serenity, his independence of control by favorite or friend. He never deceived himself as to the power of fate and the ability of man; he felt that in all things fortune—accident—must bestow success, and this perhaps is the reason why he often chose to play so desperate a game.

Caesar was from the beginning of his political career emphatically a statesman; his aim was the regeneration, political, military, intellectual, and moral, of his own and of the Hellenic nation. He was a brilliant and masculine orator, an author of an inimitable purity and simplicity of style; as a general he disregarded routine and tradition, and conducted each campaign with regard to its own requirements. Like William of Orange, he stood always ready for battle after defeat, and in the rapid movement of masses of men— the highest and most difficult element of warfare—he was unrivaled. But he was all these things only secondarily, and merely because he was a statesman: they were but the means to an end. His original plan had been to compass his aim, like Pericles, without force of arms, and it was not till the age of forty that he found himself at the head of an army. This improvised generalship is seen in the temerity with which, in many instances, notably when he landed in Epirus, he set aside, without absolute necessity, the best-founded principles of war. But, though a master of the art of war, he did his utmost to avert civil strife, and, after the struggle, he allowed no hierarchy of marshals or government of pretorians to arise. He had every quality which makes the statesman. He was a born ruler, and compelled men of all natures to work in his service. His talent for organization was unsurpassed, and is seen in the creation and management of his political alliances and of his army. He never made the blunder, which so many others have made, of carrying into politics the tone of military command; he was a monarch, but never a tyrant. In his life there were doubtless many mistakes, but there was no false step of passion for him to regret; nothing to be compared with the murder of Kleitos or the burning of Persepolis, in the life of Alexander. Whatever his task, he always recognized its natural limits; where he recognized that fate had spoken, he always obeyed. Alexander on the Hyphasis, Napoleon at Moscow, turned back because they were compelled; Caesar turned back voluntarily on the Thames, and on the Rhine; and on the Danube and the Euphrates he thought, not of unbounded conquests, but of well-considered frontiers.

Such was the man—so easy and yet so difficult to describe. Tradition has handed down copious and vivid information regarding him, and yet no man is more difficult to reproduce to the life. The secret lies in his perfection; the artist can paint anything except only consummate beauty. Normality admits, doubtless, of being expressed, but it gives us only the negative notion of the absence of defect. In the character of Caesar, the great contrasts of existence meet and balance each other. He was of the mightiest creative power, and yet of the most penetrating judgment; of the highest energy of will and the highest capacity of execution; filled with republican ideals, and at the same time born to be king. He was the entire and perfect man; and he was this because he was the entire and perfect Roman; he was in the full current of his time, and possessed in perfection the special gift of his nation—practical aptitude as a citizen.

In the work of regenerating the state Caesar started at once from the principle of the reconciliation of parties—so far as antagonistic principles can be reconciled at all. The statues of Sulla, overthrown by the mob in the capital after Pharsalus, were ordered to be set up again; the men who had been banished in the Cinnan and Sertorian times were recalled, and the children of those outlawed by Sulla were restored to their full rights. In the same way all who had suffered loss of rights in the early stages of the recent struggle, especially through the impeachments of 52 B.C., received full restitution. The only exceptions were made in the case of those who had put to death the proscribed for money, and of Milo, the condottiere of the senatorial party.

These steps were easy; but it was much more difficult to deal with the parties, which even now, after the war, confronted each other with undiminished hatred. Caesar's own adherents were among the most dissatisfied with the results of the struggle. The Roman popular party expected Caesar to accomplish for them what Catilina had attempted; and loud was their outcry when it became plain that the most which debtors could expect from him was some alleviations of payment and modifications of procedure. They began even to coquet with the Pompeians, and during Caesar's

THE MONARCHY 365

long absence from Italy, in 48 and 47 B.C., to instigate a second civil war.

Just before the battle of Pharsalus the pretor Marcus Caelius Rufus promised to the people laws granting to debtors a respite of six years free of interest and canceling all claims from loans or house rents. When deposed by the Caesarian senate he entered into negotiations with Milo for a rising in Italy. Milo raised his standard in the region of Thurii, and Rufus formed a plan, which was frustrated, to seize Capua. The fall of the two leaders put an end to the incident, in 48 B.C., but in the following year Publius Dolabella revived the laws of Rufus, and disturbances took place, which had to be put down by Marcus Antonius, the commandant of Italy, by military force.

At the same time that Caesar repressed with a strong hand the ebullitions of his own left wing, he tried to pave the way for the gradual extinction of the republican party by a policy of combined repression and conciliation. He refused to triumph on the ground of victories won over his fellow-countrymen. The statue of Pompeius was restored to its former distinguished place in the senate-house, and political prosecutions of his opponents were confined within the narrowest limits. The papers found in the enemy's headquarters after Pharsalus and Thapsus were burned unread; all the common soldiers, except those burgesses who had enlisted under King Juba, escaped with impunity. Even the officers obtained free pardon until the close of the Spanish campaign of 49 B.C.; after that date all who served as officers in the enemy's army, or who sat in the opposition senate, forfeited property and political rights, and were banished from Italy for life. Any who had fought once more after accepting pardon forfeited life at once. But these rules were applied in the mildest possible manner; the punishment of death was rarely inflicted; many were pardoned or escaped with fines, and in fact almost all were pardoned who could bring themselves to ask favor of Caesar. Ultimately, in 44 B.C., a general amnesty was issued.

But the opposition was none the more reconciled. Open resistance there was none, but secret agitations and, above all, the literature of opposition gave expression to the seething republican discontent. The praise of Cato was the favorite theme of opposition pamphlets, which were replied to by Caesar and his confidants. The republican and Caesarian scribes fought round the dead hero of

Utica like the Trojans and Hellenes round the dead body of Patroclus. But, naturally, the Caesarians had the worst of it with a republican public. Hence literary men, like Publius Nigidius Figulus and Aulus Caecina, found more difficulty than any other class in obtaining permission to return to Italy; and in Italy itself they were subjected to a practical censorship whose punishments were purely arbitrary. But though risings of republicans and Pompeians were perpetually preparing in every part of the empire, and conspiracies were formed even in the capital itself, Caesar was not induced to surround himself by a bodyguard, but contented himself with making known the plots, when detected, by public placards. His clemency and his indifference were not the fruit of sentiment, but of the statesmanly conviction that vanquished parties are absorbed within the state more rapidly than they can be exterminated by proscription. Besides, he needed for his own high objects all the talent, culture, and distinction which the aristocratic party embraced; for here, in spite of all, was still to be found all that remained of a free and national spirit among the Roman burgesses. Like Henry IV. of France and William of Orange, Caesar found that his difficulties only began with victory. For the moment all parties united against their chief, and against his own great ideal. But what Caesar lost the state gained; voluntarily or compulsorily, men of all parties worked at the erection of the new and mighty edifice; and if the reconciliation was but external, no one knew better than Caesar that antagonisms lose their keenness when brought into outward union, and that only in this way can the statesman anticipate the work of time.

In attempting to give a detailed account of the mode in which the transition was effected from the old to the new, it must be remembered that Caesar came not to begin, but to complete. The principles of the popular party, which Caesar had from the beginning adopted to the full, were the principles of Gaius Gracchus, and had, since his time, been the essential principles of the democracy. They were: the alleviation of the burdens of debtors; transmarine colonization; equalization of the differences of rights existing between the classes in the state; emancipation of the executive from the senate. And these remained the principles of Caesar as monarch; for his monarchy was like the monarchy of Pericles and of Cromwell, the representation of the nation by the man in whom it puts supreme and unlimited confidence.

With regard to the judgment to be passed upon Caesar, too much care cannot be taken to avoid the common blunder of using historical praise and historical censure, applied to particular circumstances, as phrases of general application; and, in the present instance, of construing praise of Caesar as praise of what is called " Caesarianism." History is instructive with respect to the present only as she reveals the necessary organic conditions of civilization—the fundamental forces everywhere alike, and the manner of their combination everywhere different—the knowledge of which leads men. not to slavish imitation, but to independent reproduction. The history of Roman imperialism is in reality the bitterest censure of modern autocracy which could be written by the hand of man. Every constitution which gives play to the free self-determination of a majority of citizens infinitely surpasses the most brilliant and humane absolutism, just as the smallest organism is superior to the most artistic machine; the former is living and capable of development, but the latter cannot develop, and is therefore dead. Caesar's work could bring no blessing in itself, but was necessary and salutary because the ancient political organization, based upon slavery and ignorant of representative government, ended logically in military monarchy as the least of evils.

Formally the position of the new monarch assumed a singular shape.

First, he was invested with the dictatorship, at first temporarily, after his return from Spain in 49 B.C.; again for an indefinite time after Pharsalus; finally from January 1, 45 B.C., as an annual office, which was in 44 B.C. conferred on him for life.

Second, he held the consulship for 48 B.C.—the office which immediately occasioned the civil war; afterwards he was appointed for five and finally for ten years—once without colleague.

Third, he was invested with tribunician power for life, in 48 B.C.; with the first place and the leading vote in the senate; with the title of imperator for life; and, though already pontifex maximus, he became a member of the college of augurs.

Fourth, numerous decrees of the senate intrusted him with the right of deciding on war and peace, the disposal of armies and treasure, the nomination of provincial governors, and many other privileges; together with such empty honors as the title of *pater patriae,* and the designation of the month in which he was born by the name of Julius.

It is difficult in this confused union of offices to determine by
what formal shape Caesar chose to express the new absolute power,
but the new name of imperator is in every respect its appropriate
formal expression, just because it is new, and no outward occasion
for its introduction is apparent. It expresses concisely all the functions of the chief of the state—the concentration of official power
in the hands of a popular chief independent of the senate. The
title prevails on Caesar's coins, especially those of the last period,
by the side of the dictatorship; in his law as to political crimes the
monarch is designated by this name; and, what is most decisive, the
authority of imperator was given to Caesar for his bodily or adopted
descendants. The new monarchy was to be hereditary. The new
office was based on the position which consuls or proconsuls occupied outside the pomerium, and included not only the military, but
the supreme administrative and judicial power. Moreover, the imperator, unlike the consul, had never been checked by the right of
provocatio or been obliged to respect the advice of the senate.

In fact, the new office of imperator was nothing else than the
regal office reëstablished; as the consulship was only the kingship
with certain restrictions imposed, so for the new office these restrictions were once more removed. Almost every feature of the
old monarchy reappears in the new: the union of supreme military,
judicial, and administrative power in the hands of the prince; the
religious presidency over the commonwealth; the right of issuing
binding ordinances; the reduction of the senate to a council of
state, the revival of the patriciate and of the prefecture of the city;
the power of the prince to nominate his successor under the form of
adoption. Again, as the old kings of Rome had been the protectors
of the commons against the nobility, so Caesar came not to destroy
liberty, but to fulfill it. Nor had the idea of the regal office ever
become obsolete at Rome; at various times, in the republican dictatorship, in the decemviral power, in the Sullan regency—there
had been a practical recurrence to it. And as mankind have infinite
difficulty in reaching new creations, and therefore cherish the once
developed forms as sacred heirlooms, it was natural for Caesar to
connect himself with Servius Tullius, as Charlemagne connected
himself with Caesar, and as Napoleon attempted to connect himself
with Charlemagne. Accordingly, beside the statues of the traditional seven kings on the Capitol, Caesar ordered his own to be
erected as the eighth. He appeared in public in the costume of the

old kings of Alba; in the formula for political oaths the genius of the imperator was added to the Jovis and the Penates of the Roman people; from the year 44 B.C. the head of Caesar appears on the coins—the recognized outward badge of monarchy. There could be no doubt as to Caesar's view of his position; it is even possible that he wished to assume the title of king; certainly he was often pressed by his adherents to assume it—most strikingly when Marcus Antonius, as consul, offered him the diadem before all the people. But it is probable that Caesar was resolved to avoid the name as tainted with a curse, and as familiar to the Romans of his day chiefly as applied to the despots of the East; and the scene with Antonius may have been designed to put an end once and for all to rumors on the subject.

Whatever the title, the sovereign was there, and all the due accompaniments of royalty at once made their appearance. Caesar appeared in public, not in the consular robe with purple stripes, but in the robe wholly of purple, and received without rising from his chair the procession of the senate. Rents rose in the quarter of the city where he lived; personal interviews became so difficult that Caesar was often obliged to communicate in writing even with his nearest friends. A new monarchical aristocracy arose to replace the old patriciate, which still existed but had dwindled away until not more than fifteen or sixteen genuine patrician families remained. Caesar had the right of creating new patrician gentes conferred on him by popular decree, and thus established a new nobility entirely dependent on himself.

Thus the regal tradition was completely renewed; the burgess assembly remained by the side of the king as the ultimate expression of the sovereign will of the people; the senate was reduced to its old function of giving advice to the ruler when requested; and the whole magisterial authority of the state was concentrated in the monarch.

In legislation the primitive maxim of Roman law was reverted to, that the assembly in concert with the king can alone alter the law of the state; and Caesar regularly had his enactments confirmed by the people. Though the authority of the comitia was only a shadow, yet their existence was a standing acknowledgment of the principle of the sovereignty of the people, and an energetic protest against sultanism.

But at the same time the other maxim of state law was revived, that the command of the supreme magistrate is binding at least as long as he remains in office; and hence the royal edict now obtained the force of law.

On the other hand, while Caesar formally acknowledged the sovereignty of the people, it was no part of his plan to divide his authority with the senate. He made use of it as a council to advise him with regard to new laws, and for issuing important administrative regulations. The latter were usually issued formally in the name of the senate, and there are instances of such decrees of which none of the senators recited as present had any knowledge. In order to make it representative as far as possible of all classes, and also in order to take from it its character as headquarters of the opposition, it was raised at once to the number of nine hundred; and, to maintain this increase, the number of questors—all of whom became annually members of the senate—was raised from twenty to forty. Of these, twenty were nominated by the imperator, who had also the privilege of conferring the honorary rights of the questorship on whomsoever he pleased. The immediate extraordinary increase was carried out solely by Caesar's nomination, and the new members included many non-Italians and persons of humble or dubious origin.

At the same time, the whole executive was concentrated in the hands of the monarch. Every question of any moment was decided by the imperator in person; and Caesar was able to carry personal government to a height which seems incredible to men of modern times. The Roman house was a machine, and the intellectual powers of slaves and freedmen were as much at the disposal of the master as their manual labor. So, whenever circumstances permitted, Caesar filled up any post demanding special confidence with slaves, freedmen, or clients of humble birth. It was the beau-ideal of bureaucratic centralization.

In matters strictly political Caesar of course avoided, whenever possible, any delegation of his functions; when this was inevitable, as when he was compelled to be absent from Rome, his representative was usually no political personage, but his banker, the Phoenician Lucius Cornelius Balbus, without regular official jurisdiction. In finance, the private means of the monarch were kept strictly separate from the property of the state; but the whole financial management, the levying of the provincial revenues and the coinage—were intrusted to the slaves and freedmen of the imperator. The provincial governors, now that they were relieved of all financial business by the new imperial tax receivers, became little more than military commanders. Egypt, on account of its great resources, and its geographical isolation, which rendered it peculiarly liable to be broken off from the central power under an able leader, was intrusted to Rufio, the son of a freedman, a man little likely to abuse his position. The more important of the other provinces were given to those who had been consuls, the others to those who had been pretors, and the distribution of provinces among qualified candidates was vested in the imperator. The consuls for the year were often induced to abdicate to make room for other men; moreover the number of pretors was raised from eight to sixteen, and the nomination of them intrusted to the imperator; finally, the prince could nominate titular pretors or questors, and by these various means could always count upon a sufficient number of candidates favorable to himself. As a rule the consular governor remained not more than two years, the pretorian not more than one, in his province. The Roman magistrates— consuls, pretors, ediles, tribunes, and questors—retained substantially their former powers; but their position was radically changed. Formerly they had been magistrates of the empire, now they were magistrates of the city of Rome, and the consulship became little but a titular post, important only as implying the reversion of a higher governorship. The election of consuls, tribunes, and plebeian ediles was free from restriction; but half of the pretors, curule ediles, and questors were nominated by the monarch. The tribunician power was left in the main untouched, but a refractory tribune would of course be summarily dealt with.

Thus, for all general and important questions, the imperator was his own minister; he controlled the finances by his servants and the army by his adjutants; the old state magistracies were again converted into magistracies of the city of Rome; and, in addition to all this, he acquired the right of nominating his successor. The autocracy was indeed complete.

In spiritual matters Caesar made little alteration, except to attach the supreme pontificate and the augurship to the person of the monarch. Such support as religion could give to the state was now transferred to the monarchy, but it can scarcely have been worth having.

With regard to the administration of the law, Caesar revived the ancient regal right of bringing both capital cases and private

suits before himself for sole and final decision. He often sat, like
the ancient kings, in the Forum to try burgesses in cases of high
treason; client princes accused of the same offense were tried in
Caesar's house: so that the only privilege of burgesses in this
respect was that of publicity. But for all ordinary cases the former
republican procedure was retained. Criminal causes went before
the several jury commissions appointed to deal with them; civil
cases came either before the centumviri, as the court of inheritance
was called, or were referred to single judges. The general superintendence of judicial proceedings was conducted in the capital chiefly
by the pretor, in the provinces by the governors. Political crimes
were still referred to a special commission; the law on this subject
was laid down with great precision, and excluded all prosecution of
opinions, while it fixed as the penalty, not death, but exile. The
question of the selection of jurymen was left, as before, according
to the law of Cotta, except that the rating of jurymen was twenty
thousand dollars.

The old republican jurisdiction and that of the king were on
the whole coördinate, and any case once decided upon before
either bar was regarded as closed. But by his tribunician power the
king might interfere with any sentence (unless where the law
specially forbade the veto of the tribunes) so as to cancel it, and
might then, by virtue of his judicial supremacy, order the case to be
tried anew before himself. This was the germ of the system of
appeal to a higher court, a thing entirely unknown to earlier procedure.[1]

But these innovations—which cannot with certainty be pronounced improvements in themselves—could not cure the evils
from which the Roman administration of justice was suffering. In
the first place, criminal procedure could never be sound in a slave
state. For the duty of proceeding against a slave must be left, *de
facto* at any rate, to the master, who will punish crime in a slave
only so far as it impairs his value; slave criminals at Rome were
sold to the fighting booth, just as an ox given to goring was sent to
the butchers; but punishment for crime as crime could scarcely exist
for slaves. Again, during the long course of political disturbance
criminal prosecutions, even against freemen, had become mere
faction fights, to be fought out by means of favor, money, and
violence. All classes bear the blame of this demoralization, but the

---

[1] This cannot be proved to have existed anterior to Augustus.

class of advocates must take the lion's share. Among all the numerous pleadings in criminal causes which have come down to us from this epoch, scarcely one makes a serious attempt to fix the crime and to put the proof or counterproof into proper shape. Civil procedure suffered in the same way, though, from the nature of the case, of course in a minor degree. Caesar retained and even made more severe the curb imposed on forensic eloquence by Pompeius, and under his rule of course open corruption and intimidation of the courts came to an end. But he could not pluck up the roots of the evil, or reproduce in the minds of the people the sacred sense of right and reverence for law which alone can insure the purity of judicial administration.

Nowhere was the general decay of the state more conspicuously exemplified than in the condition of the military system. This was now in much the same condition as that of the Carthaginians in the time of Hannibal. The governing classes furnished the officers; the subjects, plebeians and provincials, the rank and file. The general was left practically to himself, and to the resources of his province. All civic or national spirit had deserted the army; *esprit de corps* alone held it together; it had ceased to be the instrument of the commonwealth, and had become that of the general who commanded it. Under the ordinary wretched commanders it became a rabble, but in the hands of a capable leader it attained a perfection of which the burgess army was incapable. The higher ranks in the state became more and more averse to arms; so that the military tribuneship, once so keenly competed for, was open to any man of equestrian rank who chose to serve. The staff of officers usually gave the signal for mutiny and desertion. Caesar himself has described the scene at his own headquarters when orders were given to advance against Ariovistus—the cursing and weeping, the making of wills, the requests for furlough. The levy was held with great unfairness; and soldiers once levied were kept thirty years under the standards. The burgess cavalry had degenerated into an ornamental guard; the "burgess" infantry was a troop of mercenaries collected from the lowest dregs of the populace. The subjects furnished the whole of the cavalry and light-armed troops, and began to be employed extensively in the infantry. The post of centurion went by favor, or was even sold to the highest bidder: the payment of the soldiers was most defective and irregular. Of the decay of the navy enough has been said before; here, too, as elsewhere, everything that could be ruined had been reduced to ruin under the oligarchic government.

Caesar's military reorganization was limited substantially to the tightening and strengthening of the reins of discipline. The system itself he did not attempt—perhaps he did not wish—to reform. He did indeed enact that, in order to hold a municipal magistracy or sit on a municipal council before the thirtieth year, a man must serve, either three years as an officer, or six years in the ranks; and thus attempted to attract the better classes into the army. But he dared not associate the holding of an honorary office unconditionally with the fulfillment of the time of service. The levy was better arranged, and the time of service shortened; for the rest, the infantry continued to be raised chiefly from the lower orders of burgesses, the cavalry and light infantry from the other subjects. Two innovations must be placed to Caesar's account: one the use of mercenaries in the cavalry, to which he was driven by the untrustworthiness of the subject cavalry; the other the appointment of adjutants of the legion with pretorian powers. Hitherto the legion had been led by its military tribunes, who were appointed partly by the burgesses, partly by the general, and who, as a rule, commanded the legion in succession. But henceforward colonels or adjutants of the whole legion were nominated by the imperator in Rome, and were meant chiefly as a counterpoise to the governor's authority. The most important change in the military system was, of course, the new supreme command; for the first time the armies of the state were under the real and energetic control of the supreme government. In all probability the governor would still retain the supreme military authority in his own province, but subject to the authority of the imperator, who might take it from him at any moment and assume it for himself or his delegates. There was no longer any fear, either that the armies might become utterly disorganized or that they might forget that they belonged to the commonwealth in their devotion to their leaders.

Perhaps it was the sole illusion which Caesar allowed himself to cherish that the monarchy he had founded could be otherwise than military. That a standing army was necessary he saw of course, but only because the nature of the empire required permanent frontier garrisons; and to the regulation of the frontier his military plans were substantially limited. He had already taken measures for the tranquillization of Spain, and had provided for

THE MONARCHY

the defense of the Gallic and the African boundaries; he had similar plans for the countries bordering on the Euphrates and the Danube. Above all, he was determined to avenge the day of Carrhae, and to set bounds to the power of Boerebistas, king of the Getae, who was extending his dominions on both sides of the Danube. Fabulous schemes of world-wide conquest are ascribed to Caesar, but on no respectable authority, and his conduct in Gaul and Britain gives little countenance to such traditions. At any rate it is certain that

THE ROMAN EMPIRE
AT THE DEATH OF CÆSAR

he did not intend to rest his monarchy primarily on the army, or to set the military power above the civil. The magnificent Gallic legions were dissolved as incompatible with a civic commonwealth; only their glorious names were perpetuated by newly founded colonies. The soldiers who obtained allotments were not settled together to form military colonies, but scattered throughout Italy, except where, as in Campania, aggregation could not be avoided. Caesar attempted in every way to keep the soldiers within the sphere of civil life: by allowing them to serve their term, not continuously, but by instalments; by shortening the term of service; by settling the *emeriti* as agricultural colonists; by keeping the army aloof from Italy, on the distant frontiers. No corps of guards—

the true criterion of a military state—was even formed by him; even as general he dropped the bodyguard which had long been usual; and, though constantly beset by assassins in the capital, he contented himself with the usual escort of lictors. But this noble ideal, of a kingship based only on the confidence of the people, could but be an illusion; amid the deep disorganization of the nation it was impossible for the eighth king of Rome to reign merely by virtue of law and justice. Just as little could the army which had placed him on the throne be really absorbed again into the state. The Campanian mutiny and the battlefield of Thapsus showed how the legionaries had learned their lesson. Thousands of swords still flew at Caesar's signal from their scabbards, but they no longer returned to their scabbards at his signal. Caesar's creation could not but be a military monarchy; he had overthrown the *régime* of the aristocrats and bankers only to put in its place a military *régime*. Nevertheless, it was important that at the outset Caesar labored, however uselessly, to avoid military rule; and it is owing to his exertions that for centuries the emperors of Rome used the army in the main, not against the citizen, but against the foe.

The financial embarrassment in which the state had found itself during recent years was not caused by deficiency of revenue, which had lately been increased by $4,250,000 since the formation of the provinces of Bithynia-Pontus and Syria. The taxation of foreign luxuries, too, yielded a constantly increasing revenue; and immense sums had been brought into the state chest by Lucullus, Metellus, Pompeius, Cato, and others. But expenditure had likewise increased, and the whole department had been mismanaged. The corn distribution had gradually come to absorb one-fifth of the revenue; the military budget had risen with the addition of Cilicia, Syria, and Gaul to the list of provinces. Again, special warlike preparations had swallowed up enormous sums. Still, such were the resources of the empire, the exchequer might have met all these claims upon it but for mismanagement and corruption.

Apart from these last two causes there were two institutions, both introduced by Gaius Gracchus, which ate like a gangrene into the Roman financial system—the corn distributions and the leasing system. The latter was retained for the indirect taxes; but the direct taxes were in future either paid in kind, like the contributions of corn and oil from Sardinia and Africa, or converted into fixed money payments, the collection being intrusted to the communities

THE MONARCHY

themselves. The corn distributions could hardly be abolished; but in their present form they were an assertion of the principle that the ruling community had a right to be supported by its subjects. Caesar reduced the number of persons relieved from 320,000 to 150,000, which number was fixed as a maximum, and he excluded from the list all but the most needy, thus converting the institution from a political privilege into a provision for the poor.

A thorough revision of income and expenditure was carried out. The ordinary items of revenue were fixed anew. On many communities and districts total exemption from taxation was conferred, either directly or by bestowal of the franchise. Many others had their tribute lowered: that of Asia was reduced by one-third; in the newly conquered districts of Illyria and in Gaul the tribute was fixed at a low rate; all Gaul paid but $2,000,000. On the other hand, some communities, as Little Leptis in Africa, had their tribute raised; the recently abolished Italian harbor dues were reimposed. And to these ordinary sources of income were to be added great sums raised from booty, temple treasures, forced loans and fines imposed on subject communities or on individuals; above all, from the proceeds of the estates of the defeated party. The fine of the African capitalists who sat in the senate at Utica amounted to $5,000,000, and the property of Pompeius sold for $3,500,000. These confiscations were necessary, because the strength of the aristocrats lay in their colossal wealth; but the proceeds were scrupulously devoted to state purposes, and the purchase money was always rigidly exacted, even from Caesar's closest adherents, such as Marcus Antonius.

The expenditure was largely diminished by the restriction of the corn distributions, and these, together with the supply of oil for the baths, were now provided for by contributions in kind from Sardinia and Africa, and thus kept separate from the exchequer. But the military expenditure was increased, both by the augmentation of the standing army and by the raising of the pay from $25 to $45 annually. Both steps were necessary: the first owing to the want of any efficient defense of the frontiers; the second because the former pay of 6½ cents per day had been fixed at a time when money had an entirely different value, and when the soldier entered the army, not for pay, but for the irregular gains which he made at the expense of the provincials. The new scale was fixed at 12 cents per day, the ordinary day's wages at the same period

being 15 cents.   Caesar's extraordinary expenses during and after
the civil wars were enormous.   The war had cost immense sums;
every common soldier in Caesar's army received $1,000 at its close,
every neutral burgess in the capital, $15.   Buildings undertaken in
the capital cost in all $8,000,000.   Yet, in spite of these immense
disbursements, in March, 44 B.C., there was in the public treasury a
sum of $35,000,000, in that of Caesar $5,000,000—tenfold the
amount which the treasury had held in the most flourishing times
of the republic.

But the task of breaking up the old parties and furnishing the
state with a suitable constitution, an efficient army, and well-
ordered finances was not the most difficult part of Caesar's work.
It remained to regenerate the Italian nation, to reorganize Rome,
Italy, and the provinces.

As to Rome itself, nothing could be more deplorable than the
condition into which it had fallen.   In it, as in all capitals, were
congregated the upper classes who regarded their homes in town
as mere lodging places, the foreign settlers, the fluctuating population of travelers on business or pleasure, the mass of indolent,
criminal, bankrupt, and abandoned rabble.   All real communal life
had ceased in Rome; it was a center to which people flocked from
the whole extent of the empire for speculation, debauchery, intrigue, or crime.   All the evils inseparable from great capitals were
found intensified at Rome, and there were others peculiar to itself.
No city, perhaps, was ever so completely without free industry of
any kind, which was rendered impossible by the importation of
foreign commodities and by the extensive employment of slaves in
domestic manufacture.   Nowhere, again, were such masses of
slaves congregated; nowhere were the slaves of so many different
nationalities—Syrians, Phrygians, half-Hellenes, Libyans, Moors,
Getae, Iberians, and, of late years, Celts and Germans in daily
increasing numbers.   Still worse were the masses of freedmen—
often free only *de facto*—a mixture of beggars and of rich par-
venus, no longer slaves, but not yet burgesses, economically and
even legally dependent on their masters.   Retail trade and minor
handicrafts were almost entirely in their hands, and in riots and at
elections their influence was supreme.   The oligarchical government had done nothing to mend these evils.   The law prohibiting
persons condemned for capital offenses from living in the capital
was not enforced; the police supervision over clubs and associations

THE MONARCHY

was first neglected and then forbidden by law. Popular festivals had been allowed to increase so largely that the seven principal celebrations alone occupied sixty-two days. The grain supply was managed with the greatest remissness, and the fluctuations in prices were fabulous and incalculable. Lastly, the free distributions were a standing invitation to all destitute and indolent burgesses to come and take up their abode in the capital. Out of all this neglect sprang the system of clubs and bands, the worship of Isis and other religious extravagances. Dearth and famine were ordinary incidents; life was nowhere more insecure than at Rome. The condition of the buildings and streets was equally disgraceful; nothing was done to prevent the constant overflows of the river, and the city was still content with one bridge over the Tiber. The streets were narrow and steep, the footpaths small and ill-paved. Ordinary houses were wretchedly built, and of a giddy height, while the palaces of the rich formed a striking contrast to the decaying temples of the gods, with their images still carved for the most part in wood. If we try to conceive to ourselves a London with the slave population of New Orleans in our mid-century and the police of Constantinople about that time, with the non-industrial character of modern Rome, and agitated by politics after the fashion of the Paris of 1848, we shall acquire an approximate idea of the republican glory, the departure of which Cicero and his associates in their sulky letters deplore.

Caesar could not, of course, alter the essential character of the city, nor would this have suited his plan. To be the head of the Roman empire it must remain what it was, the denationalized capital of many nations, situated at the meeting point of East and West; and for this reason Caesar tolerated the new Egyptian worship, and even the strange rites of the Jews, alongside of those of Father Jovis; while at his popular festivals he caused dramas to be performed, not only in Latin and Greek, but in Phoenician, Hebrew, Syrian, and Spanish. The primary evils could not be eradicated; Caesar could not abolish slavery or conjure into existence a free industry in the capital. But by his extensive building operations he at any rate gave to the willing an opportunity of honorable employment, while the limitation of the distributions must have stopped the influx of the destitute into Rome. The existing proletariate was reduced by measures of police and by comprehensive transmarine colonization. Eighty thousand settlers were sent abroad during the few years of Caesar's government. The grain supply was placed upon a regular and efficient basis, and intrusted to the two newly appointed corn ediles. The club system was checked by laws, and came to an end of itself as the elections ceased to be of practical importance. In future, with some few exceptions, the right of forming associations depended upon the permission of the monarch and the senate. At the same time, the laws regarding violence were rendered more severe, and the right of the convicted criminal to withdraw himself from part of the penalty by self-banishment was set aside. The repair of the streets and footpaths was laid as a burden upon house proprietors, and the whole regulation of the streets was intrusted to the four ediles, who each superintended a distinct police district. Building in the capital received a stimulus which put to shame everything that had been accomplished in former days. And the new buildings were not merely monuments of splendor, but contributed largely to the public convenience. The crowded Forum was relieved by the construction of a new comitium in the Campus Martius, and of a new place of judicature, the Forum Julium. In the same spirit, oil was supplied to the baths free of cost, as a measure of sanitation. Other and more brilliant projects, such as the alteration of the whole lower course of the Tiber, so as to provide more space for public edifices, to drain the Pomptine marshes, and to provide the capital with a safe seaport, were cut short by the death of Caesar.

But when all was done, Rome, just because it was incapable of a real municipal life, was essentially inferior to other municipalities of the period. The republican Rome was a den of robbers, but it was at the same time the state; the Rome of the monarchy, although it began to embellish itself with all the glories of the three continents, and to glitter in gold and marble, was yet nothing in the state but a royal residence in connection with a poorhouse, or, in other words, a necessary evil.

The reorganization of the police of Rome was, of course, a small task compared with the social reorganization of Italy. The plague spot in the condition of Italy was, as it had long been, the disappearance of the agricultural and the unnatural increase of the mercantile population. In spite of numerous attempts to foster the system of small holdings, farm husbandry was scarcely anywhere predominant in Italy. In the districts of Tibur and Tusculum, on the shores of Terracina and Baiae, where the Italian farmer had once sowed and reaped, there was now to be seen only the barren splendor of the villas of the nobles, with all the appurtenances of gardens and fish-ponds, salt and fresh, nurseries of snails and slugs, game preserves, and aviaries. The stock of a pigeon-house was valued at $5000; the fishes left behind by Lucius Lucullus brought $2000. Accordingly the supply of such luxuries developed into a trade which, if intelligently prosecuted, brought large profits. Gardening, the production of vegetables, fruit, and flowers, especially roses and violets, in Latium and Campania, and the production of honey, were the most profitable. The management of estates on the planter system gave results which, from an economic point of view, far surpassed anything which the old system of small cultivators could have given, especially in central Italy, the districts of the Fucine Lake, of the Liris and Volturnus. Even some branches of industry, such as were suitable accompaniments of a slave estate, were taken up by intelligent landlords, and inns, weaving factories, and brickworks were conducted on the demesne. Pastoral husbandry, which was always spreading, especially in the south and southeast, was indeed in every respect a retrograde movement, but it too participated in the general progress, and accomplished much in the way of improvement of breeds.

The dimensions which money-dealing assumed by the side of this unnaturally prosperous estate husbandry, and the extent to which capital flowed to Rome, is shown by the singular fact that at Rome the ordinary rate of interest was six per cent.; that is, one-half the average rate elsewhere in ancient times.

The result of this economic system, based upon masses of capital, was the most fearful disproportion in the distribution of wealth. Nowhere is the phrase "a commonwealth composed of millionaires and beggars" so applicable as at Rome in the last stages of the republic; nowhere has the essential maxim of the slave state, that the rich man who lives by the exertion of his slaves is respectable, and the poor man who lives by the labor of his hands is necessarily vulgar, been so widely recognized. A real middle class there can never be in any fully developed slave state; the nearest approach to it in the Roman commonwealth was composed of men who were either too cultivated or too uncultivated to go beyond their own sphere of activity, and to take any share in public life. Of the former class, Cicero's friend, Titus Pomponius At-

ticus. is a typical example. He acquired a large fortune by estate
farming and by extensive money transactions; but he was never
seduced into soliciting office, or even into money transactions with
the state; his table was ample, but moderate, and was maintained
at a cost of five dollars per day; he was content with an easy existence, which included all the charms of a country and a city
life, together with intercourse with the best society of Rome and
Greece, and all the enjoyments of literature and art. Of the less
cultivated rural gentleman (*pater familias rusticanus*) an example
is furnished by Sextus Roscius, who was murdered in 81 B.C. He
manages his thirteen estates in person, and comes seldom to the capital, where his clownish manners contrast strangely with those of the
polished senator. In such men and in their country towns the discipline, manners, and language of their fathers were best preserved.
Traces of such a class appear wherever a national movement arises
in politics, and from it sprang Varro, Lucretius, Catullus, and all
the freshest literature of the time. An excellent picture of this
simple landlord life may be found in the graceful introduction to
the second book of Cicero's treatise " *De Legibus.*"

But the vigorous class of landlords is completely outbalanced
by the two predominant classes in the state, the mass of beggars
and the world of quality. The relative proportions of poor and rich
we have no means of accurately knowing. But fifty years earlier
the number of families of established wealth did not amount to
two thousand; and the disproportion had probably increased. The
growth of poverty is shown by the crowding into the army, and
into the city for the corn largesses; that of wealth, by the fact
that an author of this generation describes an estate of $100,000 of
the Marian period, as " riches, according to the circumstances of that
day," and by the enormous fortunes possessed by individuals. The
estate of Pompeius amounted to $3,500,000; Crassus, who began
with a fortune of $350,000, died, after lavishing enormous sums
on the people, worth $8,500,000. The result was, on both sides,
economic and moral disorganization. The Roman plebeian became
a lazy mendicant, fonder of gazing in the theater than of working.
The gladiatorial games flourished as never before; freedom had
so fallen in value that freemen often sold themselves for board and
wages as gladiatorial slaves. In the world of quality essentially
the same features occur. As the plebeian lounged on the pavement,
the aristocrat lay in bed till late in the·day; unbounded and taste-

less luxury everywhere prevailed; huge sums were lavished on politics and on the theater, to the corruption of both. In 54 B.C. the first voting division alone was paid $500,000, and all intelligent interest in the drama vanished amid the insane extravagance of decoration. Rents in Rome were four times as high as in the country; the house of Marcus Lepidus, at the time of Sulla's death the finest in Rome, was, a generation later, not the hundredth on the list of Roman palaces. A palatial sepulcher was a necessity to every noble who wished to die as became his rank; horses, dogs, furniture, dress, plate, all cost outrageous sums. But it was the luxury of the table, the coarsest luxury of all, which flourished most bravely. There were dining-rooms for winter and summer; sometimes the meal was served on a platform in the deer-park, and the guests were entertained by a theatrical Orpheus, at whose notes trained roes and wild boars gathered round. Italian delicacies had become vulgar, and even at popular festivals three sorts of foreign wine, Sicilian, Lesbian, and Chian, were distributed. Emetics were commonly taken to avoid the consequences of a meal. Debauchery of every sort had become a profession, by which instructors in the theory and practice of vice could gain a living. Of course no fortune could bear the ravages of such expenditure. The canvass for the consulship was the usual high-road to ruin. The princely wealth of the period is far surpassed by the more than princely liabilities. Caesar in 62 B.C. owed $1,250,000 more than his assets. Marcus Antonius owed at the age of twenty-four $300,000, fourteen years later $2,000,000; Curio owed $3,000,000; Milo, $3,500,000. The borrowing of the competitors for the consulship once suddenly raised the rate of interest from four to eight per cent. Insolvency was usually prolonged by the debtor as long as possible, and when the final crash came the creditors perhaps got —as in the case of Milo—four per cent. of their lendings. The only man who profited by such a condition of things was, of course, the cool banker. The debtors were either in servile subjection to their creditors, or ready to get rid of them by conspiracy and civil war. Hence the cry of "clear sheets" (*novae tabulae*), the motto of Cinna and Catilina, of Caelius and Dolabella.

Under such circumstances morality and family life had become antiquated things; poverty was the only disgrace, the only crime; the state, honor, freedom were alike sold for money. Men had forgotten what honesty was, and a man who refused a bribe was regarded as a personal foe. The criminal calendars of all ages and countries could scarcely furnish a tale of crime so horrible, so varied, and so unnatural as the trial of Aulus Cluentius reveals in the bosom of a respectable family in an Italian country town. Nevertheless, the surface of life was overspread with a veneer of polish and professions of universal friendship. All the world exchanged visits. At houses of quality the crowds of visitors were admitted in a fixed order, the more notable one by one, the others in groups, or in a body at the close. Invitations to dinner and the customary domestic festivals became almost public ceremonials, and even at his death the Roman was expected to provide each of his countless friends with a keepsake. Instead of the genuine intimacy of family ties there was a spectral shadow of " friendship," not the least of the evil spirits which brooded over the horrors of the age.

Another equally characteristic feature was the emancipation of women—not merely the economic emancipation from father or husband, which had long ago been accomplished, but a freedom which allowed them to interfere in every department of life. The ballet dancers and all their tribe pollute even the pages of history; liaisons in even the best circles were so common that only a very extraordinary scandal could excite comment. The intrusion of Publius Clodius at the women's festival of the Bona Dea, a scandal hitherto unparalleled, passed almost without investigation. The carnival time for license of this sort was the watering-place season, in April, at Baiae and Puteoli, but the women were not content with their own domain. They invaded the realm of politics, attended political conferences, and took their part in all the coterie intrigues of the time. The lightness with which divorce was regarded may be inferred from the conduct of the stern moralist Cato, who did not hesitate to divorce his wife for a friend who wished to marry her, or to marry her again after the death of his friend. Celibacy and childlessness became increasingly common, especially in the upper classes; even with Cato and his circle the same maxim was now current to which Polybius had traced the decay of Hellas, that it is the duty of a citizen to keep great wealth together, and therefore not to beget too many children.

During all this period the population of Italy was growing steadily smaller. The amount of talent and working power necessary for the government of the empire was no longer forthcoming from the peninsula, especially as a large part of its best material was continually being lost forever to the nation. The aristocracy lost the habit of looking on Italy as their home. Of the men enlisted in the army large numbers perished in the numerous wars, and many more were wholly estranged from their native land by the long period of service. Speculation kept many of the landholders and merchants away from their country, and their itinerant habits estranged them from civic and family life. In return for these sound elements Italy received a rabble of slaves and freedmen, handicraftsmen and tradesmen from Asia Minor, Syria, and Egypt, who moreover flourished chiefly in the seaports and in the capital; in many parts of Italy there was not even this compensation, and the population visibly declined. The pastoral districts, such as Apulia and the region round Rome, became every year more desolate: many towns, such as Labici and Gabii, could hardly find representatives for the Latin festival; Tusculum consisted almost solely of families of rank who lived at Rome but retained their Tusculan franchise. In some portions of Italy, especially Campania, things were not so bad; but in general, as Varro complains, " the once populous cities of Italy stood desolate."

It is a terrible picture, but not one peculiar to Italy; wherever the government in a slave state has fully developed itself, it has desolated God's fair world in the same way. As in the Hellas of Polybius, and the Carthage of Hannibal's time, the all-powerful rule of capital ruined the middle class, raised trade and estate-farming to the highest prosperity, and ultimately led to a moral and political corruption of the nation.

The evils of Italy were in their deepest essence irremediable; the wisest government cannot give freshness to the corrupt juices of the organism, or do more in such a case than remove obstructions in the way of the remedial power of nature. The worst excrescences vanished under the new rule, such as the pampering of the proletariate, the impunity of crimes, the purchasing of offices. But Caesar was not one of those overwise men who refuse to embank the sea because no dyke will keep out a sudden influx of the tide. Though no one knew better than himself the limits of his power, he applied all his energies to bring back the nation to home and family life, and to reform the national economy by law and decree.

In order to check the absence of Italians from Italy, the term of military service was shortened, and men of senatorial rank were prohibited from living out of Italy except on public business. Other Italians, of marriageable age, were forbidden to be absent for more than three consecutive years. In his first consulship Caesar had especially favored fathers who had several children, in founding his colony of Capua. As imperator he offered rewards to fathers of numerous families, and treated divorce and adultery with great rigor. In order to repress some of the worst forms of luxury, extravagance in sepulchral monuments was cut down by law, the use of purple robes and of pearls was restricted, and a maximum was fixed for the expenditure of the table. Even the semblance of propriety enforced by these police measures was, under the circumstances, not to be despised. The laws designed to meet the existing monetary crisis, and for the better regulation of monetary dealings in future, were more serious and promised better results. The law which was produced by the outcry against locked-up capital, and which provided that no one should have on hand more than three thousand dollars in gold and silver, was probably only meant to allay the public indignation, and can hardly have been enforced. The treatment of pending claims was a more serious matter. Two important concessions were made to debtors in 49 B.C. First, the interest in arrear was struck off, and that already paid was deducted from the capital. Secondly, the creditor had to accept as payment the property of the debtor at its estimated value before the general depreciation caused by the civil war; which of course was only fair, inasmuch as it compelled the creditor to bear his share of the general fall in values. But the first provision, which in practice compelled the creditor to lose, besides the interest, an average of twenty-five per cent. of his capital, amounted to a partial concession to the cry for a total canceling of debts. But the democratic party had always taken their stand upon the illegality of all interest: interest was, in fact, forbidden by the *Lex Genucia*, which was extorted by the plebeians in 342 B.C., and which was still formally valid; in the confusion of the Marian period it had even been enforced for a time. And though Caesar can hardly have shared the crude views of his party, he could not entirely repudiate its traditional maxims; especially as he had to decide this question, not as the conqueror of Pharsalus, but even before his departure for Epirus.

Besides assisting the debtor of the moment, Caesar did what

he could permanently to repress the fearful omnipotence of capital. According to Roman law the insolvent debtor became the slave of his creditor; and though modified in secondary points, the principle had remained unaltered for five hundred years. It was Caesar who first gave to an insolvent the right of saving his personal freedom, though with diminished political rights, of ceding his property to his creditors, and beginning a new financial existence. Claims arising from the earlier period could be enforced against him only if he could meet them without renewed financial ruin. At the same time, Caesar did not disown the antipathy of his party to usury. In Italy, for the future, no single capitalist was allowed to lend sums amounting to more than a fixed proportion (perhaps one-half) of the value of his landed estate. In consequence of this law every money-lender was compelled to be also a landowner, and the class of capitalists subsisting wholly on their interest would disappear from Italy. It was also forbidden to take a higher interest than one per cent. per month; or to take interest on arrears of interest, or to claim interest to a greater amount than the capital—provisions which were probably first introduced by Lucius Lucullus in Asia Minor, and which were extended to all the provinces by decree of the senate in the year 50 B.C.

For the improvement of agriculture the first necessity was the improvement of the administration of law and justice. Hitherto neither movable nor immovable property had been secure. The leaders of armed bands, when their services were not required in the capital, had applied themselves to rounding out the country estates of their masters by violently expelling the rightful owners. Such proceedings were now at an end. A high road was made from Rome through the passes of the Apennines to the Adriatic, and the level of the Fucine Lake was lowered for the benefit of the Marsian farmers. In order to check brigandage and encourage free labor, Italian graziers were required to take at least a third of their herdsmen from free-born adults. In the encouragement of small holdings Caesar showed himself scrupulously observant of every legitimate title, whether derived from Gracchus or Sulla; but the commission of twenty was revived to revise all Italian titles, and the whole of the actual domain land of Italy which was suitable for agriculture was destined for distribution. In the selection of farmers the veterans were first considered, and thus Caesar restored to his country as a farmer the proletarian whom he

had levied as a recruit. Desolate Latin communities, such as Veii
and Capena, were provided with new colonists. The new owners
were forbidden to alienate their lands for twenty years.

The newly organized municipal system, which had been developed out of the crisis of the social war, was regulated by Caesar
in two ordinances of 49 B.C. and 45 B.C., the former of which applied to Cisalpine Gaul only, while the latter remained the fundamental law for all succeeding time. It proceeded on the line of
purifying the urban corporations from all immoral elements, and
of restricting centralization to the utmost. The communities were
still allowed to elect their own magistrates, and to exercise a limited
civil and criminal jurisdiction.

Such were Caesar's regulations for the reform of the social
economy of Italy. It would be easy to show that they were in-
sufficient, and that they acted in some respects injuriously—still
easier to show that the evils of Italian economy were incurable.
But Caesar did not hope or expect from them the regeneration of
Italy. This he attempted to attain in a very different way, for the
understanding of which it is necessary to review the condition
of the provinces as Caesar found them.

The provinces in existence at this time were fourteen in num-
ber: seven European—Farther Spain, Hither Spain, Transalpine
Gaul, Italian Gaul with Illyricum, Macedonia with Greece, Sicily,
Sardinia with Corsica; five Asiatic—Asia, Bithynia with Pontus,
Cilicia with Cyprus, Syria, Crete; two African—Cyrene, Africa.
To these Caesar added three more—Lugdunese Gaul, Belgica, and
Illyria, which was now erected into a separate province.

Under the oligarchy the provinces were reduced to a condition
of hopeless misery which it seems impossible for any government
ever to surpass. It is true that, before the Romans had their day,
the rule of Greeks, Phoenicians, or Asiatics had almost everywhere
driven from the nations all sense of right and liberty. The Roman
provincial, when accused, was obliged to appear personally at
Rome; the Roman governor interfered at pleasure in every detail
of administration; the Roman administrators and their train were
bound by no rule of morality and justice, and outrages, rapes,
murders with or without the form of law, were of daily occurrence.
But these things had gone on from time immemorial under Carthaginian overseers and Syrian satraps, and the well-being of the
provincials was far less disturbed by them than by the financial

exactions, in which the Romans outran all former tyrants. The ordinary taxes were rendered doubly oppressive by the mode of levying them. As to the quartering of troops, Roman statesmen themselves confessed that a town suffered nearly as much from it as when stormed by an enemy. The taxation was properly an indemnification for the burden of military defense undertaken by Rome, and the communities taxed had a right to be exempt at any rate from the ordinary service. But garrison duty was still for the most part imposed upon the provincials, as well as the whole burden of cavalry service; and the extraordinary contributions for the supply of grain to the capital, the costly naval armaments and coast defenses against the pirates, the military requisitions in time of war, were frequent and oppressive in the extreme. In Sicily the number of farms decreased fifty-nine per cent. during three years of the administration of Gaius Verres, and the ruined cultivators were not small farmers, but considerable planters and Roman burgesses! In the client states the burdens were, if possible, heavier. In addition to the Roman exactions came those of the native courts; farmer and king were alike bankrupt. And to these, to some extent regular exactions, are to be added the plunderings of the governor and of all his friends, each of whom expected to return to Rome a made man. The advocates and jurymen at home expected to share the spoil; so that the more the governor stole, the greater his security. And these were the successors of the men who had brought nothing home from the provinces but the thanks of the subjects and the approval of their countrymen!

Nor is this all. The tyranny of the Italian men of business was even worse than that of the governors. Much of the landed property and most of the commerce and finance of the provinces were in their hands. Usury flourished as never before. The small landowners managed their estates as the debtor-slaves of their creditors. Communities had sometimes to pay four per cent. per month for loans. Frequently a man of business got the title of envoy conferred on him, and sometimes had men put at his disposal for the more effective prosecution of his affairs. On one occasion a banker who had a claim on the town of Salamis in Cyprus kept its council blockaded in the town-house until five members died of hunger. And still to all these miseries and oppressions there remains to be added general calamities, for some of which, such as war, brigandage, and piracy, the inefficiency of the Roman government was responsible. The general result, even in the comparatively prosperous provinces of Spain and Narbonese Gaul, was total ruin. Towns like Samos and Halicarnassus stood empty; even the patient Asiatic was weary of life. The statesmen of Rome allowed that the Roman name was unutterably hateful throughout Greece and Asia; and when the men of Heraclea, in Pontus, put to death the whole of the Roman tax collectors, the only matter for regret was that such things did not occur oftener.

The wounds inflicted could only be healed by time; but Caesar took care that there should be no new inflictions. The new governors were the servants of a stern master, and were practically appointed by him. Their functions were largely restricted by the new supreme command in Rome and by the new adjutants associated with them. The raising of the taxes, too, was probably already committed to imperial officials, so that the governor was now surrounded by an independent staff, directly responsible to the imperator. The law against exactions had been made more stringent by Caesar in his first consulate, and was applied with inexorable severity. At the same time, the extraordinary burdens were limited to the necessary requirements, and the ordinary burdens materially lessened. Exemptions from tribute were liberally granted, the direct taxes lowered, the system of *decumae* confined to Africa and Sardinia, and the system of middlemen in the collection was set aside. That Caesar, like Sertorius, tried to free the subjects from the burden of quartering troops cannot be proved, but it was in this spirit that the heirs of his policy created military camps, and converted them into towns which formed rallying-points in the barbarian frontier districts.

To deliver the provincials from the tyranny of Roman capital was a far more difficult task. Its power could not be directly broken, and a radical cure could only be hoped for from the gradual revival of prosperity. Isolated abuses were abolished, and palpable acts of violence or flagrant wrong were sharply punished; but this was all. Caesar had, as governor of Farther Spain in 60 B.C., assigned to the creditors two-thirds of the income of their debtors in order to pay themselves; and Lucius Lucullus had in Asia canceled a portion of the arrears of interest, and assigned to the creditors a fourth part of the produce of the lands of their debtors. It is probable that similar liquidations were instituted in the provinces generally after the civil wars. As to the remaining evils of piracy and brigandage, these might be expected to disappear through the fresh vigor of the new *régime*. At any rate, with Caesar hope dawned afresh, and the first intelligent and humane government which had appeared for centuries began to rule. " Well might the subject in particular mourn along with the best Romans by the bier of the great liberator."

We have now surveyed in outline the principal measures by which Caesar attempted to reorganize existing institutions, to get rid of abuses, and to reform the whole system of government. But this was, on the whole, but the negative part of his task. For the regeneration, it might almost be said the re-creation, of the state he tried to lay a firm foundation upon which might be realized that conception which had first been grasped by Gaius Gracchus, and which was afterwards taken up by Sertorius in Spain. Like those great statesmen, Caesar looked forward to the time when the provinces, as such, would disappear, and when a new Helleno-Italic nation should arise in a new and wider home, with a fresher, broader, grander national life, which would of itself be the extinction of the sorrows and wrongs of the nation for which there could be no redress in old Italy. The emigration of Italians to the provinces had been going on for centuries. Gaius Gracchus was the first to guide the Italians systematically to settle beyond the bounds of Italy by his colonization of Carthage and Narbo. Sertorious had done his best to Latinize the Spaniards of rank, and to introduce Italian culture into Spain, and by Caesar's time there was a large Italian population ready to his hand in nearly every province of the empire. On the other hand, the interpenetration of the Latin and the Hellenic character was as old almost as Rome. The Roman legionary was followed everywhere by the Greek schoolmaster, and the Latin higher culture was nothing but Hellenism proclaimed in the Latin tongue. Everywhere it was felt that Rome was the protector and avenger of Hellenism. The idea of a new Italo-Hellenic empire was not new, but Caesar was the first to grasp it, and systematically to carry it out. The first conditions for the realization of this idea were the extension and preservation of the two nations which were destined jointly to rule, and the absorption of the barbarian races. There was, indeed, a third nationality—the Hebrews—which might almost have claimed a place by the side of the other two. The Jews were numerous and powerful in the city of Rome, and influential everywhere as traders;

but the Jewish nation is denied the gift of political aptitude. The Jew stands in a relation of indifference to the state, clothes himself readily with any nationality, and is unfit to be a member of a governing hierarchy. But for this very reason he seemed made for the purposes of this new state, which was to be built upon the ruins of a hundred different nationalities, and accordingly Judaism was everywhere protected by Caesar as an effective leaven of cosmopolitanism and of national decomposition.

The Greek nationality was protected wherever it existed, notably at Massilia and Alexandria, but the Italian none the less remained everywhere in the ascendent. Hellenism was too dangerous by its intellectual superiority, by its wide extension, and by the firm hold which it had obtained in Italy, to make it desirable for the government to extend it by direct action. The rule of the Greek lackeys had already begun with Theophanes, the confidential servant of Pompeius, and his influence was at once a sign of the times and a warning full of ill omen for the future. But the Roman element was everywhere promoted by the government, both by means of colonies and by Latinizing the provincials, and to further this object the principle that all the land in the provinces not ceded by special act of the government to communities or private persons was the property of the state, was retained by Caesar, and raised from a democratic party theory to a fundamental maxim of law. Cisalpine Gaul in 49 B.C. received *de jure* the full citizenship which it had already enjoyed *de facto* for forty years, and remained for centuries the headquarters of Italian manners and culture. Transalpine Gaul henceforth occupied the place of the old sister province, and became more and more an Italian land. Four new colonies were founded in it, at Baeterrae (Beziers), Arelate (Arles), Arausio (Orange), and Forum Julii (Fréjus), with which were connected the names of the most famous of the Gallic legions. Other communities, such as Nemausus (Nimes), received Latin rights. In other non-Greek and non-Latin regions centers of Italian civilization were established: in northern Gaul, Noviodunum (Nyon) arose on the Leman Lake; in Spain, Emporiae was founded; and the ancient city of Gades was admitted to full rights in 49 B.C. A few years later other communities were similarly favored, and others received Latin rights. In Africa, the project of Gaius Gracchus was renewed, and a Roman Carthage arose on the old site; Utica had apparently already received Latin rights, and Cirta was constituted as a Roman military colony. In Greece the restoration of Corinth was energetically carried out, and a plan formed for cutting through the Isthmus. In the remote East, Heraclea and Sinope were reinforced by bodies of Roman colonists; Berytus in Syria received an Italian constitution, and even in Egypt a Roman station was established on the island of Pharos.

Through these arrangements the Italian municipal system was carried into the provinces in a manner far more comprehensive than ever before. The fully enfranchised communities of the provinces were on an equality with those of Italy in two respects: namely, that they administered their own affairs and exercised a limited legal jurisdiction, while the more important processes of law came before the Roman authority, usually the governor of the province. The autonomous Latin communities had probably unlimited jurisdiction, as well as administrative freedom, though the governor could of course interfere in virtue of his general power of control. There was now for the first time a whole province, that of Cisalpine Gaul, consisting entirely of Roman burgesses; and this fact marked the disappearance of the first great difference between Rome and the provinces. The second began soon to disappear, at any rate in practice. It is true that the legal distinction between Italy as the sphere of civil law and of the consuls and pretors, and the provinces as the sphere of martial law and of the proconsuls and propretors, remained; but the procedure of martial and of civil law had for long been practically the same: what had been the true and vital point of distinction vanished when legions ceased to be stationed ordinarily in the provinces, and were kept only where there was a frontier to be guarded. The rule of the urban community of Rome over the shores of the Mediterranean was at an end; in its stead came the new Mediterranean state; and the restoration of Carthage and Corinth showed clearly that the *régime* of political tyranny which had destroyed those two famous centers of commerce was over, and that a new era of national and political equality had begun.

The new united empire was, of course, rather an inanimate product of art than a vigorous growth of nature; it needed unity of institutions as well as unity of government; unity in constitution and administration, in religion and jurisprudence, in money, weights, and measures. In all these departments Caesar did little but lay the foundations; only here and there the lines which he drew can still be traced.

As to administration, the three most important elements of unity have already been noticed: the transition of the sovereignty from the municipal council of Rome to the sole master of the Mediterranean monarchy; the conversion of that council into a supreme imperial council representing Italy and the provinces; above all, the transference, which was now begun, of the Roman and Italian municipal organization to the provinces. One other important work in this department was undertaken by Caesar—an improved census of Italy, which was to be taken in future, not at Rome, but simultaneously in each Italian community; and a survey of the whole empire, which was ordered, suggests that Caesar intended to make arrangements for a similar census in the provinces. It was of the first importance to the new empire that the government should have at its disposal a comprehensive view of the resources in men and money at its command.

In religion, men had for long been busied in forging together the Italian and Hellenic worships, a task which was rendered easier by the abstract formless character of the Roman gods. At the same time, local faiths were tolerated and protected.

In the field of law, the criminal department, in which the government must always interfere directly to a large extent, was easily made uniform by judicial enactment throughout the empire.· In civil law, commercial intercourse had long·ago developed naturally the code which the united empire required. Roman urban law was still based formally upon the Twelve Tables. But commercial intercourse between Romans and non-Romans had long ago developed an international private law (*jus gentium*), a body of maxims relating chiefly to commercial matters, according to which Roman judges gave judgment when from the nature of the case they were compelled to revert to the common notions of right underlying all commercial dealings. This body of law arose originally out of proceedings between Romans and non-Romans; but, in practice, dealings between Romans and Romans, particularly commercial matters, had come to be judged by the standard of what was substantially a compromise between this new law and the old Twelve Tables. Secondly, this new law was to a certain extent in use throughout the whole extent of the empire as subsidiary law; the various local statutes were retained for transactions be-

THE MONARCHY

tween members of the same legal district, while those between members of different districts were regulated according to the principles of the new law as expressed in the pretor's edict. Caesar's design for a new code was never carried out; but it is easy to guess what must have been his intentions. It was most necessary, first, that the new urban law should be extended as subsidiary law to the provinces where it had properly no application; and, secondly, that the old law of the Twelve Tables with its accretions, which still formally outweighed the later code, should be set aside in favor of this newer and spontaneous growth.

In respect of money, measures, and weights, and kindred matters the Roman standard was alone used in all official intercourse; and the non-Roman systems were restricted to local currency, and placed in a fixed ratio to the Roman. Under the republic the coinage had been exclusively silver, gold being given and taken by weight. But from Caesar's time gold obtained the first place; the new Caesarian gold piece (worth about five dollars) was coined to an enormous extent. In a single treasure, buried only a few years after his death, eighty thousand of them were found. The mint of Massilia was closed, but the coining of small silver and copper money was permitted to many Western communities. Later the arrangement found in existence is this: that the Roman silver coin, the denarius, has everywhere legal currency, while local coins are in circulation at a tariff unfavorable to them as compared with the denarius.

The calendar, like every other institution, had become hopelessly confused under the oligarchical government, and had come to anticipate the solar time by sixty-seven days, so that, e. g., the festival of Flora was celebrated on July 11, instead of on April 28. This evil was finally removed by Caesar, and the Italian farmer's year was introduced, together with a rational system of intercalation, into religious and official use. At the same time the beginning of the year was altered from March 1 to January 1. This latter date had already been long predominant in civil life owing to the fact that the supreme magistrates entered upon office on that day. The new Julian calendar, which is still in the main the standard of the civilized world, came into use on January 1, 45 B.C.

Such was the manner in which Caesar attempted to lay the foundations for the regeneration of the Roman state. There was doubtless much corruption in this regeneration; as the unity of Italy was accomplished over the ruins of Samnite and Etruscan nations, so the Mediterranean monarchy built itself on the ruins of countless states and tribes once living and vigorous; but it was a corruption out of which sprang a rich growth, part of which remains green to the present day. Caesar ruled as king of Rome for about five years and a half; the intervals of seven great campaigns, which altogether gave him but fifteen months in the capital, were all the time allowed him to regulate the destinies of the world. This very rapidity proves that the plan had long been meditated and its parts settled in detail. The outlines were laid down, the future alone could complete the structure; and, indeed, Caesar was heard himself to say that he had lived long enough.

BIBLIOGRAPHY

BIBLIOGRAPHY

SOURCES

ONLY the more important sources and such as are easily accessible in English translation are here given.

Appian.—Trans. by Horace White: "The Roman History of Appian of Alexandria." New York, 1899. 2 vols.

Caesar.—Trans. by W. A. McDevitte and W. G. Bohn: "Caesar's Commentaries on the Gallic and Civil Wars; with the Supplementary Books attributed to Histius, including the Alexandrian, African, and Spanish Wars"; with notes. New York, 1898.

Cicero.—Trans. by E. S. Shuckburgh: "The Letters of Cicero," the whole extant correspondence in chronological order. London, 1899-1900. 4 vols.

Trans. by C. D. Yonge: "Select Orations of Cicero." New York. 4 vols.

Dio, Cassius.—Trans. by H. B. Foster: "Cassius Dio's Roman History." Troy, N. Y., 1905-1906. 4 vols.

Livy.—Trans. by D. Spillan: "The History of Rome by Titus Livius." New York, 1890.

Plutarch.—Trans. by A. Stewart and G. Long: "Plutarch's Lives of Famous Greeks and Romans." New York, 1889. 4 vols.

Polybius.—Trans. by E. S. Shuckburgh: "The Histories of Polybius," from the Text of F. Hultsch. New York, 1889. 2 vols.

Sallust.—Trans. by A. W. Pollard: "Sallust's Conspiracy of Catiline and the Jugurthine War." New York, 1882.

GENERAL HISTORIES

Duruy, V.—"History of Rome and the Roman People." Trans. by W. J. Clarke and ed. by J. P. Mahaffy. Boston, 1883. 8 vols.
Extends from the earliest times to the barbarian invasions. One of the best popular histories.

How, W. W., and Leigh, H. D.—"A History of Rome to the Death of Caesar" London and New York, 1896.
Interestingly written and scholarly.

Ihne, W.—"History of Rome." London, 1882. 5 vols.
Originally written in German, but the English version prepared by the author. Based on opposition to Mommsen's views. Less interesting but more judicial than the latter. Full evidence given on both sides of controverted questions.

Mommsen, T.—"History of Rome." Trans. by W. P. Dickson. London, 1894. 4 vols. (4th ed. of English version.)

Niebuhr, B. G.—"History of Rome." Trans. by J. C. Hare, C. Thirlwell, W. Smith, and L. Schmitz. London, 1859. 3 vols.
The chief importance of this work is historiographic. It first appeared in Germany in 1812 and really began the modern study of Roman history. Many of Niebuhr's views have since been rejected.

Pelham, H. F.—"Outlines of Roman History." 3d ed. London, 1900.
The best single-volume work covering the whole period down to 476 A. D.
The author's views are independent and authoritative.
Shuckburgh, E. S.—"A History of Rome to the Battle of Actium." New York,
1894.
A good one-volume work.

PARTICULAR PERIODS

Allcroft, A. H., and Mason, W. F.—"History of Rome." London. 4 periods:
The Struggle for Empire (287-202 B. C.); Rome under the Oligarchs
(202-133 B. C.); The Decline of the Oligarchy (133-78 B. C.); The Making
of the Monarchy (78-31 B. C.).
These small books give abundant details, but do not attempt to present a
philosophical survey.
Arnold, T.—"The Second Punic War: being Chapters in the History of Rome."
Ed. by his grandson, W. T. Arnold. London, 1886.
A republication of the 3d volume of Arnold's unfinished history, with full
notes. It is probably the most spirited and interesting account of the
Second Punic War in English.
Church, A. J.—"The Story of Carthage." (Story of the Nations Series.) New
York and London, 1886.
A popular book, illustrated. Deals with religious and commercial, as well
as with political history.
Fustel de Coulanges.—"The Ancient City." Trans. by W. Smalls. Boston, 1877.
A brilliant and suggestive study of the religion and institutions of Greece
and Rome, but somewhat vitiated by untenable theories.
Fowler, W. W.—"The City-State of the Greeks and Romans." New York, 1893.
More sane, though less brilliant, than the work of Fustel de Coulanges.
Greenidge, A. H. J.—"A History of Rome during the Later Republic and Early
Principate to Vespasian." New York, 1905.
The best work in English on the period. It is to be in 6 volumes, but only
the first, from 133-104 B. C., has yet appeared.
Holmes, T. R.—"Caesar's Conquest of Gaul." London, 1899.
The first portion gives an able narrative of the Gallic campaigns; the
second deals with the difficult questions of topography, institutions, etc.,
suggested by the text of Caesar's Commentaries.
Ihne, W.—"Early Rome." (Epochs of Ancient History.) London, 1876.
A small popular book on the history of the city down to its destruction
by the Gauls.
Long, G.—"Decline and Fall of the Roman Republic." London, 1864-1874. 5
vols.
Covers the period from the end of the Punic Wars to the time of Augustus.
Dry, but accurate.
Merivale, C.—"The Fall of the Roman Republic." London, 1853.
Covers the same ground as Long, but is briefer and more interesting.
——"The Roman Triumvirates." (Epochs of Ancient History.) New York,
1878.
——"History of the Romans under the Empire." London, 1850-1862. 7 vols.
As this work begins with the death of Sulla the earlier volumes constitute
a history of the fall of the Republic.
Smith, R. B.—"Rome and Carthage: The Punic Wars." (Epochs of Ancient
History.) London, 1881.
An abridgment of the author's longer work on Carthage.

Smith, R. B.—"Carthage and the Carthagenians." London, 1878.
A careful study of the city and of the careers of Hamilcar Barca, and Hannibal.

BIOGRAPHY

Beesly, A. H.—"The Gracchi, Marius and Sulla." (Epochs of Ancient History.) New York, 1878.
Well written. Is based largely on Long and Mommsen.
Beesly, E. S.—"Catiline, Clodius and Tiberius." London, 1878.
A collection of essays, originally published in the *Fortnightly Review*, giving a good picture of the times.
Boissier, G.—"Cicero and his Friends." Trans. by A. D. Jones. London, 1897.
Deals with the literary rather than the political side of his activity.
Dodge, T. A.—"Hannibal." Boston, 1891.
A military history.
——"Caesar." Boston, 1892.
A study of Caesar as a general.
Forsyth, W.—"Life of Marcus Tullius Cicero." New York, 1871. 2 vols.
Rather out of date, but describing Cicero's career in great detail.
Fowler, W. W.—"Julius Caesar and the Foundation of the Roman Imperial System." New York, 1892.
The best account of Caesar in English.
Froude, J. A.—"Caesar: a Sketch." New York, 1892.
A rather partisan defense of Caesar.
How, W. W.—"Hannibal and the Great War between Rome and Carthage." London, 1899.
Morris, W. O.—"Hannibal." London and New York, 1897.
An excellent, well-balanced account; in many ways the best biography in English.
Napoleon III, Emperor of the French.—"History of Julius Caesar." New York, 1865. 2 vols.
The work of many hands prepared under the direction of Napoleon III. Treats with special fullness of Caesar's career in Gaul.
Oman, C. W. C.—"Seven Roman Statesmen of the Later Republic." 2d ed. London, 1902.
Gives interesting studies of the Gracchi, Sulla, Crassus, Cato, Pompey, and Caesar.
Scott, F. J.—"Portraitures of Julius Caesar." London, 1903.
A discussion of the various busts and other representations of Caesar that have come down to us.
Strachan-Davidson, J. L.—"Cicero and the Fall of the Roman Republic." New York, 1894.
Valuable and charmingly written, but rather prejudiced in Cicero's favor.
Trollope, A.—"Life of Cicero." New York, 1881. 2 vols.
A vivid and sympathetic portraiture of Cicero, giving the personal rather than the political side of his career.

INSTITUTIONS

Abbott, F. F.—"Roman Political Institutions." New York, 1901.
The best brief survey in English of the Roman constitution.
Arnold, W. T.—"Roman System of Provincial Administration to the Accession of Constantine." London, 1879.
An interesting study, but largely superseded by the dryer but more scholarly work of Mommsen.

Greenidge, A. H. J.—"Roman Public Life." London, 1901.
Gives a good general survey of the growth of the Roman constitution and an explanation of its workings.
Hadley, J.—Introduction to Roman Law. New York, 1875.
Mommsen, T.—"*Römisches Staatsrecht.*" Leipzig, 1887. 3 vols. (Found in Marquardt and Mommsen's "*Handbuch der römischen Alterthümer.*")
This is the great authority on the Roman constitution, but it has not been translated into English.
——"The Provinces of the Roman Empire." Trans. by W. P. Dickson. New York, 1887. 2 vols.
While this work deals with the provinces under the emperors much may be gathered from it regarding conditions in the republican period.
Morey, W. C.—"Outlines of Roman Law: Comprising its History, Growth and General Principles." New York, 1884.
This book and the similar one by Hadley give an excellent popular survey of the subject.
Muirhead, J.—"Historical Introduction to the Private Law of Rome." 2d ed. revised and edited by H. Goudy. London, 1899.
A standard treatise.
Sohm, R.—"The Institutes: a Text-Book of the History and System of Roman Private Law." Trans. by J. C. Ledlie, with an introduction by E. Grueber. Oxford, 1901. 2d ed.
The best comprehensive survey of the law in one volume, giving (1) its history and development, and (2) the principles of the law.

LIFE AND MANNERS

Church, A. J.—"Roman Life in the Days of Cicero: Sketches drawn from his Letters and Speeches." London, 1884.
A picture of social conditions both in the provinces and at Rome during the period 100-40 B. C.
Cunningham, W.—"Western Civilization in its Economic Aspects. Part I. Ancient Times." Cambridge, 1898.
A suggestive book; the first attempt to give a general survey of all antiquity from an economic point of view.
Johnston, H. W.—"The Private Life of the Romans." Chicago, 1903.
Similar in purpose to Preston and Dodge.
Lanciani, R.—"Ancient Rome in the Light of Recent Discoveries." Boston, 1891.
Popular but interesting account of the results of excavations in Rome up to 1890.
——"Ruins and Excavations of Ancient Rome." Boston, 1897.
Mackail, J. W.—"Latin Literature." London, 1896.
The best brief account of the subject, charmingly written.
Middleton, J. H.—"The Remains of Ancient Rome." London, 1892. 2 vols.
Preston, H. W., and Dodge, L.—"Private Life of the Romans." Boston, 1893.
Prepared as a text-book, but giving an interesting account of the daily life in Rome.
Ramsay, W.—"Manual of Roman Antiquities." 15th ed. revised and partly rewritten by R. Lanciani. New York, 1895.
Teuffel, W. S.—"History of Roman Literature." Trans. by G. C. W. Warr from the 5th German edition. London, 1891-1892. 2 vols.
The best of the larger works on Roman literature accessible to the English reader.

INDEX

INDEX

A

Abgarus of Edessa: betrays the Roman army, 323

Achaean League: faults of, 138; joins Rome, 140; declares war against Sparta (146 B.C.), 166

Achaeans: found Sybaris, 26

Achaeus: general in the slave revolt, 173

Achaia: province of, formed, 166; surrenders to Mithradates, 217

Adherbal: king of Numidia, 188

Aegusa: battle of, 105

Aemilius, Lucius: commands campaign against Tarentum, 75

Aequi: wars with Rome, 22

Aetolian League: faults of, 138; joins Rome in third Macedonian War, 149

Afranius, Lucius: flees to Macedonia, 343; defeated by Caesar, 340; at the Corcyra council of war, 350; arrival in Africa, 359; death, 359

Africa: province of, formed, 165

Agrigentum: founded, 28; surrendered to Rome, 125; seized by the slaves, 173

Ahala: defeats Celtic horde, 64

Alba: center of the Latin League, 9; conquered and destroyed, 20; battle of, 59

Albinus Spurius: his campaign against Jugurtha, 189

Alesia: siege of, 306

Alexandria: sends embassy to Rome, (273 B.C.), 86; influence of, 137; insurrection of, 352

Alexander, the Molossian: his campaign in southern Italy, 68

Allia: battle of, 59

Allobroges: attack Hannibal, 115

Ambiorix, king of the Eburones: leader of Gallic rebellion, 305

Ancona: founded, 57

Anicius, Lucius: captures Scodra, 150

Antiochus (III) the Great, king of Syria: forms an alliance with Philip of Macedon, 139; war with Rome, 143; death, 145

Antiochus (IV) Epiphanes, king of Syria, submits to Roman interference, 151

Antiochus (XIII) Asiaticus, king of Syria: deposed, 274

Antonius, Gaius: Caesar prosecutes, 266; elected consul, 281; at battle of Dolabella, 343

Antonius, Marcus (143-87 B.C.): commissioned to clear the seas of pirates, 260; death, 223, 260

Antonius, Marcus (ca. 85-30 B.C.): his campaign against recruiting officers of Pompeius, 337; joins Caesar in Greece, 346; puts down insurrection of Dolabella, 365; offers the crown to Caesar, 369

Apennines: boundary of Italy, 3

Apollonia: founded, 27

Appuleian Laws: passed, 200; canceled, 202

Apulia: in Rome's hands, 70

Aquae Sextiae: founded, 192; battle of (102 B.C.), 194

Aquileia: founded, 133; battle of, 193

Aquillius, Manius: quells slave revolt in Sicily, 187; encourages uprising of Bithynian king, 215

Aquilonia: battle of (293 B.C.), 72

Aquitania: conquered by Caesar, 304

Aratus of Sicyon: dispute with Sparta, 138

Arausio (Orange): battle of, 193; founded, 392

Archelaus: at battle of Chaeronea, 218

Archidamus III, king of Sparta: attempts to aid Tarentum, 68

Archimedes: at the siege of Syracuse, 124

Arelate (Arles): founded, 392

1 See also under C